Perennial Decay

New Cultural Studies

Series Editors
Joan DeJean
Carroll Smith-Rosenberg
Peter Stallybrass
Gary A. Tomlinson

A complete list of books in the series is available from the publisher.

Perennial Decay

On the Aesthetics and
Politics of Decadence

Edited by Liz Constable, Dennis Denisoff,
and Matthew Potolsky

PENN

University of Pennsylvania Press

Philadelphia

10 9 8 7 6 5 4 3 2 1

Published by
University of Pennsylvania Press
Philadelphia, Pennsylvania 19104–4011

Library of Congress Cataloging-in-Publication Data

Perennial decay : on the aesthetics and politics of
decadence / edited by Liz Constable, Dennis Denisoff,
and Matthew Potolsky.
        p.   cm.
    Includes bibliographical references and index.
    ISBN 0-8122-3470-7 (hardcover : alk. paper). —
ISBN 0-8122-1678-4 (pbk. : alk. paper)
    1. Decadence (Literary movement)   2. Decadence in
art.   3. Arts, Modern — 19th century.   4. Arts,
Modern — 20th century.   5. Aesthetics, Modern — 19th
century.   6. Aesthetics, Modern — 20th century.
I. Constable, Liz.   II. Denisoff, Dennis, 1961–   .
III. Potolsky, Matthew.
PN56.D45P47   1999
809′.911 — dc21   98-34373
                                                 CIP

Contents

Introduction   1
Liz Constable, Matthew Potolsky, and Dennis Denisoff

Defining Decadence

1. Interversions   35
Barbara Spackman

2. Unknowing Decadence   50
Charles Bernheimer

3. Decadent Paradoxes   65
Michael Riffaterre
Translated by Liz Constable and Matthew Potolsky

Visualizing Decadence

4. Posing a Threat: Queensberry, Wilde, and the Portrayal of
Decadence   83
Dennis Denisoff

5. Decadent Critique: Constructing "History" in Peter Greenaway's
The Cook, the Thief, His Wife & Her Lover   101
David Wayne Thomas

6. Opera and the Discourse of Decadence: From Wagner to AIDS   119
Marc A. Weiner

7. Spaces of the Demimonde / Subcultures of Decadence: 1890–1990   142
Emily Apter

Identifications of Decadence and Decadent Identities

8. "Comment Peut-on Être Homosexuel?": Multinational
(In)Corporation and the Frenchness of *Salomé*   159
Melanie C. Hawthorne

9. The Politics of Posing: Translating Decadence in Fin-de-Siècle
Latin America   183
Sylvia Molloy

10. Improper Names: Pseudonyms and Transvestites in Decadent
Prose   198
Leonard R. Koos

11. Imperial Dependency, Addiction, and the Decadent Body   215
Hema Chari

Decadence, History, and the Politics of Language

12. Pale Imitations: Walter Pater's Decadent Historiography   235
Matthew Potolsky

13. "Golden Mediocrity": Pater's Marcus Aurelius and the Making
of Decadence   254
Sharon Bassett

14. Fetishizing Writing: The Politics of Fictional Form in the Work
of Remy de Gourmont and Joséphin Péladan   268
Jennifer Birkett

15. "Ce Bazar Intellectuel": Maurice Barrès, Decadent Masters,
and Nationalist Pupils   289
Liz Constable

List of Contributors   309

Index   311

Introduction

Liz Constable, Matthew Potolsky, and Dennis Denisoff

Stripped of its mysticism, its necessity, of all its historical genealogy, the idea of literary decadence is reduced to a purely Negative idea, to the simple idea of absence.
            Remy de Gourmont, "Stéphane Mallarmé and the Idea of Decadence"

"There is not a man or a woman in the English-speaking world possessed of the treasure of a wholesome mind who is not under a deep debt of gratitude to the Marquess of Queensberry for destroying the high Priest of the Decadents," exclaimed the *National Observer* when Oscar Wilde was convicted of gross indecency in 1895. This image of Wilde as the quintessential embodiment and model of decadence — and its apparent containment — reflects a diverse collection of cultural anxieties and biases that were not, of course, to be dispatched with one individual, despite the newspaper claims. The *Observer*'s confident obituary of decadence was greatly exaggerated, and today — just over one hundred years after the famous trials — cultural phenomena designated as decadent continue to exercise a significant force. Indeed, contrary to the sometimes narrow connotations of its name, decadence was in the nineteenth century and has more recently proved to be a concept whose analysis yields a very broad set of resonances and associations. Many of these associations open up new perspectives on the fin(s)-de-siècle(s), and extend the critical field of decadence beyond its conventional reduction to a few stock themes proffered by a small group of late nineteenth-century European writers and artists subsequently deemed "decadent" by critics. The study of decadence — and, as we shall suggest, the study of many recent studies of decadence — indicates that, contrary to its image as a rarefied ivory-tower aesthetic or a merely parodic hiatus before the inception of Modernism, decadence poses serious literary, political, and historical questions. This collection of original essays by major scholars in the field seeks to evaluate from the vantage point of our own fin-de-siècle the continuing importance for contemporary literary and cultural studies of both late nineteenth-century decadence and our current understanding of so-called decadent cultural phenomena.

It is the overarching claim of this collection that the critical study of decadence should not be confined to its traditional association with, for example, morbidity, a cult of artificiality, exoticism, or sexual nonconformism. Granted, these topics often dominate the thematic texture of decadent writing, and their literary representations constitute, to a great extent, its most lasting influence upon twentieth-century culture. Yet decadence, we shall argue, can and should be understood as something more than the mere compendium of transgressive themes and images by which it is usually identified. Beginning with a brief account of the ideological biases that have shaped much of the criticism on decadence and that have contributed to rather literalist approaches to defining decadence, this introduction will offer a background to current scholarship on the subject and will point to several aspects of decadent writing that the criticism has consistently (and symptomatically) misread or undervalued. Rather than seeking merely to dismiss any particular critic or critical approach, or to minimize the importance of both past and contemporary scholarship, we hope here to raise what we consider significant questions about the academic reception of decadence, questions that we believe indicate and redefine the pertinence of decadent art and writing to contemporary theoretical concerns. The sketch provided by this introduction is filled in by the individual chapters, which seek to evaluate the continuing interest in decadence and to map out the possible future directions for critical work on the topic.

*   *   *

While the general concept of decadence (from the Latin *de* + *cadere*, to fall away or from) centers on decline, decay, and the loss of traditional values, the study of decadence has seemed strangely and almost compulsively occupied with reinstating values by introducing, cataloging, and presenting an object it deems already defined or hopelessly undefinable. Throughout its twentieth-century reception, decadence has found its way to the shelves of research libraries (in France and Germany, as well as in English-speaking countries) almost exclusively by means of academic studies that seek to do little more than survey, summarize, and taxonomize their topic, but rarely, if ever, question the assumptions conveyed by the topic itself. Where a departure from traditional values can suggest innovation and experimentation, rather than decline, criticism on decadence is almost wholly literalist in its implicit reassertion of the very values dismantled by decadent texts. Many early studies of decadence suffer from what we might call "Nordau sprawl," after Max Nordau's influential work *Degeneration* (1892). Nordau's hostile tome collapses understandings of literary and cultural decadence into biological degeneration, treating decadent literary strategies (characterized in absurdly broad strokes) as simply the aesthetic manifestation of degenerate minds. Despite the continuing work of devoted scholars (many of whom contribute to this volume), the study of decadence has suffered under the legacy of Nordau's unreflective syncretism, his sensationalism, and the hostility of his approach. Nearly every book from the past century that purports to discuss decadence does so in the same broad strokes that characterize Nordau's work, even while trying to avoid his disparaging tone and updating his critical methods. Aside from studies of major authors such as Oscar Wilde and Joris-Karl Huysmans, specialized approaches to decadence that question the term, that interrogate the assumed continuity between decadence and degeneration, or that even move beyond plot summary or strictly thematic accounts are difficult to come by.

There are, of course, commonsense reasons for this "introductory" orientation in the criticism of decadence. For example, the writings of decadent authors are often so voluminous, and the associations of the word *decadent* so far-reaching, that the critic can understandably become enmeshed in simply making sense of his or her subject matter. Many of the most impressive studies of the field (such as Mario Praz's *Romantic Agony* and Jean Pierrot's *Decadent Imagination*) have emerged from precisely this desire to account for what seems a hopelessly chaotic, but nevertheless compelling, grouping of texts. This drive merely to introduce and characterize decadence, rather than to interrogate the strategies of decadent texts, marks even studies from the 1990s (such as David Weir's *Decadence and the Making of Modernism*). Another problem facing the critic of decadence is the sheer difficulty— both linguistic and thematic—of decadent writing. Decadent style is so notoriously challenging that an entire critical cottage industry has sprung up to confront its near "unreadability," and the combination of sexuality, violence, and esoteric thought that constitutes the thematic texture of decadence renders it foreboding to even the most patient and receptive of contemporary readers. It is, then, hardly surprising that critics have largely satisfied themselves with plot summaries (and extrapolations based on such summaries) rather than close readings or more extensive historical research. Add to the foregoing problems the almost total unavailability of decadent texts—few titles remain in print, either in their original languages or in translation (although this situation is rapidly improving), and even the best libraries often lack important primary and scholarly works—and one has a convincing set of reasons for the prevailing tendencies of much criticism on decadence.

But if the considerable challenges—material, thematic, and theoretical—facing critics of decadence offer at least a tentative explanation for the state and quality of criticism on the subject, the specific praxis of that criticism deserves further attention. Although twentieth-century critics have generally dispensed with the evangelical zeal of Nordau's antidecadent crusade, there nevertheless lingers in many critical studies a barely concealed distaste and contempt for decadent writers and texts and a concomitant drive toward classification and taxonomy. Like certain antipornography activists who meticulously catalog and classify examples of the representations they despise, critics of decadence often seem engaged in a drama of attraction to and repulsion from the texts they study, a drama that plays itself out with little attention to the gap between the act of reading and what is read. Nordau is surely the paradigmatic example of this recurring critical psychomachia, having lavished far more attention on the work he targets than almost any other critic. But even among presumably sympathetic and tolerant critics, one finds palpable traces of Nordau's distaste and discomfort. Thus A. E. Carter, whose *Idea of Decadence in French Literature* did much to further study of the field, begins his work by dismissing most decadent writing as "morbid" and "a pretentious mummy" (viii), valuable as a document, but merely "amusing" or "unreadable" in and of itself (143). And the nineteenth-century British writer Arthur Symons, who in his essay on "The Decadent Movement in Literature" (1893) was among the first openly to champion the movement in England, introduces his subsequent book *The Symbolist Movement in Literature* (1899) by suggesting that the decadent movement was a perverse product of "lesser men" and "a straying aside from the main road of literature" (6–7). Examples of this attitude can be drawn nearly at random from even the most respected studies. Such studies, as we see in Symons's reference to "lesser men," are all too often based on an implicit shift from Nordau's biologism to a barely disguised psychologism, from a focus on decadent bodies to what we might call decadent subjects.[1]

These disparaging characterizations of decadence have become so common as to seem mere received wisdom, yet their very prevalence is perhaps telling — indeed symptomatic — of a problem lying within criticism itself, and not within the supposedly decadent subjects that it so eagerly catalogs. For in their attempts to distance themselves by means of taxonomy and description from their object of study, critics of decadence inadvertently become decadent critics of sorts, deploying the same oppositions and the same evaluative categories that they find problematic in their subject matter. To call a decadent writer "morbid" or "perverse" or "artificial" is to speak in the very idiom by which these writers originally defined themselves. It is for this reason that one so often finds critics struggling to dissociate themselves from the works they study. Nordau, as usual, provides a classic case of this struggle. Nordau's work seeks to diagnose the symptoms of hysteria and hereditary degeneration in what he describes as "the *fin-de-siècle* disposition" (15). Ranging with an often striking familiarity over much of the late nineteenth-century literary scene, Nordau finds the stigmata of these afflictions in such far-flung matters as mysticism, pessimism, the formation of literary schools, and the "irresistible desire . . . to accumulate useless trifles"

(27). Yet, whereas Nordau writes from the confident perspective of the scientific investigator, he nevertheless seems at many points inadvertently, and yet significantly, to breach the boundary between himself and his pathologized "subjects." In his chapter "Decadents and Æsthetes," for example, Nordau repeatedly finds himself agreeing with the decadents' characterizations of themselves, citing as proof of his own hypothesis Gautier's famous description of Baudelaire's literary style (although he quibbles with Gautier's account of late Latin writing), scolding Huysmans for misusing the very scientific concepts upon which Nordau based his own study, and accusing Wilde of advocating claims "long ago established by me" on the relation of art and life (321). The chapter culminates in a tedious and confused attempt by Nordau — as if to reassure himself of his difference from the decadents — to produce his own speculative account of "how works of art and art in general originated" (323). In the decadents, Nordau hopes to find confirmation of his theories, but instead he finds himself staring into a kind of fun-house mirror. What Nordau seeks to describe in life, the decadents have already described (and, crucially, ironized) in their art. His "diagnosis" of their degeneracy thus turns into an effort of the presumptive "physician" not simply to ascertain "symptoms" and to pinpoint an "illness" but also (and most strenuously) to differentiate himself thereby from his textual "patient."[2]

We find similar dramas of differentiation played out in critical works that apparently maintain none of Nordau's hostility or ideological baggage, and yet which do not question the potentially telling connection between the notion of decadence and the playing out of these dramas. Karl Beckson, for example, dedicates his important anthology of British decadent writing to his wife and sons, who, he asserts, "are neither Aesthetes nor Decadents." The obvious implication of Beckson's dedication — the first words a reader is likely to encounter in opening the book — is that the "danger" of decadence can be counteracted by a strong conventional family structure. While Beckson's attempt to differentiate himself and his family from the subject matter of his book may be quite lighthearted, it in fact inscribes him within the very discourse from which he seeks to move away. The characters in decadent writing are almost always presented as the products of "degenerate" ancestral lines, the feeble last buds of dying family trees. Decadent texts, moreover, are often centrally concerned with questions of reproduction. Working from an implicit association between sexual and artistic reproduction, these texts repeatedly stage the relationship between a writer and his or her textual "progeny," or lack thereof: author and text, author and reader, mentor and student. Where conventionally one thinks of the writer "generating" his or her textual progeny (the text as child being among the well-worn Humanist topoi), decadent texts tend to undermine such straight, filial lines of reproduction, supplementing and supplanting them with figures of nonreproductive or overproductive textual generation. A notable example of this conflating of reproductions may be found in the case of Des Esseintes, Joris-Karl Huysmans's "degenerate" protagonist from *A rebours* (1884) who marks his conversion to the "unnatural" and ultimately unproductive pursuits he undertakes throughout the narrative with a funeral for his virility. Beckson's assertion of the family structure and secure filial descent as a bulwark against decadence thus plays out in reverse the plot of a decadent novel — the evidence of "good" and "normal" reproduction (a wife and two straight sons) will presumably defend against the "bad" and "perverse" reproduction depicted in and embodied by decadence — yet without any interrogation of its own inverse mirroring of its decadent subject.[3]

Critics have long characterized decadent writing in similar terms, as the product of an unnatural (pro)creation, weak and deficient yet dangerously prolific. This characterization is, of course, the basis of Nordau's attack on his "degenerate" literary contemporaries; and it finds its way into Beckson's more sympathetic relation to the movement. We also find a surprising recapitulation of this topos in Vladimir Jankélévitch's substantial and widely respected essay "La Décadence" (1950). For Jankélévitch, the decadent text is one that spawns mutants in what he describes as a "fever of proliferation." Decadence, he argues, begins in an excessive self-consciousness: "Once consciousness is aware of itself, it keeps splitting from itself like a cancer metastasizing, becoming ever more abstract, evanescent and subtly intelligent" (339). Contrasting this malignant splitting of consciousness with the focus, precision, and control he deems essential to artistic creation, Jankélévitch goes on to define decadence as a form of unhealthy introversion and narcissism. The tendency of decadent writing to turn in upon itself, to replace the "fecundity of synthesis" with the "sterile and feverish delights of self-analysis" (342), marks for Jankélévitch a sort of degenerate textual inbreeding. Whereas creative genius, he suggests, finds "its harmonious moderation and law of temperance in the very progeny it brings into the world," and thus practices what one might call a prudent textual family planning policy, the "immoderate" but sterile decadent does not know where to cease its unnatural reproduction, generating not artistic masterpieces but "new families of monsters" (345). The stable family structure and clear lines of descent that mark artistic creativity are here threatened by the monstrously dysfunctional family of what Jankélévitch calls the "ogres" (a tendency toward grandiosity and hyperbole) and "dwarves" (the valorization of details) produced by decadent procreation.

Although critics may distance themselves from the "improper" but strangely overproductive nonreproduction to which they attribute the origin and dissemination of decadence, an interesting reversal takes place when these critics treat the relationship of so-called decadent women writers to the predominantly male literary phenomenon. For here the familial metaphors that, as we have seen, generally brand the male decadents as figurative deviations from the norms of "healthy" heterosexual procreation, seem instead to present decadent women as products of the very family structure their male counterparts ostensibly threaten. Thus Maurice Barrès, for example, famously dubbed Rachilde "Mlle Baudelaire." Jean Lorrain wrote an article on Rachilde entitled "Mlle Salamandre." And the contemporary critic Jean de Palacio, along similar lines, writes an entire chapter on the French writer Jane de la Vaudere with the goal of noting that her "feminine discourse of decadence" is "curiously imitative of the masculine discourse" of her literary father Huysmans (197).[4] By means of such a reassertion of genealogical descent, Barrès, Lorrain, and Palacio foreclose the modes and means of women writers' relationships to decadence by figuring them merely as dutiful and imitative daughters who work in the shadow of exemplary fathers. The obvious implication of this selective use of genealogical metaphors is that artists must be "good" enough (i.e., be male) in order to be "bad" (i.e., to deviate from faithful aesthetic reproduction). In this manner, critics defend themselves against improper reproduction, yet also implicitly define such reproduction as the aesthetic prerogative of male writers, indeed set it up as a chief trope of decadence itself. However, as the growing critical interest in women's perspectives on decadence attests, women's contributions (women aesthetes, New Women, decadent women), often published under pseudonyms, constitute a significant intervention into, and rearticulation of, decadence and related fin-de-siècle artistic modes.[5]

The strangely congruent approaches of such different critics as Nordau, Beckson, Jankélévitch, and Barrès (spanning a century, and encompassing a wide range of ideological assumptions) highlight the common function of decadence as the bad, weak, or insignificant (but nevertheless essential) backdrop to something implicitly good, strong, and crucial. This logic of the "other" shapes much of the criticism on decadence, even (indeed especially) where such a logic might seem least applicable. In the case of Nordau, who works explicitly from a normative model of human development—the degenerate writer being, he suggests, "a morbid deviation from an original type" (16)—decadence functions, not surprisingly, as the deviation, the literary expression of biological degeneracy. But one finds a strikingly similar logic at work in the unlikely context of literary history. The genetic patterns that largely govern the writing of literary history produce diachronic narratives in which one period, movement, or school gives "birth" to another in linear fashion. While Nordau's model of decadence as deviation reinforces the moralizing end of what he assumes to be normal (and normative) human development, we also find a curious normative orientation in attempts by critics to inscribe decadence within the presumably value-neutral genealogies of literary history.

Critics tend to treat decadence, in this regard, as the weak other of some "strong" literary movement, distinguishing the (good) Aesthetes from the (bad) decadents, the (transcendent) Symbolists from the (materialistic) decadents, or the (original) Romantics from the (imitative) decadents who merely parrot or plagiarize their imagery and doctrines. Thus, for example, James M. Smith surveys more than a century of commentaries on decadence only to end up defining the movement, in terms evocative of Jankélévitch, as the "non-creative imitation of a preceding and superior literary expression [namely, Romanticism]" produced by writers "whose creative faculties have been impaired through hyperanalysis and sterile erudition" (651). Clyde de L. Ryals characterizes decadence as a hubristic inversion of Romanticism that marks the "complete disintegration" of classical aesthetic ideals (86). And John Reed, in his book-length attempt to distinguish decadence from the numerous coeval movements with which it is often confused, suggests that whereas "Symbolism is the direct descendant of Aestheticism and Art-for-Art's Sake," and thus a legitimate heir to their concerns, decadence is by contrast hybrid, "self-consciously transitional," and best understood as "an illegitimate by-blow sired by Naturalism upon Aestheticism" (14). As in the case of the figurative dysfunctional decadent family we found in other accounts, Reed's fantastic implications of bestiality and illegitimacy subtly shade into the normative judgments that literary history claims to avoid. Decadence here uncannily seems less the object of criticism than its informing model. And yet this drama of differentiation—which produces, like a decadent Sorcerer's Apprentice, so many uncontrollable decadent others—also suggests that the patterns we find in the criticism of decadence challenge in significant ways the methodological presuppositions of literary history.[6]

The paradigmatic example of this gesture is surely that of the critic Désiré Nisard, whose *Etudes de moeurs et de critique sur les poètes latins de la décadence* (1834) definitively introduced the term *décadence* into French aesthetic discourse. Nisard declares that decadent poetry results from cultural and aesthetic exhaustion, from a state "where the richest of imaginations can do nothing more for real poetry, and have merely the strength to destroy languages in scandalous fashion" (xi). Comparing passages from Virgil and Horace with those of the later poet Lucan, Nisard asserts that the two unmistakable signs of decadent poetry are the prevalence of description and the display of erudition. He ascribes this double failing to a writer's need to appeal to a jaded public (211), to the writer's own desire to avoid imitation of the "Greats," and to a presumed turn by later writers from human subjects toward an obsession with inanimate objects. Most important for Nisard, however, is the relation of decadent writing to its age. In the case of Lucan and his presumptive heirs among Nisard's contemporaries, this age is one "which satisfies itself with trifles, which has cravings for desserts, capricious and feminine, rather than virile desires" (318). Nisard here figures the question of aesthetic "taste" in the most literal of terms. While he feminizes the decadent writer as a whimsical, fanciful character with a sweet tooth, in fact his references to food associate decadence not only with overindulgence, but also with an impoverished diet, with both excess and lack, a double transgression of imaginary norms.[7] Throughout his analysis, an ideal aesthetic regime of "virile" moderation and propriety hangs as the normative backdrop to the decadent feast of scraps. And yet, Nisard's own book feeds itself on precisely such scraps, as its "only moral" (381) — the alignment of decadent poets with Nisard's Romantic contemporaries — is left to a vague eight-page coda that follows four hundred pages of copious commentary, description, quotation, and ostentatious displays of erudition. As in the decadent works he criticizes, the means of Nisard's book have engulfed their end, the text itself has taken over from its so-called pretext. Somehow the object of criticism, as Nisard himself stoically noted in the preface to the 1849 edition of his work, has gotten the better of its critic.

Twentieth-century commentators have by no means dispensed with the normative orientation that inflects Nisard's account of decadence. A recent and striking example of this strange production of a decadent "other" under the guise of literary history may be observed in Regenia Gagnier's essay "A Critique of Practical Aesthetics." For Gagnier, the crucial distinction between decadence and aestheticism is political: while the aesthetes (she includes Ruskin, Morris, and Wilde) sought equality and liberation by applying the freedom associated with art to life, the decadents sought to "derail" this project by subordinating life to art (265). That is, if the aesthetes were serious about their claims regarding the liberatory powers of art, the decadents merely mimed such claims in an attempt to avoid or to discredit such powers. Yet no sooner has Gagnier drawn this distinction between decadence and aestheticism then she herself begins to mime precisely the subordination of life to art that she finds at the pernicious heart of decadence. This subordination begins with her transition between a discussion of the two movements, which turns on an extended contrast between the thoughts and actions of Wilde and those of Huysmans's character Des Esseintes: the aesthetes are represented by a real person, while the decadents are represented by a literary figure. But the subordination becomes all-encompassing in Gagnier's discussion of Frederick Rolfe's 1906 novel *Desire and Pursuit of the Whole*. Here she repeatedly attributes the bizarre acts and attitudes of Rolfe's protagonist Crabbe to Rolfe himself, tellingly joining the two throughout her reading by calling him Crabbe/Rolfe (or sometimes Rolfe/Crabbe) and at points eliding Crabbe altogether by simply attributing his actions in the narrative to Rolfe himself. In the process of identifying the "decadent fear of the freedom of others," a fear she claims "effectively terminated the liberatory aesthetics" of Ruskin, Morris, and Wilde (276), Gagnier denies Rolfe any distance from his creation, and so displays the fear she attributes to her own decadent "other."

In much the same way as critics from Nisard and Nordau to Gagnier have tended to present decadent texts as the insignificant, second-rate, or retrograde others of literary and cultural expressions deemed more worthy of serious attention, commentators have also consistently figured decadence as a dangerous national "other," a threat emanating from beyond the borders. Just as the medical and genealogical figures deployed by critics of decadence seek to ward off a perceived threat to the body, so the critics' topographical distancing of decadence acts to defend against an apparently insalubrious, if not poisonous, "foreign commodity." The nineteenth-century reception of (or reaction to) decadence in England is a case in point. Derided as a "French disease" (like syphilis), and linguistically bracketed by its designation as "*décadence*" (as in Richard Le Gallienne's satirical poem "The *Décadent* to His Soul"), decadent art and writing appear to critics as nefarious and exotic French imports. The popular British writer Marie Corelli, for example, implicitly denounced decadent writing in 1895 by designating its geographical source in "Zola, Huysmans and Baudelaire" (qtd. in Palacio 19). Walter Pater is known to have effaced all references and allusions to Gautier and Baudelaire in his writings following the controversial reception of his first book, *Studies in the History of the Renaissance* (1873). And Wilde's "questionable" relationship to French literature (and presumably French "morals") was a pivotal aspect of the prosecution against him.

This nineteenth-century exoticizing of decadence also characterizes, in somewhat less defensive terms, much of the more recent twentieth-century criticism on the topic. English language discussions of British decadence generally continue to characterize the phenomenon as an exotic French import carried across the channel by figures such as Swinburne, and perilously grafted to token native trends. Even the 1989 edition of the *Oxford English Dictionary* still defines decadence as something "said of a *French* school which affects to belong to an age of decadence" (emphasis added). But the image of decadence as an exotic other also arises in criticism of French writers. A. E. Carter, for example, presents decadence primarily as a hostile reaction to Rousseau's social theories, picturing the decadent artist as a kind of "photographic negative" of the Noble Savage, still "vigorous and primitive, breathing the air of his virgin forests or fighting superbly for his tribal gods" (151). Carter here supplements the typically exotic atlas of decadence by treating urban landscapes, theater wings, brothels, and clinics as a kind of degenerately primitive internal other. Similarly, the Italian critic Mario Praz, despite his usual sensitivity to the exoticizing tendency in decadent texts, colors in a few maps in the imaginary atlas in his important work, *The Romantic Agony*.[8] Praz was among the first to appreciate the ways in which decadent writing seeks to "localize" decadence, to project its deviations into the representation of a "particular cultural atmosphere" (201). He points in particular to the familiar decadent topos of the Fatal Woman, who is almost inevitably placed within a nebulous Orientalized space. Yet even Praz at points tellingly Orientalizes the Orientalist writing he seeks to explain. For example, he entitles his chapter on decadence "Byzantium," thus localizing the phenomenon according to its own criteria. And in a passage redolent of the best decadent style, he describes decadent writers' fascination with "the long Byzantine twilight, that gloomy apse gleaming with dull gold and gory purple, from which peer enigmatic faces, barbaric yet refined, with dilated neurasthenic pupils" (397). Here again, we find the familiar pattern of a criticism "seduced" by its ostensibly inert object of study. Like the decadent topographies that even such sensitive critics as Praz highlight as themes *in* decadent texts, the equally exoticizing topographies of decadence offered by critics to *explain* this writing provide no real analysis of decadence, but instead map the specific concerns or anxieties of the critics or writers in question. And as with the other attempts by critics to defend the "inside" by othering the "outside," what often seems safely distant or contained by these dramas of differentiation may in fact be but an unrecognized aspect of oneself.

*   *   *

The subtle (and often not so subtle) hostility directed against decadent writers by even their best critics attests to a uneasiness produced not only by the oft-derided or unreflectively celebrated thematic universe of decadent writing (the familiar constellation of perversions, artificialities, illnesses, and blasphemies) but also by a potentially destabilizing effect of that writing itself. Decadence, as the contributors to this book demonstrate, functions as more than the collection of themes, tropes, and stock characters that critics have largely focused upon. Instead, decadent textual strategies interfere with the boundaries and borders (national, sexual, definitional, historical, to name but a few) that criticism normally relies upon to make its judgments, producing what we call a "perennial decay" of those boundaries and borders. We suggest that the many dramas of differentiation between critic and text that have shaped the academic reception of decadence are not simply incidental but in fact have everything to do with the task of rethinking both decadence and the various critical approaches to it. Whereas the critics we have examined here depend—explicitly or implicitly—on the essential "being" and definability of their subject matter, on a stable referential corpus that can be called "decadence," whatever specificity we might attribute to the decadent text pertains in fact to its "doing," to the *way* it deploys the tropes that seem to define and contain it.[9] As Jankélévitch perceptively notes, "There are no historical contents that are decadent 'in themselves.' Decadence is not *in statu*, but *in motu*; it is not a structure, it is a manner and a tendency" (365). To this extent, decadence requires a criticism receptive not merely to its themes and styles but also to its particular textual means, strategies, and procedures.

The very notion of a "decadent" movement bears this observation out. The idea of literary decadence was, from its initial application by Nisard, a term of opprobrium. All of its most resonant associations—overrefinement, sterility, morbidity, intimations of sickness and decline—had, and continue to have, largely negative inflections. The self-defined decadent "school" in France, however, constituted itself by means of an appropriation and re-mobilization of the word and its associations.[10] According to Anatole Baju, the founder of the short-lived journal *Le Décadent,* the name *decadent* was adopted precisely because of its status as a dismissive critical term: "To avoid the damaging comments about us that this somewhat despised word might generate, and then to have done with the whole thing, we opted to take the term as our emblem" (12). In much the same way—although for often starkly different cultural and political purposes—as segments of the con-temporary gay community have appropriated the previously derisive term *queer,* some of the writers we now identify as "decadent" shaped themselves and their works by ironizing and revaluing the judgment of their critics.[11] And just as one would hardly attempt to characterize the gay community by examining the meaning of the word *queer,* so the critics who attempt to define decadence by taking literally the figurative associations of an iron-ically adopted appellation inevitably place themselves in the midst of an interpretive illusion. Decadence, Richard Gilman perceptively argues in this regard, "is a word chosen to fill a space," an epithet that relies entirely on the norm it implicitly calls up and points to no substantive condition (159). It is, as Remy de Gourmont notes, in the passage that serves as our epigraph, "a purely negative idea" (70).[12] As such, decadent writing is no more "deca-dent" than realist writing is "real." Only when critics begin to recognize the consequences of this insight and examine the *uses* of decadence, rather than its *meaning,* can critical discussions of the topic move beyond assumptions (often unwittingly) inherited from Nordau.

The most interesting decadent writers, we would argue, unlike the major-ity of their contemporary and twentieth-century readers, actively cultivated the illusion of decadence in their works and, in so doing, attempted to render problematic both the moralizing dismissals of their critics and the apparent enthusiasm with which those critics tellingly brandished the con-cept of decadence in their efforts to dismiss it. Indeed, it might be argued that the critics' response to decadence is no mere misunderstanding but an important consequence of decadent literary strategies. The dramas of dif-ferentiation we noted in the critical response to decadence are not simply one more potential response among others. Rather, as we shall suggest, the production of precisely such dramas—and not the commonly identified senses of revulsion or titillation—is the pivotal effect that decadent texts have upon their readers. Generations of critics have accounted for decadent writing by pointing to the "deviance" of its authors, its protagonists, or its prevalent thematic concerns. Decadence, according to this model, is quite simply—and tautologically—decadent, fundamentally limited by its de-viance (wilful or not) from some cultural, political, biological, ethical, or artistic norm. We would suggest, however, that decadent writing poses a challenge to precisely the kinds of literary and artistic judgments that would allow one to call a text "decadent" or to measure its deviation from the norm. The familiar textual markers (thematic, stylistic, or characterologi- cal) that critics point to in their identification of a work's decadence are never presented clearly or distinctly. Instead, we would argue, these markers are inevitably framed in decadent writing by a complex series of inversions, displacements, and qualifications that renders their status as evidence high- ly questionable. This textual strategy throws into relief not the decadence of a work, an author, or a character but the theoretical assumptions that under- lie any attempt to make such a determination.

Charles Baudelaire, to take a pivotal example of this strategy, often found himself at the center of the polemical aftermath following upon Nisard's work. While he did not consider himself a "decadent" writer (Gautier, how- ever, would make a tentative connection in his famous 1868 "Notice" to the first posthumous edition of *Les Fleurs du mal*), he did not simply deny the applicability of the term. Rather than rejecting the implications of deca- dence out of hand, he effectively mobilized its associations in order to prob- lematize its use. In his essay "Further Notes on Edgar Poe" (1857), for example, he suggests that the literary shortcomings attributed to decadent writing mark instead a failure of critical insight:

> "Literature of decadence!" Empty words that we often hear dropping, with all the resonance of a flatulent yawn, from the lips of those sphinxes-without-a-riddle which stand guard before the holy portals of Classical Aesthetics. Each time that the dogma- tic oracle echoes forth, you can be certain that you are in the presence of a work more entertaining than the *Iliad*. It is undoubtedly a question of some poem or novel in which all the parts are skillfully interwoven to create surprise, a work superbly rich in style, in which all the resources of language and prosody have been employed by an unerring hand. (93; trans. modified)

Baudelaire here caricatures the detractors of decadence as humorlessly literalist, even deficient, readers (atypical sphinxes with no secrets), whose dogmatic criteria lead them to overlook the literary value of anything more recent than Homer. Rather than simply inverting the critics' dogmatism by claiming that so-called decadent writing is in fact "better" than the works accepted by Classical Aesthetics, however, Baudelaire questions the anthro- pomorphic implications of the metaphor itself. If, he suggests, one insists on anthropomorphizing literary history, on claiming that "there is a scale of literatures, one infantile, one childish, one adolescent, etc., etc.," then writers can hardly be blamed for acting according to the "fatal and foreor- dained" logic of "such a mysterious law" (93). In this way, Baudelaire sets up a double relationship to the idea of decadence, at once working with the term, while working against its naturalizing (and hence moralizing) implica- tions.[13] As opposed to those who take literally the setting suns and decaying empires evoked by decadence, Baudelaire proposes that "the sunset will in fact seem . . . like a wonderful allegory," a nonmimetic figure, and not the image of some actual decline (94).

Baudelaire similarly destabilizes the ideologically charged boundaries constructed by his critics in the section of *The Painter of Modern Life* (1863) entitled "In Praise of Cosmetics." Baudelaire's text (in many ways a development of Gautier's preface to *Mademoiselle de Maupin* [1834], and an important model for Wilde's "Decay of Lying" [1891]), argues that artificial means of improving upon natural beauty should be valued and not disparaged. Although many introductory approaches to decadence refer (reductively yet quite legitimately) to this text's role in promoting an aesthetics of artifice, Baudelaire's "decadent topography" here goes much further than a mere substitution of art for nature. For Baudelaire, artifice is by no means the supposedly decadent option of overcivilized societies. While eighteenth-century aesthetics saw nature as the source of all good and beauty — and thus defined modern artifice as antinatural and deceptive — Baudelaire sardonically insists that social good is in fact a product of artificiality rather than its antithesis. Whereas nature counsels self-interest, only the artificial laws of society and religion teach us virtue. "Evil," Baudelaire writes, "happens without effort, naturally, fatally; Good is always the product of some art" (32). Baudelaire finds further support for this claim in the example offered by the children and "primitives" whose way of life eighteenth-century "Arcadian" writers critically contrasted with decadent modernity. For these supposedly more "natural" and less "decadent" groups are no less fascinated with artifice than are the moderns: "Those races which our confused and perverted civilization is pleased to treat as savage, with an altogether ludicrous pride and complacency, understand, just as the child understands, the lofty spiritual significance of ornamentation" (32; trans. modified). By questioning the conflation of two oppositions frequently taken for granted — artifice vs. nature, civilized vs. primitive — Baudelaire challenges the logical and historical assumptions informing literalist understandings of decadence. Modern society is decadent, he insists, only to the extent that it has fallen away from ideals of *artifice* and not those associated with nature. In this context, the key concept of decadent aesthetics ironically (and strategically) becomes the norm and not the deviation it is generally assumed to be. "Woe to him," Baudelaire concludes, "who . . . carries his degeneracy [la dépravation] to the point of no longer having a taste for anything but nature unadorned" (32).[14]

We find a further example of this simultaneous mobilization and undermining of the concept of decadence in the later writings of Friedrich Nietzsche. Nietzsche's complex use of the term *decadence* (often emphasized in his text by the French *décadence*, on the likely model of the similarly complex term *ressentiment*) is quite different from that of Baudelaire, but tends toward the same critique of its moralizing and naturalizing implications.

Nietzsche, of course, cast himself as an opponent of decadence, not its champion. But he, like Baudelaire, was deeply skeptical of those who used the term as a means of disparagement. Nietzsche characterizes decadence not as a natural process but as a psychological disposition, a "will" to sickness informing modern morality, a morality that nonetheless presents itself as the very norm of health. As he writes, for example, in the *Case of Wagner* (1888), the "typical decadent" is one who "has a sense of necessity in his corrupted taste, who claims it as a higher taste, who knows how to get his corruption accepted as law, as progress, as fulfillment" (620). To critique decadence, in this regard, is not merely to point out the "symptoms" of decline (which for readers such as Nisard amounted to little more than the presence of certain themes or stylistic traits), but radically to question the "physicians" themselves, to turn their own "diagnosis" against them.

But Nietzsche takes this critique a step further. For rather than adopting unproblematically the physician's role he denies to the "typical decadents," Nietzsche insists upon questioning the entire doctor/patient dynamic of the received discourse on decadence. While he continues to mobilize the rhetoric of health and sickness — and indeed makes it a central trope of his later writings — Nietzsche significantly complicates this dynamic by repeatedly asserting his own status as a "recovering" decadent. As he writes in his autobiography, *Ecce Homo* (1888), his interest in and analytical sensitivity toward the "symptoms" of decadence cannot be dissociated from his own "decadent" genealogy:

The good fortune of my existence, its uniqueness perhaps, lies in its fatality: I am, to express it in the form of a riddle, already dead as my father, while as my mother I am still living and becoming old. This dual descent, as it were, both from the highest and the lowest rung on the ladder of life, at the same time a *decadent* and a beginning — this, if anything, explains that neutrality, that freedom from all partiality in relation to the total problem of life, that perhaps distinguishes me. I have a subtler sense of smell for the signs of ascent and decline than any other human being before me; I am the teacher *par excellence* for this — I know both; I am both. (678)

The effect of Nietzsche's assertion here is to render the opposition between doctor and patient hopelessly confused. If, as he suggests, the only competent "doctor" is necessarily also a "patient," if the healer is necessarily sick, then any clear distinction between the two positions — a distinction insisted upon by Nordau and other critics — must break down. But this confusion in roles extends implicitly to the relationship between reader (as physician) and text (as patient). To the extent that Nietzsche defines the decadent as above all a dissimulator, his apparent confession does little more than set us in a disarming interpretive abyss. If we believe his confession, we risk falling for a decadent ruse; but if we reject it, we must also question Nietzsche's definition of decadence, which grounds our very rejection. In neither case can we confidently take on the role of "physician," or even grasp onto a definition of decadence that would inform our perspective.

All of Nietzsche's accusations of decadence function along similarly paradoxical lines. Take the case of Nietzsche's well-known "borrowing" of Paul Bourget's definition of decadent style. For Bourget, a French novelist and conservative cultural critic, literary decadence is a sign that the broader social "organism" has lost control of its individual "cells," subordinating the greater good of the whole to the independent demands of the parts.[15] Such a failure of subordination is reflected in Bourget's famous image of decadent writing as a chaos of insubordination: "A decadent style is one in which the unity of the book breaks down [se décompose] to make room for the independence of the page, in which the page breaks down to make room for the independence of the sentence, and the sentence to make room for the independence of the word" (24). In Bourget's account, decadence comes across as a deviation from a norm: where the part should be subordinate to the whole, decadence gives precedence to the part over the whole. In *The Case of Wagner*, Nietzsche recasts Bourget's image of textual insubordination, but in so doing subtly changes the image and its meaning: "What is the sign of every *literary decadence*? That life no longer dwells in the whole. The word becomes sovereign and leaps out of [springt aus] the sentence, the sentence reaches out and obscures the meaning of the page, the page gains life at the expense of the whole — the whole is no longer a whole" (626). Aside from shifting Bourget's metaphorical register to emphasize the vigor of decadent style (e.g., instead of the sentence "making room" for the word, the word "leaps out" of the sentence), Nietzsche's most consequential alteration is to reverse the *direction* of Bourget's account. Both Nietzsche and Bourget begin with a notion of the whole. But whereas in Bourget's image this whole figuratively decomposes (from the book, to the page, to the sentence, to the word), in Nietzsche's version the whole is, as it were, recomposed (from the word, to the sentence, to the page) in the very process of its presumptive decomposition. Although Nietzsche seems to be saying the same thing as Bourget, his reordering questions the naturalistic and historical implications of the organic metaphor upon which Bourget's notion rests. The whole, for Nietzsche, is not a norm from which decadence deviates, but is rendered "no longer a whole."

Both Baudelaire and Nietzsche, we might suggest, appropriate the concept of decadence primarily in order to question the conceptual groundings that critics frequently attribute to it, and to challenge the easy conflation of organic, historical, and aesthetic metaphors to which the term lends itself so easily. The critics to whom Baudelaire and Nietzsche respond treat decadence as a real quality of a civilization or an individual, a quality that can be ascertained by means of textual traces (either thematic or stylistic) which presumably reveal evidence of some organic or social disorder. Baudelaire and Nietzsche, as we have seen, ask instead whether the practice of such a textual symptomatology is itself symptomatic of something unexamined in the critics' method. The decadent text here becomes something

like a two-way mirror, in which the reader's effort to see through the glass —
an effort seemingly encouraged by the text's themes and style — is frustrated
by the persistence of his or her own reflection. The very tool that allows one
to identify and understand decadence — here the metaphorical conflation
of text and symptom — necessarily blocks that understanding.

Baudelaire's poem "To the Reader," which serves to preface *Les Fleurs du
mal* (1858), offers a striking example of just this strategy played out in terms
of broader concerns. The poem seems throughout to present a series of
tableaux depicting the decadence of Second Republic France. Intoning like
a street-corner prophet, Baudelaire's lyric voice condemns in almost lascivi-
ous detail the "folly and error, stinginess and sin" that possess our bodies
and souls (5), and the false tears and hollow gestures of remorse that allow
us to explain away the consequences of our actions. Among all of the sins
the poet enumerates, though, one "dainty monster" is, he writes, "most foul
and false," Ennui (7). But the danger of this allegorical monster, unlike that
of the more conventional sins to which Baudelaire's speaker points, stems
less from its directly harmful effects than from its hypocrisy and self-
deception:

> Though making no grand gestures, nor great cries
> He willingly would devastate the earth
> And in one yawning swallow all the world;
>
> He is Ennui — eye weighted with an involuntary tear,
> He dreams of scaffolds, as he puffs his water-pipe.
> (7; trans. modified)

Ennui here seems to be a type of the decadent hero made familiar by
Huysmans and Wilde. He is, as Ross Chambers has noted in his fine reading
of this poem, ensconced in stereotypically "oriental" luxury, and — much
like Des Esseintes at his "refined Thebaid" or Dorian Gray at the opium
den–he dreams of violent spectacles while drying his crocodile tears with a
puff of narcotic smoke (98). Tellingly, however, Baudelaire quite explicitly
figures this most "decadent" of sinners in a way that unmistakably applies as
well to his readers. While Ennui "would" devastate the earth or swallow the
world, he most certainly does find pleasure in observing its more horrifying
spectacles. Ennui's "decadence," in other words, is a product of its spectacular attitude toward sin, and not its hereditary, sexual, or political disposition.
This distinction allows Baudelaire's speaker to turn his apparent description
of decadence against his reader: "Reader, you know this dainty monster /
— Hypocrite reader — my semblance — my brother!" (7; trans. modified).
Baudelaire's speaker refuses to allow his reader the comfort of looking upon
Ennui as if he were merely a freakish captive of the "infamous menagerie of
vice" in which the poem places him (7). Rather, precisely this comfortable

assumption of aesthetic distance becomes the chief emblem for the sin itself. In the passive spectatorship of Ennui, the poem insists, the reader should find his or her own reflection and not the moralizing lesson he or she is led to expect. The reader, it turns out, is the very "monster" whose decadence the poem puts on display.

Many of the pivotal decadent novels elaborate a similar mobilization and critique of the major concept that seems to define them. Much as, we would argue, Baudelaire and Nietzsche take up the notion of decadence chiefly in order to question its assumptions, so the novels of Huysmans, Wilde, and others, conspicuously present themselves as accounts of decadence, but at the same time they severely challenge the possibility of giving such an account. Perhaps the best example of this procedure is the "Notice" to Huysmans's *A rebours*. This brief preface gives an account of Des Esseintes's origins and education, and details the events leading up to his quintessentially "decadent" retreat from Paris. The account begins with a guided tour of the family portraits preserved in Des Esseintes's ancestral home, the Château de Lourps. As a group, the narrator notes, these portraits depict the "degeneration" of the family. The earliest portraits show "sturdy campaigners with forbidding faces," whose vitality is so evident that the picture frames "were scarcely wide enough for their broad shoulders" (17). At the other end of the spectrum stands a single portrait, which presents "a strange, sly face, with pale, drawn features; the cheekbones were punctuated with cosmetic commas of rouge, the hair plastered down and bound with a string of pearls, and the thin, painted neck emerged from the starched pleats of a ruff" (17). To explain this apparent aberration of the family line, an aberration that recurs in Des Esseintes, who "bore a striking resemblance to his distant ancestor," the narrator draws upon a discourse all too familiar to readers of Nordau. In this portrait, the narrator insists, "the defects of an impoverished stock and the excess of lymph in the blood were already apparent" (17). These defects and excesses, the reader is left to infer, explain the "decadence" of the novel's protagonist, the last scion of his family. "Since then," the narrator writes, "the degeneration [la décadence] of this ancient house had without a doubt followed a regular course" (17; trans. modified).

The English translator's decision in this passage to replace Huysmans's word "décadence" with the biological concept of "degeneration," however contextually and historically appropriate it may seem, throws into relief a tension within the text itself between the narrator's self-assured explanatory model of degeneracy and the questionable supporting evidence offered by the text.[16] To begin with, the portrait that seems to indicate the "regular" degeneration of the family is the sole remaining portrait between those depicting the founders of the family and the narrator's own "portrait" of Des Esseintes himself: "There was, in fact, a gap in the pictorial pedigree [filière des visages], with only one canvas to bridge it, only one face to join past and present" (17). This gap renders the narrator's genealogical interpretation somewhat more shaky than it might at first appear, for the single portrait can thereby provide no evidence of a continuous decline.[17] The narrator's confident assertions that the portraits form a consistent chain or line pointing — "without a doubt" — to hereditary decadence would suggest, on the contrary, that there is no positive (or positivist) evidence to support the idea that Des Esseintes's decadence can be explained in terms of biological degeneracy. Contrary to the narrator's implicit assimilation of decadence to degeneration, Huysmans's text drives a wedge between the two ideas, refusing to allow one to account for the other. This tension surrounding the narrator's initial explanatory model for the protagonist's actions is supported over the course of the narrative as a whole, which offers numerous competing explanations for Des Esseintes's decadence, from the details of his childhood, to his Jesuit education (Des Esseintes's own explanation), to his youthful debaucheries, to the encroachments of modern society.

Moreover, just as Huysmans's text disallows ready-made, naturalistically determined, definitions of its protagonist, so too the narrator's interpretation of the pictorial pedigree relies on theoretical claims about the artwork that Des Esseintes explicitly disputes. The narrator's reading of the portraits is mimetic; it assumes that art imitates nature, that a picture can tell us something about the person it depicts.[18] Whereas the narrator tells us that a given picture represents somebody who preexists the form of the representation itself, Des Esseintes consistently argues against such mimetic assumptions, claiming that "Nature . . . has had her day" as the grounding for artistic interpretation (36). For Des Esseintes, the once-clear distinctions between nature and artifice have ceded to a more mottled aesthetics drawing upon the interdependence of their meanings. The narrator's mimetic interpretation of the portraits thus fundamentally contradicts the claims of Des Esseintes's new aesthetic creed, a creed enthusiastically imparted by the very same narrator. We cannot accept the coherence of one model without inherently rejecting the coherence of the other. On both explanatory and theoretical grounds, then, Huysmans's narrative undermines the seemingly authoritative claims made by its narrator about the protagonist's decadence. Huysmans nowhere explicitly argues against these claims, and thus lures his readers — including his English translator — into accepting them. But to do so requires us to go against the grain, as it were, of the competing claims scattered throughout the work. The "decadence" that Huysmans appears to exemplify does not in fact offer predictable explanatory examples of decadence. Decadence does not stand as a basic fact from which the work can be assumed to proceed. Rather, it functions as a critical designation for a work whose textual strategies are in constant tension with its supposed explanations and examples.

We find a similarly complicated relationship between decadence and interpretation in Wilde's *Picture of Dorian Gray* (1890). Critics seem never to tire of attributing Wilde's decadence to his "slavish" imitations of more illustrious French and British forerunners (even the normally judicious Graham Hough could suggest, for example, that Wilde's ideas are "little more than a series of attitudes and undigested notions" held together by the thread of personality [203]). But Wilde arguably took far more from his ostensible influences than the empty catalogs of tropes and themes that critics identify. Indeed, much as Nietzsche, Baudelaire, and Huysmans offer "portraits" of decadence that inevitably become reflections of the reader's interpretive processes, so Wilde's own treatment of decadence turns crucially on the question of interpretation. In *The Picture of Dorian Gray*, as in *A rebours*, much of this treatment centers on a painting. Throughout Wilde's narrative we are encouraged to find the decadence of the work's titular protagonist in the portrait that seems to provide visible evidence of his increasing moral decay. Painted by an admiring artist, this portrait initially "teaches" Dorian about his beauty, but following the apparently supernatural fulfillment of Dorian's plea for eternal youth, it ages in his place. The legacy of his sins, and the consequences of his decadence, appear to manifest themselves on the painted canvas, not on Dorian's body: "The portrait was to bear the burden of his shame" (117). Here we find an absurdly literal version of the narrator's reading of the "pictorial pedigree" in the "Notice" to *A rebours*. The painting of Dorian seems to present a portrait of degeneration in process and within a single generation, not over the course of centuries. Its mimesis is, as it were, more real than the original.

Tellingly, however, this supernatural interpretation of the portrait's transformation (an interpretation voiced by Dorian and shared, significantly, by the suspiciously unreliable narrator) is only one among several readings of the work presented in the course of the narrative. As Wilde writes in his preface to the novel, "It is the spectator, and not life, that art really mirrors" (4). Far from being merely an abstract theoretical claim, this statement succinctly describes the responses of Wilde's fictional characters to Dorian's portrait. Each major character in the novel finds his own reflection, and precisely not that of the sitter, in the picture. The artist, Basil Hallward, for instance, resists showing the painting in public because, he says, "I have put too much of myself into it" (6). The work, he believes, tells the autobiographical story of the artist's idolatry, not the story of the sitter's decay. Basil's friend Lord Henry, who plays Mephistopheles to Dorian's Faust, instead finds in the portrait an image of "the real Dorian Gray" (33). But this Dorian is for Lord Henry simply another version of himself, whom he has "fashioned into a marvelous type," and who echoes Lord Henry's intellectual views "with all the added music of passion and youth" (42). Like Basil, Lord Henry finds his own image in the work. Dorian reads the work along this line as well. At first, he finds in it "the sense of his own beauty" (30). Later, he notes "a real pleasure" (118) in watching the changes on the canvas, and describes the work as "a diary of my life from day to day" (169).

And in a scene that explicitly recalls the "Notice" to *A rebours*, Dorian gazes
at the portraits of his ancestors and wonders whether the strange quality of
his own portrait can be attributed to his family history, to some poisonous
hereditary "germ" that has passed from body to body (158).[19]

Juxtaposed with the opinions of Basil and Lord Henry, Dorian's interpretation of the portrait's decadence becomes much less authoritative than
at first it seems to be. Whatever the portrait may "actually" look like, and to
whatever extent it "really" depicts Dorian's decadence, all we are given by
the text is a series of mutually exclusive interpretations of what the portrait
presents. There is simply no way to verify any of the interpretations. Wilde's
text, in this respect, becomes a "portrait" of competing interpretations and
not just the parable about the impossibility of living a decadent life that it
has long been made out to be. As Wilde himself wrote in a public response to
newspaper criticisms of his book, "Each man sees his own sin in Dorian
Gray. What Dorian Gray's sins are no one knows. He who finds them has
brought them" (*Artist* 248). These words, let us note, can apply both to
Wilde's protagonist and to the book that bears his name. Just as Wilde gives
us no general description of Dorian's portrait, only a series of reactions to it,
so readers of his work can never "find" the decadence that portrait seems to
offer. For any attribution of decadence — both within the novel and in its
reading — returns readers and characters alike to their own interpretive
strategies.

*   *   *

Decadence was in the nineteenth century — and remains today — a term
that moved easily across disciplinary boundaries, settling in different contexts with distinct connotations and effects. The mobility of the term itself,
we suggest, demands an interdisciplinary critical response, one able to track
the term's relocations, recontextualizations, and redefinitions across historical and geographical boundaries. The readiness of critics to expel decadence from their own borders suggests that they fear not just a "decadent"
contagion within their national, biological, or disciplinary realms, but rather a phenomenon that highlights the conventional nature of boundaries
themselves. We see this "perennial decay" of boundaries — the insistence on
at once mobilizing and undermining boundaries and differences — as a central quality and effect of decadent writing, and all of the essays in this
volume address it explicitly or implicitly. To rethink decadence in this manner, we suggest, is not only to engage matters of aesthetics and politics,
rhetoric and ideology, art and life, but also to begin to understand the part
that decadence has played in the development, and the dissolution, of such
oppositional boundaries.

The individual essays in *Perennial Decay* all address the long underappreci-
ated aesthetic and political complexity of decadent cultural phenomena.

They examine this complexity across several national boundaries, and detail the significance of decadence in a variety of contexts, from literature, to theater and film, to the visual arts, to the social arena, and to the adumbration of sexual, national, and political differences. Amid this wide range of subjects, three basic theoretical and methodological questions inform all of the essays. Perhaps the most characteristic gesture of many of the contributors is to take the antimimetic claims of decadence seriously as a textual and social strategy rather than simply as one more decadent theme. Barbara Spackman, for example, questions the conventional approach to decadence as an inversion of mimesis, where nature now imitates art. While the simple binary inversion substituting artifice for nature is often seen as synecdochal of decadent aesthetics as a whole, Spackman demonstrates, in a reading of asymmetrical "interversions" in Huysmans's *A rebours*, that decadent aesthetics destabilizes the very opposition between nature and artifice. Matthew Potolsky similarly examines the uses of imitation in decadent writing. Exploring in detail the effects of imitation in a short story by Walter Pater, Potolsky suggests that decadent imitation is a method of critical resignification and not the final recourse of exhausted intellects that it is frequently taken to be.

The destabilizing effect of the decadent conception of mimesis is also apparent in several essays that focus on the problem of posing and performativity. Looking at the Latin American response to Oscar Wilde, Sylvia Molloy argues that the poses, discourses, and clothing in which any identity is performed are often highly ambiguous, all the more so when these signs are transposed from one culture to another. As she points out, the individuals responsible for transferring the coded disourses of London's fin-de-siècle decadents to Latin America — for abetting the "correct" interpretation of a Latin American author's or artist's actions and creations–were often the same individuals whose careers depended on the cultural excision of these same codes and identities. Dennis Denisoff begins by analyzing the almost identical poses struck by Wilde and his legal nemesis, the Marquess of Queensberry, in separate photographic portraits–a genre that demanded the communication of a forced "naturalness," a simultaneous acknowledgment and denial of self-fashioning–in order to demonstrate the similar performative and strategic overlap in Wilde's and Queensberry's efforts to attain authority and maneuverability within their society. The portraits, Denisoff argues, reveal a decadent space, also articulated in the men's writings and public performances, in which *both* men hoped to institute different cultural values and desires. Emily Apter's essay focuses on the depiction of the shadowy realm of the demimonde in the photography of Nan Goldin and Brassaï. For Apter, the demimonde constitutes a subset of decadence in its performance of marginality. Like the decadent, the resident of the demimonde is a kind of internal exile, a "squatter" within the dominant culture, whose poses make visible the margins of that culture.

Questions of performance are, of course, inextricably linked to the play-ing out of identity—national, sexual, political, colonial—in decadent writ-ing. In his contribution to *Perennial Decay*, Leonard Koos examines the way proper names in decadent writing paradoxically disrupt nominal, genealogi-cal, and sex- and gender-based identity. The use of the pseudonym and the figure of the transvestite, Koos argues, distorts the very models on which selfhood and difference rely. Koos's insights complement Marc Weiner's and Melanie Hawthorne's examinations of the decadent construction of male sexual identity. Weiner traces the decadent identification of homosexuality, opera, and disease from its origins in the writings of Wagner and Nietzsche to its recent reappearance in the film *Philadelphia*. For Weiner, this reappear-ance of a fin-de-siècle topos in the climactic moment of a contemporary film attests to the (unthinking) persistence of a decadent thematics in twentieth-century culture. Hawthorne examines the role of French in discursively con-stituting homosexual identity, using the case of Wilde's *Salomé* as an illustra-tion. The zone of "otherness" created by national borders, Hawthorne ar-gues, offers a way to articulate an identity that could not otherwise speak its name.

Liz Constable, Hema Chari, and Jennifer Birkett all approach the prob-lem of decadence by way of national and political identification. Constable focuses on Maurice Barrès, turn-of-the-century French decadent and, subse-quently, extreme nationalist. Highlighting the naming and identification of decadence in Barrès's work, she shows that, in his transition to nationalism, Barrès freezes the dynamic resistance of decadent strategies into rigidly oppositional allegorical poles of a nationalist unconscious, now menaced by phenomena identified as decadent. Constable argues that the decadence named by Barrès, for which he furnishes a nationalist, anti-Semitic causal explanation, in fact identifies the threat of reading against the grain, of interpreting texts, as opposed to following ideological interpretive direc-tives. Birkett's essay challenges some of the family resemblances attributed to decadent artists by turning to stylistic similarities between writers that in fact coexist with, and disguise, stark political differences. Comparing the work of Remy de Gourmont and Joséphin Péladan, Birkett demonstrates that, despite stylistic similarities, the two writers generate notably different political implications. Chari argues that Wilkie Collins's novel *The Moonstone* constructs and identifies an Orientalized decadent body through mobiliz-ing a complex ideological matrix of addiction, foreignness, male effemin-acy, and nonprocreative sexual desire. Chari analyzes the textual strategies through which Collins's narrative fetishistically disavows British dependency on the opium trade, while constructing the addictive, dependent body of the colonized in order to justify British imperialist incursions.

Other essays in this collection demonstrate that the rewriting of history that Chari notes is, however, reconstituted in some intentionally decadent works as a means of critically revising ideals and images of the past. Charles

Bernheimer, for example, reexamines the common critical dismissal of the term *decadence* on the grounds that its metaphorical, rather than referential, function invalidates its use. Highlighting the way in which *decadence* suggests either a subversive, defiant refusal of norms or a reprehensible transgression of such norms through a failure in sublimation, Bernheimer redirects our attention to the role of the norm for decadent artists, and points to the ways in which their texts are self-consciously aware that essentializing norms are projections, even as they may fantasize the existence of such unquestioned norms. Michael Riffaterre similarly looks at the way decadent writing is based upon a "paradoxical" rewriting of Romantic themes and topoi. Decadence, he suggests, goes against the "doxa" (opinion, common sense) by transforming Romantic conventions into parodic or hyperbolic repetitions. This focus on decadence as the scene of a literary-historical agon should, according to Riffaterre, foster an understanding of the movement that avoids the essentializing biological or chronological criteria assumed by many previous critics. Both Sharon Bassett and David Wayne Thomas examine decadent revisions of history and historical judgment. Although *Marius the Epicurian* is often read as Pater's timid effort to erase the decadent impression his earlier works had made on critics, Bassett argues that this erasure might better be understood not as a retreat from decadence but as an amplification on the level of style and language. In an analysis of the figure of Marcus Aurelius, highly valorized by contemporary Victorians, Bassett shows the extent to which Pater's rewriting of this figure demonstrates his investment in maintaining, if at the same time, concealing, his decadent cultural project. David Wayne Thomas begins with the familiar premise that history constructs itself through narrative, when he analyzes the decadent means by which Peter Greenaway's film *The Cook, the Thief, His Wife & Her Lover* defamiliarizes the narrative process. The film, Thomas demonstrates, relies on shifts in narrative perspective to restructure history even as its dominant narrative unfolds.

* * *

Of course, the revised "portrait" of decadence that we have argued for should by no means be taken to depict a family trait. Indeed, this portrait itself is very much a product of the taxonomizing approach (here applied to scholarly rather than literary texts) that we question in the writings of earlier critics. It is in this way perhaps no less symptomatic in its characterization of decadence than the criticism of Nisard or Nordau. Moreover, much of the work produced under the decadent banner has much different ideological effects than the writings we have examined. Often this work drains the potentially disruptive textual strategies that mark certain decadent texts of their critical power by reducing these strategies into conventionalized thematic models. A crucial case in point is the phenomenon of "baudelairisme" that marked much of the so-called decadent movement of the 1880s and 1890s in France. Baudelaire, as we have seen, often deployed "decadent" tropes and themes as a means of challenging his readers' interpretive assumptions. Later writers, however, often sought to turn the essentially critical, provocative, and problematically unaccountable textual strategies of his work into a source-model for their own productions. Catherine Coquio, in an important discussion of Baudelaire and the decadents, describes this process as a "sexualizing, demonizing, [and] pathological intensification" of Baudelairian elements (95). As such, these writers "create" Baudelaire retrospectively as a model, where, in fact, his texts resist providing any model for their semiotic disruptions. For example, in his novel *Méphistophéla* (1890), Catulle Mendès literalizes and pathologizes the Baudelairian tropes of drug use and lesbianism in the moralistic tale of a lesbian morphine addict. As Barbara Spackman notes, Mendès here "recycles" Baudelaire's themes, but ignores the larger strategic purposes which these themes may originally have served. Mendès, she writes, adds "an ideological glue absent from Baudelaire's texts," a glue that binds the tropes to "petty bourgeois concerns foreign to Baudelaire himself."

By contrast, the examples of Baudelaire (as opposed to "baudelairisme"), Nietzsche, Huysmans, and Wilde suggest that decadent literary strategies can offer a powerful challenge to entrenched manners of reading and interpretation. Many of the other writers and artists discussed by our contributors—from Rachilde to Gourmont, Djuna Barnes to Georges Brassaï, Nan Goldin to Peter Greenaway—present in their own works a similar challenge, and thus attest to the continuing relevance of decadent cultural phenomena. That said, it remains to ask the question implicitly posed by the subtitle to this collection and repeatedly addressed by our contributors: "What are the political implications of decadence and decadent aesthetics?" If, as we have suggested, decadence aims to undermine conventional boundaries and borders, to what extent can this undermining be understood as a political—and even politically useful—gesture?

Critics have long treated decadent writing as a conservative, even reactionary, mode. On some levels, this interpretation seems sound. Unlike many of the Romantics and Naturalists before them, the decadents almost uniformly reject the democratic, secularist, and egalitarian developments of the modern world, preferring instead to seek out the aristocratic and spiritual trappings of an imagined old regime. Decadent texts often set themselves implicitly against a wide range of despised others: woman, the bourgeoisie, non-Europeans, the clergy. Even the ornate and allusive style of decadent writing seems addressed to a privileged minority. And yet the examples of decadent textual strategies we have discussed above suggest that, far from being simply reactionary, decadent texts also question the interpretive validity of their own claims. Indeed, as we have seen, statements that initially seem reactionary often turn out to suggest a radical critical interrogation of the very tropes they deploy. The critique of organicism we found in the works of Baudelaire and Nietzsche, for instance, makes use of a major reactionary trope in order to question it. Similarly, Huysmans and Wilde draw upon the discourse of degeneracy that Nordau would later take up for his own purposes, but they subject this discourse to a rigorous theoretical challenge.

Even on the level of strategy, however, decadence produces no consistent political implication, for the disruptions of decadent writing regularly have supported starkly opposed political aims. The case of Nietzsche's appropriation by Nazi philosophers is surely the paradigmatic example of this problem, but similar instances are not difficult to find.[20] For example, the Italian decadent writer Gabriele D'Annunzio — often called the "John the Baptist of fascism" — notoriously commanded an occupation of the city of Fiume in 1919, presenting a significant political challenge to Mussolini. In response, Mussolini appropriated many of D'Annunzio's slogans and stylistic gestures, and sought, with a certain degree of success, to bring him into the fascist fold.[21] The French novelist Maurice Barrès, likewise, forged connections between decadent aesthetics and an aggressively anti-Semitic nationalist politics. Critics generally seek to treat the decadent and the political dimensions of Barrès's work as chronologically and ideologically distinct, associating his decadence with writings from the 1880s and early 1890s, and his politics with later nationalistic writings. However, much as D'Annunzio saw little distinction between his decadence and his proto-fascism, Barrès moved quite deliberately between decadence and nationalism, giving an explicitly political form to the intuitive and instinctive aesthetics of sensation he described as his "éducation baudelairienne" (7). On the other end of the political spectrum, though, we find numerous assertions of the way decadent writing can serve the interests of progressive, and even radical, political aims. Poststructuralist theory finds important examples of radical thought in the works of many fin-de-siècle figures closely associated with decadence. Theorists such as Julia Kristeva, Jacques Derrida, Sarah Kofman, and Gilles Deleuze, for example, have pointed to the radical implications of Mallarmé's poetic experimentation and Nietzsche's philosophy.[22] More recently, Jonathan Dollimore finds in Wilde's strategy of sexual and aesthetic inversion a valuable contribution to contemporary theoretical debates on dissident, nonessentializing, and antihomophobic forms of cultural resistance.

Given the complex implications of these examples, we would maintain that the critical task posed by the analysis of decadence, a task begun by the contributors to this collection, lies less in simply noting the disruption of conventional boundaries that characterizes decadent writing (although noting it is a crucial first step) than in accounting for the ways in which such disruptions make any effort to cross over from aesthetics to politics highly unpredictable. While the decadent textual strategies we have discussed seem to offer a potentially progressive counterpart to the apparently reactionary tendencies of much decadent writing, we would argue that the most resonant political lesson of this writing lies less in the strategies themselves than in what these strategies imply about the entire relationship between literature and politics. For no strategy can be said to have a determinate political content. Strategies offer ways and means of achieving some end, but do not constitute the end itself. If the politically protean quality of decadent writing seems troubling, this is perhaps because it continues to hold a mirror up to the concerns and anxieties of our own fin de siècle. And to this extent, at least, decadence did not die with Oscar Wilde.

Notes

1. For further instances of the tendency to disparage decadence, see Ruth Temple (esp. 214–16). Probably the best brief treatment of the idea of decadence is that of Matei Calinescu. Also quite useful are R. K. R. Thornton's discussion of *decadence* as a critical term in France and England (14–70), Koenraad Swart's wide-ranging discussion of decadence in nineteenth-century France, and Richard Gilman's extensive and highly perceptive study of the word's history.

We should note that recent years have seen the publication of some fine attempts to treat decadent writing according to less immediately dismissive criteria. Along with the many earlier works of the contributors to this volume, and some works we discuss in what follows, we would also direct interested readers to, among other recent publications, the relevant chapters of Rita Felski's *The Gender of Modernity*; Linda Dowling's *Language and Decadence in the Victorian Fin de Siècle*; Séverine Jouve's *Obsessions et perversions dans la littérature et les demeures à la fin du dix-neuvième siècle*; David Weir's *Decadence and the Making of Modernism*; and Michele Hannoosh's *Parody and Decadence*.

2. Interestingly, as Hans-Peter Söder pointed out in a recent essay, when *Degeneration* is seen in the context of Nordau's situation as a bourgeois Jew in fin-de-siècle Germany, it looks less like a philistine's pseudo-scientific attack on the literary avant-garde than "a preemptive strike against those conservatives for whom decadence and degeneration were synonymous with being Jewish" (478). Such an interpretation of the work largely explains Nordau's palpable anxiety at finding so many of his own hypotheses prefigured in the texts he disparages, for it would constitute yet more ammunition for the conservative anti-Semites. Georg Lukács notably mobilizes a similar collection of tropes in the interest of a Marxist attack on "modern decadence" in his essay "Healthy or Sick Art?" The degeneracy that for Nordau has a hereditary origin emerges for Lukács from an "abnormal attitude toward life" following upon "a sterile, impotent opposition to the dominant social system" (108). For further discussion of the doctor/patient dynamic surrounding literary judgments of health and sickness, see Barbara Spackman (1–32). And for more on Nordau, see George Mosse's excellent introduction to the English translation of *Degeneration*.

3. Our thanks to Elaine Showalter for directing us to Beckson's loaded dedication.

4. Jane de la Vaudere (1862–1908) wrote exoticist novels, amongst them *Le Mystère de Kama*, *Le Harem de Syta*, *L'Amazone du roi de Siam*, *L'Amante du pharaon*, and *Les Courtisanes de Brahma*. She also wrote a collection of fantastic tales entitled *Les Sataniques*.

5. We should acknowledge at this point the groundbreaking work being done in this area by a number of contemporary scholars, including Elaine Showalter, whose

anthology *Daughters of Decadence* brought together the writings of many neglected "New Women" writers; and Melanie Hawthorne, who was among the first scholars in this country to draw attention (by means of translations and articles) to the writings of Rachilde. While the British writers Vernon Lee and Ada Leverson, and Rachilde in the French context, have occupied much of the critical attention, important research is currently being done (much of it as yet unpublished) on many other fin-de-siècle women writers.

6. For an important preliminary attempt to question the genetic presuppositions of literary history, see the first few pages of Paul de Man's essay "Genesis and Genealogy." As de Man notes, the narrative orientation of modern literary history cannot confidently be distinguished from the narratives it seeks to classify and situate.

A recent exception to the predominant literary-historical denigration of decadent writing is David Weir's *Decadence and the Making of Modernism*. For Weir, decadence is best understood as a transitional and translational stage between romanticism and modernism and not a falling away from the established or incipient ideals of either. If decadence is largely indefinable in itself, Weir argues, it nevertheless functions in literary history as a kind of "mystical sphere whose circumference is everywhere but whose center is nowhere" (xix), encompassing or explaining aspects of nearly every late-century avant garde aesthetic (from realism to aestheticism, naturalism to parnassianism) and facilitating their twentieth-century transformations. Although, as we shall argue below, we would question Weir's efforts to rehabilitate decadence as a coherent concept, his insistence on placing the phenomenon at the center (rather than the disreputable margins) of nineteenth-century literary culture offers a useful corrective to past treatments of the topic.

7. It is worth noting, in this regard, that in both English and French, the verb "to consume" (*consommer*) paradoxically denotes both beginnings and endings, as well as the ambiguous intermediary stages that partake of both. The verb (etymologically, in fact, two different words) functions literally to designate ingestion; but it also functions figuratively to designate the exhaustion and depletion of something (its end) or its fulfillment, as in the consummation of a marriage. Most significant for the image of decadence, however, is its passive usage (as in "he is consumed by fear"), which suggests an eating away, a suggestion inevitably echoed in the nineteenth century by the common name for the "wasting disease" tuberculosis, namely, consumption. Nisard's culinary metaphors for decadence echo through the contemporary food world, where the ubiquitous Chocolate Decadence cake — and its evocations of dangerous and transgressive pleasures — lurks on many a dessert menu. Indeed, today decadence is often treated as a mere synonym for indulgent consumption. On the nineteenth-century resonances of the word and idea of consumption, see Rosalind H. Williams (esp. 1–15).

8. Italian scholars, Praz among the most prominent among them, have taken the concept of decadence — or *decadentismo* — far more seriously as a literary-historical category than their American, French, or German counterparts. For a brief survey of the importance of this concept in Italy, see Calinescu (211–21).

9. To this extent, we might challenge the claim of the Marxist critic Peter Bürger that only the modernist avant-garde can be said to intervene in critical ways to expose the bourgeois institutionalization of the work of art, as well as the ideologies reproduced through such complicity. For Bürger, the avant-garde critiques bourgeois ideology by exposing the stylistic means, or processes, of works of art: "Certain categories essential to the description of pre-avant-gardiste art (such as organicity, subordination of the parts to the whole) are in fact negated in the avant-gardiste work" (19). As we suggest, however, such challenging of aesthetic means, and their ideological implications, is well under way in the phenomenon of decadence.

10. It is a matter of considerable debate whether such a "school" can in fact be said to have existed. Baju set up *Le Décadent*, along with Jules Barbey d'Aurevilly, Paul Verlaine, Maurice du Plessys, and others, as an official organ for a movement they felt themselves to be spearheading. But many of the most prominent "decadents" were either long dead (Baudelaire) or quite unwilling to accept the title (Mallarmé and, to a lesser extent, Huysmans), and the journal lasted only a brief time. As Séverine Jouve has noted, moreover, since all of the ostensible "founders" of decadence in France were also its first detractors, decadence is wholly "unlocatable" as a school (2). In England, the "school" question is complicated by the fact that journals now identified with the decadents (notably *The Yellow Book*) often printed essays and fiction by writers who had little relation to the supposed movement, and hence they can hardly be called organs. The closest thing to an English "manifesto," Symons's "Decadent Movement in Literature" deals almost solely with French writers, and it was later superseded (probably as a result of the Wilde trials) by his book on symbolism. In the German-speaking world, the situation is even more complex, as few if any of the writers now associated with decadence (e.g., Hofmannsthal, Bahr, Nietzsche, Schnitzler, the early Rilke) can be said to form anything like an organized school or movement. The decadent writers of other countries — Russia, Italy, or various Latin American nations — despite their local interests and concerns, generally cast themselves as followers of their ostensible French or English "fathers." For this reason, and in light of what we have found in the critical reception of the subject, we prefer to leave open the question of whether decadence should be called a school, a movement, a cultural phenomenon, or even an identifiable phase of literary and cultural history. This does not mean, though, that we find the term of no importance, and so we continue to use it here.

11. On the significance of this strategy of appropriation in the gay community, see Judith Butler: "The public assertion of 'queerness' enacts performativity as citationality for the purposes of resignifying the abjection of homosexuality into defiance and legitimacy" (21).

12. Gourmont, in an analytic process he defines as the "dissociation of ideas," takes on the task of "dissociating" decadence from the clichéd meanings that have accrued to it. He suggests that, if it is used at all, the term *decadence* should designate servile aesthetic imitation and not the poetic innovations he finds in the work of Mallarmé.

13. Here we would direct our readers to Louis Marvick's recent discussion of decadent paradox as a social strategy. For Marvick, the importance of paradox to the texture of decadent style is part of a larger effort by the decadent writer simultaneously to confront and reject his or her world. Just as the contradictory elements of any paradox are dependent upon one another (otherwise there would be no paradox), so the decadent writer seeks to persuade the bourgeois reader that decadence is the epitome of late nineteenth-century society and not an aberration. For further discussion of the decadent paradox, see Michael Riffaterre's essay in this volume.

14. Baudelaire's critique of artifice, we should note, is problematically allied with a seemingly misogynistic valorization of women's inherent artificiality. The pervasive misogyny of much decadent art and writing, its relation to the antiessentialist claims of modernism, as well as its potential relation to the problems raised by contemporary gender studies, is a vast topic that we cannot even begin to treat here in anything like the detail it deserves. We refer readers to the important discussions of the topic by Christine Buci-Glucksmann, Rita Felski, and Barbara Spackman. It is worth asking, though, whether the complex critique of naturalism offered by Baudelaire should be weighed against the misogyny associated with his contribution to the understanding of decadence.

15. On Bourget and the idea of decadence, see Raymond Pouilliart. On Bourget's pivotal influence in Germany and Austria, see J. C. Fewster.

16. Huysmans's modern French editor, Marc Fumaroli, assumes a similar slippage between decadence and degeneration, writing in a note to the passage in question, "The 'commonplace' of heredity, dear to Naturalism, is here put to work in the service of the myth of 'Decadence' " (338).

17. For another account of the "gap" in Des Esseintes's pedigree, see Rodolphe Gasché. As Gasché notes, the novel's beginning epitomizes its preoccupation with and complication of origins and beginnings.

18. Let us note, too, that the narrator foreshadows (and proleptically critiques) Nordau in seeking to read symptoms of degeneration "through" a work of art, examining the portrait both in terms of its "decadent" subject and for evidence of its deviation from the proper genealogical line. Like Nordau and his often unwitting followers, that is, Huysmans's narrator conflates body and work, symptom and subject.

19. For another discussion of the portraits in Wilde's novel, see Dennis Denisoff's essay in this volume.

20. For a discussion of Nietzsche's role in the adumbration of Nazi thought, see Walter Kaufmann (esp. 284–306). Kaufmann insists that Nazi philosophers simply misread Nietzsche or deliberately distorted his clear intentions in an effort to use some of his ideas. Although his reading is doubtless more nuanced than that of the "thinkers" he criticizes, we would maintain that Kaufmann, too, is mistaken in seeking to extract a determinate political message from Nietzsche's writings.

21. For an account of D'Annunzio at Fiume, see Michael Ledeen.

22. For an overview of Nietzsche's importance to French theory, see the essays collected by David B. Allison. On Mallarmé, see Derrida and Kristeva.

Works Cited

Allison, David B., ed. *The New Nietzsche*. New York: Dell, 1977.

Baju, Anatole. *L'Ecole décadente*. Paris: Vannier, 1887.

Barrès, Maurice. "La Folie de Charles Baudelaire." *1884 Taches d'Encre*. Paris: Les écrivains réunis, 1926.

Baudelaire, Charles. *The Flowers of Evil*. trans. James McGowan. Oxford: Oxford University Press, 1993.

———. *The Painter of Modern Life, and Other Essays*. Ed. and trans. Jonathan Mayne. 1863. New York: Da Capo, 1964.

Beckson, Karl, ed. *Aesthetes and Decadents of the 1890s*. Chicago: Academy, 1982.

Bourget, Paul. *Essais de psychologie contemporaine*. Paris: Lemerre, 1893.

Buci-Glucksmann, Christine. *La raison baroque: De Baudelaire à Benjamin*. Paris: Galilée, 1984.

Bürger, Peter. *Theory of the Avant-Garde*. Trans. Michael Shaw. Minneapolis: U of Minnesota Press, 1984.

Butler, Judith. *Bodies that Matter: On the Discursive Limits of Sex*. New York: Routledge, 1993.

Calinescu, Matei. "The Idea of Decadence." *Five Faces of Modernity*. Durham: Duke University Press, 1987.

Carter, A. E. *The Idea of Decadence in French Literature, 1830–1900*. Toronto: University of Toronto Press, 1958.

Chambers, Ross. "Poetry in the Asiatic Mode: Baudelaire's 'Au Lecteur.' " *Yale French Studies* 74 (1988): 97–116.

Coquio, Catherine. "La 'Baudelairité' décadente: Un modèle spectral." *Romantisme* 82 (1993): 91–107.

de Man, Paul. "Genesis and Genealogy." In *Allegories of Reading*. New Haven: Yale University Press, 1979.

Derrida, Jacques. "The Double Session." *Dissemination*. Trans. Barbara Johnson. Chicago: University of Chicago Press, 1981.

Dowling, Linda. *Language and Decadence in the Victorian Fin de Siècle*. Princeton: Princeton University Press, 1989.

Felski, Rita. *The Gender of Modernity*. Cambridge: Harvard University Press, 1995.

Fewster, J. C. "Au Service de l'ordre: Paul Bourget and the Critical Response to Decadence in Austria and Germany." *Comparative Literature Studies* 29 (1992): 259–75.

Gagnier, Regenia. "A Critique of Practical Aesthetics." In *Aesthetics and Ideology*, ed. George Levine. New Brunswick, N.J.: Rutgers University Press, 1994.

Gasché, Rodolphe. "The Falls of History: Huysmans's *A Rebours*." *Yale French Studies* 74 (1988): 183–204.

Gilman, Richard. *Decadence: The Strange Life of an Epithet*. New York: Farrar, Straus and Giroux 1979.

Gourmont, Remy de. *Selected Writings*. Trans. Glenn Burne. Ann Arbor: University of Michigan Press, 1966.

Hannoosh, Michele. *Parody and Decadence: Laforgue's* Moralités légendaires. Columbus: Ohio State University Press, 1989.

Hough, Graham. *The Last Romantics*. London: Duckworth, 1949.

Huysmans, Joris-Karl. *A rebours*. Ed. Marc Fumaroli. Paris: Gallimard, 1977.

———. *Against Nature*. Trans. Robert Baldick. Harmondsworth: Penguin, 1959.

Jankélévitch, Vladimir. "La Décadence." *Revue de métaphysique et de morale* 55 (1950): 337–69.

Jouve, Séverine. *Obsessions et perversions dans la littérature et les demeures à la fin du dix-neuvième siècle*. Paris: Hermann, 1996.

Kaufmann, Walter. *Nietzsche: Philosopher, Psychologist, Antichrist*. 4th ed. Princeton: Princeton University Press, 1974.

Kristeva, Julia. *La Révolution du langage poétique*. Paris: Editions du Seuil, 1974.

Ledeen, Michael. *The First Duce: D'Annunzio at Fiume*. Baltimore: Johns Hopkins University Press, 1977.

Lukács, Georg. "Healthy or Sick Art?" *Writer and Critic and Other Essays*. Ed. and trans. Arthur Kahn. London: Merlin, 1970.

Marvick, Louis W. "Aspects of the Fin-de-Siècle Decadent Paradox." *Clio* 22 (1992): 1–19.

Nietzsche, Friedrich. *Basic Writings of Nietzsche*. Ed. and trans. Walter Kaufmann. New York: Modern Library, 1968.

Nisard, Désiré. *Etudes de moeurs et de critique sur les poètes latins de la décadence*. 1834. Paris: Hachette, 1878.

Nordau, Max. *Degeneration*. 1892. Lincoln: University of Nebraska Press, 1993.

———. *Degeneration*. Intro by George L. Mosse. New York: Howard Fertig, 1968.

Palacio, Jean de. *Figures et formes de la décadence*. Paris: Seguier, 1994.

Pouilliart, Raymond. "Paul Bourget et l'esprit de décadence." *Les Lettres romanes* 5 (1951): 199–229.

Praz, Mario. *The Romantic Agony*. Trans. Angus Davidson. Oxford: Oxford University Press, 1970.

Reed, John. *Decadent Style*. Athens: Ohio University Press, 1985.

Ryals, Clyde de L. "Toward a Definition of *Decadent* as Applied to British Literature of the Nineteenth Century." *Journal of Aesthetics and Art Criticism* 17 (1958): 85–92.

Showalter, Elaine, ed. *Daughters of Decadence: Women Writers of the Fin-de-Siècle.* New Brunswick: Rutgers University Press, 1993.

Smith, James. "Concepts of Decadence in Nineteenth-Century France." *Studies in Philology* 50 (1953): 640–51.

Söder, Hans-Peter. "Disease and Health as Contexts of Modernity: Max Nordau as a Critic of Fin-de-Siècle Modernism." *German Studies Review* 14 (1991): 473–87.

Spackman, Barbara. *Decadent Genealogies: The Rhetoric of Sickness from Baudelaire to D'Annunzio.* Ithaca: Cornell University Press, 1989.

———. "Recycling Baudelaire: The Decadence of Catulle Mendès (1841–1909)." In *The Decadent Reader.* New York: Zone, 1998.

Swart, Koenraad. *The Sense of Decadence in Nineteenth-Century France.* The Hague: Nijhoff, 1964.

Symons, Arthur. *The Symbolist Movement in Literature.* London: Heinemann, 1899.

Temple, Ruth Z. "Truth in Labelling: Pre-Raphaelitism, Aestheticism, Decadence, Fin de Siècle." *English Literature in Transition* 17 (1974): 201–22.

Thornton, R. K. R. *The Decadent Dilemma.* London: Arnold, 1983.

Weir, David. *Decadence and the Making of Modernism.* Amherst: University of Massachusetts Press, 1995.

Wilde, Oscar. *The Picture of Dorian Gray.* Harmondsworth: Penguin, 1985.

———. *The Artist as Critic: Critical Writings of Oscar Wilde.* Ed. Richard Ellmann. 1969. Chicago: University of Chicago Press, 1982.

Williams, Rosalind H. *Dream Worlds: Mass Consumption in Late Nineteenth-Century France.* Berkeley: University of California Press, 1982.

Defining Decadence

Chapter 1
Interversions

Barbara Spackman

Perhaps no text provides more fertile ground for the commonplace that the master trope of decadence is inversion than J. K. Huysmans's *A rebours*. Lining itself up on the culturally devalued side of a series of familiar oppositions — feminine vs. masculine, degeneration vs. evolution, decadence vs. progress, sickness vs. health, artifice vs. nature, false vs. true, perversion vs. normalcy, and so on — the text seems merely to occupy the position *à rebours* (against nature) and to accomplish an inversion that ends up reaffirming the "positive" side of the opposition on which it depends, negatively, for its own definition. Both Françoise Gaillard and Charles Bernheimer have formulated versions of this argument, Gaillard in reference to Huysmans's text in particular and Bernheimer in reference to decadence in general. In a 1976 essay, Gaillard argues that Huysmans's text functions through denegation and ends up reaffirming the existence of Truth, Authenticity, and God; Des Esseintes, for Gaillard, is a prisoner of the *doxa* that he follows *à rebours*. Although Gaillard addresses only *A rebours*, one could certainly apply her conclusions to other decadents, in particular the eminently paradoxical Oscar Wilde, whose witticisms depend upon such inversions of the *doxa*.[1] Bernheimer takes a different tack in a 1992 essay, where he argues that, although decadence shows the constructedness of both sides of such oppositions, it must forget the constructedness of the norm against which it defines its own deviance. Implicit in Bernheimer's formulation is the logic of fetishistic disavowal; decadence thus may know very well that, as Bernheimer puts it, "every normative standard is already inhabited by otherness," yet all the same, it acts as though they were not. Trapped by binary oppositions that it can reverse, invert, rub the wrong way, or disavow, decadence, it would seem, can be of little interest in a second fin de siècle in which we have learned not merely to reverse but also to rewrite such structuring oppositions.

But we have also learned to reread, and I would like to revisit the Breviary of Decadence in order to reexamine this commonplace, its validity as well as its fragility. That it grew luxuriantly from the pages of *A rebours* is undeniable. Exemplary might be the way in which the text plays with and within the binary opposition that constitutes sexual difference as a logic of absolute difference. As Jean Laplanche makes clear in *Castrations/Symbolisations*, such a logic posits "difference" as existing between two and only two terms that are understood as contradictories, such that not $x = y$, not male = female. There is no need, in fact, for two terms in such a system, since the presence or absence of one feature, say, y (and not coincidentally!), is sufficient to distinguish between the two. This is the logic that produces male and female as one sex and its (castrating because castrated, mutilating because mutilated) negation, and that is familiar to us as that of Freud's infantile theorist, as the logic of the same that is the object of Luce Irigaray's critique, as "sexual indifference."[2] And this is the logic that seems to govern the most narratively engaging section of the novel: the series of episodes that begins with Des Esseintes's recollection of his traumatic visit to a dentist, continues with visions of decapitation, evacuation, and toothlessness in the description of Gustave Moreau's *Salomé* and the dream of the Pox, and culminates in the memories of Miss Urania and the ventriloquist. Motored by inversions and reversals, the series recycles a limited number of figures: the extraction of teeth and decapitation are first figured on male bodies (Des Esseintes's own, and that of John the Baptist), then displaced onto female bodies (the toothless bulldog-woman, and Salomé, "nailed to the spot . . . her hand clawing convulsively at her throat" [67], by way of the extraction of the tortoise from its shell, and that of the woman's innards in Egyptian funereal rites); permutations of "male" and "female" produce figures of androgynes, hermaphrodites, eunuchs, and equivocal creatures "sans sexe"; Des Esseintes's sex exchange with Miss Urania produces a symmetrical inversion whereby she is masculinized and he is feminized. However acrobatic or ventriloquistic, androgynous or hermaphroditic, the figures produced by the text can only recombine two terms, male and female, in predictable ways. Even the text's figures for recombination seem programmed by a variation of the trope of inversion: Des Esseintes's attempt to breathe masculine thoughts into the ventriloquist's female body recalls the model of sexual inversion as the soul of one sex trapped within the body of the other.

Things do not look much better when we turn to the relation between nature and artifice. From the "nuit factice" in which Des Esseintes lives, to the artificial hothouse flowers and simulacra of a monk's quarters and sea voyages, *A rebours* celebrates the artificial and the factitious. Yet, argues Gaillard, this celebration is governed by and trapped within another opposition, that between the true and the false, in such a way as to reaffirm the priority of the "positive" terms in both oppositions. Gaillard astutely opposes what she calls the "realist illusion" to "decadent imitation": "A l'opposé de *l'illusion réaliste* qui s'efforce de gommer tous les indices de sa fab-

rication afin de susciter un effet de présence, de transparence du réel,
l'*imitation décadente* souligne toutes les marques du leurre pour mettre l'accent sur l'artificialité du produit. Faire du 'vrai faux'!" [Contrary to the
realist illusion that takes pains to cover over all the marks of its fabrication in
order to produce an effect of presence, of transparency of the real, *decadent
imitation* underlines all the marks of trickery in order to accentuate the
artificiality of the product. To make a "true fake"!] (131). This "true fake"
would be one that always retains the sign of its own artificiality, that announces itself as copy and thereby remains dependent upon the thing copied, upon nature, or the real. For Gaillard, Des Esseintes's simulacra, such as
his sea voyage or his trip to London, must never entirely detach themselves
from their natural reference, for the pleasure that he takes in them is "le
plaisir sacrilège à l'inversion des signes. Or qui dit sacrilège dit foi, le plaisir
à la transgression n'est plaisir que sur fond de croyance" [the sacrilegious
pleasure in the inversion of signs. Now whoever says sacrilege says faith; the
pleasure in transgression is only pleasure against a background of belief]
(139–40). In Huysmans's case, that faith is, for Gaillard, a belief in Truth,
and Des Esseintes's simulacra function to homogenize and restore to the
real its lost oneness, and its truth: "Voilà pourquoi la recherche de la facticité reste totalement enfermée dans l'opposition bipolaire entre le vrai et
le faux, opposition qui n'a de sens que parce que, même dans ce monde
dégradé que le décadent méprise, le vrai reste encore la référence obligée,
le fondement suprême de la valeur" [That's why the search for the factitious
remains totally enclosed within the binary opposition between true and
false, an opposition that has meaning only because, even in the degraded
world that the decadent disdains, the true is still the obligatory reference,
the supreme foundation of value] (140). At best, then, Des Esseintes manages to be paradoxical, in both the logical and rhetorical senses: the "vrai
faux" goes against the grain of the doxa by combining apparently contradictory terms, yet finally it is that "vrai" which provides the program and the
titillation; no wonder, she suggests, that Huysmans himself should turn to
God in the end.

In the course of her compelling argument, Gaillard warns the reader not
to be fooled by what might seem to disturb this notion; don't be fooled by
the bric-a-brac, she writes: "Ne nous laissons pas prendre à l'aspect bric-à-brac ou bricolage si évident à la lecture d'*A rebours*, car cette improvisation
apparente masque la véritable logique qui est à l'oeuvre dans la surcherie: celle d'une réduction sémiotique du réel. Peu importe l'hétérogénéité
des éléments utilisés; leur provenance, leur appartenance, leur valeur différentielles comptent peu" [Let us not allow ourselves to be taken in by the
bric-a-brac or *bricolage* aspect so evident in reading *Against the Grain*, for this
apparent improvisation masks the true logic that is at work in trickery: that
of a semiotic reduction of the real. The heterogeneity of elements utilized is
of little importance; their provenance, their belonging, their differential

value counts for little] (135). By warning us away from an alluring appearance of heterogeneity to look at a homogeneous truth "masked" by artifice, Gaillard contains any potential disturbance within the appearance/reality model and thus in effect performs a semiotic reduction similar to what she finds is the "véritable logique" of the text. Such containment seems not merely an analysis but almost an enforcement of a binary opposition, a righting of its relation so that the "appearance" of the text is put in its proper place and value is restored to its "essence."

In an essay entitled "Huysmans: Writing Against (Female) Nature," Bernheimer also warns us away from an alluring heterogeneity that, he argues, is a fetish covering over a nasty truth. Bernheimer is interested in the relation between the lists, the "textual surface that, like the tortoise's shell Des Esseintes orders encrusted with precious stones, is studded with elements alien to biological life," and the "traumatic perception of female castration" that his argument associates with the referential function of language (384–85).[3] This textuality, Bernheimer argues, is produced by the fetishist's disavowal; it functions to repair the "female wound" and "deny the female sexual body" (385). Bernheimer's own language insists upon the hardness of this surface: "dense," "encrusted," "studded," his description of the surface implicitly recalls the apotropaic display that, in Freud's Medusa's Head essay, says "I have a penis. I defy you" (18:274). Like Gaillard, Bernheimer sees heterogeneity in the text, but he suggests that it is only apparent: "But however heterogeneous their referential contents may be, these carefully cultivated fantasies all have the same function of denying the real" (384). This is a suggestive reading and one that deserves more attention than I can give it here. What strikes me about it, however, is the way in which it seems to enforce the logic of absolute difference by reinscribing the relation between the lists and the "female sexual body" *within* the logic of absolute difference. The terms that structure his argument line up neatly, with surface, appearance, artifice, rhetoric ("rare difficult words and a deliberately tortured syntax"), the factitious and fetishistic all on one side, and nature, fact, the referential function of language, truth, and the female sexual body all on the other. Bernheimer is on the side of "truth" in this model, for not only does he take no distance from the identification of the "female sexual body" with the "traumatic perception of female castration" (thereby naturalizing what even in Freud is not a perception but an interpretation imposed, *nachträglich*, on a perception), but he also recommends, at the end of his essay, that Huysmans, and all the French modernists, should face facts: "The modernist movement in the arts . . . with its emphasis on the discontinuous, the self-reflective, the opaque, was involved in a sublimating, fetishizing effort to deny the female sexual body. This defensive effort, however, was doomed by the very terms of its expression. As long as (female) nature remains at the origin, the supplement can never take the place of that which it augments" (385). What I find disturbing about this alignment is that it relies upon a hermeneutic model (appearance conceals reality, surface conceals depth, artifice conceals truth, rhetoric conceals plain speech and reference) that is not innocent in relation to the question of sexual difference, that in fact implies a model of sexual difference in which "woman" stands as the privileged figure of absence. This relation is most familiar to us in the figure of the enchantress turned hag (not a few of which are to be found in Huysmans's texts), in which an alluring enchantress (appearance, artifice, cosmetic rhetoric) is revealed to be a toothless old hag (essence, truth, plain speech). As Derrida has argued in *Spurs*, the relation here between tenor and vehicle is not an accidental one; rather, a decision concerning sexual difference underlies the hermeneutic model such that the truth *is* the "truth of woman." If this is the case, and I am convinced that it is, then one would want not to speak as a secret advocate of a logic that must necessarily speak of woman as the negation of man, not to perform a reinscription, but rather to insist on whatever in the text might work to destabilize such a reinscription and such a truth. That would mean reading the lists not as a cover-up but rather as systems of diversity that destabilize the binary oppositions that structure the text. Let us, then, follow Nietzsche's lead in the *Preface to the Gay Science* and stop at the appearance, decadently linger over the differential value of those heterogeneous elements, and suggest that from it may emerge a different logic, a logic, as it turns out, not of the "vrai" but of the "véritable."

*   *   *

Any reader of *A rebours* will remember the endless lists of gemstones, flowers, colors, and authors, the bric-a-brac that we have come to consider a fingerprint of decadence. Unlike the simulacra that Gaillard analyzes (the Trappist's cell, the sea voyage), these lists seem to go nowhere, never reach a totalizable conclusion, re-create nothing in particular but rather seem to form independent semiotic systems. I quote a passage from early on in the novel:

> Lentement, il tria, un à un, les tons.
> Le bleu tire aux flambeaux sur un faux vert; s'il est foncé comme le cobalt et l'indigo, il devient noir; s'il est clair, il tourne au gris; s'il est sincère et doux comme la turquoise, il se ternit et se glace.
> A moins donc de l'associer, ainsi qu'un adjuvant, à une autre couleur, il ne pouvait être question d'en faire la note dominante d'une pièce.
> D'un autre côté, les gris fer se renfrognent encore et s'alourdissent; les gris de perle perdent leur azur et se métamorphosent en un blanc sale; les bruns s'endorment et se froidissent; quant aux verts foncés, ainsi que les verts empereur et les verts myrte, ils agissent de même que les gros bleus et fusionnent avec les noirs; restaient donc les verts plus pâles, tels que le vert paon, les cinabres et les laques, mais alors la lumière exile leur bleu et ne détient plus que leur jaune qui ne garde, à son tour, qu'un ton faux, qu'une saveur trouble. (96)

[Slowly, one by one, he went through the various colours.

Blue, he remembered, takes on an artificial green tint by candlelight, if a dark blue like indigo or cobalt, it becomes black; if pale, it turns to grey; and if soft and true, like turquoise, it goes dull and cold. There could, therefore, be no question of making it the keynote of a room, though it might be used to help out another colour.

On the other hand, under the same conditions the iron greys grow sullen and heavy; the pearl greys lose their blue sheen and are metamorphosed into a dirty white; the browns become cold and sleepy; and as for the dark greens such as emperor green and myrtle green, they react like the dark blues and turn quite black. Only the pale greens remained — peacock green, for instance, or the cinnabar and lacquer greens — but then artificial light kills the blue in them and leaves only the yellow, which for its part lacks clarity and consistency.] (28–29)

The thematic interest here is primarily in metamorphosis, in the shifting of one color into another as a result of its reaction to the light, but what strikes one about the "logic" that organizes the passage is that it is not one of difference, understood as absolute difference, but rather would seem to belong to what Jean Laplanche, in *Castrations/Symbolisations*, has called a system of diversity. I draw again on his exposition of the distinction between *difference* [Unterschied] and *diversity* [Verschiedenheit] in Freud's texts on sexual difference. In those texts ("Infantile Genital Organization," "The Disappearance of the Oedipus Complex," and "Some Psychological Conse-quences of the Anatomical Distinction Between the Sexes"), *diversity* refers to the child's knowledge of the distinction between the sexes prior to the castration complex, whereas *difference* refers to the child's understanding after its onset. Before the delivery of the threat of castration that causes the child to reread his vision of female nudity, the child is aware of a distinction between, say, his mother and father, but that distinction is characterized by a number of features, including but not limited to anatomical ones — mother wears pearls and perfume and has breasts; father smells of cigars, has a deep voice and hairy arms, and so on. The threat of castration and the interpreta-tion through deferred action of the sight of female nudity causes a system of difference to be imposed onto those features, rendering them meaningless in relation to that one familiar feature whose presence or absence will there-after serve to figure sexual difference. Given the presence of such a logic and such themes in *A rebours*, the Freudian context is not without interest, nor is the example on which Laplanche relies to explain the distinction between these two logics, these two systems: that of the spectrum of colors. Different organizations of the spectrum provide examples of both systems. Thus, in a system of "diversity," there are an infinite number of colors, and no color defines itself as the negation of another; it may contain two elements, but it may also contain x number of elements. In such a system, there may be contraries but not contradictories; blue and green, for example, are contrar-ies, but in a system of diversity "not-green" will automatically signify not blue, but all of the remaining colors. As with the child's understanding of the distinction between the sexes, this, too, may be transformed into a system of difference; were one to set up two teams (or factions, or races) and give them jerseys of different colors (or insignia, as Laplanche calls them), say, green and blue, one will have set up these colors as contradictories such that "not-green" necessarily signifies blue. And as Laplanche points out, one really only needs one color for such a system since all other colors have now been defined as "not-green"; either you're green or you're not, either you're a marked term or you're not, or, to draw the obvious analogy, either you're castrated or you're not. One has only to think of the redundancy of asking of new parents, "Is it a boy or a girl?" since the answer "No, it's not a boy" necessarily implies "Yes, it's a girl." In a system of difference, the answer, "Well, uh, actually . . . neither," would be taken to refer to a monstrosity, for the logic of absolute difference constitutes all hybrids as monstrosities (and as we have seen, it is in this sense that it programs the production of hermaphrodites, androgynes, chimera, and sphinx in Huysmans's text).

I would like to argue that the passage above not only coincidentally shares the theme of "colors" with Laplanche's example, but that it puts into play a system of diversity in contrast to the logic of absolute difference linked to the themes of sexual difference, castration, mutilation, and so on. Cinnabar, peacock green, pearl gray, myrtle green . . . no color can be said to be the negation of another. "Not-cinnabar" is not only not necessarily peacock green, but it sends the reader to the dictionary to find out what "cinnabar" is to begin with. This logic of diversity programs Des Esseintes's other lists as well: his sorting of precious stones, his listing of perfumes, the invention of the alcoholic organ on the analogy of another system of diversity, that of the orchestra, and so on. What, then, is the relation between these two logics within the text itself? I would like to argue that, in the most interesting cases, this relation is one of contamination whereby the logic of diversity functions to contaminate and introduce an asymmetry into the logic of absolute difference.[4]

A first, faint glimmer of this is already evident in the passage above. It concerns the opposition that emerges as the dominant one in both Gaillard's and Bernheimer's arguments, that between the "vrai" and the "faux." What is interesting about the color passage is that it puts "faux" into play within a system of diversity and skews its relation to the "vrai." The term *faux* appears twice, first in reference to "un faux vert" and then in reference to "un ton faux." In the first case, "faux" comes to be one of a number of kinds of green — "foncés, empereur, myrte, paon, cinabres, laques" — and one of several adjectives modifying colors — "clair, doux, gros, sincère." Both "faux" and "sincère" are made to function not oppositionally but as one of a number of possibilities; blue may be a "faux vert" under certain conditions, but in others it may become black, or gray, or it may go dull and cold. "Bleu sincère" is opposed not to a hypocritical blue but to light blues and deep blues. In the second appearance of *faux,* the "ton faux," "falseness" has to do with a dissonance introduced into a harmony, and it appears in apposition (and not opposition) to "une saveur trouble," an indistinct taste. As so often happens in this novel, the "synaesthetic" combination of the senses — here of music, tastes, and colors — also piles one system of diversity onto another; in this case, the dominant tone of the "pièce" is at once that of a room and that of a musical composition, and it is by apposition related to the system of taste. Not coincidentally, the "saveur" in question is not one of the "oppositional" tastes, not sweet or sour, but "une saveur trouble," an equivocal taste that muddies the opposition. In neither case is the "false-ness" involved an epistemological one; rather, it is recycled into a system of diversity.

A second example of an asymmetry introduced into a logic of absolute difference brings us to a passage in which we seem to get the most pared-down system possible: a color system, again, but this time one in which there are only two terms, only black and white, and the relation described would seem to be a straightforward inversion:

Ainsi qu'une haute tenture de contre-hermine, le ciel se levait devant lui, noir et moucheté de blanc.
Un vent glacial courut, accéléra le vol éperdu de la neige, intervertit l'ordre des couleurs.
La tenture héraldique du ciel se retourna, devint une véritable hermine, blanche mouchetée de noir, à son tour, par les points de nuit dispersés entre les flocons. (137)

[Like a great canopy of counter-ermine, the sky hung before him, a black curtain spattered with white.
Suddenly an icy wind blew up which drove the dancing snowflakes before it and reversed this arrangement of colours. The sky's heraldic trappings were turned round to reveal a true ermine, white dotted with black where pinpricks of darkness showed through the curtain of falling snow.] (57–58)

Black dotted with white is reversed, inverted, and turned into white dotted with black; a counter-ermine is inverted and returns to its "true" form. Yet here again we find that the "truth" at stake is not epistemological, for this "true" ermine is not "vrai" but "véritable"; the sky has not literally become fur but is deserving of the figural designation "ermine." Indeed, when *véritable* appears before the noun, it may refer to that which is precisely named, that which merits its name, and by extension, it may reinforce or introduce a metaphorical or figural term, which, as the Petit Robert nicely puts it, "n'est justement pas 'véritable' mais dont on veut souligner l'exacti-tude" [is precisely not "veritable" but whose exactitude one wishes to em-phasize]. In other words, *véritable* may tell you that the correspondence between name and thing named is a precise one or that the noun modified is used not literally but figuratively, and that the figure is an apt one. Web-ster's provides as an example of this last usage, "a veritable mountain of references"; the Petit Robert offers, from Georges Sand, the image of two bulls, "veritable patriarchs of the prairie." Of course, what is "veritable" may or may not be "real" as opposed to counterfeit; in the example above, we clearly have a fur that is so only metaphorically. What thus appeared (especially in translation) to be a simple opposition between a true and a false ermine turns out to be a relation between two kinds of ermine, one deserving of the metaphor and the other, the "contre-hermine," a technical term that has an English equivalent in the term *ermines*. The verb translated as "reversed" also contains within it the possibility of the sort of skewing we have been exploring. That verb is not *invertir*, which would have given us, by definition, a symmetrical reversal, but rather *intervertir*. What is of interest is that again we have to do with a relation to language: *intervertir* is defined by the Petit Robert as "to displace the elements of a whole, by reversing their original order, to displace the natural, logical, or habitual order; to change, to permute." The examples of usage all have to do with language: one may "intervertir" the words in a phrase, the pages in a manuscript, the letters in a word, the positions of interlocutors. *Interversion* is defined as "derangement, reversal of a natural, habitual, or logical order," and comes to French from the Latin "interverto-vertere": to intercept, hence to embezzle or purloin, or to cheat, to rob of (curiously, *me muliere* is the example given). Nothing about the verb requires that there be only two elements insofar as a displacement, a shuffling or permutation is indicated by it. Returning to the passage cited, we might note that the verb itself is being used in a sense that displaces its normal use, for not only is the "original, natural, or habitual order" that is "interverted" already marked linguistically as an inversion, as "*counter*-ermine," but, as a heraldic term, it belongs to no "natural" order: the fictional fur called "ermines" has never been worn by a living animal; it exists only in the world of heraldry.[5]

A trace of a similar skewing inhabits Des Esseintes's aesthetic theory which would seem to be a cosmetic, rather than mimetic, one; true to his Baudelairean genealogy, he cites as counterexample Tertullian's condemnation of what Baudelaire called "the vulgar art of face painting":

. . . [T]out au plus, lisait-il quelques pages du *De cultu feminarum* où Tertullien objurgue les femmes de ne pas se parer de bijoux et d'étoffes précieuses, et leur défend l'usage des cosmétiques parce qu'ils essayent de corriger la nature et de l'embellir.
Ces idées, diamétralement opposées aux siennes, le faisait sourire. (120)

[(A)t the very most he sometimes read a page or two of the *De Cultu Feminarum* where Tertullian exhorts women not to adorn their persons with jewels and precious stuffs, and forbids them to use cosmetics because these attempt to correct and improve on Nature.
These ideas, diametrically opposed to his own, brought a smile to his lips.] (45)

To correct and embellish nature: this is the theory that governs his production of perfumes, which he compares to that art of cutting precious stones:

"En résumé, l'artiste achève l'odeur initiale de la nature dont il taille la senteur, et il la monte ainsi qu'un joaillier épure l'eau d'une pierre et la fait valoir" (223) [In short, the artist in perfumery completes the original natural odour, which, so to speak, he cuts and mounts as a jeweller improves and brings out the water of a precious stone] (120). This means that the artificial or "factice" is not merely a copy that announces itself as copy, but a cosmetic improvement upon the original. Paradoxically, this cosmesis may accomplish its effects through mimesis — but a mimesis with a decadent twist, one that will create a second-order artificial nature.

Is this merely an inversion of mimesis, such that, as Oscar Wilde will put it, it is not art that imitates life but life that imitates art? A first passage from the "flower chapter" would suggest that this is so:

Ces plantes sont tout de même stupéfiantes, se dit-il; puis il se recula et en couvrit d'un coup d'oeil l'amas; son but était atteint; aucune ne semblait réelle; l'étoffe, le papier, la porcelaine, le métal, paraissaient avoir été prêtés par l'homme à la nature pour lui permettre de créer ses monstres. Quand elle n'avait pu imiter l'oeuvre humaine, elle avait été réduite à recopier les membranes intérieures des animaux, à emprunter les vivaces teintes de leurs chairs en pourriture, les magnifiques hideurs de leur gangrène. (197)

["These plants are really astounding," he said to himself, stepping back to appraise the entire collection. Yes, his object had been achieved; not one of them looked real; it was as if cloth, paper, porcelain, and metal had been lent by man to Nature to enable her to create these monstrosities. Where she had not found it possible to imitate the work of human hands, she had been reduced to copying the membranes of animals' organs, to borrowing the vivid tints of their rotting flesh, the hideous splendours of their gangrened skin.] (101)

The second function is less interesting than the first for, in the second, nature copies itself as it does in camouflage; nature imitates nature. In the first case, however, we have a nature that imitates artifice, a decadent nature that inverts the mimetic relation between nature and art and produces a natural artifice. This is a symmetrical inversion, Gaillard's "vrai faux." Indeed, this relation finds expression in a chiasmus, the figure *par excellence* of reversals and inversions: "Après les fleurs factices singeant les véritables fleurs, il voulait des fleurs naturelles imitant des fleurs fausses" (191) [Tired of artificial flowers aping real ones, he wanted some natural flowers that would look like fakes] (97). The sentence compacts the terms of the inversion in a chiasmus that, in the version given us by Baldick's translation, is neatly symmetrical. If we diagram the crossing of terms, as Baldick translates them, we get the following scheme:

Here the natural is to the real as the artificial is to the fakes; these terms belong to two orders of opposition, an ontological one and an epistemological one such that nature is opposed to art and truth is opposed to falsehood. In the chiasmus that the translation produces, these get lined up symmetrically, so that in effect what is produced is the following chiasmus, in which the crossing of terms aligns nature with the order of truth and art with that of falsehood.

Art — Truth

Nature — Falsehood

This, then, would be the doxa that Des Esseintes inverts yet reaffirms. And the inversion is underscored by the choice of verbs: artificial flowers, those made by humans, "ape" true flowers, while natural flowers, presumably those not of human origin, "imitate" fake flowers; human activity is described with the naturalizing verb, while the work of nature is characterized by the verb we would expect would be applied to the work of the human hand: again, a naturalized artifice and an artificial nature.

But something is slightly askew in the sentence that sets forth the terms of this inversion—something that appears only if we refuse to discard the "surface" of the text in order to gain access to its "essence." Whereas Baldick's translation enforces the neatness of the chiasmus, a literal translation would give us the following sentence: "After factitious flowers aping veritable flowers, he wanted natural flowers imitating false ones."

Factitious — Veritable

Natural — False

Baldick's rendering of *véritable* as "true" is one possibility, but as we know from the "ermine" passage, the English *veritable* is equally apt. What would it mean to read the flowers of our chiasmus as "veritable ones"? As with the example of the ermine, "veritable flowers" would not be "true" flowers in the sense that they are "real" as opposed to "counterfeit." Rather, the "trueness" of veritable flowers depends on their relation to a designation within language. Flowers correctly so-called might be opposed to flowers incorrectly so-called, but these might equally well be "real" or "artificial." And if those flowers were indeed precisely not literal but rather already figurative, then the orders of opposition would also no longer be quite the same, but would appear as follows, in which art is to falsehood what nature is to a correct relation to language.

Art — Language

Nature — Falsehood

Here the relation between artificial and natural has been "freed" of its entrapment within true/false opposition, and nature and language are not opposed, as in the arguments of Gaillard and Bernheimer. Rather, the naturality of reference assumed by both Gaillard and Bernheimer finds itself unsettled by the introduction of a nature not true but "veritable," always linked to questions of figural language.

Indeed, the cosmetic "correction" necessary to Des Esseintes's aesthetic theory would suggest that only the factitious and artificial correspond to all the features of a designation, be it "flower" or "London" or "sea voyage," since their "real" manifestation is always found to be lacking. Thus, to return to the example of the perfumes, Des Esseintes finds that:

Presque jamais, en effet, les parfums ne sont issus des fleurs dont ils portent le nom; l'artiste qui oserait emprunter à la seule nature ses éléments, ne produirait qu'une oeuvre bâtarde, sans vérité, sans style, attendu que l'essence obtenue par la distillation des fleurs ne saurait offrir qu'une très lointaine et très vulgaire analogie avec l'arôme même de la fleur vivante, épandant ses effluves en pleine terre. (223)

[Hardly ever, in fact, are perfumes produced from the flowers whose names they bear; and any artist foolish enough to take his raw materials from Nature alone would get only a hybrid result, lacking both conviction and distinction, for the very good reason that the essence obtained by distillation from the flower itself cannot possibly offer more than a very distant, very vulgar analogy with the real aroma of the living flower, rooted in the ground and spreading its effluvia through the open air.] (119)

In the art of perfumery, an intervention on the part of the "artist" is necessary in order that perfumes deserve the name they carry and that their figural relation to the real be more than a "distant, very vulgar analogy." The skewing introduced here might be summed up in a skewing of Gaillard's formulation of the goal of decadent imitation; rather than making a true fake, decadent imitation would here seem to set out to produce a *veritable fake*. To return to the term introduced in the "ermine" example, we might say that the relation between nature and truth has been interverted by language.

Is sexual difference, understood as a logic of absolute difference, ever similarly skewed, "interverted," as it were, by the logics of diversity and of the veritable that govern the bric-a-brac of the text? I would argue that we have had to wait for our own fin de siècle for a full-blown contamination to have extended to our understanding of genders and sexualities. But I would also want to argue that these logics appear in *A rebours* not as a denial of a "truth" but rather as an attempt to reconceive of a logic of difference that has baleful consequences for all concerned. It is significant in this regard, I think, that the narrative sequence that begins with the dentist episode and ends with the ventriloquist episode — the sequence that is most obviously obsessed with castrations and mutilations and sexual inversions — in fact is followed by what on the face of it is a minor coda. If more critical attention has been given to the fantasies set in motion by the description of Moreau's paintings of Salomé or by the dream of the Pox, this is perhaps because those passages reaffirm that familiar cultural fantasy of the castrating-because-castrated woman and reinstate the logic of absolute difference. The culmination of the narrative sequence however, is the encounter of Des Esseintes with a young man who approaches him in the street, and asks after the quickest route to the Rue de Babylone. Both follow the way pointed out by Des Esseintes, a way which leads to a friendship that brings with it delight and "satisfaction mingled with distress." Brief and apparently of little importance to the narrative, this episode is remarkable for the fact that it represents same-sex relations without the trappings of inversion that dress them elsewhere in the text; examples that leap to mind are Elagabalus, who "se faisait appeler Impératrice et changeait, toutes les nuits, d'Empereur" (121) [calling himself Empress and bedding every night a new Emperor] (45), and the sex exchange and role reversal with Miss Urania and its winking allusion to "uranisme," a nineteenth-century French term for male homosexuality. The invocation of the pederastic model, as the younger man asks for direction from the older man, twists the representation of male homosexuality away from the male/female opposition that recodes it as a version of heterosexuality and, in terms of narrative economy, seems to represent both solution and resolution to what has come before.[6] As solution it can be understood as an interversion, rather than inversion, of the "logical" order that preceded it, for it replaces the male/female opposition with that between older and younger man and the passage concentrates on the boy's "figure": "La figure était troublante: pâle et tirée, assez regulière sous les longs cheveux noirs, elle était éclairée par de grands yeux humides" (217). Thematically and literally, of course, what is at stake here is simply a description of the boy's disquieting face. Yet that face is also "la figure." The text here introduces a final "female figure" into the narrative sequence, but one that is only grammatically (and not thematically) so. One might say that gendering is thus displaced from the terms of the heterosexual relation (homosexuality understood as inversion) onto language, as both grammar and figure. In other words, what is feminized is not one of the participants in the exchange but rather language and figuration: on that level one might say that "la figure était troublante" [the figure was exciting] also because, in the context of *A rebours* and its logic of the veritable, figuration creates desire, and Des Esseintes's primary "heterosexual" relation is to language, to that "rhétorique de mots postiches" (118) [rhetorical jargon of invented words] (43) that he so admires in Petronius and that stands as an accurate description of the "bric-a-brac" of *A rebours* itself.

It is not by chance that, like Bernheimer and Gaillard, we have ended up with a fetishistic formulation, here invoked by the "mots postiches," and present in the two critics' arguments as the "fetishization of codes" (136) and the fetishization of the surface of the text. But it is at this point that

Gaillard and Bernheimer draw a line in the sand. On one side there is decadence, the text, and the factitious; on the other, there is fact, reality, and antidecadence. Both adopt an antidecadent position when they plant themselves firmly on the side of a facticity that remains unquestioned, indeed, that goes by the name of "nature." For Gaillard, that nature is the necessity of the passage of time and, finally, of death; for Bernheimer, as we saw in the beginning of the essay, that nature is something called the "female sexual body." Yet if fetishism is the battleground here, then it is worth remembering that fetishism works not simply to deny "female castration" but also to deny its facticity, to refuse to grant an interpretation the status of nature, and thus it rebels against the logic of absolute difference in which it is of course not possible (to return to Freud for a moment) to be castrated and not castrated at the same time. The fetishist, one might say, oscillates not only between "she's castrated — she's not castrated" but also between a logic of absolute difference and one of diversity. From our point of view — in another fin de siècle — it is this latter oscillation that rings true, as we continue to rewrite the opposition between what is "fact" and what is "factitious," find "truth" to be the product of discursive formations, and work to "intervert" what goes by the name of "nature." The "interversions" of our own turn of the century come in less flamboyant dress than those of a Huysmans or a D'Annunzio; they appear in the understanding of discourse as that which precedes any opposition between language and action, and show up as the continued exposure of the natural as "constructed." But it is this, rather than the thematics of excess, that stands as the legacy of decadence.

Notes

1. On decadence as paradoxical, see Michael Riffaterre's essay in this volume.

2. For Irigaray's critique, see *Speculum of the Other Woman* and *This Sex Which Is Not One*. On sexual difference as "indifference," see de Lauretis.

3. Rita Felski suggests instead that the lists and dense surface of the text are "reminiscent of nothing other than the lavish prose of a consumer catalogue" (100).

4. This is not to say that this is the only relation; particularly striking is the example of the dinner in black, given in honor of Des Esseintes's deceased virility. The menu of all black food and drink is a very pedagogically effective example of Roman Jakobson's poetic function of language: the paradigmatic axis of similarity (metaphor) projected onto the syntagmatic axis of combination (metonymy).

5. And, color conscious as the logic of diversity has taught us to be, we might also point out that "inter*vertir*" introduces a third color into the system of black and white: the green of "vert" made more visible by the repetition of the "er."

6. For a discussion of inversion as a strategy to preserve the heterosexuality of desire, see Christopher Craft. It is significant, I think, that both of Des Esseintes's encounters with young men — the episode at hand and the encounter with Auguste Langlois — are staged as "interceptions" that take place in the street and concern the "way" to be chosen. In the latter case, Des Esseintes attempts to turn the boy into a

criminal by getting him used to the caresses of prostitutes at an early age and then depriving him of the means to satisfy his habit. The goal is to create and then deprive the boy of a habitual order — "intervert" it, as it were.

Works Cited

Bernheimer, Charles. "The Decadent Subject." *L'Esprit Créateur* 32: 4 (1992): 53–62.
———. "Huysmans: Writing Against (Female) Nature." In *The Female Body in Western Culture*, ed. Susan Suleiman, 384–85. Cambridge: Harvard University Press, 1985.
Craft, Christopher. " 'Kiss Me with Those Red Lips': Gender and Inversion in Bram Stoker's *Dracula*." In *Speaking of Gender*, ed. Elaine Showalter, 216–42. New York: Routledge, 1989.
de Lauretis, Teresa. "Sexual Indifference and Lesbian Representation." *Theatre Journal* 40.2 (1988): 155–77.
Felski, Rita. *The Gender of Modernity*. Cambridge: Harvard University Press, 1995.
Freud, Sigmund. *Standard Edition of the Complete Psychological Works of Sigmund Freud*. 24 vols. London: Hogarth Press, 1966–74.
Gaillard, Françoise. "*A rebours* ou l'inversion des signes." In *L'esprit de décadence*, Colloque de Nantes 1, 129–40 Paris: Librairie Minard, 1980.
Huysmans, Joris-Karl. *A rebours*. Ed. Marc Fumaroli. Paris: Gallimard, 1977.
———. *Against Nature*. Trans. Robert Baldick. 1959. New York: Penguin, 1979.
Irigaray, Luce. *Speculum of the Other Woman*. Trans. Gillian C. Gill. Ithaca: Cornell University Press, 1985.
———. *This Sex Which Is Not One*. Trans. Catherine Porter and Carolyn Burke. Ithaca: Cornell University Press, 1985.
Laplanche, Jean. *Castrations/Symbolisations*. Paris: Presses Universitaires de France, 1980.

Chapter 2
Unknowing Decadence

Charles Bernheimer

Imagine the following scenario: at a dinner party I am telling a friend about the vacation from which I have just returned. I describe lolling naked in a hot tub at a luxurious resort, sipping chilled French champagne, nibbling delicious chocolate truffles, and flirting with a beautiful woman — or was it a beautiful boy? — who is soaking next to me. "How decadent!" exclaims my friend. Although perfectly current, this usage of the word warrants some reflection. It conveys quite a complex set of conflicted feelings. There is, of course, envy: my experience sounds *wonderfully* decadent to my friend in the sense of its being self-indulgently hedonistic and sensuously stimulating, with hints of loosened inhibitions and sexual transgression. All of this made possible by an enviably large outlay of money. But there is also a suggestion of moral censorship: my friend may have chosen this word to convey his sense of my conduct's being *excessively* self-indulgent, of its having *reprehensibly* failed to respect the proper social norms, of its demonstrating *insufficiently* repressed and sublimated instinctual appetites. The first meaning makes me morally superior to my friend, in the subversive sense that I have shown myself not to be subject to the dictates of traditional morality. The second meaning makes my friend morally superior to me insofar as he recognizes the value of those dictates and judges me to have violated them. In the first instance, my friend envies me the potential unraveling of my stable identity through sensuous pleasure and erotic adventure. I am, as it were, tempting fate, and succeeding, by seductively lifting repression. I am not so much indulging myself as undoing the self's coherence by liberating the perverse force of desire. In the second instance, my friend implicitly asserts the self's claim to wholeness and stands by the importance of that wholeness for the dynamic progress of civilization. From this perspective my decadence is regressive, counterproductive, even childish. Continue along that path, my friend implies, and you'll become an impoverished, obese, alcoholic pervert with one foot in a watery grave.

All this goes to show that, even in current parlance, the notion of decadence is inhabited by a doubleness that puts fundamental moral and social values in question. There is an implicit appeal to a norm that sustains society's assumptions about what is natural, good, right, life-sustaining, progressive, and so forth. But there is also the suggestion that this appeal constricts human potential, denies opportunities for pleasure, and discredits the attraction of the perverse and destructive.

*   *   *

In 1979, Richard Gilman, a respected literary and cultural critic, published a short book entitled *Decadence: The Strange Life of an Epithet*. Gilman's attitude toward his subject — the word *decadence* itself and its uses, or rather misuses, throughout western history — is passionately censorious. He presents himself as an arbiter of cultural value whose purpose is to draw attention to the contemporary degradation of language. The word *decadence* is representative for him of a class of words that, he says, "injure meaning and bring about confusion" (5) by evading truth and obscuring reality with a veil of illusion. But Gilman's dismissal of the word *decadence* as a tool for insight can itself serve as a tool for insight. His book is actually very useful, for in arguing that the term *decadence* has no specific referent, that "*all* the forms in which we think we detect the phenomenon of decadence are products of the word's prior uses and not stable realities of the objective world" (14), by so arguing Gilman succeeds less in proving the emptiness of decadence as a subject than in proving its coherence as a subversive agent in language and culture. It is against the appeal of this subversion, evident in Gilman's fascination with his slippery, duplicitous topic, that he defensively reacts.

One of Gilman's strongest objections to the term *decadence* is that it corrupts what he calls the "proper" distinction between a metaphorical use of language, which, he claims, "relieves us of the burden of the world's facticity" (161), and an epistemologically accurate use of language through which that facticity is made intelligible. Decadence, he complains, is a poetic metaphor that speakers mistakenly employ as if it described documentable actualities in the real world. The Romans were the first to use the term in this way to account for their sense of loss in relation to a projected image of their own earlier vigor. But this loss, Gilman argues, cannot be measured in any concrete, historically specific terms. Late Roman art was different than, rather than inferior to, its classical predecessor. Thus Rome's sense of its decline was a fictional construct posited on the premise of a preceding ideal performance. Change, brought on largely by factors over which Rome had little control, was interpreted poetically, metaphorically, narcissistically, as degradation and loss.

For Gilman, this is a culturally destructive mistake that blinds a society to its own innovative potential. He claims that the fault lies largely in the failure of the society to perceive the purely constructed fictive quality of the ideal in relation to which it judges its own inferiority. If, that is to say, the notion of "progress" were to be recognized as an arbitrary fiction, rather than a natural function of civilized life, then the epistemological value of "decadence" as its logical negative complement would be immediately suspect. Once revealed as poetic lies and discredited as instruments of knowledge, both words, *progress* and *decadence*, would presumably have to retreat to their "proper spheres" (161) of metaphorical operation, and Gilman could finally relax his vigilant policing of their harmful vagaries.

Such vagaries, Gilman claims, are harmful to proper semantic function and to what he terms "the integrity and wholeness of communal experience" (163). Like certain figures of late nineteenth-century liberalism — such as Max Nordau, author of the massive attack on fin-de-siècle decadence entitled *Degeneration* (1892) — he refuses to acknowledge the possibility that the subversion of communal wholeness could have cultural value.[1] He fails to see that the transgression of conventionally "proper" spheres of verbal operation — for instance, the use of metaphor in the context of history — need not be symptomatic of epistemological confusion and may reflect a lucid skepticism about asserting distinctions between fiction and history, writing and what is outside it.

The most useful of the revaluations one can make of Gilman's critique concerns his model of decadent constructedness. In order for the term *decadence* to have any meaning at all, he argues, a positive norm must be constructed in relation to which certain modes of behavior can be designated as regressively deviant. The arbitrary, fictional quality of this construct must be forgotten, however, if decadence, linked to the norm as its abnormal, depressive opposite, is to appear to have any subject matter proper to it, such as decline, loss, degradation, and so forth. In other words, the notion of decadence depends, according to Gilman, on a prior essentializing gesture whereby a cultural metaphor is mistakenly taken to be a truth of nature.

He's right, I think, though I don't read the founding mistake of decadence the way he does, as grounds for linguistic eviction. And he's only partially right, as I propose to demonstrate in the rest of this essay.

*   *   *

Reviewing Flaubert's newly published novel *Salammbô*, the critic Sainte-Beuve complains about the insignificance of the book's subject, the brutal war between Carthage and its mercenary army in 241–238 B.C. "Why should I interest myself in this lost war, buried in the mountain passes or the sands of Africa?" (437) he asks, foreshadowing the puzzled, irritated response of numerous subsequent readers. This war made no difference to the future of European civilization, he protests; there is no "live communication" (437) between it and the present; its story reveals nothing about how we got where we are. Sainte-Beuve's complaint amounts to this: Flaubert's historical novel is unhistorical because the author has perversely chosen a subject in history that had no effect on history. Although Sainte-Beuve does not use the word, he is accusing Flaubert of decadence, decadence displayed as the failure of historical understanding.

Sainte-Beuve's Romantic perspective is echoed in our century by the materialist critique of the philosopher Georg Lukács, who accuses Flaubert of failing to understand "the real driving forces of history as they objectively worked" (177) and of transforming history from a means of dramatizing social and economic contradictions into "a collection of exotic anecdotes" (182). The appeal of this exoticism, Lukács argues, motivated Flaubert in his choice of a historical subject that would have no connection with the modern bourgeois society that he so passionately hated. But, notes Lukács in a perception that goes well beyond Sainte-Beuve's insights, "this lack of connection — or rather the illusion of such — is at the same time the subjective factor which connects Flaubert's exotic historical subject matter with the everyday life of the present" (185). Here Lukács is linking the disconnected meaninglessness of Flaubert's historical subject in *Salammbô* with the disconnected impersonality and disinterestedness of the authorial attitude that Flaubert wished to assume in *Madame Bovary*. Since Lukács considers this wish a reflection of Flaubert's regrettable detachment from the material processes of historical change, he has little sympathy for it. Reading Flaubert against Flaubert, he attributes the greater success of *Madame Bovary* to the author's failure to remain distant and impersonal.

However, what Lukács interprets as a failure of historical vision may be an assertion that history lacks vision. What he sees as the decadence of historical fiction may be a fiction generated by history's decadence. Flaubert feels himself to be at an end — which he variously describes as that of nineteenth-century France, of the Latin race, even of the world — but he associates this ending not with a poverty of history but with its excess: "Wretched as we are," he observes to his friend Louis Bouilhet from Cairo in 1850, "we have, I think, a good deal of taste because we are profoundly historical, admit everything, and adopt the point of view of the thing in order to judge it. But," he asks rhetorically, "do we have as much innateness as we have comprehensivity? Is a fierce originality even compatible with so much breadth?" (*Correspondance* 645). This passage suggests that, for Flaubert, in direct antithesis to Sainte-Beuve, a highly developed historical sense is a symptom of decadence, of a falling away from an ideal of imaginative originality. Flaubert's conception of what it means to be historical destroys history as a mode of insight and understanding. To be historical, he says, is to *lose* any elevated perspective, any distance from events and objects, and to adopt an entirely contingent point of view, "le point de vue de la chose." History for Flaubert is no more than its objects and exists nowhere else than in its objects. Sainte-Beuve criticizes just this myopic narrative stance in *Salammbô*: "The author does not maintain himself above his work," he observes; "he applies himself too closely, he's got his nose on top of it. He never distanced himself enough from his work to adopt the point of view of his readers" (436). Those readers, Sainte-Beuve suggests, want Flaubert to present history as a teleological narrative capable of explaining progress and decadence in terms of causes and effects.

Flaubert, in contrast, suggests that he is constrained to write from *within* decadence, which he views as a historical moment incapable of reading itself from a historically significant perspective. In this he agrees with Nietzsche's analysis of the consequences of the oversaturation of the modern age with history: "To take everything objectively," Nietzsche observes in "On the Uses and Disadvantages of History for Life," "to grow angry at nothing, to love nothing, to understand everything, how soft and pliable that makes one" (105). Nietzsche measures the decadent loss of vitality, as does Flaubert, against a Romantic ideal of the demiurgic imagination. This comparative measure betrays the de-historicizing contingency of the decadent moment by constructing an ideal in relation to which decadence can be narrativized as such.

My formulation here echoes Gilman's model for decadence but with two crucial differences. First, Gilman describes the projection of an essentialized norm as an epistemological *mistake* that necessarily discredits any oppositional structure built on its premise. In contrast, I see the projection of the norm as *betrayal* that, far from discrediting the idea of decadence, actually enables its articulation. Second, Gilman claims that the fictive dimension of the projected norm must be forgotten in order to mask the vacancy of its decadent opposite. I believe that decadent artists are self-consciously aware of the norm's uncertain ontological status.

Flaubert silences this awareness when he defends the accuracy of his depiction of Carthage against the criticism of Sainte-Beuve. The norm against which Sainte-Beuve measures Flaubert's deficiency is, as we have seen, historical meaning — and Flaubert's response appears to be addressed to this issue. He takes great pains to defend the exactitude of his documentation, often citing the precise volume and page number of his source. "You may be sure," he tells Sainte-Beuve, "that I have not created a fantastic Carthage. Documents on Carthage do exist" (451). The reader of Flaubert's open letters to Sainte-Beuve and to the archaeologist Froehner is surprised to realize, upon reflection, that Flaubert nowhere interprets the historical significance of his subject. He simply cites his sources. No model of epistemological coherence determines his choices: it suffices that some detail can be found in an author of antiquity for him to accept it as true.[2] What he calls the comprehensivity of his historical sense in the letter to Bouilhet is manifested by the sheer magnitude of his scholarly research. Inspiration in a decadent age is born in the library; it is secondary, derivative, and quantitative. Flaubert's textual documents are like the body parts strewn across the battlefields in his novel: they are the cultural remains that constitute history's resistance to meaning.

This resistance is thematized in *Salammbô* by the collapse of the difference between disputing opponents, supposedly civilized Carthaginians and supposedly savage barbarians.[3] Although their confrontation is motivated at the outset by a grievance — the mercenaries' claim to their unpaid wages — this complaint is soon forgotten and the motive of opposition on both sides becomes the pure desire to oppose and dominate. Flaubert grants neither side any kind of comprehension of its historical position, any moral project or political vision. The warring opposites, as in *Bouvard et Pécuchet*, are purely structural. The violence of their clash does not produce a meaningful distinction between civilization and savagery, culture and nature, or any other dualism. History is pictured on the micro level as mutilation and dismemberment — think of Hanno's leprous flesh hanging in rotten shreds; of Mâtho's bleeding body picked and scratched to death by the whole population of Carthage; of the barbarians trapped in the Défilé de la Hache cutting up and devouring their comrades; of any battle scene, for that matter, where detached body parts proliferate and are even recycled for new uses — human fat to grease war machines, human nails to fabricate armor, and so forth. Indifferently Carthaginian or barbarian, the dismembered body emblematizes the absence of historical direction when everything has become history. The confrontation of enemies turns into a duplication of the same, and barbarism is revealed to be an attribute projected onto the Other to create the illusion of differential superiority, progressives on one side, decadents on the other. Indeed, in Flaubert's usage, *barbarism* is just another term for decadence.

The reader who, like Sainte-Beuve, condemns Flaubert's novel as barbarous is thus doubly entrapped by the structural dynamics of decadence. First, the novel deconstructs the opposition on which his condemnation depends. Second, if he tries to speak from a position outside the collapse of difference and to read this collapse historically as itself a symptom of decadence, his reading is always already included within decadence as the betrayal of its indifference to historical knowledge.

*   *   *

"Nature has had her day," reflects Des Esseintes in Huysmans's *A rebours*. "The time has come to replace her, to the degree possible, by artifice" (107, 108). This project is probably what first comes to most people's minds when they think of decadence as a style in art and literature. Decadent style is artificial, ornamental, superficial, decorative. It fetishizes the particularized detail at the expense of the organic whole. It is a style of decomposition and disintegration, best appreciated by the kind of myopic point of view Flaubert considered characteristic of his age. "What is the style of every *literary deca-*

dence?" asks Nietzsche in *The Case of Wagner*. Paraphrasing Paul Bourget's earlier formulation, he answers: "That life no longer dwells in the whole. The word becomes sovereign and leaps out of the sentence, the sentence reaches out and obscures the meaning of the page, the page gains life at the expense of the whole — the whole is no longer whole" (170).

While this description applies perfectly to Nietzsche's own fragmentary, inconclusive writing style — showing that he failed to overcome what makes him, as he says, "a child of this time; that is, a decadent" (*Case of Wagner* 15) — it seems far removed from the style of literary naturalism. Zola's sentences don't have the tortured syntax and densely encrusted verbal surface of Huysmans's. But the decadence is not only a matter of style. Huysmans began as a disciple of Zola, and his first novels are characteristically naturalistic in language and theme. Indeed, one could argue that Nietzsche's borrowed description simply projects onto the plane of literary style what is at the thematic center of much naturalist writing, that is, the decomposition of organic wholes, the failure of nature to sustain meaning, and a decentered instability that Nietzsche, speaking of Wagner, associates with physical degeneration and hysteria.

Des Esseintes's favorite novel by Zola, *La faute de l'abbé Mouret*, seems to be written in praise of the same qualities that Nietzsche also champions, that is, in Nietzsche's terms, "the vibration and exuberance of life" (*Case of Wagner* 10) and "the return to nature, health, cheerfulness, youth, *virtue*" (159–60). But just as Nietzsche observes in *The Will to Power* that "man reaches nature only after a long struggle — he never 'returns'" (73), so Zola, in a novel that appears to offer just such an ideal liberating return, shows that nature is always already decadent, that is, unhealthy, decomposing, derivative, like Nietzsche's definition of decadent style.[4]

The first part of the novel paints an antithesis between Serge Mouret, an ascetic young priest who exults in his contemptuous denial of nature, of sensual pleasure, and of the sexual body, and his sister Désirée, "une belle bête" [a beautiful animal] (93), who, sexually and intellectually innocent herself, exults in the pullulating fertility of the barnyard animals she maternally tends. The siblings live in a tiny, isolated village where promiscuous sexual activity defines the relation of the brutish peasants both to each other and to the land they till, with which they are described as "fornicating" (65). The alternatives Zola offers are both singularly unappealing: an embrace of nature as teeming animal generation or a violent repression of life in the flesh, so violent, indeed, that it leads to psychosomatic collapse. At the end of part one, Serge, in a masochistic delirium, calls on the Virgin Mary to castrate him so that he can unite with her without sin.

In the novel's second part, Serge wakes up from his long illness to find himself in the symbolically named Paradou, which was a country domain in the eighteenth century and is now a decaying manor surrounded by an immense, luxuriantly overgrown garden. There Serge, who has forgotten his past, is reborn and nursed back to life by the generous, spontaneously loving Albine. An exuberant child of nature, she teaches Serge to love the beauty of the garden's abundant flowers, plants, trees, and animals. The sensuous appreciation of organic life, his own included, is Albine's cure for Serge, which enlists the indulgent cooperation of the erotically charged garden — roses reveal their delectable nakedness, fragrant perfumes fill the air, sap exudes from the fruit-laden trees. Soon the garden becomes an active force in encouraging Serge and Albine to consummate their love. Hesitant and anxious at first, when they finally "exceed to the exigencies of the garden," Zola calls their act "a victory for the animals, plants, and things that had wanted the entry of these two children into the eternity of life" (248).

Thus, the novel's message seems to reverse the Edenic myth: instead of being a fall, a sin, an act against man's better nature, sex is a celebration of love and of the integration of man and woman into "l'éternité de la vie." But this message becomes confused when, immediately after their carnal climax, Serge and Albine feel shame, and Serge's religious past returns to his consciousness. Overwhelmed by guilt, he flees from Albine and the Paradou to resume his priestly duties. At the outset of the last of the novel's three parts, he has once again dedicated himself to the negation of life and fervently wishes for death. This wish is not for just any death, however, but for an inorganic one that would "save [him] from all putrefaction." "Your garden," he tells Albine, who has come to take him back, "is a charnel house where the cadavers of things decompose" (317).

Serge's claim is that apparently unfallen nature, nurturing and therapeutic, is actually no different from nature in its decadence, where sex is mere animal instinct and death feeds life by corrupting it. The text justifies this perception. At the garden's most intimate moment of complicity with the lovers, when it seems to be offering them the liberating ecstasy of sexual union, Zola describes it as pullulating with fecund couplings and fertile fornications — a description that resembles nothing so much as the rampant sexual promiscuity in the village and in Désirée's farmyard. The liberating benefits of a natural sexuality are thus equated with the repugnant repetitions of a futile fertility. And woman as savior becomes woman as libidinal vampire.

Not only is the Paradou's ideal nature decomposed by organic process, it is also undermined by representation and artifice. The Paradou is not actually a wilderness but the luxuriant overgrowth of what was initially a sophisticated design: a cultural intention is at the origin of this natural efflorescence. And at the origin of Zola's evocation of this efflorescence is his research in botanical dictionaries, not his promenades in pristine nature. Cultural also are the incitements to sex that Serge and Albine derive from the suggestive paintings of human and mythological couplings in the château's bedrooms. Thus the lesson in love is not taught only by animals and plants. Finally, there is the Biblical intertext, which often asserts itself so insistently that the reader becomes less interested in the mimetic rendition of nature's flora and fauna than in the Paradou's relation to its Edenic prototype.

One could summarize these observations by saying that, for Zola, "Nature is no great mother who has borne us. She is our creation. It is in our brain that she quickens to life" (*Artist as Critic* 312). So opines Oscar Wilde, an author with whom Zola is rarely linked and who condemned his French contemporary for his "unimaginative realism" (299). But in *La faute de l'abbé Mouret*, which Wilde may not have known, Zola takes his realism to its imaginative limit, where nature's organic decomposition is shown to be analogous to its cultural constructedness. Life here certainly no longer dwells in the whole. Nature is no great mother. Yet just as Flaubert plays with the possibility of meaningful history, so Zola plays with a fantasy of nature's beneficent meaning. Both writers are highly invested in their projected norms. I don't want to give the impression that these projections are mere tactical gestures. Flaubert's defense of his historical accuracy is passionate and sincere. Zola's desire to redeem nature is so convincing that the critic introducing the Garnier-Flammarion edition calls the novel "a magnificent hymn to nature" (*La faute* 32). But both writers subvert their own dreams of making sense of their decadence. They reveal the abnormality of the normative position from which this judgment could be made. The revelation has a strong masochistic motive: the renunciation of judgment charges the decadent world erotically with deviance, disintegration, fragmentation, even castration. Emblematic is Father Mouret's desire to be nailed to the cross, to have his limbs pierced and his side opened. Nature having failed as nurturing mother, decadent masculinity defines itself in homoerotic relation to a punitive father, who, in fantasy, denaturalizes his son's body.

*   *   *

It is largely because Wilde's *Picture of Dorian Gray* appears firmly to know and to judge its decadent subject that it has become the canonical example of literary decadence in English. The normative standard subverted by Flaubert in *Salammbô* and by Zola in *La faute de l'abbé Mouret* is embodied by Wilde in Basil Hallward's magical portrait of the beautiful Dorian. The painting acts as an unimpeachable moral arbiter, "the visible emblem of conscience," expressing on the surface of the canvas the truth of Dorian's sinful, degenerate life. While Dorian goes about the world looking eternally youthful and innocent, the picture unsparingly records the physical impact of his moral failures. For example, when, at the novel's end, he imagines that he has done a good deed in not seducing a peasant girl who loves him, the portrait adds a look of cunning to the eyes and a hypocritical wrinkle to the mouth, thereby convincing Dorian that "through vanity he had spared her. In hypocrisy he had worn the mask of goodness. For curiosity's sake he had tried the denial of self" (192). Disgusted by what he calls "this monstrous soul-life" (192), Dorian decides to get rid of the painting. The result is a novelistic ending that has the didactic quality of a fairy tale finale: in stabbing the picture, Dorian kills himself, and the dichotomy between life and representation returns to "normal." The picture reverts to its original youthful appearance and the dead man is revealed to be "withered, wrinkled, and loathsome of visage" (193).

This scenario reduces the notion of decadence to a catalog of moral perversions — Dorian is condemned for his aestheticism, his self-indulgent narcissism, his callous indifference to the suffering of others. Wilde's book then becomes, as Richard Ellmann maintains, "the tragedy of aestheticism, [proof that] life cannot be lived on such terms" (315), and this most famous of English decadent novels is reassuringly interpreted as a devastating critique of decadence. Interestingly, Wilde himself was worried about this likely misreading of his novel, of which he simultaneously acknowledged the validity. Responding to a critical review of the book's first edition, he insisted that his story had a moral. "And the moral is this: All excess, as well as all renunciation, brings its own punishment." Basil, he claimed, is punished for "worshipping physical beauty far too much," Dorian for "having led a life of mere sensation and pleasure," and Lord Henry for attempting to be "merely the spectator of life." Then, in a remark that is surely tongue-in-cheek, Wilde says that his "terrible moral" may not be accessible to the prurient but "will be revealed to those whose minds are healthy. Is this an artistic error? I fear it is" (*Artist as Critic* 240–41). Thus Wilde recognizes that the moral structure of his book betrays decadent art, which, having no standard of health or ethics, is constitutionally morbid and in error. But that error requires the fiction of truth in order to be judged as such.

Critics who side with the portrait's moral righteousness are repeating the demonic pact whereby Dorian fixes his essence on the canvas. That pact, in my view, does not signal the onset of Dorian's decadence but rather his failure to espouse decadent subjectivity.

The first scenes of Wilde's novel show the creation of Dorian Gray as the subject of the verbal and visual representations of two male admirers. Looking at his finished portrait, Dorian feels "as if he had recognized himself for the first time" (25). But the self he claims to be recognizing is actually entirely new, for it is the locus of the conjunction, as Ed Cohen puts it, "between Basil's visual embodiment of his erotic desire for Dorian and Lord Henry's verbal sublimation of such desire" (806). Basil says that he has invested the portrait with his soul and heart (13); similarly, Lord Henry claims to have projected his soul into Dorian's gracious form, a projection whose effects the painting must certainly register, since Basil is completing it while Lord Henry is verbally seducing Dorian. Thus the identity that Dorian recognizes is his only insofar as it is not his. Dorian's subjectivity is constituted as decadent insofar as it is a function of the desire of the Other.

It is this dynamic of identity de-formation and alienation that Dorian rejects when he falls in love with his painted alter ego and volunteers to give up his soul to always look like it. Thereby Dorian equates his soul, that is, his moral center, his essential being, with a perfectly static image of his unchanging physical beauty. The equation is explicit in a number of his reflections after the portrait's appearance has begun to change. For instance: "As it had revealed to him his own body, so it would reveal to him his own soul" (93). The image of his body, ideally beautiful, ideally whole, expresses for Dorian the essence of his soul's moral integrity. But he has misread himself. His painted body image is actually the projection of the souls of his lovers. Their souls are mobile instruments of desire; Dorian's, in contrast, is a repressive agency that punishes transgression. By identifying with this soul, Dorian ensures that his decadence will be massively condemned, as it has been by countless readers eager to associate themselves with his right-thinking spiritual essence. But such condemnation mistakes Wilde's decadent subject, which is betrayed by Dorian's overly conscientious soul.

"No artist has ethical sympathies," Wilde observes in the preface to *The Picture of Dorian Gray*, in response to criticism of the novel's first edition. "An ethical sympathy in an artist is an unpardonable mannerism of style" (*Artist as Critic* 236). This aphorism suggests that, from the point of view of the (decadent) artist, an ethical sympathy may actually *be* pardonable if it is revealed to be no more than a stylistic mannerism. I believe that the ending of *Dorian Gray*, with what Wilde called "its extremely obvious moral" (245), is just such a pardonable mannerism. Rather than embodying a lesson in ethics — if you destroy your soul you kill yourself — it offers a sort of comic send-up of this message. Nor is Dorian's death a form of atonement, as if art were somehow able to redeem a ruined life. Wilde's message, insofar as there is one, concerns rather the mistake of imagining that life is anything other than art, that a soul is anything other than a style of representation, that a normative standard of ethics is anything more than a mannerism, or that decadence can judge itself in any other way than by betraying its own aesthetic premises.

The effects of those premises are evident throughout Wilde's text, which is a collage of artistic styles and conventions. There is the witty, epigrammatic dialogue that seems to be lifted from Wilde's plays; there is the naturalistic, "slice-of-life" subplot involving the actress Sybil Vane and her brother, whose return to revenge his sister's death is the stuff of Victorian melodrama; there is the unacknowledged imitation, which Wilde probably considered "decorative," of whole sections of Huysmans's *A rebours* — about Dorian's study of perfumes, music, jewels, and so forth — as well as the borrowing of Huysmanian techniques and themes; there are repeated echoes of Pater in Lord Henry's speech; there are sentences in a highly artificial, aestheticized style that appear in the midst of naturalistic description; there are obvious references to Faust's pact with the devil and to the imagery of fairy tales.

This heterogeneous hodgepodge of imitated styles and borrowed themes constitutes Wilde's decadent subject. It corresponds to an interpretation of subjectivity that Dorian, insofar as he identifies with his essential soul, would have to find abhorrent. Yet none other than Dorian offers as a normative picture of man's psychology just such a version of the multiple, decomposed subject of decadence. Looking at pictures of his ancestors, he wonders how anyone could be so naive as to "conceive the Ego in man as a thing simple, reliable and of one essence. To him, man was a being with myriad lives and myriad sensations, a complex multiform creature that bore within itself strange legacies of thought and passion, and whose very flesh was tainted with the monstrous maladies of the dead" (124).[5] Here it is precisely the stimulus of representations in paint that pushes Dorian to reflect on the ego's constitution in and through otherness. Yet, earlier, when he identified with his portrait as the permanent embodiment of his essence, Dorian had rejected any notion that he might be constitutionally tainted, monstrous, multiform, that his essential self might be dissolved by anteriority, plurality, and difference.

By seeing his morbid taint simply as the physical consequence of sin, Dorian denies the complex multiformity of his decadent constitution. He also closes off the implications of the most sophisticated of his earlier ideas about the formation of the ego: "One had ancestors in literature as well as one's own race," he says to himself, "nearer perhaps in type and tempera-ment" (125). This observation is particularly pertinent at this point in the narrative since Dorian's entire meditation about genealogy is stolen from Des Esseintes's thoughts in the opening pages of A rebours. So the rot invad-ing Dorian's portrait from inside can be seen not only as the sign of his disintegration through "strange legacies of thought and passion" but also as the effect of his being poisoned at birth by the legacies of the library, the famous yellow book and many others. It is a poison similar to the one that infected Zola's Paradou and Flaubert's Carthage. A century later this mor-bid agent becomes a crucial ingredient in the witches' brew of postmodern-ism, whose subject, according to Terry Eagleton, is "a dispersed, decentered network of libidinal attachments, emptied of ethical substance and psychi-cal interiority" (145).

*   *   *

I have spoken of decadence's being betrayed by attaining knowledge of itself, a formulation that obviously reflects on my position as author of this article about decadence. If I'm right, then I must be in error about my subject. But, then again, that depends on how you define knowledge. If I assume the place of judgment and speak as if I had access to truth, then I enter into the decadent subject as an agent of its betrayal. Theoreticians of decadence, of whom — not surprisingly — there have been few, have often made this mistake. They have become Manichean allegorists, or mythomans like Camille Paglia, dividing the world up into the good and the bad, the healthy and the sick, the progressive and the degenerate. Even Nietzsche, who thought about decadence obsessively, had a tendency to want to put decadence behind him by defining it in stark opposition to life, health, and creativity. But he also observed, "The phenomenon of decadence is as necessary as the increase and advance of life: one is in no position to abolish it" (*Will to Power* 25).

My word *betrayal* is inspired by Walter Benjamin's meditations on the structure of German baroque allegory. Although not everything that Benjamin says about allegory is relevant to decadence, certain aspects of his analysis are illuminating in this context.[6] He describes the allegorical world as containing nothing but ruins, fragments, scraps, the products of unending erosion and decay. " 'History,' " writes Benjamin, "is inscribed on the face of nature in the sign-script [*Zeichenschrift*] of transience" (353). Flaubert's "documents sur Carthage," Zola's biblical and botanical intertexts, Wilde's decorative borrowings from the library are all such sign-scripts, inscribing representation on the face of nature, disrupting natural process with alien script. The allegorical protagonist tries to give sense to these enigmatic fragments and lives in a melancholy state of contemplation. Finally his patience is rewarded when an *Umschwung* (406), an about-turn, occurs and redemptive meaning is revealed. This about-turn corresponds, in the terms of my analyses in this essay, to a vision of history's significance (Flaubert), to a knowledge of nature's purpose (Zola), or to a picture of moral rectitude (Wilde). Allegory turns to metaphysical truth as its teleology. Decadence, in contrast, is antiteleological and antimetaphysical — yet it cannot do without the illusions of metaphysics. In this sense, it cannot not judge its own value negatively from the point of view of history, nature, or ethics. But this judgment is not final, as it becomes in allegory after the *Umschwung*. Decadence holds judgment in suspension. It fights against betraying the materiality of signs and objects and tries to adhere to surfaces and sensations. It wants to claim autonomy in its own realm, commandeering death to undertake its own work rather than serve the interests of life. Thus diverted from its natural function, this agency promotes unnatural practices and generates perverse pleasures. Decadence wants to do without truth. But its moment, at least as regards the nineteenth century, is that precisely defined by Nietzsche in his writings on European nihilism, when God has died but his place remains empty, tempting man to fill it — with art, science (decadence and positivism are not necessarily opposites, as degeneration theory demonstrates), mysticism, diabolism, even a return to religion. Decadence is haunted by its Other, yet also knows that this Other is no more than an illusory projection, a false turn away from the materiality of an allegorical world without redemption.[7]

Notes

1. Nordau mounts an attack on language far more sweeping than Gilman's. He considers all use of language to be contaminated by mysticism. The only reliable knowledge, in his positivist view, is "derived from direct perception" (68).

2. This point was first brought out forcefully by Jacques Neefs in his important article. Other pieces of value for seeing *Salammbô* in the context of decadence are by Liz Constable, Eugenio Donato, and Françoise Gaillard.

3. The best discussion of this aspect of Flaubert's novel is Michal Ginsburg's chapter in her book on Flaubert.

4. The critic who reads Zola with the greatest sensitivity to this aspect of his creative vision is Jean Borie. Illuminating articles on *La faute* are those listed below by Mieke Bal, Janet Beizer, and Dorothy Kelly.

5. Wilde puts basically this same idea into the mouth of one of his dialogists in "The Critic as Artist," first published in 1890. "And so, it is not our own life that we live, but the lives of the dead," says Gilbert, "and the soul that dwells within us is no single spiritual entity, making us personal and individual, created for our service, and entering into us for our joy. It is something that has dwelt in fearful places, and in ancient sepulchres has made its abode. It is sick with many maladies, and has memories of curious sins" (*Artist as Critic* 383).

6. The relation of Benjamin's ideas to an analysis of decadence has been explored by Christine Buci-Glucksmann in her stimulating book *Baroque Reason*.

7. This article is an elaboration from the point of view of epistemology of a model I first developed in a shorter essay, "The Decadent Subject," and incorporates passages from that essay.

Works Cited

Bal, Mieke. "Quelle est la faute de l'abbé Mouret? Pour une narratologie diachronique et polémique." *Australian Journal of French Studies* 23.2 (1986): 149–67.

Beizer, Janet. "This Is Not a Source Study: Zola, Genesis, and *La Faute de l'abbé Mouret*." *Nineteenth-Century French Studies* 18 (Fall-Winter 1989–90): 186–95.

Benjamin, Walter. *Ursprung des deutschen Trauerspiels in Gesammelte Schriften*. Ed. Rolf Tiedemann and Hermann Schweppenhäuser. Frankfurt: Suhrkamp, 1974.

Bernheimer, Charles. "The Decadent Subject." *L'Esprit Créateur* 32:4 (Winter 1992), 53–62.

Borie, Jean. *Zola et les mythes: Ou de la nausée au salut*. Paris: Seuil, 1971.

Buci-Glucksmann, Christine. *Baroque Reason: The Aesthetics of Modernity*. Trans. Patrick Camiller. London: Sage, 1994.

Cohen, Ed. "Writing Gone Wilde: Homoerotic Desire in the Closet of Representation." *PMLA* 102.5 (Oct. 1987): 801–13.

Constable, Liz. "Critical Departures: *Salammbô*'s Orientalism." *MLN* 111 (1996): 625–46.

Donato, Eugenio. *The Script of Decadence: Essays on the Fictions of Flaubert and the Poetics of Romanticism*. New York: Oxford University Press, 1993.

Eagleton, Terry. *Against the Grain: Essays 1975–1985*. London: Verso, 1986.

Ellmann, Richard. *Oscar Wilde*. New York: Knopf, 1988.

Flaubert, Gustave. *Correspondance.* Vol.1. Ed. Jean Bruneau. Paris: Pléiade, 1973.

———. *Salammbô.* Paris: Club de l'Honnête Homme, 1971.

Gaillard, Françoise. "La révolte contre la révolution (*Salammbô*: Un autre point de vue sur l'histoire)." In *Gustave Flaubert: Procédés Narratifs et Fondements Epistémologiques,* ed. Alfonso de Toro. Tübingen: Gunter Narr, 1987.

Gilman, Richard. *Decadence: The Strange Life of an Epithet.* New York: Farrar, Straus and Giroux, 1979.

Ginsburg, Michal Peled. *Flaubert Writing: A Study in Narrative Strategies.* Stanford: Stanford University Press, 1986.

Huysmans, Joris-Karl. *A rebours.* Ed. Marc Fumaroli. Paris: Gallimard, 1977.

Kelly, Dorothy. "Experimenting on Women: Zola's Theory and Practice of the Experimental Novel." In *Spectacles of Realism: Body, Gender, Genre,* ed. Margaret Cohen and Christopher Prendergast. Minneapolis: Minnesota University Press, 1995.

Lukács, Georg. *The Historical Novel.* Boston: Beacon, 1963.

Neefs, Jacques. "*Salammbô*, textes critiques." *Littérature* 15: 52–64.

Nietzsche, Friedrich. *The Case of Wagner.* Trans. Walter Kaufmann. New York: Vintage, 1967.

———. "On the Uses and Disadvantages of History for Life." In *Untimely Meditations,* trans. R. J. Hollingdale, 57–123. Cambridge: Cambridge University Press, 1983.

———. *The Will to Power.* Trans. Walter Kaufmann and R. J. Hollingdale. New York: Vintage, 1967.

Nordau, Max. *Degeneration.* New York: Howard Fertig, 1968.

Sainte-Beuve, Charles. "*Salammbô* par M. Gustave Flaubert." Appendix. *Salammbô.* 410–52.

Wilde, Oscar. *The Artist as Critic: Critical Writings of Oscar Wilde.* Ed. Richard Ellmann. Chicago: University of Chicago Press, 1969.

———. *The Picture of Dorian Gray and Other Writings.* New York: Bantam, 1982.

Zola, Emile. *La faute de l'abbé Mouret.* Paris: Flammarion, 1972.

Chapter 3
Decadent Paradoxes

Michael Riffaterre
Translated by Liz Constable and Matthew Potolsky

The very meaning of the word *decadent* has encouraged critics to make value judgments that do little more than translate biological or chronological notions — such as senescence, exhaustion, the "end" of the century — into aesthetic terms. Among decadent writers themselves these notions produced a thematic universe whose most characteristic and frequently evoked traits include ennui and morbidity, and whose characters take a bitter pleasure in their disgust with life and cultivate an unhealthy sensibility — a taste for excess, a predisposition toward artifice, sadomasochistic experiments, and so on — in a quest to palliate their *acedia*. This aspect of decadence — both the content of these forms and the rhetoric of these contents — has already been well documented.

It remains difficult, however, to differentiate these tropes and themes as a group from similar ones found in the writings of the Romantics. Critics have wanted to minimize their role in Romanticism, to see them as marginal phenomena found primarily in the works of minor writers like the Bouzingos, already cast out of the temple by such parodic texts as Gautier's *Jeunes-France*. But this distinction is illusory, since decadent traits are evident in texts that are in no way marginal, such as Gautier's *Comédie de la mort* or Sainte-Beuve's *Poésies de Joseph Delorme*. Indeed, these traits reach their stylistic apogee in Baudelaire's *Les Fleurs du mal*. Critics have also been tempted to base the difference between decadent writing and its Romantic models on the existence of characteristics determined by historical factors. Thus such themes as the corruption of values and world-weary cynicism would reflect the senescence characteristic of the fin de siècle. Yet Romanticism itself also coincided with a turn of the century and even maintained its millenarian symbolism well into the next century (for example, in Lamennais's *Paroles d'un croyant*).

I believe that the difference between Romanticism and decadence is to be found elsewhere, namely, in its tropological nature. I propose to discern a figure always present in decadent texts but generally absent in Romantic style: paradox.

My claim has this advantage for criticism: paradox is a formal and semantic characteristic. It is inscribed in the text and is thus wholly evident. It does not demand any recourse to ideological or aesthetic explanations. Paradox also has the advantage of being something necessarily perceived by the reader, assuring us that it is indeed an element of the text's literarity. In fact, it cannot escape the reader, because the utterance in which it occurs contrasts with a previous utterance, in relation to which it is absurd, or it simply strikes the reader because its use of words goes blatantly against standard usage. Paradox does not only offer statements contrary to the reader's expectation—or even to his or her idea of reality—but expresses them disconcertingly, unpleasantly, or worse, ridiculously, thereby arousing in the reader reactions ranging from an initial incredulity, to irritation, to a sense of amusement before the too-evident artifice of the procedure. Its mechanism is thus similar to that of humor. Just as in the more spontaneous literary forms, the hold that paradox exercises over the imagination works like humor but is carried out in two stages. It first proposes an object, and then offers an aberrant point of view that falsifies the representation of that object. The effect of surprise caused by an expression that seems inadequate, or even by a systematic mismatch between form and content, is a consequence of the combination of the two stages. The first, prior to the paradoxical transformation, is the *given*. The second, following the transformation, is the *derivation*, the form of the incongruity. Paradox resides in the polarity between the given and the derivation, since the given is not in itself paradoxical, and the derivation that it generates would be gratuitously bizarre, or arbitrarily false, if it were presented alone.

As the derivation develops, each descriptive detail, each narrative episode that complicates it, accentuates the difference and underlines the contrast between what the given would allow one to conceive or foresee and what the derivation has drawn from it.

But the contrast in itself does not vary; the variants that successively actualize it never cease to reinforce the same oxymoron. It opposes either the denotations of the given to those of the derivation (for example, representing nature in terms of artifice, or vice versa), or the connotations of the given or specific value judgments founded upon them (for example, a repulsive or horrible object described in terms of beauty or in a sublime style). The given is enunciated one time only. It can be explicit, presented unambiguously in the text, or implicit, in which case it is presupposed by the text in the form of a reference to a theme or to an intertext. By contrast, the derivation produced from the given is a complex enunciation that is always explicit and that occupies more space than the given. The derivation transforms the given by means of either a periphrasis or a paradigm. The periphrasis develops each aspect of the given successively through paradoxical representations. The paradigm is a sequence of variations on the given, each paradoxical, and each repeating the same pattern under different but synonymous forms. The paradigm veers toward hyperbole, initially by its repetitions, but then by means of a snowball effect, in which each variant moves a level beyond that of the previous one in an ascending gradation.

The given is at one and the same time the generator of the verbal derivation, the point of reference for measuring the degree of paradoxical displacement, and the "program" regulating the mode of this displacement. I will differentiate among three types of derivation.

The first type is *metalinguistic*. In this instance, the given presents, on the one hand, an object, in the form of a word or a descriptive phrase and, on the other hand, a commentary indicating how this object can serve as a decadent experience or can be interpreted from a decadent point of view. This commentary (metalinguistic in the proper sense of the word, since it refers to the language of the text itself) is thus the program of the derivation.

The second type is *thematic*. Here a theme is evoked and recognized by the reader. The derivation then transforms the stereotypes that constitute the theme as a paradoxical discourse.

The third type is *intertextual*. In this case, the reader infers — as a result of difficulties that halt or slow his or her interpretation — the trace of a latent intertext from which the paradox will construct a narrative or descriptive supplement that would be incomprehensible or unacceptable if one were not to retrieve the intertextuality in which its meaning is concealed.

*   *   *

My example of the first type of derivation will be the botanical nomenclature in Joris-Karl Huysmans's novel *A rebours* (*Against the Grain*) that generates the second narrative variant of a quest for rarefied sensations. Huysmans's aesthete, Des Esseintes, loves flowers, but as a decadent aesthete he particularly loves the eccentricities of flowers, which he seeks out in two directions. First, he tries artificial flowers: "his inborn taste for the artificial had led him to neglect the real flower for its copy, faithfully and almost miraculously executed in indiarubber, and wire, calico and taffeta, paper and velvet" [son penchant naturel vers l'artifice . . . l'avait conduit à délaisser la véritable fleur pour son image fidèlement exécutée, grâce aux miracles des caoutchoucs et des fils, des percalines et des taffetas, des papiers et des velours] (97). This elementary paradox is but a first step toward a more perfect paradox, as it is in the very heart of nature that he verifies the law of artifice: "tired of artificial flowers aping real ones, he wanted some natural flowers that would look like fakes" [Après les fleurs factices singeant les véritables fleurs, il voulait des fleurs naturelles imitant des fleurs fausses] (97).

It is thus not the artifice itself that constitutes the paradox, but the contradiction in terms— artifice in nature. The metalinguistic pattern for this contradiction is provided for us by the oxymoron that describes Des Esseintes's mentality: his "natural penchant for artifice." The text constructs a succession of variants on this pattern out of a paradigm of analogous contradictions. The object, described in such a manner as to bring out these contradictions, is the flower. The word *flower* brings together the following semantic traits (semes): beauty, naturalness, multiplicity of forms, variety of color. Normally, these semes are actualized hyperbolically and are positively marked. As a consequence, the paradoxical derivation will take place by associating the essential seme, *beauty*, with negative actualizations of the other semes.

The seme *natural* is thus replaced by its contrary, *artificial*. The rarest flowers, born in foreign climates, miracles of nature's imagination, must be "kept alive with cunning attention in artificial tropics created by carefully regulated stoves" [entretenues avec des soins rusés, sous de faux équateurs produits par les souffles dosés des poêles] (96–97). This description is, of course, merely a periphrasis for *hothouse*, but it is clear that the function of the syntagme generated by this compound word is less to describe plants protected by glass than to multiply the synonyms for artificial: "cunning attention," "artificial tropics," "carefully regulated." In the works of other authors, the given of the hothouse has generated paradigms in which the cumulative effect of the tautological series noted above is demonstrated by a transgressive culmination of the sequence: when the paradigm arrives at the end of its roll of synonyms, it sets off again with renewed vigor by crossing the frontier separating figurative from literal. And having reached the bounds of the figurative, it passes another limit and goes from metaphors to extended metaphors. The hothouse, which is simply a locus of artificial nature, thus becomes a microcosm for pathological nature and is represented as an alcove, a theater of unbridled sexuality (this is the hothouse of Zola's novel *La Curée*), or as a hospital room — a metaphor for the vegetative life of sick people — in the poems gathered by Maeterlinck under the title *Serres chaudes*.[1]

Huysmans prefers a different variant of the inversion of natural into artificial: applying the earlier metalinguistic model literally, his plants resemble artificial plants, such as this tropical variation on the artichoke from our gardener: "the *Encephalartos horridus*, a gigantic artichoke, an iron spike painted rust, like the ones they put on park gates to keep trespassers from climbing over" [l' "Encephalartos horridus," un gigantesque artichaut de fer, peint en rouille, tel qu'on en met aux portes des châteaux, afin d'empêcher les escalades] (100; trans. modified). The paradox is double: the exotic artichoke, made more exotic by its wild name, resembles an artichoke made of iron; but if it were only a matter of expressing the physical resemblance of two objects — the one vegetable, the other metal — we would have nothing more here than a comparison highlighting the bizarre appearance of the plant, yet it would not be a paradox. The paradox is that the comparison, a figure which describes similarity in the midst of difference, is inverted, replaced by a similarity in identity, since it takes a metaphor literally. This artichoke "resembles" an artichoke, since the word *artichoke* refers both to the plant and to the assemblage of teeth and spikes that keeps trespassers away (in fact, this assemblage is so named because it is shaped like the head of an artichoke bristling with leaves). The homonymy fuses two objects that are separated syntactically at the same time as they are brought together on the level of meaning. And the paradox is reinforced by the visual proof, by the detail that seems to demonstrate that the vegetable is made of iron: "painted rust" is a solecism (one would say "rust colored"). The solecism, derived from *painted black*, *painted red*, and so on, treats the natural color of the plant as if it were produced by a layer of paint. But this painting is a contradiction in terms, since one paints iron so that it does not rust. And further — why stop on such a fruitful path? — *rust* also designates a disease of plants. This demonstrates once again that the plant resembles its imitation. But this tautology of nature and artifice is only made evident as a syllepsis, that is, as a play on words, when in fact the play on words cancels all similarity or, better, is the paradox of a false similarity.

Let us move on to another semantic transformation. This one affects the two semes that make up the word *flower*, the example par excellence of nature's exuberance: *formal multiplicity* and *variety of colors*. Taken negatively, these semes generate the descriptive derivations that transform the flower into a monster. The negative transformation consists in translating *multiple* into *hybrid*, the defining trait of deformity and the fantastic. Hybridity results from partial substitutions: moving from a floral given, the paradigm replaces the floral with the animal or even the human and with the mineral. These incompatibilities are assembled through a montage of separate pieces, like a collage, or the useless mechanisms that constitute the "ready mades" of Marcel Duchamp:

Now they were getting a fresh batch of monstrosities down from the carts — the Echinopsis, thrusting its ghastly pink blossoms out of the cotton-wool compresses . . . the Cypripedium, with its complex, incoherent contours devised by some demented draughtsman. It looked rather like a clog or a tidy, and on top was a human tongue bent back with the string stretched tight, just as you may see it depicted in the plates of medical works dealing with diseases of the throat and mouth; two little wings, of a jujube red, which might also have been borrowed from a child's toy windmill, completed this baroque combination. (99)

[On descendait des voitures une nouvelle fournée de monstres: des Echinopsis, sortant de compresses en ouate des fleurs d'un rose de moignon ignoble; . . . des Cypripedium, aux contours compliqués, incohérents, imaginés par un inventeur en démence. Ils ressemblaient à un sabot, à un vide-poche, au-dessus duquel se retrousserait une langue humaine, au filet tendu, telle qu'on en voit dessinées sur les planches des ouvrages traitant des affections de la gorge et de la bouche; deux petites ailettes, rouge de jujube, qui paraissaient empruntées à un moulin d'enfant, complétaient ce baroque assemblage.]

Let us again verify the rule of the paradigm's acceleration toward superlative summits — an acceleration entirely pertinent to the decadent quest for excess and satiety. One expects an ever more elaborate description, swarming with technical terms. But here an orgy of concrete representations, in which the realism ends in a "naturalism" of repugnant notations, is followed by a highly abstract clause that takes us by surprise. The paradigm stemmed from an oxymoron overlaid with the fantastic: *vegetable ghouls*. With these words Huysmans opens the door to a teratological museum of "carnivorous plants." For each of these insect-eating flowers, destined one day to inspire the man-eating plants of modern horror films, a new variant of the monster will be a further step toward a paroxysm of the imagination. This paroxysm is, however, reached paradoxically, when, at the end of the catalog of ghouls, a clause takes "imagination" literally and leaves the initiative to the reader: "and finally the Nepenthes, in which fantasy passes the known limits of eccentric forms" [enfin le Népenthès dont la fantaisie dépasse les limites connues des excentriques formes] (100; trans. modified). It is clear that "fantasy," "eccentricity," and "passes the known limits" are redundant: the sentence seems to progress from subject to predicate, but each term only repeats the impossibility of speaking the unspeakable. Here the derivation is faithful to a given in which the flower escapes botanical nomenclature and is only found in the poetry of dream, for the Nepenthes only grows in the *Odyssey*. Homer tells us that the magic sap of this plant removes all afflictions but that no one has ever seen it. It is no longer even a question of carnivorous plants here: since the name of the plant had been generated backwards from the derivation that paraphrases it, the Greek word seems to materialize both fantasy and the unimaginable themselves.[2]

*   *   *

The second manner of engendering paradoxes is *thematic*. The reader sees the paradox when he or she recognizes a literary theme in the decadent text's aberrant version. Such is the case with the theme of the setting sun, the contemplation of which provides one of Romanticism's commonplaces: critics have railed at Hugo for having made his strolls at dusk into a theatrical encounter with the orb, for having posed as the artist in communion with nature. It was inevitable that the decadents should seize on a theme whose images of death correspond to their penchant for morbidity, and whose *décor* lends itself to staging the twilight of an ideology, the end of a century, and the deconstruction of Romanticism.

Baudelaire, last Romantic and first decadent, had provided the model for

this deconstruction in the sonnet entitled "Le Coucher du soleil romantique" [Romantic sunset], published as an introduction to *Epaves* in 1866.

> Fair is the sun when first he flames above,
> Flinging his joy down in a happy beam;
> And happy he who can salute with love
> The sunset far more glorious than a dream.
>
> Flower, stream, and furrow! — I have seen them all
> In the sun's eye swoon like one trembling heart —
> Though it be late let us with speed depart
> To catch at least one ray ere it fall!
>
> But I pursue the retreating god in vain,
> For conquering Night makes firm her dark domain,
> Mist and gloom fall, and terrors glide between,
> And graveyard odours in the shadow swim,
> And my faint footsteps on the marsh's rim,
> Bruise the cold snail and the crawling toad unseen.
>   (*Flowers* 208–9; trans. modified)

[Que le Soleil est beau quand tout frais il se lève, / Comme une explosion
nous lançant son bonjour! / — Bienheureux celui-là qui peut avec amour
/ Saluer son coucher plus glorieux qu'un rêve! / Je me souviens! . . . J'ai
vu tout, fleur, source, sillon, / Se pâmer sous son oeil comme un coeur
qui palpite . . . / — Courons vers l'horizon, il est tard, courons vite, / Pour
attraper au moins un oblique rayon! / Mais je poursuis en vain le Dieu qui
se retire; / L'irrésistible Nuit établit son empire, / Noire, humide, fun-
este et pleine de frissons; / Une odeur de tombeau dans les ténèbres
nage, / Et mon pied peureux froisse, au bord du marécage, / Des cra-
pauds imprévus et de froids limaçons.]

A note in the text informs us that this poem responds to Banville's sonnet
entitled, "Le Lever du soleil romantique" [Romantic sunrise]. In fact, by
replacing "coucher de soleil" [the setting sun] with "coucher du soleil"
[the setting of the sun] Baudelaire renders the note superfluous. The luminous sky, "more glorious than a dream" in the quatrain, contrasts, in the
tercets, with "graveyard odours in the shadow" and the nocturnal life of a
marsh: "conquering Night makes firm her dark domain." The departure of
the orb here becomes a flight or a defeat. Verlaine sounds a similar note the
same year with a crepuscular discourse that one can only decipher as a fin-
de-siècle code, in three of the "Paysages tristes" of the *Poèmes saturniens*:
"Soleils couchants" where *melancholic* becomes synonymous with the ves-
peral, "Crépuscule du soir mystique," "Promenade sentimentale" ("and

then, upon / The sun's last rays there fell a murky pall, / A ghostly tide which drowned the sun" [25]). Verlaine himself invites us to read it in this way in his "Critique des Poèmes saturniens," published in 1890, precisely in order to claim the paternity of a decadent aesthetic: "Are these poems not in some sense the embryo, the clutch of eggs, of a whole flight of poetic nightingales [vers chanteurs], vaguely gathered and defined, of which I remain perhaps the first bird-catcher to date?"

It is in relation to the Baudelairian model, to a sunset already interpreted as the end of a literary movement, that we can measure the decadent contribution, and determine what exactly decadence substitutes for Romanticism: in place of the direct interpretation of natural symbols (which characterizes Romanticism), it substitutes a reinterpretation of that first interpretation. This reinterpretation no longer takes natural spectacles as its immediate object, but instead takes these spectacles mediated by their presentation in a preexisting text, and either reinterprets themes in their potentiality, as they float in the collective imaginary, or the literary versions, already written, of these same themes.

It is in this reinterpretation that we come upon the paradox again, for a very simple reason: since the theme is already an interpretation of nature, positive or negative, one can only go further by continuing the descriptive or narrative derivations beyond the limits indicated by verisimilitude or beyond the limits of the connotation of the natural phenomenon, those which have allowed, in the first place, the production of a positive or negative symbol.

Two examples, both taken from the writings of Jules Laforgue, should suffice. First, the parodic setting sun in "Persée et Andromède," a burlesque version of the myth from *Moralités légendaires* [Moral tales] the first three editions of which — in 1887, 1894, and 1904 — span the length of a fashion exactly contemporary with the decadent movement:

The wind has fallen, the sea is calm, and the horizon lays out a melancholy tabula rasa for the ceremony of the setting sun . . . morning and springtime signify happiness . . . twilight and autumn signify death. (And since nothing tickles superior organisms more than to feel themselves dying when they know they aren't, twilight and autumn like the drama of the sun and death constitute the highest aesthetic.) (*Moral* 121–22; trans. modified)

[Le vent est tombé et c'est les accalmies et l'horizon qui fait table rase mélancolique pour la cérémonie du couchant . . . le matin et le printemps sont de bonheur . . . le crépuscule et l'automne sont de mort. (Mais comme rien n'est plus chatouilleux aux organismes supérieurs que de se sentir mourir tout en sachant qu'il n'en sera rien, le crépuscule et l'automne, le drame du soleil et de la mort sont esthétiques par excellence.)]

This passage, it must be emphasized, refers not to a moment of the day, nor to a particular season, but to a theme of the passage of time. Decadent writing here is nothing other than an exercise upon a verbal given. The thematic given differs, however, from the metalinguistic type of given in its complexity, since it combines both the theme in its pure state (a mininarrative or minidescription, or a fragment presupposing one or the other) and the valorized or interpreted theme (which is already an initial derivation from the theme as such). It is this combination that the paradox transforms. Since the thematic complex has already developed the setting sun as a theatrical sunset, as a grand natural spectacle, or better, as an example of the sublime in nature, and since this sublime is the mark of Romanticism, the decadent paradox deconstructs the sublime version of the sunset. In order not to alter its poetic value, it retains all its givens but replaces the marks or indices of the natural by marks or indices of the theatrical, a special case of the artifice specified by the given "grand spectacle"; and it inverts the marks of the sublime, transforming them into marks of the grotesque.

Here is the "theatrical" version:

Off there on the flashing horizon where Sirens hold their breath,
The scaffolding of the setting sun goes up,
From lighthouse to lighthouse rise vast stage sets;
The pyrotechnists make their final preparations.
Golden moons blossom forth like the bells of many trumpets on which
the batallions of heralds will thunder forth their messages.

(*Moral* 124; trans. modified)

[Là-bas, à l'horizon miroitant où les sirènes retiennent leur respiration, / Les échafaudages du couchant montent; / De phares en phares, s'é-tagent des maçonneries de théâtre; / Les artificiers donnent le dernier coup de main; / Une serie de lunes d'or s'épanouissent, comme les embouchures de buccins rangés dont des phalanges de hérauts annonciateurs fulmineraient!]

The settings, the stage hands, and the extras transform the Romantic theme of the fantastic architecture of the clouds, a theme whose success stems from the oxymoron representing what is most mobile and most impalpable in nature together with the most massively immobile in art. This oxymoron had already been exploited by Hugo in 1828, in his "Soleils couchants" [Setting suns]:

Behind the last mists, further still
Suddenly appear thousands of golden towers
Of an edifice of clouds
. . . .

The eye believes it sees climbing, climbing further
With its stairways, its bridges, its great towers
Some kind of excessive Babel.

[Derrière les derniers brouillards, plus loin encore, / Apparaissent soudain les mille étages d'or / D'un édifice de nuées; . . . L'oeil croit voir jusqu'au ciel monter, monter toujours, / Avec ses escaliers, ses ponts, ses grandes tours, / Quelque Babel démesurée] (*Oeuvres poétiques* 788–89)

The paradox is somewhat reminiscent of the artichoke that resembled, so strikingly, an artichoke. The text takes literally the Romantic metaphor, or rather the sham of the figurative discourse is realized by the trompe-l'oeil of the setting. Then comes the intermission and the time to change the setting. The main character leaves the stage: "Silence and horizon! After all the wild activities of the afternoon, the air is calm again, contemplative, before the classic retreat of the Sun" [Silence et horizon! l'air est dans l'accalmie et se recueille devant la retraite classique de l'Astre] (*Moral* 124; trans. modified).

The personification of the air is absurd, but we should be cautious about reducing it to a facile comic effect. In fact, it continues the artifice. In the most baroque of his plays, Shakespeare had already had an eye-witness report of the magical appearance of Cleopatra sailing on the Nile to meet Antony: if this witness holds its breath, it is because even the air, drawn by the crowd of dumbfounded spectators, has departed to see the galley of the royal seductress: "Purple the sails, and so perfumed that / The winds were love-sick with them. . . . The city cast / Her people out upon her; and Antony / Enthron'd i' th' market-place, did sit alone, / Whistling to th' air, which, but for vacancy, / Had gone to gaze on Cleopatra too, / And made a gap in nature" (*Antony* 2.2.193–94, 213–18). The "classical retreat of the Orb" (a metalinguistic formula that translates Baudelaire's image of "the retreating god" in his "Coucher du soleil romantique") triggers a derivation in which the anti-sublime and anti-reality render another technique of the staging absurd — the change at sight, the tumultuous and yet methodical picking up of the accessories and the props before the spectators, while the curtain is still raised. But in keeping with the rule of the intensification of the paradigm, the movement accelerates, as in a farcical pursuit, and the *retreat*, through a characteristic play on words, becomes a *defeat*, the fall of the monarch sun. A play on words, without doubt, but at the expense of the Romantic given, of which we find an example in Walter Scott's novel *The Antiquary*: "The sun was now resting his huge disk upon the edge of the level ocean, and gilded the accumulation of towering clouds through which he had traveled the livelong day, and which now assembled on all sides, like misfortunes and disasters around a sinking empire and falling monarch" (59). The end of a world, then, dusk, and images of the stage lights going out. Laforgue combines the nostalgia for the light that departs (Baudelaire again: "Though it be late let us with speed depart / To catch at least one ray ere it fall!"), the jostling of the stage hands, the tumult in the wings, the panicked flight, and a satire of the conventional style (official accessories):

Rows of trumpets come down, ramparts crumble with the prismatic carafes of the lighthouses! Cymbals fly off, courtiers trip over the standards, tents are folded, the army breaks camp, carrying off in its panic the occidental basilicas, the wine-presses, the idols, the bundles, the vestal virgins, the desks, the ambulances, the bandstands — all the official accessories.

And they all fade into a pink golden dusty haze. (*Moral* 125)

[Les rangées de buccins s'abaissent, les remparts s'écroulent, avec leurs phares de carafes prismatiques! Des cymbales volent, les courtisans trébuchent dans les étendards, les tentes sont repliées, l'armée lève le camp, emportant dans une panique les basiliques occidentales, les pressoirs, les idoles, les ballots, les vestales, les bureaux, les ambulances, les estrades des orphéons, tous les accessoires officiels.

Et ils s'effacent dans un poudroiement d'or rose.]

The coda, as musical as it is visual, remains nevertheless compatible with the Romantic sublime, whereas its replacement by the grotesque calls for a systematic modification, an inversion of the marks of each significant word, as the terms are both literally mimetic (because they represent the setting sun) and metaphoric (because they evoke the beheading of a king — the "Soleil cou coupé" of Apollinaire).

Or let us take the most famous stanza of Baudelaire's "Harmonie du soir" [Evening harmony]: "In its own *congealing blood* the *sun* lies drowning" [Le *soleil* s'est noyé dans son *sang* qui se *fige*] (*Flowers* 60; trans. modified). A periphrasis, based on each of the words I emphasized, reduces each sublime image to the level of the abject: these periphrases do not aim to deprive the setting sun of its prestige but, through humor, to render poetic what the preceding school had rendered sublime. The procedure takes from the intertext what it needs in order to reject it. Again Laforgue, this time from the poem "Le Mystére des trois cors" ("The Mystery of the Three Horns"):

First of all, the dying sun!

The sun takes off his pontiff's stole,
Opens the sluices of the Main Sewer,
Releasing a thousand golden streams,
Which our most sophisticated distilleries
Mix with hundreds of phials of exotic vitriol! . . .
The pool of blood spreads afar
It suddenly rises drowning the mares of the four-in-hand
They rear up and splash about and then get mired
In these floods of bengal lights and alcohol!
But over the horizon hard sands and cinders
Soon absorb all of this display of poisoned wine.

(*Poems* 375; trans. modified)

[Mais, le soleil qui se meurt, avant tout! / Le soleil dépose sa pontificale étoile, / Lâche les écluses du Grand-collecteur / En mille Pactoles / Que les artistes / De nos liquoristes / Attisent de cent fioles de vitriol oriental! . . . / Le sanglant étang, aussitôt s'étend, aussitôt s'étale, / Noyant les cavales du quadrige / Qui se cabre, et qui patauge, et puis se fige / Dans ces déluges de bengale et d'alcool! / Mais les durs sables et les cendres de l'horizon / Ont vite bu tout cet étalage de poisons]

The *blood*—lake of blood in the lofty style (for example, in Baudelaire's "Phares")—is here merely a pool [*étang*] rendered yet more grotesque through the internal rhyme with *s'étend*. Without tampering with the mimesis, this rhyme creates something like a mocking echo. In the same way, the horses of the Sun's chariot are changed into *cavales* [mares] to rhyme with the verb *s'étale*. Moreover, the word *cavales* lacks the conventional high style connotations of *coursiers* [steeds]. As a result, Baudelaire's image of the sun drowning in its own blood, itself modeled on a cliché of the grand dramatic style, here gives way to a carriage that gets stuck in the mud, parodying the classical image of the chariot of Phoebus plunging into the mythological river ancient poets called the ocean, an image that Laforgue had already analyzed in the "Complainte à Notre-Dame des soirs" [Complaint to Our Lady of Eventide]: "lakes, lost in the sunset's long dying / . . . the Sun, who spills the blood of his rearing horses, / and crucagulates in their blood!" [lacs éperdus des longs couchants défunts / . . . Soleil qui, saignant son quadrige, / Cabré, s'y crucifige] (*Poems* 39; trans. modified). I am not quoting this poem for the satisfaction of one more comparison, but because the sentence shows the slippage from the theme to the intertext. The transformation of a theme could not lead to a nonsense phrase like "lake of the sunset," of a quadriga being bled, and of "crucigeals," for a theme is an outline rather than a fully completed text. The transformation of an intertext, on the other hand, requires the simultaneous double decoding of the text being read and of the intertext in which the key to its meaning is concealed. The combination of "to crucify" and "to coagulate" that we find in "crucagulate" can be easily understood as a variation on the theme of the monarch sun tortured and crucified. But the last syllable only has any meaning if we go back through the blood coagulating on the horizon of Baudelaire's "Harmonie du soir."

*   *   *

The third type of paradox is *intertextual*. In order to describe it I return to a passage in *A rebours* (chapter 13) that would seem completely unmotivated as a narrative episode, and gratuitous as a decadent symbol, were it not that its absurdity leads the reader to retrieve its first appearance in the intertext upon which it depends, in this case, one of the *Petits Poèmes en prose* [Short prose poems] by Baudelaire, "Le Gâteau" [The cake]. In this poem, the narrator evokes the memory of a moment of perfect happiness during a journey on foot through the Pyrenees, a journey which was as much a Romantic topos as an actual excursion: "In short, thanks to the compelling beauty around me, I was at peace with myself and with the universe. . . . I was beginning to think the newspapers might not be so ridiculous, after all, in wanting to make us believe that man is born good" [Je me sentais, grâce à l'enthousiasmante beauté dont j'étais entouré, en parfaite paix avec moi-même et avec l'univers . . . , j'en étais venu à ne plus trouver si ridicules les journaux qui prétendent que l'homme est né bon] (*Paris* 28). Seated facing this panorama, our traveler partakes of a frugal lunch of cold water and white bread. He is interrupted by a starving beggar child, to whom the bread appears as good as cake. The traveler has scarcely given him a slice when another wretched beggar attacks the happy beneficiary and a "hideous fight" ensues. "The cake traveled from hand to hand and changed pockets at every instant, changing, alas! in size as well, and when finally, exhausted and panting and covered with blood, they stopped . . . the piece of bread had disappeared, and the crumbs, scattered all around, were indistinguishable from the grains of sand with which they were mingled" (*Paris* 29) [Le gâteau changeait de poche à chaque instant, mais hélas! il changeait aussi de volume, et lorsque enfin, exténués, haletants, sanglants, ils s'arrêtèrent . . . le morceau de pain avait disparu . . . éparpillé en miettes semblables aux grains de sable auxquels il était mêlé]. The observer's optimism about humanity crumbles together with the cake.

Let us compare this intertext with the decadent text that depends upon it. This second text would seem the height of ludicrousness and improbability if it were simply an isolated narrative incident. On the other hand, what appears ludicrous and improbable in the narrative disappears as soon as we stop considering it as a narrative progression motivated in a normal fashion; that is, if we no longer consider it as a narrative teleologically determined by the goal to be attained, by the final line to which it must lead at all costs, but consider it instead as an antinomy overdetermined by the intertext. The incident recounted by Huysmans is composed against the grain of Baudelaire's apologue. The realist model of the intertext is followed only so as to take the opposite tack to the plausible lesson that infused the prose poem with humanity. The rewriting transforms its lesson (the unconscious evil in the hearts of innocents) into the paradox of having a conscience and committing evil. Nothing has any meaning, or any truth, in the Huysmans passage unless one sees there a paradox on the pleasure derived from being evil and in pitiful objects metamorphosed into objects of desire.

Each element of the prose poem is inverted. Baudelaire's narrator is hungry, but it is an appetite stimulated by a walk in the wilderness, whereas Des Esseintes, gnawed and needled by boredom, suffering from the neurasthenia of a sedentary individual, has lost all appetite. In Baudelaire's poem, the narrator's lunch attracts the little beggars, and the bread he gives to them out of charity provokes their battle. In the passage from *A rebours*, the lunch of some "vicious brats" seduces Des Esseintes; they are already in the process of fighting over it savagely — "abominable law of the struggle for life" [abominable loi de la lutte pour l'existence] (170) — a natural law which inspires him to reproduce it artificially. Baudelaire's children fight for some white bread, a healthy and simple form of nourishment. Huysmans's children snatch from each other a "disgusting white mess" [immonde tartine], spotted with something green, either the green of chives or the green of the snot which is dripping from the beggar's nostrils onto his "lips . . . coated with a revolting white dirt" [lèvres dégoûtantes entourées de crasse blanche] (169; trans modified). Our decadent convinces himself that "his stomach . . . would digest this frightful food and that his palate would enjoy it as a real treat" [digérerait cet affreux mets et que son palais en jouirait comme d'un régal] (169; trans. modified). He sends his servants to look for the ingredients to reproduce it, and has it served up to him as a royal delicacy "on a silver-gilt salver" [sur un plat de vermeil] (172). Then, no longer hungry, he has this substitute given to the children. And whereas in Baudelaire's example, the fratricidal struggle for a scrap of bread was an object of meditation on an unfortunate child, Des Esseintes ponders a birth-control crusade, which becomes actively Malthusian, and conducts himself like a decadent Roman at the circus: " 'You see those children fighting on the road?' he said to the man. 'Well, throw the stuff to them. And let's hope that the weaker ones get maimed, that they don't get so much as a crumb of bread, and that on top of it they get a beating when they come home with a black eye and their breaches torn' " ["Jetez cette tartine," dit-il au domestique, "à ces enfants qui se massacrent sur la route; que les plus faibles soient estropiés, n'aient part à aucun morceau et soient, de plus, rossés d'importance par leurs familles quand ils rentreront chez elles les culottes déchirées et les yeux meurtris"] (172; trans. modified). Read in isolation, in terms of the reality which it would then represent, this text is perverse or artificial. But read intertextually, it really appears to be an exercise, a variation on a model, and its pathos, far from being unbearable, is like a musical score to be played and is therefore a legitimate source of pleasure. In the artifice, we then find a basic law of literary narrative: *emotion recollected in tranquillity*. And beyond the excess, beyond the improbability, we become aware of another law of literariness: literary representation does not depend on referents outside the text, but on a constant intertextual exchange.

Everything lies in the internal games of writing, and this provides an extra point of interest in the decadent text (one which redeems the rather wearisome aspects of their procedures), the power they have to make this truth visible through their formal eccentricity, and to require of us a reading that demands full awareness and complete participation.

Notes

1. See Riffaterre, "Decadent Features in Maeterlinck's Poetry" and "Paradox and Presupposition." Huysmans only makes these variants bloom: "Gathered together, these sickly blooms struck Des Esseintes as even more monstrous than when he had first come upon them, mixed up with others like patients in a hospital inside the glass walls of their conservatory wards" [ces fleurs . . . plus monstrueuses que lorsqu'il les avait surprises, confondues avec d'autres, ainsi que dans un hôpital, parmi les salles vitrées des serres] (98).

2. I have not overlooked the fact that modern botanical taxonomy has created a family of Nepenthaces, which however only includes a single plant, exotic and carnivorous, and it is doubtless by means of this taxonomy that Huysmans made the connection with the Homeric Nepenthes. But what he made of it is in fact merely the equivalent of a punctuation mark, of an *etc.*, open to an infinite number of possible combinations itself symbolized by a beyond of mimesis: any verbal sequence that has exhausted the Latin terminology is ready to start again from ground zero with the Greek nomenclature.

Works Cited

Baudelaire, Charles. *The Flowers of Evil*. Ed. Marthiel and Jackson Mathews. New York: New Directions, 1963.

———. *Paris Spleen*. Trans. Louise Varèse. New York: New Directions, 1970.

Hugo, Victor. *Oeuvres poétiques*, vol. 1. Ed. Pierre Albouy. Paris: Editions Pléiade, 1964.

Huysmans, Joris-Karl. *Against Nature*. Trans. Robert Baldick. Harmondsworth: Penguin, 1982.

Laforgue, Jules. *Moral Tales*. Trans. William Jay Smith. New York: New Directions, 1985.

———. *Poems of Jules Laforgue*. Trans. Peter Dale. London: Anvil, 1986.

Riffaterre, Michael. "Decadent Features in Maeterlinck's Poetry." *Language and Style* 7 (1974): 3–19.

———. "Paradox and Presupposition." In *Le Paradoxe en linguistique et en littérature*, ed. Roland Landherr and Paul J. Smith. Geneva: Droz, 1996.

Scott, Walter. *The Antiquary*. New York: Harper, 1829.

Shakespeare, William. *Antony and Cleopatra*. In *The Riverside Shakespeare*. Boston: Houghton Mifflin, 1974.

Verlaine, Paul. *The Sky Above the Roof: Fifty-six Poems by Paul Verlaine*. Trans. Brian Hill. London: Davis, 1957.

Visualizing Decadence

Chapter 4
Posing a Threat
Queensberry, Wilde, and the
Portrayal of Decadence

Dennis Denisoff

On April Fool's Day, 1894, John Sholto Douglas, the ninth Marquess of Queensberry, sent off a letter to his son Alfred Douglas in which he complains about the young man's relationship with Oscar Wilde: "To my mind to pose as a thing is as bad as to be it. With my own eyes I saw you both in the most loathsome and disgusting relationship as expressed by your manner and expression. Never in my experience have I ever seen such a sight as that in your horrible features. . . . Your disgusted so-called father, Queensberry" (qtd. in Ellmann 394). The Marquess's reference to himself as the "so-called" father suggests that the connection between an intentionally decadent pose and what he saw as a degenerate "thing" is so complete that it risks displacing Douglas's identity as his son. Although such a gesture of delegitimation comes across more as a threat than as actual doubt, Queensberry was deeply troubled by his belief that an offspring's biological degeneracy reflected a weakness in the family line. The situation was no better, as far as he was concerned, if his son were simply playing a faddish decadent role, because people might still interpret the pose as reflecting inherited flaws. His only hope of absolving himself of any blame, therefore, was to persuade the public that Douglas's external signs of degeneracy were nothing more than artifice. Ironically, in order to do so, the oppressive, insensitive patriarch had to convince the court of his own pose as the concerned and caring father.

More was at stake for the Marquess than his son's reputation. Despite the unnuanced affiliation of artifice with decadence, conscious self-fashioning was far from an exclusively decadent strategy. Indeed, Max Nordau himself saw value in self-decoration, as long as "the instinct of vanity" is ultimately "a result of thought about others, of preoccupation with the race" (318). But if the costume is *purposely* intended "to cause irritation to others," to "lend itself to ridicule," and to excite "disapproval instead of approbation," then the "predilection for strange costume is a pathological aberration of a racial instinct." It was when one's gestures were used to acknowledge the subterfuge through, for example, exaggerated physical gestures or excesses in literary form that they were perceived as decadent. Nordau's effort to suture such cultural performance to a biological degeneracy would not have left the Marquess feeling absolved of responsibility. Queensberry's concern about his son's pose is only partially an issue of hereditary taint; his anxiety also reflects a growing social recognition that acknowledging the performative aspects of identities exacerbated the effects of conceptual shifts–regarding things such as the nation, the family, class, and sex–that already threatened the essentialist hierarchies from which the Marquess drew his own authority–as a father, as a nobleman, as a heterosexual, as a man. A comparison of his and Wilde's writing and photographic portraits shows that what Queensberry hoped to curtail, as much as his son's sexual proclivities, was the decadent exposure of the pervasive performance of identities and the radical reconceptualization of social authority that he felt such a revelation could induce.

Decadence and Portraiture

A glance at a couple of late Victorian photographic portraits — one of Wilde and Douglas, the other of the Marquess — suggests the difficulty in distinguishing between Wilde's and Queensberry's everyday use of performance, while also nevertheless revealing the revisionary decadent trace.[1] Late Victorian portraiture often brought attention to both a disjuncture regarding the genre's ability to capture the "essence" of a sitter, and the increased strain being placed on it to remain a strong signifier of the nation's and family's stability. Portraits, like most heirlooms, were generally expected to reinforce the view of genealogy as a fundamental measure of worth and to support established hierarchies. Indeed, simply owning painted portraits of blood relations suggested that one's family had a history of financial stability. As Pierre Bourdieu has argued, "Family heirlooms not only bear material witness to the age and continuity of the lineage and so consecrate its social identity, which is inseparable from performance over time; they also contribute in a practical way to its spiritual reproduction, that is, to transmitting the values, virtues and competences which are the basis of legitimate membership in bourgeois dynasties" (76–77). Portraits helped defend the authority of the family against individualism and extra-familial communities. This model of authority, moreover, reverberated through British society's approach to broader issues concerning culture and the nation.

The Victorian association of portraiture with concerns regarding economic and political growth extended through to the end of the century. Kenneth McConkey notes that, even during the Edwardian era, "the disposition of the age was to monumental social realism, to landscape and to portraiture. This latter genre was born of the desire for confident self-projection associated with the exercise of power" (*Edwardian* 16). The late nineteenth century, however, was also a time of economic uncertainty, and the portrait reflected concerns regarding the dissipation of both Britain's class system and its national vitality. The increased mixing of new and old money and the growing commodification of identities such as the male and female dandy brought about a destabilization of the wealth/heredity equation that turned the portrait into a signifier of riches without any immediate association with lineage, refinement, or dignity. The important significatory role of the genre is apparent from the fact that, during the second half of the nineteenth century, portraiture was among the most lucrative artistic activities (McPherson 19). However, by the end of the century, the financial wealth signified by ownership of portraits was less readily seen as a reflection of hereditary values (McConkey "Well-Bred" 353). The tenuousness of the portrait's actual significance inevitably became disconcertingly apparent.

Portraiture's "identity crisis" (McPherson 19) was exacerbated by a growing community of photographers who frequently broke the rules of the genre while also undermining its exclusivity by lowering the price of the end product. During this "decadent" period of portraiture (Mayne 93), portable photograph shops complete with comic costumes and props dotted towns and vacation spots throughout Britain. At the same time, some photographers' intentions of having their work recognized as high art, combined with the growing interest among artists in general for expressing their personal sense of their subjects, resulted in portrait theory shifting attention further away from communicating a subject's public standing to the task of presenting an individual's "essence," which was understood to be some moral or psychological dimension inherent to the sitter.[2] The distilled "essence" was, of course, not actually captured but signified through such elements as color, shading, fashion, posture, and facial expression. The confusion of external signifiers with moral or psychological "essence," however, made portraiture a useful context for Wilde's analysis of surface and depth models of identity and their relation to sexual politics.

During the nineteenth century, reserve and restraint were seen as the most appropriate posing attributes, with the subject encouraged to adopt physical signifiers of high social rank. The metaphoric affirmation of the individual's authority and self-assurance was more frequently rendered in male, rather than female, physiognomy and posture.[3] In posing for a portrait, men were allowed "greater assurance and assertiveness. This was achieved by means of crossed legs, elbows out at angles, with canes and umbrellas projecting into the space around them" (Linkman, 46; see also McConkey "Well-Bred" 356). Wilde's photograph (Figure 4.1) would have made a satisfactory technical illustration of Victorian portrait conventions of masculinity; his facial expression is restrained, one of his feet is placed

Figure 4.1. Oscar Wilde and Alfred Douglas, 1892.

confidently forward, while an elbow juts boldly away from his body. The image is reflected even more precisely in the photographs of Wilde taken in 1897 and 1900 in Rome (see Ellmann, between pages 432 and 433). The exiled Wilde — famous at this time as much for his illegal sexual pleasures as for his writing — presents himself as the perfect model of his society's masculine ideal; his pose, suggesting no sense of parody or irony on his part,

effectively demonstrates the constructed quality of late Victorian masculinity as it participated in a web of issues involving sexuality, gender, class, age,
and nationalism.

Since Wilde was aware that he was being photographed, the image in
Figure 4.1 cannot be seen as mimetically representative of his everyday
public persona, the image with which Queensberry had taken offense. The
picture of the two lovers was shot in the autumn of 1892, when they were
staying alone at a country house in Norfolk. ("What about your country
house, and the life that is led there?" Basil had asked Dorian a couple of
years earlier. "Dorian, you don't know what is said about you" [118].) The
fact that he and Douglas are not in a public space, however, combined with
his awareness that he had some control over the image, means that Wilde
could more likely have chosen to include some signifier of his adoration for
Douglas. Notwithstanding the facts that Wilde *is* touching Douglas, and that
someone might read the men's white or light-colored clothing as an "excessive" refinement of taste, there is nothing strongly suggesting what Queensberry probably recognized as sodomitical or degenerate characteristics. Indeed, it would not be difficult to read the image — if the subjects were
unknown — as a father affectionately showing off (or possibly supporting)
his son. The element of display derives from the placement of Wilde's right
hand on the back of Douglas's left shoulder. Had Wilde draped his arm
across Bosie's neck, the gesture would have been a blatant one of acceptable
male camaraderie, as suggested by casual photographic portraits of the
time. But Wilde is discreet and seemingly self-conscious in his display of
affection. More than half-hidden, Wilde's hand implies that his gesture
signifies, for him, something less accepted than conventional friendship. So
gentle, so tentative, the fingers connote not only the caution in Wilde's
effort to display same-sex erotic affection, but also the general fragility at
this time of relations that undermined conventional family-based notions of
love.

Compare this portrait to one of the Marquess, taken in 1896 for *The
Cycling World Illustrated* (Fig. 4.2). The latter photograph is in many ways
similar to the one of Wilde and Douglas. Both pictures have the subjects
positioned outdoors against a bucolic background of foliage, and all three
men stand on solid ground. Wilde and Queensberry look to be about the
same height, weight, and general shape, and they hold almost the exact
same pose. Each man appears on the right side of the photograph, his body
angled to the camera and leaning slightly forward. Each has his left foot
planted before him, and each has that "masculine" angle in the left arm.
The men are even dressed in similar hats and sharp suits. These similarities
between the images of Queensberry and Wilde as secure and supportive
patriarchs signal the jockeying for position that was taking place with regard
to the men's relations to Alfred Douglas.

Even Moisés Kaufman's successful play *Gross Indecency: The Three Trials of*

Figure 4.2. The Marquess of Queensberry, *Cycling World Illustrated*, 1896.

Oscar Wilde, which opened in New York in September 1997, offers a sartorial echo that accentuates the sociopolitical maneuvering of the two men. The play opens with nine actors forming two lines on a simple set colored red, white, and black. The pervading structural order accords with the sense of inevitability that gradually permeates the performance, as characters offer mechanical banter and motions, stylized shifts in scenario, and precise, eloquent language much of which is taken directly from the works and reminiscences of Wilde, Douglas, and others. The story of Wilde's adult life becomes a familiarly tragic scenario in which an individual's fall from fame appears in part encouraged by his own arrogance. Kaufman takes Wilde's cue that he stood in symbolic relation to his cultural era and refashions the person as a symbol of the ostracized and persecuted, a relation reinforced by the play's costuming. As participants in a courtroom scene, the characters are dressed in dark, simple suits and basic ties of judicial colors. Against this structured and muted backdrop, one quickly notices Wilde's yellow boutonniere and loose, red cravat, despite their lack of excess. In fact, the latter is echoed by Queensberry's own black cravat. In *Gross Indecency,* the difference that Queensberry and Wilde for the most part successfully establish between themselves is called into question from the start by their similarly authoritative personae as defined by their sartorial distance from the rest of the actors. When, during the first trial, Wilde reminds the court that *he* is the prosecutor, the interchangeability of Wilde's and Queensberry's roles becomes uncomfortably apparent. This performative echo only accentuates the anxious need that Queensberry felt for establishing his, and his son's, distance from Wilde.

Likewise, in the two men's photographs, the similarities in their self-presentations function to accentuate notable differences. Wilde's light-colored wardrobe, for example, contrasts with the Marquess's darker outfit. Ironically, the sportsman's knee socks, breeches, and white shirt under dark clothing echo the garb that Wilde wore for the dandiacal portraits taken during his 1882 lecture tour in North America. The main difference between the two photographs, however, is in the additional subjects. Wilde is shown displaying, supporting, caressing Douglas in a way that confuses Wilde's pose as possibly that of lover or that of father. At the time the picture was taken, Wilde was finishing writing *A Woman of No Importance,* the message of which Richard Ellmann summarizes as follows: "We are not what we think we are or what other people think us, and our ties to them may be greater or less than we imagine" (357).

Lytton Strachey presents Wilde's challenge to conventional identity hierarchies more boldly, describing the play's character Lord Illingworth as "a wicked Lord, staying in a country house, who has made up his mind to bugger one of the other guests—a handsome young man of twenty. The handsome young man is delighted; when his mother enters, sees his Lordship and recognises him as having copulated with her twenty years before, the result of which was—the handsome young man. She appeals to Lord [Illingworth] not to bugger his own son. He replies that that is an additional reason for doing it (oh! he's a *very* wicked Lord!)" (qtd. in Holroyd 357n.). Strachey obviously had to take full advantage of any coded discourse that the play may have offered in order to attain this interpretation, but he was encouraged to do so because of the decadent persona already attached to

Wilde. Strachey's reading of the play, with its dependence on a knowledge of Wilde's public image, reinforces the idea that the author could expect his caress, in the portrait, to be recognized by many as more than just display.

Eve Kosofsky Sedgwick, in her analysis of *The Importance of Being Earnest* (58), wants us to "Forget the Name of the Father" (58); Wilde's own pose seems to demand that we forget old what's-his-name entirely. Meanwhile, in the portrait in *Cycling World Illustrated*, Queensberry—having won the legal right to a say regarding the people with whom Douglas maintains relations, having put all that sodomitical business behind him—now has the free time to proudly display, support, and caress . . . his bicycle.

The Heredity of the Phantom Son

> I say it is a pity and a disgrace that our laws are often such that to obey a social law we must disregard a natural one; and *vice versa*, that in obeying a natural one we have to violate the social. I blame not the so-called offenders, but the wrong law for the present time. (*Marriage* 5)

In the late Victorian period in which it was written, this argument, vague as it is in its terms, could have been read as a criticism of the laws opposing sodomy. It is, however, a statement made by Queensberry in defense of what he called a "plurality of marriage" and what others called polygamy. The Marquess goes on to argue, "We are now imperfect in both health and morals, and we require a social system adapted to men and women as they are" (12). A society's official laws, he proposes, should accommodate its level of degeneracy. Queensberry hoped to prove that sodomy, however, did not warrant such an understanding approach because, at least when his sons were involved, it was not a sign of natural degeneracy but of decadent bourgeois-bating. The point to realize is that there was more at stake for Queensberry than Douglas's public image; he saw his son's performance as partly constructing his own identity as well.

The Marquess strongly believed that he was fundamentally responsible for his children's behavior, that he was, in Foucault's words, "in a position of 'biological responsibility' with regard to the species" (118). In a speech entitled "The Religion of Secularism and the Perfectibility of Man," Queensberry argues that, because "[w]e reproduce our children bodily . . . [and] the Soul is the effect of the body, then we certainly reproduce *their Souls as well*, and thus become directly responsible for what those Souls may be and are" (6). His poem *The Spirit of the Matterhorn* brings out the parental anxieties associated with this responsibility:

Dark flows the blood impure within their veins,
To scourge their children with their fathers' sins.

"Behold their sickly frames and stunted growth:
Their pallid cheeks and eyes, that should be bright,
Already show a weariness of life.
Alas, that such a cruel wrong should be,
Of sins upon the children visited! . . ." (27)

Contrary to what it might initially seem, the depiction of a youth with "pallid cheeks and eyes" and a "weariness of life" is not a description of the Marquess's youngest son; Douglas was only six when the poem was published and possibly not even born when it was written. The poem, however, voices the common Victorian notion that posture, physiognomy, and pathognomy (facial expression) signify a person's moral standing.[4] What Foucault refers to as the "perversion-heredity-degenerescence system" (119) remains obtuse unless written on the body or, an equal possibility, read into the body. One can do more than speculate whether, once Douglas had become a decadent aesthete, Queensberry recognized in his son the profile that his poem personifies as the sins of the father — his own verbal portrait of degeneracy somehow having come to life.

The Marquess's sense of potential personal inadequacy arose most prominently with regard to marital difficulties. Seven years after his first wife, Sybil Montgomery, divorced him for adultery, his second wife, Ethel Weedon, also began divorce proceedings by accusing her husband of impotence. Montgomery's accusation was not unbearable for Queensberry because, while he saw heterosexual monogamy as the familial ideal, he frequently spoke out in favor of a "plurality of marriage" whereby a husband, in certain situations, would take more than one wife. Impotence, conversely, he probably would have interpreted as a sign of degenerate inadequacy. Queensberry's theory of hereditary responsibility, combined with his marital difficulties, would have strongly suggested to him that he was himself at fault for any degeneracy that he might detect in his children.

Unfortunately, in Queensberry's eyes, his children exhibited many such flaws. He was aware that his eldest son, Francis, had probably had a sexual relationship with Lord Rosebery, Gladstone's foreign minister. In addition, the secularist's second son, Percy, married the daughter of a Cornish clergyman. And now Alfred was — through pose, telegram, and anything else he could get his hands on — announcing his intimate relations with Wilde. Queensberry, according to his notion of heredity, would either have to accept the blame for what he saw as his children's flaws or disown his progeny. And he was too proud to take the blame. In a letter to Douglas, he writes, "If I catch you again with that man I will make a public scandal. . . . I shall not be blamed for allowing such a state of things to go on" (qtd. in Roberts 188). In another letter in which he chastises Douglas, Queensberry once again questions, one assumes rhetorically, whether his children are legitimate, stating that "in this christian country . . . 'tis a wise father who knows his own child" (224). He also frequently threatened to disinherit his children. At one point, he writes, "Your intimacy with this man Wilde . . . must either cease or I will disown you" (qtd. in Ellmann 394). And, in another letter regarding Douglas, this time written to Percy, he complains that "this good-for-nothing, white-livered son of mine, *if he is so . . .* refuses to receive or answer letters. . . . [Y]ou will find the whole town has been reeking with this hideous scandal of Oscar Wilde. . . . [H]e has almost ruined my *so-called* son" (qtd. in Roberts 216; emphasis added). "So-called" is right up there with "white-livered" as one of the Marquess's favorite adjectives for his offspring.

Queensberry's self-depiction in court makes it apparent that a dexterous deployment of performance can be used not only, as Judith Butler has demonstrated, to displace the oppressive cultural and political orders supported by the more common essentialist views, but also to reinforce them.[5] Unlike Wilde's performance of the detached aesthete, the role of the innocent, concerned father posed no threat to public notions of social responsibility. However, while the ideal of Queensberry-as-father was a major factor in the *Wilde v. Queensberry* trials, the image of Douglas-as-son was significantly absent from the scene. Douglas's limited presence is especially peculiar since he is described as having been a major catalyst for many of the two men's actions. The Marquess apparently stated in court that it was primarily to protect his son that he had left Wilde a card inscribed with the words "Oscar Wilde / posing somdomite" at the Albemarle Club. It was this card which then led Wilde to prosecute Queensberry for libel. Within hours of the first trial, in which Queensberry was found not guilty, Wilde wrote to the *Evening News* to state, "It would have been impossible for me to have proved my case without putting Lord Alfred Douglas in the witness box against his father . . . but I would not let [Douglas] do so" (qtd. in Roberts 229). Shortly after the first trial, with his own conviction for gross indecency imminent, Wilde, in a sudden turn of mind, decided to disregard Bernard Shaw and Frank Harris's advice to leave the country; this change occurred immediately after Douglas had reaffirmed his allegiance to his friend (Ellmann 416). Wilde later implies in *De Profundis* that ultimately Douglas deserved much of the blame for the initial legal proceedings against Queensberry, the failure of the case, and his own subsequent prosecution.

Even after Wilde's death, Douglas would continue to argue that, had he been given the opportunity to testify regarding Queensberry's ill-treatment of his family, Wilde would probably have won the case. But Douglas was only allowed to appear as the phantom "Exhibit No. 1" that validated Queensberry's accusations. The more he became the essential justification of the Marquess's actions — as a member of an ideal familial bond — the less his actual presence was allowed on the scene. A letter that could have been used to prove that the Marquess had threatened Douglas with delegitimation, for example, is read instead as demonstrating his sincere paternal concern for his son's reputation. "From the beginning to end," the Marquess's lawyer would argue, "Lord Queensberry in dealing with Mr Oscar Wilde has been influenced by one hope alone — that of saving his son" (qtd. in Roberts 212). But saving his son from what exactly?

Douglas's decision to give primacy to his relation with Wilde over that with his father was a challenge to the authority from which Queensberry and the courts spoke. The gesture contested the very paradigm that allowed hierarchies such as father/son to define the main channels of identity fashioning. Claims such as Douglas's threatened to replace ostensibly substantive identities with context-dependent, positional ones: "Immoral" in relation to whom? "Sodomitical" in relation to whom? "A father, an athlete, a marquess" in relation to whom? Queensberry implicitly acknowledged the efficacy of this decadent move when he suggested that pose and artifice can be difficult to distinguish from fundamental modes of being: "to pose as a thing is as bad as to be it." It was only by saving his son from the repetitions of a pose which constructed and reinforced what he perceived to be a sodomitical identity, that Queensberry could sustain his own heteronormative, paternal role. As much as he might have been trying to save his son, he was also trying to protect himself or, more precisely, protect his own identity (and the authority and power it proffered him) from accusations of degeneracy.

A number of scholars have made the claim that Queensberry's behavior toward his family was not relevant to the case. H. Montgomery Hyde, for instance, argues, "The sole issue which the jury would have to decide was a simple one of fact. Did Oscar Wilde pose as a sodomite?" (96). Edward Marjoribanks and Brian Roberts make similar suggestions (Roberts 219). While I find the sodomitical pose a stickier concept than Hyde implies, my immediate point is that neither Queensberry nor Wilde wanted Douglas's private life to be exposed. Although it is true to say that the jury was specifically required to decide whether or not Wilde was posing as a sodomite (thus proving whether or not the Marquess's statement was libelous), the argument that Queensberry had acted solely out of concern for his son was also relevant to this first trial because it was seen to justify his risk of libel in the first place. Certain bonds, such as the hereditary ones between father and son, were viewed as fundamental to the dominant cultural model and, in particular instances, allowed a person to act according to rules that challenged aspects of the law. After all, the law and the government were intended to uphold, not supersede, an apparently inherent moral order defined, in large part, by the heteronormative family. The *Daily Telegraph* chose painfully ironic terms to describe the abusive Marquess, after his acquittal, as "this sorely-provoked and cruelly-injured father" (4 September 1895; qtd. in Roberts 228). As Roberts observes, the crowd that responded to the acquittal with "irrepressible cheering," according to the *Telegraph*, was uninterested in Queensberry's actual family life: "What did they care if he had tormented and betrayed his wife, hounded his sons and sent offensive letters to his daughter-in-law? Such behaviour was deplorable but at least it fell within the bounds of recognizable sexual conduct" (255). Unlike Wilde's views, which threatened to disempower the conventional family model, Queensberry's domestic problems were regarded as less hazardous to the Victorian sociopolitical order. The judicial context favored Queensberry's stance and therefore turned a blind eye when he took advantage of performance to retain his social position.

Wilde and the Positional Being

While the late Victorian judicial system for the most part reinforced the values and power structures that Queensberry supported, the realm of art was a domain in which Wilde had greater authority. It was nevertheless perhaps unwise of the prosecution to turn to an aesthetic discourse model to defend Wilde's statements and actions, arguing that his language must be read from a different perspective than that used for writing associated with "commercial correspondence . . . or those ordinary things which the necessities of life force upon one every day" (*Evening Standard*, 3 April 1895; qtd. in Cohen 151). When Queensberry's defense questioned Wilde on a passage from *The Picture of Dorian Gray* in which Basil Hallward describes his feelings for Dorian, Wilde is quoted as stating, "I think it is the most perfect description possible of what an artist would feel on meeting a beautiful personality that he felt in some way or other was necessary to his art and life." "You think that is a moral kind of feeling for one man to have toward another?" persisted the defense. "I say," replied Wilde, "it is the feeling of an artist toward a beautiful personality" (*Daily Telegraph*, 4 April 1895; qtd. in Cohen 162). When asked to explain the love letter/prose poem that he had written to Douglas "apart from art" (that is, outside the aesthetic model and within an assumedly more objective model), Wilde apparently replied that he was unable to do so (Hyde 115).

This aesthetic discourse model supported the persona for which Wilde was best known and appreciated. However, by 1895 when the trial was taking place, aestheticism was well into what is now often called its "decadent" phase, and the image of the aesthete had become an object of widespread derision. The couching of affection in aestheticist terminology had already been parodied over a decade earlier in Gilbert and Sullivan's comic opera *Patience*, first produced in 1881. One of the opera's "rapturous maidens," having learned all about romance from an aesthete, defines the experience of love as "aesthetic transfiguration," "a transcendentality of delirium — an acute accentuation of a supremest ecstasy — which the earthy might easily mistake for indigestion" (188). A court of law may not have been the best place for defending transfigurations beyond the seemingly more "earthy" issues of familial politics, and the juridical system would have found an aestheticist defense indigestible. In contrast to Queensberry's claim to hereditary responsibility, what Wilde presented as the source of his identity lacked the frame of any conventional depth model. This situation, however, was not a liability within the artistic sphere that Wilde held superior to any other.

Like the Marquess, Wilde was aware of the role that many Victorians saw heredity playing in degeneracy. The eponymous hero of *Dorian Gray* wonders, with regard to an acquaintance (although it sounds like he is thinking of himself), "With such blood as he has in his veins, how could his record be clean?" (118). As a collector not only of lives but also of portrait miniatures (117), Dorian — perusing the family pictures hanging in the gallery of his country house — muses to himself: "Had some strange poisonous germ crept from body to body till it had reached his own? . . . Had the lover of Giovanna of Naples bequeathed him some inheritance of sin and shame? [W]ere his own actions merely the dreams that the dead man had not dared to realise?" (112–13). Wilde moves beyond this series of passive inquiries, however, by tapping into portraiture's function as a signifier of identity, inheritance, and affection in order to challenge the conventional primacy of biological bonds.

The scene of Dorian in his private gallery echoes the opening paragraphs of Joris-Karl Huysmans's *Against Nature* (1884), which describe the portraits of the Des Esseintes family. Following the first few paintings of individuals — "imprisoned in old picture-frames" — with broad shoulders, "piercing" eyes and "bulging" chests, there is, the author tells us, a "gap in the pictorial pedigree" before one reaches the hero of the novel, Duc Jean des Esseintes. The only piece bridging the gap depicts a man who looks much like the central character: "It was a strange, sly face, with pale, drawn features; the cheekbones were punctuated with cosmetic commas of rouge, the hair was plastered down and bound with a string of pearls, and the thin, painted neck emerged from the starched pleats of a ruff" (17). Huysmans's blend of makeup and paint appropriately highlights Des Esseintes's aim of self-determination through artifice, while the gap in the hereditary chain accentuates the possibility of alternate lines of influence. This commingling of self-presentation and portraiture emphasizes a performative slippage, a destabilizing fluidity that, rather than undermining the essentializing aims of the portrait genre only, turns the same accusations against human identity itself.

Like Huysmans, Wilde challenges the notion that identity is solely the product of biological heredity. In *Against Nature*, Des Esseintes's parents both die while he is very young, his mother of "nervous exhaustion" and his father of "some obscure illness" (18). A surprising number of Wilde's heroes are also parentless. Dorian's father, "a mere nobody," is campily written out of the narrative — "The poor chap was killed in a duel at Spa, a few months after the marriage" — with his mother following quick on his heels: "The girl died too; died within a year" (39). Earnest, in the play that carries his name, is likewise free from a conventional family model until the end of the play, when his lineage is discovered. Cyril Graham — described in Wilde's "Portrait of Mr. W. H." as an "effeminate" man who "set an absurdly high value on personal appearance" — is also conveniently orphaned: "I should tell you that Cyril's father and mother were both dead. They had been drowned in a horrible yachting accident off the Isle of Wight" (1152). But as Lord Henry points out, with regard to Dorian's orphanage, "It was an interesting background. It posed the lad, made him more perfect as it were" (41). In contrast to various tools such as governesses and boarding schools by which Victorian society absented children and allowed parents greater freedom without questioning their ultimate authority, Wilde absents the parents in order to leave his young characters "posed" and ready for alternative formative influences.

Dorian envisions the individual as "a being with myriad lives and myriad sensations, a complex multiform creature that bore within itself strange legacies of thought and passion, and whose very flesh was tainted with the monstrous maladies of the dead" (112). The to-die-for aesthete also believes, however, that "one had ancestors in literature, as well as in one's own race, nearer perhaps in type and temperament, many of them, and certainly with an influence of which one was more absolutely conscious" (113).[6] Ed Cohen has insightfully argued that Basil's portrait of Dorian functions as an object of mediation for male-male desire (75–77). In a related sense, this mediatory fulcrum also operates in *Dorian Gray* to demonstrate the means by which individuals can inherit the attributes by which they identify themselves from people other than blood relations.

The three central characters of Wilde's novel all note this mutual exchange of identities. Declaring that "every portrait that is painted with feeling is a portrait of the artist, not of the sitter" (21), Basil claims that he has put too much of himself into the painting of his friend (19), has in fact contributed "the secret of his own soul" (21).[7] Soon after, however, he reverses the flow of influence, noting that Dorian's personality threatens to "absorb [his] whole nature, [his] whole soul, [his] very art itself" (21). Later he confesses to Dorian, "Your personality had the most extraordinary influence over me. I was dominated, soul, brain, and power by you" (93). This would mean that, even if it is a portrait of Basil's own soul (as he claims), the painting is to some degree still a painting of Dorian, who has so influenced Basil's identity. During the crucial period of the painting's completion, however, Dorian is mentally usurped by a third man, Lord Henry, who finds "something terribly enthralling in the exercise of influence. No other activity was like it. To project one's soul into some gracious form" (41). But the mutual influence does not end there, for Lord Henry ultimately falls under Dorian's influence, as his highly specialized portrait collection suggests. "I know you quite well by your photographs," Lady Henry tells Dorian with the driest of humor and erotic innuendo, "I think my husband has got seventeen of them" (47).

Pointing to the collection of influences that flow through Basil's artwork,

Wilde has Dorian overtly acknowledge the vital role of the painting—"It is part of myself. I feel that" (35)—while Basil similarly concludes that Dorian "is all my art to me now" (24). In addition to being a mediator of affection, the portrait functions as an ontological nexus of Basil, Dorian, and Lord Henry's identities. The three men are neither just individuals attracted to and influenced by each other nor aspects of one identity. Each is an individual combination of more than one history of identity formation that is not wholly contingent on conventional notions of biological heredity. The lines of influence energize the portrait so that it gains an identity seemingly as valid as those of the three men. Not only does it possess an almost living force (signified by its protean visage), but its own transformative power destabilizes the other three individuals' control of their own identities, overwhelming their substantive façades with dynamic positionalities of varying critical effect. Basil, Dorian, and Lord Henry all recognize to differing degrees the mediatory positionality of their own identities, an awareness that leads Dorian to revalue his identity as being no more fundamental than that of the portrait. Basil suggests his own awareness of the painting's independent energy when he replies to Dorian's proclamation that the painting is part of him with the affectionate joke, "Well, as soon as you are dry, you shall be varnished, and framed, and sent home. Then you can do what you like with yourself" (35). McConkey argues that Wilde called the novel *The Picture* rather than *The Portrait of Dorian Gray* in order to emphasize the painting's partial self-control; "picture" does not depend on the subject of the painting, while "portrait" refers only to a *representation* of some other living thing (*Edwardian* 16).

Unable to sever his relations with the painting, Dorian laments the existence of this being in the attic: "There is something fatal about a portrait. It has a life of its own" (95). Meanwhile, Basil finds that the absence of the object which he had helped bring into being fosters in him a new sense of freedom: "After a few days *the thing* left my studio, and as soon as I had got rid of the intolerable fascination of its presence it seemed to me that I had been foolish in imagining that I had seen anything in it" (94, emphasis added). Basil, however, has only suppressed his awareness of this influence on his identity; ultimately, the "thing" that Basil seems no longer to want to name leads him to Dorian's dank and dusty confines. Here, Dorian kills Basil, and then blackmails an acquaintance into destroying the corpse, which Dorian now refers to as "the thing, . . . the dead thing" (123), perversely echoing Basil's term for the portrait (and eerily foreshadowing Queensberry's reference to his sodomitical son). While the corpse is being destroyed, Dorian doodles miniatures of Basil's face, belittling Basil's affectionate painting of Dorian by himself propagating a plethora of portraits to replace the now dead man. The anxiety Dorian finally acknowledges by attacking his own portrait reflects the fact that, despite his seemingly permanent beauty, his identity is not fixed. Moreover, the structure of the novel ensures that, although those who see murder as less horrific than the destruction of an artwork are rare, the reader's emotions reach a climax not with Basil's death, but with the stabbing of the portrait. In accord with the importance that the novel places on pose and performance, Wilde shows the art object to have as great an influence as human beings on a person's identity.

*   *   *

Although artifice and pose have frequently been presented as decadent phenomena, Queensberry and Wilde's performances in portraits, the courtroom, and literature demonstrate that the actual distinction which concerned them is not between artifice and essence, but between the acknowledgment and denial of the role that pose and performance play in identity formation. Wilde turned to portraiture, as a volatile conflation of essentialist and constructed traits, in order to demonstrate that sexuality can override familial affiliations as a principal influence on identity self-fashioning. Some queer activists and theorists have voiced a logical extension to this Wildean concern by questioning the motivations behind establishing a hierarchy of influence at all. This stance was apparent, for example, in what seemed to be the *mode de jour* at a recent Pride Day parade — a T-shirt with the bold and brazen phrase "So what if it *is* a choice?" The question (which appropriately reads more like a declaration) is a response to the claim made by Queensberry and others that nonheteronormative desire is a learned pose, and therefore can and should be unlearned. However, the slogan is also an attempt to move beyond the claim that whatever is viewed as fundamental or "natural" is unarguably ethical and justified. While some gays, lesbians, and cross-gendered individuals have defended their desires by stating that they had no choice, what this piece of casual wear points out is that the right to express nonheteronormative desires should not be based on whether they are seen as inherent. Wilde, I would argue, had a similar aim in invigorating the portrait genre. By empowering artistic representation with an identity that interacted with other human identities, he did not naturalize the pose or de-essentialize the body; rather, he destabilized the very binaries of essence and construct, degeneracy and decadence, identity and pose, on which cultural hierarchies — including those of artistic genres — based their authority.

Notes

1. The most popular text addressing nineteenth- and early twentieth-century correlations of degeneracy and visual art is Max Nordau's *Degeneration*, although it focuses more on literature than on visual art. His follow-up study, *On Art and Artists* (1907), tempers somewhat his earlier, notorious position.

2. Julia Margaret Cameron, who used strong light and shade in her portraits of famous contemporaries, is the best-known Victorian who developed a style of photography intended to capture a sitter's "essence" without using signifiers beyond the individual's physiognomy.

3. One notable complication to this general structure regards the numerous painted and photographic portraits of Queen Victoria as ruler, mother, and/or wife. See Margaret Homans's " 'To the Queen's Private Apartments': Royal Family Portraiture and the Construction of Victoria's Sovereign Obedience," and Ira Nadel's "Portraits of the Queen."

4. For discussions of degeneracy and physiognomy, see Mary Cowling's *The Artist as Anthropologist: The Representation of Type and Character in Victorian Art* and Daniel Pick's *Faces of Degeneration: A European Disorder, c.1848-c.1918*. The fact that Pick's study of correlations between degeneracy and physiognomy addresses almost exclusively works by fin-de-siècle authors—including Arthur Conan Doyle, George Gissing, Bram Stoker, and H. G. Wells— suggests that the equation was reaching a critical stage at the time of Douglas and Wilde's relationship.

5. Butler argues that, although one may not see one's self as socially constructed, one's position as "I" is the result of repetitions of a performance ("Imitation" 311); more specifically, gender is a performance that fosters the "illusion of an inner sex or essence or psychic gender core . . . , the illusion of an inner depth" (317). Butler stresses, however, that gender and other aspects of one's identity are not a result of *conscious* performance; in *Bodies That Matter* she argues that performance is the generally unrecognized reiteration of norms, and that social and cultural constraints actually sustain performativity (94–95). Nevertheless, she maintains that, while performance is operative whether it is acknowledged or not, it becomes strategic when used to destabilize, and then safeguard against, essentialist notions of identity, converting identity into a site of ongoing revision ("Imitation" 312).

6. Wilde may be winking askance at the plethora of texts that influenced *Dorian Gray*. Kerry Powell offers the most extensive catalog of such works, arguing that "among the detritus of popular literature a thriving subgenre of fiction in which the props, themes, and even to some degree the dialogue and characterization of *Dorian Gray* are anticipated" (148–49).

7. Christopher Newall argues that, in fact, it was the influence of aestheticism and the Pre-Raphaelites that made portraiturists interested in "the deliberate manipulation of mood as a means of exploring the sitter's inner soul. . . . The theory of 'art for art's sake' released at least some painters from the dictates of commissions, and portraits came to be regarded as works of art in their own right rather than mere likenesses of individuals" (335).

Works Cited

Bourdieu, Pierre. *Distinction: A Social Critique of the Judgement of Taste*. Cambridge: Harvard University Press, 1984.

Butler, Judith. *Bodies that Matter*. New York: Routledge, 1993.

——. "Imitation and Gender Insubordination." In *The Lesbian and Gay Studies Reader*, ed. Henry Abelove et al., 307–20. New York: Routledge, 1993.

Cohen, Ed. *Talk on the Wilde Side: Toward a Genealogy of a Discourse on Male Sexualities*. New York: Routledge, 1993.

Cowling, Mary. *The Artist as Anthropologist: The Representation of Type and Character in Victorian Art*. Cambridge: Cambridge University Press, 1989.

Ellmann, Richard. *Oscar Wilde*. London: Penguin, 1988.

Foucault, Michel. *The History of Sexuality.* vol. 1. New York: Vintage, 1980.

Gilbert, W. S., and Arthur Sullivan. *Patience; or, Bunthorne's Bride.* 1881. In *The Complete Plays of Gilbert and Sullivan*, 184–233. New York: Modern Library, 1936.

Holroyd, Michael. *Lytton Strachey: The Unknown Years.* 1967. London: Heinemann, 1971.

Homans, Margaret. " 'To the Queen's Private Apartments': Royal Family Portraiture and the Construction of Victoria's Sovereign Obedience." *Victorian Studies* 37.1 (1993): 1–41.

Huysmans, Joris-Karl. *Against Nature.* Trans. Robert Baldick. Harmondsworth: Penguin, 1959.

Hyde, H. Montgomery. *The Trials of Oscar Wilde.* London: William Hodge, 1948.

Kaufman, Moisés. *Gross Indecency: The Three Trials of Oscar Wilde.* Dir. Moisés Kaufman. Minetta Lane Theatre, New York. 27 September 1997.

Linkman, Audrey. *The Victorians: Photographic Portraits.* London: Tauris Parke Books, 1993.

Mayne, Arthur. *British Profile Miniaturists.* London: Faber and Faber, 1970.

McConkey, Kenneth. *Edwardian Portraits: Images of an Age of Opulence.* Woodbridge, Suffolk: Antique Collectors Club, 1987.

———. " 'Well-Bred Contortions': 1880–1918." In *The British Portrait, 1660–1960*, ed. Roy Strong, 353–86. Woodbridge, Suffolk: Antique Collectors' Club: 1991.

McPherson, Heather. *Fin-de-Siècle Faces: Portraiture in the Age of Proust.* Birmingham: University Press of Alabama, 1988.

Nadel, Ira. "Portraits of the Queen." *Victorian Poetry* 25.3–4 (1987): 169–91.

Newall, Christopher. "The Victorians: 1830–1880." In *The British Portrait, 1660–1960*, ed. Roy Strong, 299–351. Woodbridge, Suffolk: Antique Collectors' Club: 1991.

Nordau, Max. *Degeneration.* 1892. Lincoln: University of Nebraska Press, 1993.

Pick, Daniel. *Faces of Degeneration: A European Disorder, c.1848-c.1918.* Cambridge: Cambridge University Press, 1989.

Powell, Kerry. "Tom, Dick, and Dorian Gray: Magic-Picture Mania in Late Victorian Fiction." *Philological Quarterly* 62.2 (1983): 147–70.

Queensberry, John Sholto Douglas, 8th Marquess of. *Marriage and the Relation of the Sexes: An Address to Women.* London: Watts, 1893.

———. *The Religion of Secularism and the Perfectibility of Man.* London: Watts, [188-].

———. *The Spirit of the Matterhorn.* London: Watts & Co., 1880.

Roberts, Brian. *The Mad Bad Line: The Family of Lord Alfred Douglas.* London: Hamish Hamilton, 1981.

Sedgwick, Eve Kosofsky. *Tendencies.* Durham, N.C.: Duke University Press, 1993.

Wilde, Oscar. *The Complete Works of Oscar Wilde.* New York: Harper and Row, 1989.

Chapter 5
Decadent Critique
Constructing "History" in Peter Greenaway's
The Cook, the Thief, His Wife & Her Lover

David Wayne Thomas

All narratives prompt one to ask at the end what progress they represent, what history they suggest. Peter Greenaway's film *The Cook, the Thief, His Wife & Her Lover* (Allarts, 1989) ratchets this question further so that we need to ask as well after the very nature of progress and history. So *Cook* urges a further step into critique — if we understand *critique* as an inquiry into foundations or conditions — and I look to this film to explore a sense in which decadent representation might pretend to such critique. And while this chapter does not aim to achieve an overarching determination of decadence, it might be well to note at the outset that a specific but still tentative notion of decadent critique motivates this discussion, namely, a notion that turns on the mutual involvement of two terms, *language* and *history*.

That motivating premise is unlikely to seem absurd. It is already a commonplace that much traditionally decadent artistry is informed, even defined, by special attentions to language. And if we look to the less usual suspect here, history, the premise will probably retain its immediate plausibility. Where *history* means generally the tracing of past events, it seems fair to say that history very often takes on thematic significance in decadent narratives, and typically as a haunting presence, something pervasive and estranged. Decadent protagonists compulsively collect and recollect, wander emotionally disenfranchised through archives and historical arcana, return to ancestral portraits and gravestones, and brood on a past that remains a burden even while it is also beyond reach and defunct. Oscar Wilde's *Picture of Dorian Gray*, to take but one example, gives us a protagonist defined and driven by an extravagant temporal disruption — his exemption from the effects of Time. And Dorian Gray is, in turn, obsessed with a quintessential object of late nineteenth-century decadence: a seductively "poisonous" novel about "a certain young Parisian, who spent his life trying to realize in the nineteenth century all the passions and modes of thought that belonged to every century except his own" (139). Such principled disconnection from historical continuity signals more than the falling away of some miscellaneous psychological disposition, and I aim to read Greenaway's *Cook* to explore how these disruptions suggest a social vision, a specifically decadent procedure of social representation.

In respect to the theme of history, *Cook* plays against a complacency that one might still easily adopt today, namely, that history and progress can be matters of simple fact. *Cook* may be seen, therefore, as a cinematic counterpart to Hayden White's 1973 study *Metahistory*, which distinguishes varieties of historical consciousness by the linguistic tropes that have regulated their particular insights. Such a notion of history was taking shape at least as far back as Hegel in the early 1800s. Writing in a context of massive revolutionary changes, Hegel observes that the German word for history (*Geschichte*) harbors two component aspects — happenings (*Geschehen*) and the telling of happenings (*Geschichte* narrowly understood). These dual aspects pertain even without the etymological kinship specific to the German: history amounts to an entangled field of the objective and the subjective, built up through a dialectical progress that involves, as Hegel has it, "both the events and the narration of the events." In this view, history is not a scene in which things happen and then narration seeks to catch up and make itself adequate to the facts. Instead, Hegel concludes, "The narration of history and historical deeds and events appear at the same time" (75).[1]

If narration plays a part at the root of history, the fact has implications worth spelling out for the following discussion. Narration presupposes perspective — there can be no story without a teller, and no teller without a viewpoint. And perspective, in its turn, is definitively specific, partial, and prey to accusations of arbitrariness. Where a narration purports to relate a communal history, that narration's communal character does not release it from its own condition of partiality. And in fact, that communal narration is all too likely to exist in a state of oblivion to its own partiality, for the narration's shared status can be supposed to certify its objectivity. It is another commonplace that ideological critique consists in showing within a social order the unacknowledged arbitrariness and constructedness of that order's supposedly "natural" forms. With such an understanding of critique, it can be argued that *Cook* affords a critical perspective on cultural production and authority and that a certain notion of decadence emerges in the character of that critique. For *Cook* cannot go so far as to adjudicate such matters or bestow moral authority on a subsequent standpoint. Its critique of cultural value and production is participatory and reflexive and does not "produce" new cultural value. Instead, it calls into question the original authoritative "saying" that would oversee the production of cultural value.

This argument's general interest hinges on the enduring and manifold relevance of the gesture I seek to identify in *Cook*. For it is a question very much to the point for current criticism, whether and how an exercise of "calling into question" is worth the doing. Is critique itself, perhaps like decadence itself, a provocatively nonprofit enterprise? And if so, how is that a strength or a failing?

* * *

In beginning to flesh out this approach to Greenaway's film, we might take a cue from the title and attend right away to four key characters. "The Cook" is Richard Boarst (Richard Bohringer), a talented and unperturbable master chef at the exquisite French restaurant Le Hollandais, located in London. "The Thief" is restaurant owner Albert Spica (Michael Gambon), a violently boorish and garrulous figure who dines nightly at Le Hollandais, surrounded by uncouth lackeys. What makes Albert a "thief" is a question I will return to; suffice it here to say that he seems to sustain his considerable wealth by extorting money from merchants in the area, in particular by threatening to introduce food poisoning at competing restaurants if the owners fail to pay him off. "His Wife" — which is to say, Albert's wife — is the elegant but abused Georgina (Helen Mirren), a connoisseur whose appreciation of the cuisine at Le Hollandais greatly exceeds that of the sloppy gourmand Albert. And "Her Lover," in turn, is Michael (Alan Howard), who lives in a deserted book depository, where he catalogs French history. Each night he arrives at the restaurant and eats alone with a book in his hand.

The story shows Albert remaining oblivious for some days to a tender, between-the-courses affair just begun between Georgina and Michael. When word of the romance is leaked to Albert, his explosive fit sends him running through the restaurant, screaming that he intends to kill and eat Michael. Michael and Georgina take refuge at the book depository, but Albert soon locates Michael there and has his goons kill the man with "style," stuffing pages from Michael's own books down his throat. As it happens, Albert leaves the dead man uneaten. Georgina, however, persuades the cook, Richard, to prepare Michael's body as a sumptuous entrée, so that she can ceremoniously force Albert to eat of this flesh at gunpoint while the living victims of Albert's various abuses stand in support behind her. After thus compelling Albert to keep his word, Georgina shoots him through the head, looks over him wryly, and casts out a final imprecation to the dead tyrant on the floor: "Cannibal!" A curtain closes on the screen, and *Cook* is done.

Here we can proceed from a rather formalistic question: how might we understand the fact that *cannibal* is the last word in this story? A theatrical curtain swings to a close just after Georgina utters this word, as if to underscore the moment's status as a formal consummation of some sort. But the character of that consummation is up for question. One might simply think that the film has proceeded from dog-eat-dog barbarism to a stern but poetic justice. (The film's opening shot does in fact show dogs competing for scraps outside the restaurant.) But we have here a problematic justice: Georgina designates the dead Albert a *cannibal*, although Albert ate human flesh only under compulsion by her. In what sense is Albert a cannibal? What does cannibalism really involve at this juncture? The word *cannibal* might seem to be merely an ironic aside, of course, a last-minute detour into sarcasm for Georgina, who has until now not been given to irony. But further reading allows a more organic — or, if you will, economic — motivation for the details of this decadent repast. *Cook*'s construction of a "cannibal" allegorizes an origin of civilization, an origin that takes shape through a moment of perspectival narration installing a communal history.

So Georgina's final utterance matters as an exercise of language through which social power is not just incidentally, but definitively, linguistic.[2] And in this light, Georgina's last word should be an unsurprising finale, for innumerable details in *Cook* have already suggested the thematic importance of words (and also wordlessness). Throughout the film, Albert's unceasing banter has been clearly opposed to the reticence shown by Richard, Georgina, and Michael. He talks constantly at the table, and during the only scene in which Georgina is at the table without Albert, the camera lingers on the scene for several seconds of silence, as if to underline this point of contrast. And as Albert gabs endlessly with his associates at the table, Georgina and Michael repeatedly pursue their passionate rendezvous without once speaking to each other. (They first speak only after they are introduced by Albert, who is unaware, at the time, that they have already become lovers.) All along, Albert has been the figure most given to speaking, so Georgina's possession of the final word highlights Albert's defeat.

What is more, the initial sequence within the restaurant, beginning and ending with explicit attention to words, suggests that a rather deliberate concern with language lies at this film's thematic foundation. In this early sequence, Albert encounters a sign — a business sign, that is, which he has just acquired for his restaurant. Large individual letters make up the sign, and they have been provisionally hung out in the cavernous kitchen. Albert notes that the letters have been misarranged. "What's that there?" he roars, exasperated. " 'ASPIC'? That's not Spica. Spell it right, for Christ's sake!" As he walks onward, we see the letter *A* trundled by one of Albert's men from the first position to the last. Albert's surname emerges, now properly constituted: SPICA.

Albert wants that sign to be a figure for his person, a proper naming. He gets his way, and the "progress" implied in the rectifying translation of that one letter from beginning to end is suggestive. Albert Spica orders that his name be set right, and the ensuing act is both a metaphorical and "literal" transposition of the letter. (The Greek *metaphorein* means "to carry over," as does the Latin *translatio* from which the English *translation* derives, and this scene shows, with amusing literalness, a *carrying-over of the letter*.) In setting the letter right, Albert blunders onto an image of narration and history. Implied in this moment is a vision of progress through language, a corrective substitution of the letter, whereby Alpha plays Omega as well (the *A* assumes a position at the end of the line, like the letter *omega* at the end of the Greek alphabet). In the last chapter of Revelation, the Lord/Christ of Judgment Day is the "Alpha and the Omega," a consummation of Word and matter that drops the curtain on a drama of human history. This biblical suggestion reemerges more concretely toward the end of the film. In a crucial discussion with Georgina, Richard explains why black foods fetch the highest prices. "Eating black food is like eating death. It is like saying, 'Death, I am eating you.'" He concludes with a comment on historical circularities that alludes to the same verse from Revelation: "Death and birth, the end and the beginning. Do you not think it is appropriate that the most expensive foods are black?"[3]

These intimations of revelation become more pointed after Albert finally has his letters set right and the grand picture has emerged — SPICA & BOARST — for signs of Georgina's eventual authority are set into play. Albert brings boyish glee to calling Richard over for the unveiling of names. We have a little impromptu fanfare from Albert, and on go the lights in these letters. Then a moment of gaudy brightness in the kitchen, whereupon the lights blow an electrical circuit in the restaurant, and all light is extinguished. In an aside to an anxious waiter, Richard credits Mr. Spica with the current state of affairs, clearly suggesting a truth extending beyond this moment: "There is darkness everywhere."

It will fall to Georgina to dispel this darkness. She accompanies Albert as Richard walks along a line of employees bearing trays with candles (the power is out, after all). As Richard lights the candles, he enumerates the evening's cold entrees, mostly in French, and Albert repeats after him in a grossly Anglicizing pronunciation. After Albert takes to reading aloud from the menu, Georgina finally finds his mangled French unendurable, and she corrects him. (He has just said *poisson* rather as one might say *poison* in English.) Albert, irascible as ever, stops short at Georgina's correction and slaps and growls at her: "What did you say? What did you say?" She repeats, with measured resolution, "It's *poisson*." At the moment of her defiant reiteration, lights are restored throughout the restaurant. And again, we have a moment that microcosmically figures the film's progress, a progress that constructs a tale of revolt against darkness, a general triumph of *enlightenment*, figured through a revolutionary usurpation of Albert by a defiant Georgina. One might even draw a lesson from the contrast between Richard's lighting of the candles — an act that copes with darkness but does not exactly remedy it — and Georgina's offering of a right pronunciation. In her case a coincidence of word and light overcomes the disorder engendered by Albert and bestows a restorative illumination.

Perhaps it seems bizarre to grant such thematic centrality to a passing incident — that is, to the goings-on with Albert's sign — but Greenaway's cinematic method is a matter of extravagantly figured fragments (not the least of his affinities with decadent procedure), and exploring the pieces is what one really has to do in any case. And indeed, the light-giving function of the word is again at issue in the film's penultimate scene. Here Georgina approaches Richard in the empty kitchen, hoping to persuade him to cook Michael. In this scene, event and language are brought forth together to forge an order of things at Le Hollandais, and for that reason one can locate here the story's truly critical moment—its moment of *crisis* and *turning*.

Georgina asks Richard to cook Michael, and Richard declines several times. Exhibiting here a disassociated sensibility that has characterized her all along, Georgina observes bizarrely to Richard that he shouldn't mind cooking Michael: "You have a reputation for a wide array of experimental dishes." Frustrated by Richard's denials, she speaks of other things: the pricing of foods, the acts of love. (Love and food have all along been entwined in *Cook*: during the first uninterrupted lovemaking of Georgina and Michael, as they are entwined within a food pantry, ostentatiously deliberate cross-cuts show facets of food preparation in the kitchen.) The decisive return to her initial project comes only after she asks Richard to tell what he saw of her relationship with Michael. Richard lists the moments of lovemaking to which he was witness, and as Georgina listens to him, she begins to weep.

When Richard narrates to Georgina her own actions, he has assumed the role of the historian. And given the timing of Georgina's emotional release, it would seem that the events become "apparent" to her only when brought out in this narration. The combination of Georgina's actual experience with this narration of it forges a connection that had been unborn for her, and that connection amounts to *history* in that Hegelian sense from which this essay proceeded, that sense integrating event and narration. The introduction of history changes everything and leads directly to the film's final scene. For when Georgina at last renews her request and it becomes clear to Richard that it is not Georgina but Albert who is to eat Michael, Richard agrees. The talk is concluded, and the finale is set: Albert will be subjected to his word, which is to say, to his promise to eat Michael.

Whereupon we are given an unusual tracking shot (a shot in which the camera rolls continually to one side). In itself, a tracking shot is the least of surprises, for throughout *Cook* the tracking shot is the most distinctive camera motion. But this particular instance is distinguished by a striking reversal in direction: this shot carries us right-to-left rather than left-to-right. *Cook*'s initial exposition, in particular, is carefully delivered through left-to-right, across-the-wall tracking shots, offering a processional motion that suggests a sort of historical progress in Greenaway's opulent *mise-en-scène*. These initial expositional shots take us from the feral domain of the parking lot, into the medieval atmosphere of the kitchen (the kitchen boy Pup [Paul Russell] singing variations on Psalm 51 in a loosely Gregorian chant), and finally to the plush-velvet, high-cultural sophistication of the dining area. If this left-to-right motion suggests the developmental progress of western reading — and perhaps, by extension, western progress in general — this late moment, with its reversed right-to-left motion, would appear to mark visually a moment of narrative reversal.

The culmination of this reversal proves to be yet another of those points when reckoning the progress implied in this story becomes suggestively problematic. As the camera dollies to the left, leaving the kitchen and moving "backward" into the parking area, Georgina's weeping slowly escalates to an anguished wailing until her voice fades out and the camera comes to rest at last on an object at the far end of the parking lot: a group portrait resembling that portrait hanging prominently in the dining area. Within the restaurant, the portrait has all along been visually linked to the goings on at the main table.[4] We cannot know whether the portrait has also been on display in the lot all along, but the deliberation with which the camera comes to rest on this image is unmistakable, and some reckoning with this appearance is in order. This moment of reversal, far from clearly reversing anything, returns us to an image associated with the very order that has prevailed to this point.

I began this discussion by declaring that all narratives prompt us to ask at the end what progress or history they have suggested. If one brings such questioning to this reversal of the tracking shot and to the revelation of this portrait at the shot's end, any interpretive solution is obliged to navigate a rather equivocal terrain. And as happens with many "literary" constructions, equivocalness can come quickly to seem a fulfillment of representational intentions rather than a failure of them. The progress in *Cook*, a progress that allegorizes an origin of history, is also a progress built to construct and sustain considerable skepticism regarding the western progress that a naive view of history might seem to accept as simple fact.

For one might propose, on the one hand, that the narrative charts a progressive and ameliorating social development. By the film's end, the new authority headed by Georgina appears to be a more familiar and morally reckonable authority, an authority that crushes only so obstreperous a lout as Albert. It is an authority figured in terms of sociality and harmonious delegation. Not only does a united group confront Albert, but the cooperative nature of that group is on display at the final scene when a waiter wrests Albert's gun from him and passes it on to Richard, who passes it on to the abused kitchen boy, who in turn passes it on to Georgina. What is more, the camera work elicits viewer identification with this group consciousness: no shots of Albert are given from behind the line-up confronting him; instead, the shots invariably assume the vantage point of the group. That is, the group is not *within* the camera's view for those shots that bear down on Albert; instead, the group *is* that view, and by extension, the group's view is

Figure 5.1. Albert with his final repast.

our view (fig. 5.1). In that brief interval between Georgina's exclamation "Cannibal!" and the closing of the curtain on this story, a final shot gives us the new order of things at Le Hollandais: Albert lies dead in the foreground, and the ascendant community gazes down on its achievement (fig. 5.2).

On the other hand, this progressive interpretation, which sees in *Cook* the story of a tyrannical oaf righteously deposed by civilized people like us, should take account of some rather ill fitting points of fact. Georgina's problematic construction of Albert as a cannibal is chief among these narrative oddities, of course. Another of these odd facts leads into that final moment. If Georgina's progress in this film is supposed to mark her liberation from Albert's domination, one has to wonder why she arrives for this final scene decked out lavishly, implicitly royalized, in a gown with a latticework train borne by an attendant. All along Georgina has been clothed very elegantly—the costumes are by Gaultier, the credits inform us—but up to this point her elegant apparel had always been figured as a sign of Albert's wealth. A more commonplace film would suggest Georgina's break from Albert by presenting her in some categorically opposed fashion, as when American formula dramas imply character progress into good wholesome values by, say, beginning with slick-haired financiers in Armani suits and converting them into denimed and plaid-flanneled common folk with superbly casual hair. It would seem, actually, that Georgina's apparel implies not so much a break with her past as a concerted extrapolation from it, a bizarre efflorescence.

Other details make even clearer the continuity between Albert and Georgina, suggesting that Georgina does not so much diverge from Albert's moral trajectory as she develops qualitatively beyond it. Of the four main characters, Georgina and Albert share the chameleonlike property of having their garments change color as they walk through the restaurant. As if by magic,

Figure 5.2. The final shot before the curtain falls.

Georgina's dresses are blue in the parking lot, green in the kitchen, red in the dining area, and white in the restroom, while Albert's sash, which he wears over his suit, changes less obviously but nonetheless identically. In contrast, Richard's white chef's frock and Michael's brown suit do not change. What is more, there are exactly two murders in the film, one each for Georgina and Albert, and Georgina's murder of Albert seems not only to mirror Albert's murder of Michael with "style," but to show up that prior murder, to go substantially beyond it by staging the matter as public spectacle.

The transition of authority between Albert and Georgina figures a progress into an order of civilization: she cultivates and installs a group-centered authority. What is more, casting this categorizing moment in terms of cannibalism recalls Freudian notions of totem and taboo and their primordial role in articulating and maintaining the group that has just stepped beyond a phase of social life in which the strength of an individual (such as Albert) reigned supreme. Freud's remarks in *Civilization and Its Discontents* state the case compactly: "In overpowering their father, the sons had made the discovery that a combination can be stronger than a single individual. The totemic culture is based on the restrictions which the sons had to impose on one another in order to keep this new state of affairs in being. The taboo observances were the first 'right' or 'law'" (55). In the light of Freud's notion, Georgina's utterance illustrates a founding gesture of civilization, a communally endorsed taxonomic prerogative on the side of right. But what sort of progress wins the endorsement of this communal authority? What "right" has this communal might brought forth? And how pertinent is Georgina's designation of Albert as a cannibal?

One can approach all of these questions by considering the act of categorization involved in Georgina's construction of Albert as a cannibal. To categorize, as Pierre Bourdieu reminds us, means "to accuse publicly" (*Lan-*

guage and Symbolic Power 121). (The Greek *kategorein* evokes the *agora* or "public space.") When Georgina calls Albert a cannibal, her dictum installs a new order in that microcosm Le Hollandais. The specific historical allegories that *Cook* so variously suggests itself to be involved in — the rise of Christianity, the hegemonic dialectic of Enlightenment, the French Revolution, the logic of Capitalism, etc. — all devolve into a fundamental allegory of an origin of civilization.

But it is a civilization of a specific character, defining itself through a new order of subjection. Albert was not a cannibal, nor was he likely ever to be one, until Georgina and the community behind her nominated him to that part. Of course, Georgina's actions are inspired by Albert's own words, a point made plain in her words to Albert in the final scene, when Georgina unveils Michael's prepared corpse for Albert:

Albert: Jesus! God!
Georgina: No, that's not God, Albert. It's Michael. My lover. You vowed you would
           kill him, and you did. And you vowed you would eat him. Now eat him.

Precisely because the finale's image of justice has taken shape here, we do well to note that any regulating notion that Albert should keep his word is alien to his character. All along, the story has illustrated Albert's capacity to pass with aplomb over any pedestrian contradiction he might happen to find himself involved in. He upbraids his men for swearing in front of the ladies, and then does so himself a moment later; he tells Georgina she shouldn't smoke in the kitchen, then takes her cigarette and extinguishes it in a nearby saucepan, ruining the preparation. Albert's word has never been his guiding authority. If Albert's rule has stood apart from any highly articulated notions of a ruler's obligation and responsibility, Georgina's determination to dictate his actions in terms of his words would seem to present, for Albert at least, a dizzying non sequitur. What has Albert to do with promises, with consistency, with self-regulation? Can it go without saying that it is "right" for Albert to be compelled to keep his word? Perhaps, but it is best to do so after this notion of "right" — this instance of poetic "justice" — is reckoned with attention to its genealogy.

In *The Genealogy of Morals*, Nietzsche traces the origins of responsibility in a way that bears on this matter of the person who promises: "The task of breeding a man with the right to make promises evidently embraces and presupposes as a preparatory task that one first *makes* men to a certain degree necessary, uniform, like among like, regular, and consequently calculable" (58–59). For Nietzsche, the human (*Mensch*) with the right to make promises is little else than modern humanity as such, with individuals designated as human and thereby subscribed to a host of prescriptions that define their material existence and their moral purview. Declared a sovereign agent in a position to make a promise — and therefore also, an agent responsible for keeping his promise—Albert is at last a proper western subject. And recalling here the remark from Hegel quoted earlier, it becomes clear that the dual aspects of history—happenings and the narration of happenings—are mutually determining at this film's consummation: Albert "being" a cannibal is inextricable from Albert being dictated or narrated as such.[5]

So the term *cannibal* is at this juncture simultaneously descriptive and prescriptive. In the language of speech-act theorists, we could say that Georgina's final word blurs the distinction between constative and performative utterance, both stating something (the constative) and "doing" something by saying (the performative—as in "I thee wed"). Not merely some last-minute detour into sarcasm, Georgina's final word exhibits an irony underlining the social operation of a properly linguistic and reflexive concern (description and prescription). Because this film's climactic moment escapes, even mocks, any merely descriptive procedure of understanding, it broaches questions about the self-sufficiency of description, questions that lead finally toward a perspectivalist conception of history as an entangled domain of description and narration. Georgina describes the already dead Albert as a "cannibal," and this last act is a historical narration written to the purposes of the latest incarnation of Le Hollandais.

Here, where rule is passed along not merely through a quantitative increase or transposition of power but through a qualitative development of power, through an overmastering and reordering articulation of power, we encounter the conception of genealogy that Nietzsche was at such pains to define.[6] And given the executionlike aspect of *Cook*'s finale, it is striking that Nietzsche's most concerted statement of his genealogical thesis takes place as an excursus in his discussion of "the origin and purpose of punishment" (76). There Nietzsche has declared it a naive confusion by moral historians to suppose that a law's "purpose"—say, revenge or deterrence—has anything to do with the "origin" of that law. Instead, he insists,

There is for historiography of any kind no more important proposition than the one it took such effort to establish but which really *ought to be* established now: the cause of the origin of a thing and its eventual utility, its actual employment and place in a system of purposes, lie worlds apart; whatever exists, having somehow come into being, is again and again reinterpreted to new ends, taken over, transformed, and redirected by some power superior to it; all events in the organic world are a subduing, a becoming master, and all subduing and becoming master involves a fresh interpretation, an adaptation [a *Zurechtmachen*—a "making-upright"] through which any previous "meaning" and "purpose" are necessarily obscured or even obliterated. (77)

This notion of impositional interpretation and *Zurechtmachen* entails that any moral order arises from an act of forcible articulation, applied not simply to a prior inarticulation, but to a prior articulation that stands to be erased, extinguished, or perhaps even cast in legend now as an inarticulation — for example, as a "Nature" before "Culture."[7]

Seen in this light, *Cook* is not simply about the fall of one sovereign authority (namely, Albert) and the rise of a replacement (Georgina, or that consenting citizenry that holds her as its figurehead). Instead, *Cook* chronicles an origin of sovereignty as such, when sovereignty has that Nietzschean sense in which the sovereign "right" to make promises is prerequisite to any responsibility one might have to keep promises. This sovereignty is a subjection to a particular vision of humanity and sociality. The order headed up by Georgina installs itself through an act of obscuring or obliterating (to use Nietzsche's terms) the regime of Albert.

Given this process of erasure, whereby prior interpretive orders are not simply sequestered away but actively transformed and obscured in the succeeding worldview, it makes a certain sense that the character of Albert's rule is an obscure matter. However tempting it is to see in *Cook* a progression from disorder to order, from anarchy to a rule of law, it seems necessary to complicate that view, for Albert is no mere figure of the primordial brute. Although hardly a monument to propriety, Albert is a man crucially defined by related notions of *property*. This restaurant owner revels in money throughout the film, and makes his first point to that effect at the film's opening scene, when he declares to the man he is abusing, "I'm Albert Spica. I've got a heart of gold and a whole lot of money to match." And if, for a certain revolutionary vision, property is theft, Albert is a "thief" quite properly. Given his taste for elevated dining, and his equally explicit (if inconsistent) taste for table manners and "proper" ways of eating, Albert embodies a loose assortment of modern psychological, social, and economic stereotypes. He is a bizarre conjunction of the infantile and the familiarly socialized — a marriage of, say, preoedipal mania (with his fixations on feces and, one could suppose, a terror of the phallic mother) and crass, bourgeois posturing. Albert's interest for the present reading consists finally in how difficult it remains to see him as some unconstructed libido, some brute of Nature.

A passage from Marx's *Grundrisse* offers terms through which this film's logic generally can be understood as a critique not of Nature / Culture but of a thoroughly cultural scene of production and consumption: "Hunger is hunger," observes Marx, "but the hunger gratified by cooked meat eaten with a knife and fork is a different hunger from that which bolts down raw meat with the aid of hand, nail and tooth" (92). Marx wishes to define a difference between animalistic hunger and "modern" humanity's typical experience of hunger, because he wishes to underscore how production serves not merely to provide objects of consumption — say, food — but how production actually creates and defines consuming subjects. And Marx's immediately ensuing comment on art allows a fancy French cuisine within its purview: "The object of art — like every other product — creates a public which is sensitive to art and enjoys beauty. Production thus not only creates an object for the subject, but also a subject for the object" (92). Much of what is compelling in Marx's theory of political economy depends on his notion that production not only serves preexisting and "natural" needs, but also furthers an ongoing creation of new needs, thus inaugurating an eccentric circling of desire and gratification, a perpetual force of revolution whose centrifugal momentum charts out an ever-expanding scene of consumption.

So the very temptation to see in Albert's world a brutish Nature, an anarchic prelude to civilized conduct, seems foiled by the fact that Albert is, at the same time, a quintessential picture of the commodity fetishist, that figure for whom money takes the place of a universalized value under which sign anything can be comprehended and rendered into a system of equivalencies. So the facets that make up Albert's character can seem rather disparate and haphazardly associated, but that very haphazardness actually meets a representational mandate to portray through character a layering and sedimentation that *Cook* proposes in its larger narrative.

Several moments in *Cook* clarify the film's larger traffic in this thematics of untidy sedimentation. The opening shot, for example, offers a scene of dogs feeding on scraps outside the restaurant, as if to suggest some savage state as prelude to the civilized forms of aggression that this history leads into. But the image's details complicate such interpretation in several respects. Conspicuous among these otherwise undistinctive dogs is one Dalmatian, a product of varietal cultivation. In addition to the primordial sounds of barking during this shot, we hear a muffled industrial pounding, as if some tremendous pile-driver is laboring in the distance. And further, one vertical pipe in a network of scaffolding rises in the center of this image, and the bracing for the horizontals is located so as to create within the image the proportions of a crucifix rising among the dogs and the scraps of meat.

Midway through the film, another scene suggests that layering of contrary indications so favored by Greenaway. The moment takes place in Michael's book depository, just after the lovers have fled the restaurant where Albert has discovered the affair and thrown his fit. That scene's violence gives way dramatically to this scene's spacious and aestheticized repose. Our introduction to this improving environment is given through one of the film's only dissolve transitions, when an image supersedes another after a moment of blurring superimposition (figs. 5.3–5.5). In the beginning of this scene, the nude figures of Georgina and Michael are postured like statuary in a classically styled interior of the book depository, standing under a shower of water directed by a third individual. At the end of this transition we see a virtually identical interior, part of the same dwelling, and here the human figures are nowhere to be seen, although countless books are now heaped between the classical columns. This dissolve suggests the replacement of these figures by these books: first there was a scene of cleansing, along with a union of classical and human forms; next there is an erasure of these human forms, and instead a union of classical forms and bookish accumulation.

Figures 5.3–5.5. Three images charting a dissolve in the interior of Michael's book
depository.

What sort of progress do we witness here? Is there a western history here? Is it a falling away, a decline? Or perhaps an extrapolation? Perhaps the very reading that could see articulated here a wholesome and pure Greco-Roman vitalism deteriorated into a dusty cultural sedimentation might do better to question that initial, wholesome purity, noting the racial difference of the man with the hose, and recalling the Greco-Roman slave economy that is still too often left unthought in celebrations of classical Western culture? To say what supersession is unfolding here is to occupy an interpretation that can exist only in the privileging of some details and subordination of others.

Greenaway's cinematic procedure bestows on such provoking details a sort of covert centrality.[8] Some notion of hyper-accumulating detail has always characterized those texts called decadent, and the present reading of *Cook* suggests that such ostentatious indifference to stylistic economy can lend articulation to a critique of psychosocial economy. Attention to literary-cinematic details, especially in their capacity to vacillate between peripheralness and centrality, urges attention to the very value formations that would recognize (or misrecognize) such formal details and decide their status as either peripheral or central. Here recognition and misrecognition are acts of *valuation*. The practical (which includes moral) organization of an audience is brought into a state of evaluative crisis through a text's capacity to present contradiction through such details—whether via irony, parody, or formal undecidability. A text's subsequent intractableness to objective and unequivocal determination frustrates any critical imperative whereby cultural valuations might seek authorization under a sign of objectivity or unequivocalness. So the decadent postures of morbid individualism and eccentricity—forms of militant, excessive perspectivalism—invite mainstream deprecation but also instate a species of reflexive social critique. For decadent excesses reflect, via caricature or other extrapolation, the same commitment to individual acts of valuation that a mainstream audience will deploy in order to deprecate decadent excess.

One scene makes nearly explicit *Cook*'s involvement in these issues of reflexive posturing and self-estrangement. Midway through the film, Georgina and Michael are alone in a pantry, and during an interlude in their lovemaking, Michael speaks of a film that had once engrossed him, but only so long as the main character had not spoken at all. After he spoke, says Michael, "I immediately lost all interest." Georgina attempts to draw out the point: "So do you mean to say, now that we have spoken, you will lose all interest in me?" Michael replies, "It was only a film." The lovers pause, and then laugh somewhat uncomfortably, as if at an irony. The pause includes *Cook*'s viewers inevitably, enforcing a stretch of time during which we too are likely to take note of our own ironic consciousness, our own investment in drawing lessons from what is, so we are told, "only a film." When a film that is so concerned to portray a critique of historical progress brackets off film's seriousness as a resource for extrapolation into the "real" world, we need to ask if we have here Greenaway's strategic irony, or perhaps an underlying cynicism that threatens to unmask the formal richness of *Cook* as an illusory and vacuous formalism. At the very least, the moment denaturalizes the narrative and all of its elaborate trappings, and implies a limit to the film's own capacity to instate a model of raised consciousness that might then go on to communicate its beneficial character to other situations and other social workings.

At the end of *Metahistory*, Hayden White sums up his discourse on history and historical consciousness with a concession that suggests a similarly unstable relation of critique and irony: "I do not deny that the Formalism of my approach to the history of historical thought itself reflects the Ironic condition from within which most of modern academic historiography is generated. But I maintain that the recognition of this Ironic perspective provides the grounds for a transcendence of it" (434). We can wonder whether or not White's confidence in transcendence is well placed. But at the end of this essay, it is more pertinent to note that White's faith in *historical* representation as a means of critique finds a counterpart in any faith that *decadent* representation might function as a means of critique. To put one's interpretive consciousness at a threshold where that which *describes* decadence borders on that which *performs* decadence — recalling that distinction whereby Georgina's final word alternately describes and performs — is to occupy that point where irony presents the uncertainty of its progressive character. Under this circumstance, the goal cannot be to transmit or produce anything in particular, much less to *reproduce* anything in particular. But this equivocal process of critique might, in its very failure to play a game of reckonable production and reproduction, construct a critical consciousness of the production of values and the conditions of interpreting and embodying those values. In this light, decadent critique shows but does not really tell, and therefore it is likely to seem suspect to anyone who wants critique to service a particular value or a particular end.

On this point of the redemptive potential in decadent representation, we find the central crux in this reading of *Cook*. It might be useful in this connection to note Bourdieu's reading of Flaubert's *Sentimental Education*, for despite his concern to show how a reflexive sociology is superior to aesthetic representation in critical potential, Bourdieu allows that "the literary work can sometimes say more, even about the social realm, than many writings with scientific pretensions." He immediately qualifies that praise by noting that literature can say what it says "only in a mode such that it does not truly say it" (*Rules of Art* 32). Bourdieu is deeply invested in the notion of "truly" saying ideas, and assessing the authority and specificity of that truthtelling is the key step in assessing Bourdieu's sociological project. For my purposes here, it is enough to show that even so putatively antiaesthetic a writer as Bourdieu allows that literary expression (into which I collapse Greenaway's *Cook*) finds its critical specificity precisely through the location of its force outside the work's declarative content. In this respect, the aspirations of social critique can be served by aesthetic procedures due to their propensity to stand apart (in instances, at least) from a narrow and instrumentalizing reduction of the work to a quantified and specified content.

Decadent representation in particular has complexly economic involvements that need further exploration if we are to understand how the most provocative and characteristic elements of decadence can be brought into the terms of fundamental critical action. These economic involvements come out in the very language one can anticipate being brought against decadent critique: What is its *yield*? What does it *get us*? What is it *worth*? What is its *value*? In *Cook*, Georgina's first remarks on entering Michael's book depository take a similar form: "What good are all of these books to you? Can you eat them?" While these questions are hardly nonsense, neither are they innocent, secure, or inevitably on target. Decadence has always been notable as a self-divided posture. To this extent it maps easily onto notions of a modern, post-French Revolution historical consciousness that internalizes a sense of its own unstable volatility. To understand better that sense in which hostile questions directed toward decadent critique are actually internal to decadent critique is to understand better something more broadly to the point today, namely, how our own procedures of critical productivity can so often harbor reflexive contradictions that perpetuate the very questions one might think oneself to be resolving. Such an inquiry must finally ask: What critique is not decadent?

Notes

1. Hegel was not the first person, of course, to suppose that history and narrative viewpoint are inextricable. Gossman refers to several eighteenth-century precursors in this terrain (229–31 and passim).

2. Bourdieu makes compelling claims for the intricate reciprocity of language acts and social power.

3. "I am the Alpha and the Omega, the beginning and the end." Revelation 21:6.

4. Gras identifies the image as a 1614 painting, *Banquet of the Officers of the St. George Civic Guard Company*, by the Dutch painter Franz Hals (137).

5. In discussing Hegel and literary historiography, Bahti touches on the figure of cannibalism in Hegel. Drawn through an image of Africa, Hegel's notion of cannibalism diagnoses in the first place a radical contempt of humanity, a contempt proceeding from a position preliminary to any properly historical consciousness. Bahti proposes that a later state of Spirit-knowledge in Hegel involves a transfigured cannibalism, emerging from the self-understanding implied in certain conceptions of "doing" history: "Hegelian scholarly (*wissenschaftlich*) history eats or cannibalizes humanity" (80).

6. See Foucault for a contemporary paraphrase of Nietzsche's concerns with genealogy.

7. Gras argues for the centrality of a Nature/Culture crux throughout Greenaway's films.

8. Schor discusses the celebration of detail as a decadent stratagem.

Works Cited

Bahti, Timothy. *Allegories of History: Literary Historiography after Hegel.* Baltimore: Johns Hopkins University Press, 1992.

Bourdieu, Pierre. *Language and Symbolic Power.* Trans. Gino Raymond and Matthew Adamson. Cambridge: Harvard University Press, 1991.

———. *The Rules of Art: Genesis and Structure of the Literary Field.* Trans. Susan Emanuel. Stanford: Stanford University Press, 1995.

The Cook, the Thief, His Wife & Her Lover. Dir. Peter Greenaway. With Richard Bohringer, Michael Gambon, Alan Howard and Helen Mirren. Allarts, 1989.

Foucault, Michel. "Nietzsche, Genealogy, History." In *Language, Countermemory, Practice: Selected Essays and Interviews,* trans. Donald F. Bouchard and Sherry Simon, 139–64. Ithaca: Cornell University Press, 1977.

Freud, Sigmund. *Civilization and its Discontents.* Trans. J. Strachey. New York: Norton, 1961.

Gossman, Lionel. *Between History and Literature.* Cambridge: Harvard University Press, 1990.

Gras, Vernon. "Dramatizing the Failure to Jump the Culture/Nature Gap: The Films of Peter Greenaway." *New Literary History* 26 (1995): 123–43.

Hegel, G. W. F. *Reason in History: A General Introduction to the Philosophy of History.* Trans. Robert S. Hartmann. Indianapolis: Bobbs-Merrill, 1953.

Marx, Karl. *Grundrisse: Foundations of the Critique of Political Economy.* Trans. Martin Nicolaus. New York: Vintage, 1973.

Nietzsche, Friedrich. *On the Genealogy of Morals.* Trans. Walter Kaufmann and R. J. Hollingdale. [With *Ecce Homo.*] 1967. New York: Vintage, 1989.

Schor, Naomi. *Reading in Detail: Aesthetics and the Feminine.* New York: Methuen, 1987.

White, Hayden. *Metahistory: the Historical Imagination in Nineteenth-Century Europe.* Baltimore: Johns Hopkins University Press, 1973.

Wilde, Oscar. *The Picture of Dorian Gray.* Harmondsworth: Penguin, 1985.

Chapter 6
Opera and the Discourse of Decadence
From Wagner to AIDS

Marc A. Weiner

Let us imagine the following scene: a young man, endowed with unusual aesthetic sensibility and great intellectual promise, attempts to communicate to those less sensitive the singular nature of an operatic air. He goes to great pains to explain the seductive realm that its sounds are intended to convey, especially the drama that the music accompanies. As his disquisition continues, his audience becomes increasingly aware of the physical strain that his enthusiasm, bordering on rapture, causes. His excitement grows to such intensity that those with whom he speaks begin to fear for his safety, for as he becomes ever more impassioned in his desire to persuade, the limits of his physical capacity to endure such passion come to the fore. His light complexion, usually bordering on a sickly pallor, is transformed by the carmine blush of his emotions, his eyes stare wildly in a troubling, introverted gaze of ecstasy, and his slight build seems scarcely able to sustain the power of his excitement evinced by the nervous character of his gesticulations and by the intoxicated swoon, bordering on sexual release, with which his rhapsody climaxes. Finally, it becomes clear that the musical-dramatic vision evoked by the young man is directly linked to his feverish and erotic state, as if the music had acted as a powerful drug, vouchsafing the initiated individual a glimpse into an imaginary realm available only to a few but experienced at a horrible price.

If asked to assign a year to this scene, I can imagine that most of us would choose a moment from the age of decadence, that purportedly voluptuous period in the development of western culture, situated at the turn of the twentieth century, that so closely associated intellectual insight with images of privileged singularity, sexual excess, moral abandon, and disease and physiological decay.[1] One could imagine such a scene, for example, in any number of literary settings from Huysmans, Proust, D'Annunzio, or, in German-speaking Europe, from Thomas Mann's *Buddenbrooks* or one of his trenchant parodies of the decadent movement, "Tristan" or "Wälsungenblut," from Ferdinand von Saar's "Geschichte eines Wiener Kindes," or perhaps from works not containing explicit references to opera, but otherwise similar, by Bahr, Beer-Hofmann, von Hofmannsthal, Graf von Keyserling, or Schnitzler.

But the scene I have in mind is found in a celebrated Hollywood film from 1993. Directed by Jonathan Demme, *Philadelphia* stars Tom Hanks as Andrew Beckett, a gay man dying of AIDS, and Denzel Washington as Joe Miller, Beckett's attorney who, in the scene in question, listens to his client wax rhapsodic on the beauties of opera. In this scene, which I will discuss in greater detail below, a series of visual icons, familiar from the collection of images we have come to associate with the decadent movement, serves to establish a connection between the music Andrew is describing, his diseased body, and his sexuality. In this way, the three components—opera, disease, and a kind of sexual activity deemed suspect by the dominant culture— form a nexus of associations that is by no means a singular reflection of our current-day sensibilities, but that, on the contrary, is the product of a set of images and attendant implications that was already firmly established in western culture over a century ago.[2] Or, to put it somewhat differently: because three of the widely accepted signs of decadence from the late nineteenth century were physiological decay, aberrant sexuality, and an aesthetics of extravagance, their conflation in the image of the dying, gay, and opera-loving Andrew Beckett—as well as the fact that this scene was repeatedly singled out, more than any other, for praise or consternation by a host of critics shortly after the film's release—may be a clue to the continued presence today of the iconic representations and ideological assumptions that attended the vocabulary of decadence at the end of the nineteenth century.

It is only recently that discussions of opera have seriously addressed the art's pervasive proximity in European culture, and in the American culture so dependent upon its European models, to notions of disease and sexual deviance.[3] While an infusion of poststructuralist theory into the confines of traditional musicology has led a new generation of scholars to examine music's capacity to convey meaning through a variety of narrative codes,[4] opera's appropriation and reflection of extra-aesthetic levels of meaning such as those associated with physiological states (especially disease and sexuality) have, with only a few noteworthy exceptions, remained largely unexplored. As only the most recent scholarship has shown, already by the early nineteenth century a host of ideologically polarized sexual metaphors were firmly in place in the cultural vocabulary of Europe that were employed in the representation, perception, and evaluation of instrumental music and opera, as clearly seen, for example, in discussions of the purportedly "masculine" music of Beethoven and the assumedly "feminine" nature of Schubert's art songs.[5] These metaphors continued to inform discussions of such works throughout the nineteenth century in general and, I will argue, in the age of decadence in particular, by which time they automatically linked notions of disease, difference, and sexuality with opera in the popular imagination, even though one of the characteristic features of the decadent movement itself was its attempt to question and to undermine such popular assumptions.[6]

Of course, there were diverse historical reasons for such a nexus, from opera's association with aristocratic patronage since its inception circa 1600, which underscored the esoteric nature of the art form in the minds of the bourgeoisie, to the long-standing perception of the theatrical world in general as a locus of low morality. There was also the horrific image of the castrati, so central to opera until the early nineteenth century, which linked the art to sexual difference and physiological damage.[7] That the association of disease, deviance, and opera can still be discerned today and still continues to evoke the value-laden binarisms of the last century, which the decadent movement so relentlessly critiqued, polarizing health-illness, masculinity-femininity, heterosexuality-homosexuality, public-private spheres, and life-art, is an indication that much of the cognitive and ideological structures associated with the age of decadence, hailed (or vilified) as the heyday of modernism, continue to inform today's purportedly postmodernist period.[8] That is, while decadence sought to challenge such binarisms as facile that were so popular at the turn of the century, they have retained their force and function today, ironically, as hallmarks of the decadent age itself.

Eve Kosofsky Sedgwick has offered some brilliant observations regarding the thematic interconnections of opera, homosexuality, and disease in an examination of Nietzsche's writings, with particular emphasis on the texts from the late 1880s devoted to the criticism of Wagner (168–69). To Sedgwick, each thematic area — art form, sexuality, and physiological pathology — is linked to and evokes the other in the philosopher's discourse, and she demonstrates that these texts provide a vehicle for examining an established discourse that they reflected, perpetuated, and criticized. I wish to show, however, that Wagner's essays on social and aesthetic reform reveal just such a discourse linking a specific kind of operatic art with cultural decay and deviant (and/or inferior) sexuality, that is, a nexus of discursive formulations and attendant assumptions that was already firmly in place nearly forty years earlier than the period in which Nietzsche would employ it in his ironic critique of Wagner.

Yet to simply identify such a discourse of sexuality and disease — related to and evoked by opera — as already occurring before the decadent movement began would hardly in itself constitute a worthwhile intellectual endeavor. Rather, I believe such an insight is important for our understanding of the implications inherent in the tenacity and pervasive legacy of the binarisms that decadence would challenge, because of the shift in sexual categorization that Foucault's celebrated *History of Sexuality* identifies as discursively manifest around 1870, that is, at a time roughly halfway between the period in which Wagner wrote his most widely read tracts on aesthetic and social reform (circa 1850) and the period in which Nietzsche labeled Wagner the quintessentially decadent artist (1888) by using the very polar oppositions that the composer had employed in his critique of modernity. The contours of this shift may be dimly discerned behind the rhetorical movement from the many contradictions within Wagner's metaphorical formulations, in which he reveals a definition of sexuality that is sometimes constructivist, and sometimes essentialist, to Nietzsche's ironically critical discourse. Foucault maintains that, in the second half of the nineteenth century, the notion that sex was defined by a set of distinct performative acts (as reflected in the term *sodomite*) and hence subject to change, modification, and even choice that had obtained in European cultural discourse in the first half of the century, gave way to the definition of sex as biologically grounded in a category of immutable gender (as reflected, for example, in the term *homosexual*, coined in 1869) (43, 101).[9] Wagner's vocabulary contains both of the cognitive models that Foucault identifies, and their contradictory implications are constitutive of his ideological agenda, but they still obtain today, reflected in the popular discursive link between opera, disease, and sexuality found in such works as *Philadelphia*. That is, the tension between these two positions of a physiologically determined understanding of sexuality and one less stable has even colored the conceptualization, representation, and reception of *opera* since this period, precisely because the art form itself has been linked to corporeal states.

Due to its association with sexuality and disease in the cultural vocabulary of late nineteenth-century Europe, opera, from the age of decadence to our own fin de siècle, has evoked—and continues to evoke—the tension between understandings of sexuality as either innately given (immutable) or as transient phenomenon (and hence distinct and open to modification). In suggesting that there may be a link between opera and the essentialist/constructivist debate concerning sexuality, I am building on the notion, put forth by the musicologist Philip Brett, that there is a link between the terms *homosexuality* and *musicality*, both of which were established during the late nineteenth century. "What happens when we separate the word *musicality* from the word *music*," Brett writes, "is comparable to what happens when we separate *homosexuality* (or *sexuality*) from *sex*. An attribute, a social role, is filtered out of a term that has socially negotiated meanings which differ according to context. . . . [Musicality] is a deviant role—for all those who identify with the label, not merely for the sexual deviants who populate the various branches of the profession" (10–11).

The same could be said of the word *opera* within the discourse that was already in place by the age of decadence and that continues to emerge, perhaps without reflection, in much criticism today. If there is a culturally pervasive (and hence constructed, though often most likely unconscious) link between categories of physiology (sexuality and health) and opera, the questions about these categories of the body regarding their social versus innate natures may attend the very perception of the art form as well. The decadent topos of a connection between art and decay, which the movement employed in order to attack the binarisms constitutive of a more bourgeois mentality, may thus be shown to have a tradition that reaches back to an age in which sexuality was only partially deemed naturally determined, and forward to our own, which continues to be fraught with questions of physiological (and aesthetic) determinism: Can one's musical sensibilities be categorized in a fashion similar to one's sexual and racial identities and one's status as healthful or diseased? Is one deemed in our culture today, by implication, *innately* musical, drawn or receptive to opera, much as one is defined physiologically as male or female, or are such proclivities constructed, developed, transient, and expressed in a series of specific acts? The question, odd though it may seem, is not unrelated to the question as to whether homosexuality, for example, is genetically determined or culturally constructed. Without the background of a debate between essentialist and constructivist camps, the ambiguities behind the notion that gay men have a purportedly special or privileged affinity with opera could not be recognized, and yet it is the contours of this very notion that may already be dimly discerned in the contradictions of Wagner's discourse linking opera to metaphorical formulations of diverse sexualities and disease. It reemerges in the cinematic, aural, and visual vocabulary of *Philadelphia*.[10]

*   *   *

It was no coincidence that Wagner repeatedly used sexual terms to describe the difference between his revolutionary music drama and the grand opera he despised because, in his mind, as well as in the discourse of mid-nineteenth century Europe that his writings reflect, opera was linked to the visual and aural spectacle of the body, and hence to sexuality, as well as to disease. At the end of part one of his most celebrated tract on aesthetic revolution, *Oper und Drama* (1851), Wagner employs sexual metaphors that serve to portray him, and the artistic tradition in which he wished his works to be understood, as heterosexual, productive, and by implication, healthy. Music by itself, he claims, is a passive or "receptive" feminine organism, while poetry is its opposite, though equally gender-specific; it is a masculine art form (*Dichtungen* 7:112).[11] The conflation of the two leads to the creation of the superior work of art, the *Musikdrama*: "The organism of music is able to give birth to the true, living melody if it is inseminated [befruchtet] by the thought of the poet. Music is the one who gives birth; the poet is the one who sires" [Die Musik ist die Gebärerin, der Dichter der Erzeuger] (*Dichtungen* 7:114). It is precisely because, within this system of thought, music by itself is deemed "feminine" that Wagner goes to great lengths to perpetuate the notion of Beethoven (his avowed forerunner and model) as a "masculine" composer (and thereby builds upon the aforementioned polarization of the "feminine" Schubert and the Rhenish composer); he emphasizes the Viennese Classicist's development as one from that of a writer of instrumental, absolute music into the exalted creator of the Ninth Symphony, which, in its final movement, incorporates Schiller's (masculine) poetry into the spirit of (feminine) music. Wagner describes the German supercomposer thus:

> With Beethoven . . . we recognize the natural life-drive to give birth to melody out of the inner organism of music. In his most important works he by no means presents the melody as something already complete, but rather he allows it, so to speak, to be born before our eyes out of its organs; he initiates us into this act of birth. . . . But the most important thing that the Master finally proclaims to us in his main work is the necessity he feels as a musician to throw himself into the arms of the poet, in order to bring about the act of *procreation* [Zeugung] of the true, unfailingly real, and redeeming melody. In order to become a *human being* [Mensch], Beethoven had to become a total, that is, collective, human being subordinate to the conditions of *the masculine and the feminine* [*des Männlichen und Weiblichen*]. (*Dichtungen* 7:109–110)

Beethoven is able to actively (and heterosexually) "produce" precisely because, instead of focusing on one aesthetic form, his artistry successfully merges the "feminine" and the "masculine" elements that will later constitute, in Wagner's hands, the *Gesamtkunstwerk* of the future. The teleology of Wagner's description underscores the (re-)union of (once) distinct parts, his goal is the total, organic, "healthy" work. Thus, the sexual imagery of the project suggests that the coupling of male and female is superior, and more natural and productive, than any other model, be it of one art functioning in isolation (which would be unproductive and, by implication, onanistic), the merging of two manifestations of the same art form (which would be unproductive, same-sexual, and hence, for the nineteenth-century imagination receptive to these metaphors, unnatural), or any other model.

It is against the background of this vocabulary of heterosexual aesthetic procreation that Wagner's disparaging anti-Semitic comments on the inferior, Judaized, nineteenth-century grand opera should be understood, for that work—the Judaized opera—constitutes the negative model against which the music drama is for him defined, and it evokes in his discourse both sexual inferiority and disease. Central to his critique of Jews was Wagner's association of the foreigner with what he perceived to be the failings of the modern and, above all, decadent age. This was characterized for him by a purported lack of rootedness within the community; emphasis on the individual over the collective; the arbitrary exchangeability of the particular within the whole negating an "organic" cohesiveness that would justify the individual (in the *völkisch* society) or the aesthetic detail (in the work of art); and a decay, nervousness, and degeneration typical for Wagner of both the physiological makeup of the Jew and, metaphorically, of the modern work of art furthered by the institutions of the purportedly Jewish culture industry.[12] (In his essay "Modern" of 1878, Wagner stressed the affinity between the modern period and decay when he pointed out that the adverb *modern* in German — the emphasis of which lies on the second syllable — has its cognative equivalent in the verb *modern* — emphasis on the first syllable, which means "to rot" [*Gesammelte* 10:60]. The modern, Judaized decadent age is a time of artistic, physiological, and general cultural decay in Wagner's imagination.)

In a letter to Ferdinand Heine of 14 September 1850, Wagner expressed his "terrible disgust over the banker-music whoring" [furchtbaren ekel für die banquier-musikhurerei], a formulation conflating his hatred of both the Jews' prominence in finance and their success and influence in the music industry and, moreover, one that evoked the realm of diseased and dangerous sexuality in conjunction with a kind of opera that he despised.[13] Wagner underscored his association of such an artwork and such malignant and salacious danger when he described the difference between his own German works and the French and Italian grand operas by employing, for the latter, images of socially degraded and sexually active women. It is "base" women who represent in Wagner's theoretical reflections the different forms of modern (Judaized) opera: the Italian opera is a *Lustdirne* [prostitute] *(Dichtungen* 7:115), and French operatic music is a *Kokette* (*Dichtungen* VII:116); both metaphors resonate with implications of the realm of the *Franzosenkrankheit*, or the dreaded "French disease" of syphilis, which had been associated with France in the German imagination since the late fifteenth century.[14] Wagner's discourse links inferior opera to sexual deviance and disease. In "Aufklärungen über 'Das Judentum in der Musik' " [Elucidations on "Jewishness in music"] (1869) he made the connection even more explicit between the corrosive influence of the Jews on German art and their physiological nature: "Of one thing I am certain: just as the influence that the Jews have gained on our spiritual life, and as it manifests itself in the distraction and falsification of our highest artistic tendencies, is not a simple, perhaps even a purely physiological coincidence, so it must also be acknowledged as undeniable and decisive" (*Gesammelte* 8:259).

That Wagner associated the music drama and opera with two different kinds of bodies can be seen in his description, from the autobiographical "Eine Mitteilung an meine Freunde" [A communication to my friends] (1851), of his initial conception of the verse his superhero Siegfried would sing, which he conceived of as a rejection of the overly intellectual artwork that he associated with Jews. Siegfried's superior, "natural" verse was to be the antithesis of the physiologically inferior body of the intellectual, rational drama:

Just as this human being moved, so his spoken expression necessarily had to be; here the merely *rationally conceived* [gedachte] modern verse with its fleeting, bodyless shape [mit seiner verschwebenden, körperlosen Gestalt] no longer sufficed; the fantastical deception of the end-rhymes no longer was able as apparent flesh to disguise the absence of all living bone structure, which this verse-body contains within itself as a work comprised of an arbitrarily expandable, disintegrating compilation of cartilage [Schleimknorpelwerk]. . . . At the primeval mythical spring, where I found the youthfully beautiful human being Siegfried, I also found automatically the sensually perfected linguistic expression in which alone this human being could express himself. It was the . . . *alliterative verse* [der . . . stabgereimte Vers] in which the *Volk* itself once created poetry, when it was still poet and creator of myths. (*Dichtungen* 6:308–9)

Here, two kinds of musical artworks—the preferred German music drama and the despised French or Italian opera—are associated with polarized images of the human body, one muscular, lithe, and healthy (and, in their dramatic representations, heterosexual), and the other weak, pale, and degenerated (and in their dramatic representations associated with suspicious sexualities). (It is not for nothing that Otto Weininger, writing at the close of the decadent period, would equate Jewishness with femininity and describe *Siegfried* in that context as "the most un-Jewish thing imaginable" [das Unjüdischeste . . . was erdacht werden konnte] (404). Little wonder, then, that it was in just these terms—in the music's purportedly dangerous affinity with, and even effect on, the body—that Wagner's art was perceived until the end of the nineteenth century.[15] By that time, the link between opera and physiology was firmly established in the cultural vocabulary of Europe.

Because of his sexual characterization of superior artistic creation as constituting a merging of the feminine and the masculine, Wagner is able to imply that the artist working solely with an individual aesthetic form is somehow lacking in something, is impoverished, and therefore, by implication, is sterile and/or deviant. It is precisely in these terms that Wagner describes the Semitic work. For Wagner, Meyerbeer, Halévy, and Mendelssohn—for him, representatives of the successful artistic Jew in the modern, decadent age—are sexually a world removed from the procreative, formative power of a Beethoven and the future Master of Bayreuth. They are unable to engage in musical-poetic union, insemination, and birth, the metaphorical-heterosexual act. He writes in *Oper und Drama*: "The superficialities of art have been made [in the works of Meyerbeer] into its essence; and we recognize this essence to be—the effect, the absolute effect, i.e., the stimulation of an artificially enticed titillation, without the activity of a true enjoyment [or act] of love" [den Reiz eines künstlich entlockten Liebeskitzels, ohne die Tätigkeit eines wirklichen Liebesgenusses] (*Dichtungen* 7: 102). The Jewish composer cannot merge the poetic and the musical, denigrating the former and focusing instead on the latter, on the *feminine*. Meyerbeer especially views his librettist Scribe as a subordinate in the process of composing an opera, according to Wagner, and thus Meyerbeer's own musical production remains impoverished and impotent (*Dichtungen* 7:95–105), because, metaphorically speaking, the Jewish composer is exclusively concerned with music, not with the procreative, generating power of words; his is a solely "feminine" artistry, grounded in the immutable destiny of his inferior racial and sexual physiology. The Jew's music, so to speak, cannot rise to the occasion of the generative-productive act.

It would be senseless, within this system of thought, to conceive of poetry as a "feminine" art or of music as "masculine." And yet, Wagner argues, that is precisely what the Jew repeatedly does. Wagner claims that "the secret of the sterility of modern [= Jewish] music" lies in its desire to have music "not only give birth, but also to sire" [nicht nur gebären, sondern auch zeugen]," which he calls "the height of madness" and associates, again, explicitly with Meyerbeer (*Dichtungen* 7:114). In "Das Kunstwerk der Zukunft" [The artwork of the future] of 1849, Wagner had already evoked the polarization of the *Volk* as fertile and the Jew as sterile in a passage describing a threat to the future of the German people:

Thus the Volk will bring about redemption by being sufficient unto itself and at the same time by redeeming its own enemies. . . . As long as the conditions [for the domination of the Volk by its enemies] exist, as long as they [its enemies] suck their life's blood from the wasted strength of the Volk, as long as they — themselves unable to sire [selbst zeugungsunfähig] — devour to no end the fertility of the *Volk* in their egotistical existence — then for just as long all interpreting, creating, changing, improving, and reforming of these conditions will be arbitrary, pointless and fruitless. (*Dichtungen* 6:21)

And similarly, in "Das Judentum in der Musik" [Jewishness in music] of 1850, Wagner makes explicit the connection between race and "production" (a term loaded with sexual connotations): "Historically we must characterize the period of Jewishness in modern music," he claims, "as that of perfected unproductivity" (*Gesammelte* 5:79).

Not all of Wagner's sexual imagery, used in his discussions of aesthetic matters, suggests immutable, essentialist states, however. It is precisely the discrepancy between sexuality as an innate, biologically grounded condition (inherent in the characterization of the artworks as Jewish and feminine) and sexuality as one of a set of distinct, performative, culturally defined identities and acts (inherent in the characterization of a kind of art as masturbatory) that emerges in Wagner's discourse. In a passage from "Eine Mitteilung an meine Freunde," such a description of music emerges metaphorically. Here, Wagner states that the modern Jewish artwork is not only feminine but, within the moral parameters of his culture, something even more pointedly insulting, yet, by implication at least, not without its potential remedy:

That which determines the artist as such are . . . the purely artistic impressions; if his power of reception [Empfängniskraft] is completely absorbed by them, so that the life-impressions to be felt later find his ability already exhausted, he will thus develop as an *absolute* artist in the direction which we must solely describe as the feminine, that is, the feminine element of art. In this we find all the artists whose activity nowadays actually constitutes the function of modern art; it is an art world fundamentally separated from life, *in which art only plays with itself* [sie ist die vom Leben schlechtweg abgesonderte Kunstwelt, *in welcher die Kunst mit sich selbst spielt*]. (*Dichtungen* 6:217; my emphasis)

Here, the artist of the modern world is not only both feminine and unproductive but also locked in a l'art-pour-l'art, masturbatory game of self-absorption with no ties to the community and to the "real" world, an "exhausted" artist whose intermittent sexual indulgences inform his diseased body and inferior aesthetics.

Students of the nineteenth century know that to the popular imagination of that time, onanism (masturbation) was a debased and reprehensible activity, but it was also an indulgence that could be remedied through abstinence.[16] That is, onanism was defined not in essentialist terms as a physiologically determined state (though it led to physiological debilitation) but as an activity resulting in conditions (deteriorating eyesight, pallor, loss of strength and mental acuity, and a weakening of the spinal cord, among others) that could be countered through a determined act of will, through abstinence or heterosexual intercourse.[17] It is precisely this glimmer of hope, based on a mutable notion of sexuality, which emerges in the texts documenting Wagner's relationship to Nietzsche.

It is well known that Nietzsche's complicated and ambivalent feelings about Wagner were in part influenced by his own feeble attempts at musical composition, by his status as a failed composer. For anyone living in a culture such as theirs, which assigned sexual meaning to aesthetic material, success or failure at artistic "production" carried with it undertones of a sexual nature as well.[18] And indeed, on more than one occasion Wagner implied that there was a link between Nietzsche's failings as a composer and the philosopher's deteriorating health and sexual identity. In 1874, he made the rather strange remark, recorded by Cosima Wagner in her diary, that Nietzsche "should either marry or compose an opera, though doubtless the latter would be such that it would never get produced, and so would not bring him into contact with life" (1:749; entry of 4 April 1874). The statement resonates with sexual implications. Within the motivic-metaphorical vocabulary of the cultural imagination of the time, to marry or to compose could be construed as comparable activities, and the success of such endeavors is measured by the degree to which they are deemed procreative — by their production of children or by the emergence of an artwork that is accepted by, and functions in, its community. (It is no coincidence that the libretto to *Die Meistersinger von Nürnberg*, the music drama most explicitly concerned with the future of German art, repeatedly describes artworks as children. Aesthetics evoked sexuality for Wagner, reflected in his use of the concept of production.) Such a union and such an artwork — as healthy and accepted — would constitute the positive models against which decadence, as a movement resisting the ethic of production and widespread consumption and associated with epithets of disease and nonheterosexual activity, would later be defined.

But already in Wagner's characterizations of the Jew, both as a racial foreigner and as the creator of an onanistic artwork, there is a tension between essentialist and constructivist categories, because, as a member of a race, the Jew's identity is physiologically determined, while one's status as an onanist, though replete for the nineteenth-century imagination with connotations of physiological danger, disease, and potential decay, was determined by a voluntary activity and hence by a kind of sexuality that could be modified. (This tension between contradictory notions of identity informs Wagner's ambiguous remarks concerning the efficacy, and even the possibility, of assimilation in solving "the Jewish problem." The essentialist would find conversion and assimilation no remedy to the physiological state of the Jew, while the constructivist would view assimilation as the sole path to the eradication of the Jew's "difference." Both positions are implied in Wagner's discourse to differing degrees at different times.) Thus it is significant that, when faced with the facts of Nietzsche's deteriorating health and the philosopher's concomitant growing criticism of the Wagnerian project, Wagner chose to characterize his wayward friend not as a man whose deviance and disease were immutably determined — not as, say, syphilitic or effeminate — but as an *onanist* — this time not metaphorically, but in a long and meddling letter of 23 October 1877 to Dr. Otto Eiser, Nietzsche's physician and friend, in which Wagner expressed his conviction that Nietzsche's deteriorating health was due to masturbation! "In my attempts to assess N.'s condition," he writes,

I have been thinking for some time of identical and very similar experiences which I recall having had with certain young men of great intellectual ability. I saw them being destroyed by similar symptoms, and discovered only too clearly that these symptoms were the result of masturbation. . . . One thing that struck me as being of great importance was the news that I recently received to the effect that the doctor whom N. had consulted in Naples some time ago advised him first and foremost — to get married.[19]

Marriage emerges here, as in the statement to Cosima regarding Nietzsche's imaginary opera, as the counter to something else that is deemed inferior — in the one case masturbation, and in the other, the creation of an impoverished, unproduceable, and by implication onanistic opera. Here, Wagner continued to associate aesthetics (both Nietzsche's criticism of Wagner's music dramas and Nietzsche's comparable inferiority as a composer) with sexuality and decay, but he vouchsafed Nietzsche a chance for redemption and a return to the healthy Wagnerian fold that he withheld from his Jewish foes when he characterized them as producing sterile works and as being essentially female. In each case, sexuality, disease, and art merge and form a constellation, part of a widespread discourse, from which would emerge the binary oppositions that decadence would critique at the close of the nineteenth century, but that would continue to inform the popular perception of opera as an extravagant aesthetic project. The tension between the two categories of sexuality—one essentialist, one constructivist—imbues Wagner's discourse and that of the post-Wagnerian age, both in Nietzsche's more self-reflexive, ironic writings and in the rhetoric of those who would follow.

*   *   *

I would like now to juxtapose this discursive analysis of material from the nineteenth century with an examination of the scene from *Philadelphia* in which the protagonist, a gay man dying of AIDS, describes an aria from the 1896 opera *Andrea Chénier* by Umberto Giordano, set in Paris during the French Revolution. Here, through its evocation of France and Italy in the narrative of the aria and the language of the opera's libretto, a visual text from the late twentieth century associates the diseased body and a minoritized sexuality with the very countries that Wagner had viewed as the locus of an inferior aesthetics of modern opera, sensuality, and physiological decay (and that Nietzsche later ironically championed as the locus of a salvation from the dangers of Wagner's "feminine," "impotent," "degenerate," and masturbatory aesthetics).[20]

Time and again, it is this scene which has been singled out for scrutiny in reviews, interviews, and discussions of the movie, and it is generally accepted that it was the performance of this scene which earned Tom Hanks the Oscar for best actor in a leading role from a film released in 1993 (and indeed, it was this scene that was shown at the Oscar ceremony to commemorate Hank's entire performance).[21] Obviously there is something about this scene that makes it appear both appropriate and persuasive to contemporary audiences. My argument will be that it is the cinematic conflation of images of a sexuality deemed deviant, disease, and opera that exploits and hence makes apparent and perpetuates this conflation, which has been within western culture at least since the middle of the nineteenth century, and that it is this nexus of associations which makes the cinematic passage appear so powerful today. In addition, I will also suggest that the film sets up a tension between essentialist and constructivist definitions of sexuality that masks a deeper essentialist model underlying the associative nexus.

The scene takes place in Andrew Beckett's loft apartment following a gay party, a flamboyant costume ball to which Joe Miller has come with his wife. After the party, Joe remains to discuss courtroom strategy for Andrew's impending testimony in a lawsuit they are bringing for wrongful termination, but Andrew is unable to concentrate and, instead, puts on a recording of Maria Callas singing "La mamma morta." As the aria unfolds, Andrew attempts to explain to Joe his passion for the musical-dramatic situation. As he does so—accompanied throughout by his I.V. as a constant visual reminder of his physical deterioration—his identification with the figure of Maddalena—a noblewoman orphaned, made destitute by the French Revolution, and in love with the poet Andrea Chénier—and his pleasure in the music increase to such intensity that they verge on intoxication. The musicologist Mitchell Morris has provided a cogent analysis of what follows:

As the music continues, Andrew becomes more and more involved in a performance that moves somewhere between a music appreciation lecture, a translation (from the music and from the Italian), and a lip-synch. . . . Andrew solicits Joe's engagement by asking for specific responses, drawing attention to salient musical gestures and timbres, translating and quoting the text, and modeling appropriate emotional reactions. These different acts constantly bleed into one another, tending to dissolve into a generalized arioso speaking. The film marks this lyrical interpolation off from the rest of the film, first by asymmetrical camera angles, and then by a (melo)dramatic shift in the lighting which, when finally displaced by the shift back to normal lighting at the end of the music, heightens the unreality of the segment.[22]

Like Morris, a number of critics have drawn attention to the "swirling camera" that "Demme swings . . . over Hanks's head" and that "swoons," producing "fancy camera angles" and a "literally condescending view of Beckett" as the scene is infused with a crimson color.[23] Clearly the "generalized arioso speaking" of which Morris writes, together with the dramatic juxtapositions of idiosyncratic camera angles and lighting, serve to fashion an identification between Andrew and the operatic material of which he speaks, which is also established if the viewing audience perceives an intertextual connection between the lighting of the cinematic narration and the scene that Maddalena narrates. (Some have seen the "brazen scarlet light" in which Andrew is bathed as an "imitation of the flames of the aria.")[24] Furthermore, the conflation of the high camera angle and the infusion of red could be said to evoke the iconography of disease, in that the angle of the shot can be seen to make Andrew into a subject of observation. It is as if he were subjected to our (micro)scopic scrutiny, an implication (of Andrew as the diseased individual) reinforced by the crimson color, which may remind the viewer not only of flames but also emphatically of *blood* (a word that he quotes in narrating and explaining the aria), especially since Andrew is nothing in this film if not the embodiment of the AIDS victim, to such an extent that his identity as an opera-loving homosexual and as diseased are presented as one and the same phenomenon, not only here, moreover, but throughout the film. It is no coincidence that the color red is inserted into the scene at the very moment that Andrew translating Maddalena's text, exclaims, "Live still! I am life!" for the audience knows that he will soon die; the carmine blush of his face underscores both his passion and the decay to which he is subject. The musicologist Carolyn Abbate has drawn attention to the pervasive acoustical metaphors in nineteenth-century opera that function as equivalents to the human body — a phenomenon that she describes, quite felicitously, as "the opera body" (112, 138) — and it reemerges in this scene in *Philadelphia*, both in the tremulous string passages in Giordano's orchestral score and in the rosy and swirling visual text so evocative of physiological interiority. Opera and the body — as the locus of both decay and sex — merge seamlessly here.

What's more, these optical and auditory metaphors for disease also function as a metaphor for the difference of the insightful, fanciful, or poetic imagination, and they thereby imply, through a host of associations, a subtext of meaning suggesting that the privileged space of such fantasy — and of aesthetics per se — is linked to physiological decay, a notion that certainly must count as the ideological trope par excellence of the decadent age. It's not for nothing that Des Esseintes's and Marcel's pallor and physical frailty conjoin with their aesthetic interests in the works of Huysmans and Proust, nor that it is an aesthetic object that marks the closeted physiological decay of Dorian Gray in a work that has been called the hallmark of the decadent age, nor that Mann's Hanno Buddenbrook is undone by playing a Wagnerian rhapsody so reminiscent of the sexually explicit music from one of the most celebrated artworks of the nineteenth century, *Tristan und Isolde*.

Both the film's critics and its supporters have drawn attention to the link this scene portrays (and thereby perpetuates) between gays and opera, and it is an issue that the film forces us to address.[25] Those who fault the scene would no doubt take even greater offence were they to examine the link between opera, homosexuality, and disease that actually emerges throughout the film as a whole, for it has been prepared long before the extravagant rhapsody involving *Andrea Chénier*. The first time the cinematic audience hears opera is also the moment it first learns that Andrew is ill, for the sounds of an operatic recording to which Andrew is listening accompany the first close-up image the audience sees of an I.V. affixed to his arm. The scene takes place in a hospital, and it is clear that such infusions have become a routine part of the man's life; Andrew sits calmly working as the fluid drips into his system, and the camera slowly pans around the room to show other men, many in pairs, emaciated and obviously seriously ill, whose images provide insight into the nature of Andrew's illness and the later trajectory of the film's plot. The connection between disease, opera, and homosexuality is immediately established. It is reinforced the second time the audience hears opera on the filmic soundtrack, when Andrew's lover, Miguel, discovers that an I.V. isn't working because a vein has collapsed in Andrew's arm. A discussion ensues regarding both the advisability of continuing the treatment and the frustrating nature of their relationship owing to Miguel's fears that Andrew will die. That is, it is not simply Andrew's demonstrated *taste* for opera that is displayed by these scenes, but his *identi-*

fication with it, as both gay and ill, through a repeated presentation of the artwork within a consistent associative nexus that appears appropriate to an audience in the early 1990s.

Andrew's identication with opera appears inaccessible and mysterious, however, to his heterosexual, black, healthy attorney, who stares in bewilderment (literally and figuratively unilluminated) at his client's (rose-colored) rhapsody. The juxtaposition of Andrew's gay attributes as diseased and esoteric versus Joe's signs of health and heterosexuality are also consistently prepared throughout the film. It is not for nothing that the opera scene opens with Andrew asking Joe what he prays for, because the exchange allows the filmmakers to underscore Joe's macho nature by having him reply that he prays for "the Phillies [to] win the penant," and shortly thereafter, when asked if he likes opera, he distinguishes between his interests and those of the gay man by claiming, "I am not that familiar with opera, Andrew." The juxtaposition of homosexual and heterosexual thus finds its cultural counterpart in that of opera and sports. The polarization of gay versus straight and operatic versus nonoperatic men makes sense to our culture because it has a long tradition and is based on other attendant polarities, the most important of which in this context, in terms of its subliminally persuasive iconographic rhetoric, is that of disease versus health.

The polarity of the opera-loving, sick, and gay man versus the aesthetically unenlightened, healthy, and straight man also merges with the binary oppositions of high versus low culture and the racial categories of white and black. Joe Miller can only look on in bewilderment as Andrew waxes operatic, and given his characterization up to this point in the film as outspokenly homophobic, athletic, and the proud father of a newborn girl, his lack of access to the musical-dramatic realm with which Andrew identifies is nothing if not culturally consistent. Certainly, American culture's discomfort with European culture — discernible, for example, in the Metropolitan Opera's compensatory need to package its elitist product through association with such popular icons as Miss Piggy and through the inane trivia quizzes of its broadcast intermissions so reminiscent of TV game shows — provides one cultural explanation for the film's (and for its audience's) need to situate opera in a realm removed from everyday cultural experience, in the realm of the exotic, identified here also as the locus of a deviant sexuality. Moreover, the cultural stereotypes linking people of color to jazz, blues, rap, and other kinds of (hetero-) "sexualized" music place Joe on one side of a divide not unlike that separating what Nietzsche described as the healthy "African cheerfulness" of Bizet from the diseased, intoxicating, feminine sensuality of Wagner in the philosopher's writings,[26] which itself simply perpetuated the split between German music's masculinity and heterosexuality versus French and Italian opera's femininity and impotence in Wagner's rhetoric. The discursive continuity between the age of the Nietzsche-Wagner exchange and the film illuminates the perpetuation of rhetorical paradigms that link the early modernist era (during which decadence was defined and theorized) and our current, purportedly destabilized, and hence less monolithic era of postmodernism. That is, despite the often-touted shifts in aesthetic paradigms that would distinguish between the ideologies of these two fins de siècle, a perpetuation of a given cultural vocabulary may be seen to demonstrate often tenacious links between the culture(s) of the mid-nineteenth century and today.

Furthermore, if the opera scene draws upon and perpetuates a culturally rooted association of sexuality, disease, and music drama, then the tensions inherent in the shift circa 1870 that Foucault describes — from the notion of sexuality as defined by acts to an essentialist category — could be said to inform the cinematic scene as well. And indeed, *Philadelphia* suggests that Andrew Beckett is somehow *innately* "operatic," rather than someone whose relationship to opera is transient or intermittent; the movie presents his identification with the art form not as an acquired taste or as an act but as an affinity, as itself one of the markers of his identity. His love for opera is so culturally constructed as to be viewed (perhaps even by himself) as second nature, as so strongly or overly determined as to appear immutable, and thus as comparable to his sexuality. The fact that the film presents the association as unquestioned, unproblematized, and as somehow automatically appropriate constitutes the ideological agenda of the culture it reflects, which constructs and assigns identity to individuals and then, when ideologically advantageous, deems such identity naturally determined. In so doing, the film reenacts the late nineteenth-century invention of the category of sexual identity as physiologically, rather than collectively, determined, and at the same time it perpetuates the same markers of such identity that the late nineteenth century had assigned to the sexual deviant: it associates him with a diseased body and with a kind of art representing difference.

As an ideological construct, however, the film wants to have it both ways: it reinforces polar oppositions through a consistent use of visual images, dialogue, and music, and it seeks to efface the binarisms separating the diseased, extravagant homosexual from the healthy, mundane heterosexual through a message of universal love. This is particularly the case in those few moments when the operatic music is employed nondiegetically, or as music not presented through mechanical or performative means to the figures in the film — that is, not as music to which these figures listen, such as in the opera scene (which is diegetic music, in this case played on a stereophonic recording, or in the earlier hospital scene, on a Sony Walkman) — but on the soundtrack, where it is available to the audience, but not necessarily, at least, to the film's protagonists.[27] Divorced from the means of its production, the nondiegetic, audience-directed music can function as a commentary on the events within scenes or as a representation of the protagonists' thoughts and auditory memories. When it does so, it provides insight into the meaning of opera in the film.

Two nondiegetic moments are significant for an understanding of the ideological function of opera in *Philadelphia*. The first occurs immediately after the scene with the aria, when Miller leaves Beckett's apartment. He is clearly embarrassed, but also quite moved, and this is significant, for up until this point in the film he has consistently been portrayed as homophobic and only grudgingly willing to concede that even homosexuals deserve legal rights. After the opera scene, however, he stops in the hallway outside Beckett's apartment and considers going back in, perhaps afraid that he has been too brusque in his exit. As he does so, there is for a moment an indeterminacy of sound, for the audience hears the strains of the beginning of Maddalena's aria, but does not know if it is being played or if Miller only recalls it. For a moment it is unclear whether the music is diegetic or nondiegetic. But then the audience realizes that Beckett has begun to play the aria again on his stereo. In the scene that follows, this indeterminacy manifestly moves into the realm of musical commentary, or the nondiegetic, through which we are allowed to hear what Miller may be listening to in a passage of interior auditory recollection divorced from the explicit connection between Andrew and opera established by the diegetic production of phonograph records. As this new scene unfolds, Miller drives home, embraces his sleeping daughter, and, clearly moved, lies down on his bed next to his wife, accompanied throughout by the aria from *Andrea Chénier* played on the soundtrack, but not on a recording within the scene. Clearly we are to assume that the music on the soundtrack is that which Miller recalls — it's what he's thinking of — and the intertextual connection between the mother's love in the aria and his love for his own daughter and wife suggests that, for the first time in the film, this music — and its message of love — is applicable not only to the homosexual but to Miller as well. For the first and only time, it has crossed the gap separating sexual orientation and become a vehicle for compassion and understanding ostensibly available to all, a purportedly universal construct that allows him to feel pity for the man so different from himself.

This is an ideologically powerful moment, because such a construct — of insight into the particular that is available to the universal — ultimately reinforces the difference it purports to transcend: it is based on the specific link between opera, homosexuality, and disease that it now seeks to disavow, a fact that is borne out by the plot. It is clearly through the opera scene, and the insight it has provided into the foreign, homosexual psyche, that Miller is finally able to feel compassion for the man he had hitherto perceived as so sexually and physiologically dangerous and alien. But when we see Beckett for the last time, following the trial and shortly before his death, he is shown lying in a hospital bed listening again to his beloved opera recordings through earphones connected to his Walkman. The diegetic music returns as an acoustical corollary to images of decay and marginalized sexual identity, and while one could argue that the filmic construct places the audience in a position similar to that of Miller following the opera scene — the fact that we have nondiegetic access to the music he recalls suggests as much — that music must return as Beckett's signature tune, because it has never ceased to function as such in a nexus that the film has previously attempted to disavow even as it ultimately reinforces it. In this way, the film's brief departures from the otherwise pervasive link between Beckett's sexual identity and his love for opera emerge as little more than gestures revealing the very tension within the essentialist/constructivist debate discernible in Wagner's discourse of the mid-nineteenth century. And beneath this tension, based on the binarisms that the decadent movement thematized and provocatively confronted, lies a set of apparently unquestioned oppositions linked to the portrayal of Beckett's identity as decadent, gay, diseased, and operatic, all of which emerge as signs of an immutable destiny. (In this context it bears mentioning that, within a recent discussion of decadence, AIDS has been described as the result of "self-inflicted injuries," a particularly pernicious perpetuation of tropes from the nineteenth century linking disease to voluntary cultural collapse.[28] According to this view, the decadent seeks self-destructive intoxication, and hence is responsible for his demise, but such a view also underscores the contradiction between viewing homosexuality sometimes as essentially determined and sometimes as the result of a willful, autonomous decision.)

It would be tempting to compare the ideological function of opera in this highly successful film with that of newer products from the Hollywood factory, such as *The Shawshank Redemption*, which concerns a relationship between a black man and a white man, homosexuality, and a connection between the privileged Caucasian and the European music drama, as manifested in the scene in which the prisoner played by Tim Robbins breaks into an office and plays a recording of *Le Nozze di Figaro* over the loudspeaker system of the prison. For I am not suggesting that opera always and only signifies the associations I have discussed here — in *The Shawshank Redemption* it clearly departs from them, though it emerges within a context that places the artwork not far from their concerns. Rather, *Philadelphia* demonstrates particularly forcefully, I think, many of the assumptions that *may* function less explicitly elsewhere when opera functions in our modern cinematic accomplishments, which are so dependent on, and constitutive of, our cultural universe.

If opera can be seen as still evoking the ideologies that attended physiology in the late nineteenth century, and if its link to notions of sexual difference and disease may thereby be questioned or deemed not automatic but culturally constructed, such insight may serve, in some small way, to deconstruct some of the assumptions that we have inherited from the last fin de siècle and that, to a remarkable degree, continue to inform our own. Such a change in the perception and cultural function of opera, however, would have to be the subject of a film very different from *Philadelphia* and one less likely to win Oscars.

Notes

1. See Richard Gilman; Thomas Whissen; Linda Williams. On the conflation of sexuality and disease in the decadent movement see Bram Dijkstra. On music and decadence see also Robert Sinai.

2. On the similarity between images of the diseased individual prior to the twentieth century and those of the AIDS patient today, see Sander L. Gilman, *Disease and Representation* (245–72).

3. See, for example, Sander L. Gilman, "Strauss, the Pervert, and Avant-Garde Opera of the Fin de Siècle," reprinted in expanded form in *Disease and Representation* (155–81); Susan McClary, *Feminine Endings*; and Linda and Michael Hutcheon. Further examples of examinations into sexuality and opera are: Philip Brett; Catherine Clement; Wayne Koestenbaum; Ralph P. Locke; Susan McClary, *Georges Bizet*; Richard D. Mohr (129–218); and a number of the essays found in Richard Dellamora and Daniel Fischlin (eds.).

4. See Carolyn Abbate; Jean-Jacques Nattiez, "Le Ring comme histoire metaphorique de la musique" and *Music and Discourse*; Rose Rosengard Subotnik; David J. Levin.

5. See Susan McClary, "Constructions of Subjectivity in Schubert's Music" and "Manliness in Music."

6. On the ideological associations attending music in the cultural vocabulary of the fin de siècle, see my *Undertones of Insurrection* (esp. 5–21).

7. See Franz Habšck; Angus Heriot; John Rosselli.

8. Eve Kosofsky Sedgwick adds to this list of oppositions the binarisms of secrecy/disclosure, knowledge/ignorance, majority/minority, innocence/initiation, natural/artificial, new/old, discipline/terrorism, canonic/noncanonic, wholeness/decadence, urbane/provincial, domestic/foreign, same/different, active/ passive, in/out, cognition/paranoia, art/kitsch, utopia/apocalypse, sincerity/sentimentality, and voluntary/addiction. See Sedgwick 11, 72.

9. See also Randolph Trumbach.

10. For a discussion of homosexuality and opera see Wayne Koestenbaum; Lawrence D. Mass.

11. Unless otherwise noted, all translations from Wagner are my own, but I should like to thank Antje Petersen for her advice on renderings into English of Wagner's more idiosyncratic and mind-boggling passages. For more extensive discussions of images of sexuality in Wagner, see my *Richard Wagner and the Anti-Semitic Imagination*. My thanks to Dr. Douglas Clayton, the Humanities Editor of the University of Nebraska Press, for permission to adapt material from the book for use in this essay.

12. In his notorious essay "Das Judentum in der Musik" [Jewishness in music] (1850), Wagner states emphatically that the Jews' financial control of European cultural institutions had come to corrupt public taste and hence the public reception of music: "That the impossibility to further create natural, necessary, and true beauty without completely changing the basis of the level to which the development of art has now advanced has brought the public taste in art under the mercantile fingers of the Jews, for that we have now to examine the causes" (*Gesammelte* 5:68). Borchmeyer omits "Das Judentum in der Musik," as well as particularly explicit anti-Semitic essays from his edition of Wagner's writings.

13. Richard Wagner, *Sämtliche Briefe* (3:406–9 [#106]), here 408. Wagner often adopted the affectation of writing nouns in lower case.

14. See Sander L. Gilman, *Disease and Representation* (248–50); see also Linda and Michael Hutcheon (22–23, 77–83, 96–99, 102–4, 109–13, 117–18).

15. The standard work on Wagner's influence on the literature of decadence, which discusses at length the notion that hearing Wagner's music was dangerous to the body, remains Erwin Koppen. See also Jean Pierrot (54, 192–93, 204).

16. The best overview of the nineteenth-century understanding of onanism is to be found in E. H. Hare.

17. Given the widespread assumption that the body would be irreparably damaged by the debilitating effects of premature and solitary sexual indulgence, many physicians in the nineteenth century came to believe that any heterosexual sex would be preferable to onanism, a notion that can be traced at least to the beginning of the eighteenth century. For example, see Simon-André Tisson (45). On occasion, nineteenth-century physicians went so far as to advise (male) masturbators to engage in intercourse with prostitutes or a mistress; such a practice forms the background to Wagner's remarks (discussed below) concerning the advice of Nietzsche's Italian physician that Nietzsche should marry.

18. On the relationship between the two men see Wilhelm Stekel; Dietrich Fischer-Dieskau; Luitpold Griesser; Roger Hollinrake; and Martin Vogel.

19. The letter was first published in an appendix to Curt von Westernhagen (527–29); it was republished in Richard Wagner, *Briefe* (597–98: #193). See also Richard Wagner, *Selected Letters of Richard Wagner* (873–74). On Wagner's correspondence with Eiser, see Robert W. Gutman (360); Dietrich Fischer-Dieskau (159); Dieter Schickling (74); Martin Gregor-Dellin (451–56); Martin Vogel (294–98); and my *Richard Wagner and the Anti-Semitic Imagination* (336–42).

20. See Nietzsche (15, 16, 18, 19, 25, 28, 32, 130, 134).

21. Owing to the fact that Maria Callas performs the aria in the recording played in the film, a National Public Radio reporter discussed the scene with Wayne Koestenbaum, who has written of a homosexual Callas cult. Transcript of the interview from 9 February 1994, *All Things Considered* (13–14). See also Stanley Kaufmann; Brian D. Johnson; Andrew Sullivan.

22. I would like to thank Mitchell Morris for providing me with a copy of "Aspects of the Coming-Out Aria," a paper he presented in December 1994 at the Modern Language Association Conference in San Diego that offers a lucid and thought-provoking analysis of the opera scene in *Philadelphia*.

23. See James M. Wall; David Denby; Stuart Klawans; John Simon; Roy Grundmann and Peter Sacks.

24. See John Simon and David Denby.

25. See especially John Simon and David Denby.

26. Nietzsche (10). On the tradition of this motivic connection between blacks and "sexual" music in German culture see my *Undertones of Insurrection* (121–34).

27. On diegesis and sexuality, see Mary Ann Doane; Linda Williams (122).

28. See Peter H. Van Ness (90).

Works Cited

Abbate, Carolyn. *Unsung Voices: Opera and Musical Narrative in the Nineteenth Century.* Princeton: Princeton University Press, 1991.

All Things Considered. Transcript of interview with Wayne Koestenbaum from 9 February 1994. National Public Radio.

Brett, Philip. "Musicality, Essentialism, and the Closet." *Queering the Pitch*. Ed. Philip Brett et al. 9–26.

Brett, Philip, Elizabeth Wood, and Gary C. Thomas, eds. *Queering the Pitch: The New Gay and Lesbian Musicology*. New York: Routledge, 1994.

Clement, Catherine. *Opera, or The Undoing of Woman*. Trans. Betsy Wing. Minneapolis: University of Minnesota Press, 1988.

— Dellamora, Richard, and Daniel Fischlin, eds. *The Work of Opera: Genre, Nationhood, and Sexual Difference*. New York: Columbia University Press, 1997.

Denby, David. "Philadelphia." *New York* (3 January 1994): 52.

— Dijkstra, Bram. *Idols of Perversity: Fantasies of Feminine Evil in Fin-de-Siècle Culture*. New York: Oxford University Press, 1986.

Doane, Mary Ann. "The Voice in the Cinema: The Articulation of Body and Space." *Cinema/Sound* (special issue). *Yale French Studies* 60 (1980): 30–50.

— Fischer-Dieskau, Dietrich. *Wagner and Nietzsche*. Trans. Joachim Neugroschel. New York: Seabury, 1976.

— Foucault, Michel. *The History of Sexuality*. Vol. 1. Trans. Robert Hurley. New York: Random House, 1990.

Gilman, Richard. *Decadence: the Strange Life of an Epithet*. New York: Farrar, Straus and Giroux, 1979.

Gilman, Sander L. *Disease and Representation: Images of Illness from Madness to AIDS*. Ithaca: Cornell University Press, 1988.

— ———. "Strauss, the Pervert, and Avant-Garde Opera of the Fin de Siècle." *New German Critique* 43 (Winter 1988): 35–68.

— Gregor-Dellin, Martin. *Richard Wagner: His Life, his Work, his Century*. Trans. J. Maxwell Brownjohn. New York: Harcourt Brace Jovanovich, 1983.

Griesser, Luitpold. *Nietzsche und Wagner: Neue Beiträge zur Geschichte und Psychologie ihrer Freundschaft*. Vienna: G. Freytag, 1923.

Grundmann, Roy, and Peter Sacks. "Philadelphia." *Cineaste* 20 (Summer 1993): 51.

— Gutman, Robert W. *Richard Wagner: The Man, His Mind, and His Music*. 2d ed. New York: Harcourt Brace Jovanovich, 1990.

Habšck, Franz. *Die Kastraten und ihre Gesangkunst*. Berlin: Deutsche Verlagsanstalt Stuttgart, 1927.

— Hare, E. H. "Masturbatory Insanity: The History of an Idea." *Journal of Mental Science* 108.452 (1962): 2–25.

Heriot, Angus. *The Castrati in Opera*. London: Da Capo, 1975.

— Hollinrake, Roger. *Nietzsche, Wagner and the Philosophy of Pessimism*. London: Allen and Unwin, 1982.

Hutcheon, Linda, and Michael Hutcheon. *Opera: Desire, Disease, Death*. Lincoln: University of Nebraska Press, 1996.

Johnson, Brian D. "Philadelphia." *Maclean's* (27 December 1993): 61.

Kaufmann, Stanley. "Philadelphia." *New Republic* (10 January 1994): 30.

Klawans, Stuart. "Philadelphia." *Nation* (3 January 1994): 31.

Koestenbaum, Wayne. *The Queen's Throat: Opera, Homosexuality, and the Mystery of Desire*. New York: Poseidon, 1993.

Koppen, Erwin. *Dekadenter Wagnerismus: Studien zur europäischen Literatur des Fin de Siècle*. Berlin: de Gruyter, 1974.

Levin, David J., ed. *Opera Through Other Eyes*. Stanford: Stanford University Press, 1994.

Locke, Ralph P. "Constructing the oriental 'Other': Saint-Saëns's Samson et Dalila." *Cambridge Opera Journal* 3.3 (November 1991): 261–302.

McClary, Susan. "Constructions of Subjectivity in Schubert's Music." In *Queering the Pitch*, ed. Brett Philip et al., 205–33.

————. *Feminine Endings: Music, Gender, and Sexuality.* Minneapolis: University of Minnesota Press, 1990.

————. *Georges Bizet: Carmen.* Cambridge: Cambridge University Press, 1992.

————. "Manliness in Music." *Musical Times* (1 August 1989): 461.

Mass, Lawrence D. *Confessions of a Jewish Wagnerite: Being Gay and Jewish in America.* London: Cassell, 1994.

Mohr, Richard D. *Gay Ideas: Outing and Other Controversies.* Boston: Beacon, 1992.

Morris, Mitchell. "Aspects of the Coming-Out Aria." Unpublished manuscript..

Nattiez, Jean-Jacques. "Le Ring comme histoire metaphorique de la musique." In *Wagner in Retrospect,* ed. Leroy Shaw et al., 44–49. Amsterdam: Rodopi, 1987.

————. *Music and Discourse: Toward a Semiology of Music.* Trans. Carolyn Abbate. Princeton: Princeton University Press, 1990.

Van Ness, Peter H. *Spirituality, Diversion, and Decadence: The Contemporary Predicament.* Albany: State University of New York Press, 1992.

Nietzsche, Friedrich. *Der Fall Wagner, Götzen-Dämmerung, Nietzsche contra Wagner.* Munich: Wilhelm Goldmann, 1964.

Pierrot, Jean. *The Decadent Imagination, 1880–1900.* Trans. Derek Coltman. Chicago: University of Chicago Press, 1981.

Rosselli, John. "The Castrati as a Professional Group and a Social Phenomenon, 1550–1850." *Acta Musicologica* 60 (1988): 145.

Schickling, Dieter. *Abschied von Walhall: Richard Wagners erotische Gesellschaft.* Stuttgart: Deutsche Verlags-Anstalt, 1983.

Sedgwick, Eve Kosofsky. *Epistemology of the Closet.* Berkeley: University of California Press, 1990.

Simon, John. "Philadelphia." *National Review* (7 February 1994): 68.

Sinai, Robert I. *The Decadence of the Modern World.* Cambridge, Mass.: Schenkman, 1978.

Stekel, Wilhelm. "Nietzsche und Wagner: Eine sexualpsychologische Studie zur Psychogenese des Freundschaftsgefühls und des Freundschaftsverrats." *Zeitschrift für Sexualwissenschaft und Sexualpolitik* 4 (1917): 22–28, 58–65.

Subotnik, Rose Rosengard. *Developing Variations: Style and Ideology in Western Music.* Minneapolis: University of Minnesota Press, 1991.

Sullivan, Andrew. "Philadelphia." *New Republic* (21 February 1994): 42.

Thomas, Gary C. " 'Was Georg Frideric Handel Gay?': On Closet Questions and Cultural Politics." In *Queering the Pitch,* ed. Philip Brett et al., 155–203.

Tisson, Simon-André. *Onanism.* New York: Collins & Hannay, 1832.

Trumbach, Randolph. "Gender and the Homosexual Role: The Eighteenth and the Nineteenth Centuries Compared." In *Homosexuality, Which Homosexuality,* ed. Dennis Altman et. al., 149–70. London: Gay Men's, 1989.

Vogel, Martin. *Nietzsche und Wagner: Ein deutsches Lesebuch.* Bonn: Verlag für systematische Musikwissenschaft, 1984.

Wagner, Cosima. *Diaries.* Ed. Martin Gregor-Dellin and Dietrich Mack. Trans. Geoffrey Skelton. 2 vols. New York: Harcourt Brace Jovanovich, 1978–80.

Wagner, Richard. *Briefe.* Ed. Hanjo Kesting. Munich: Piper, 1983.

————. *Dichtungen und Schriften.* Ed. Dieter Borchmeyer. 10 vols. Frankfurt am Main: Insel, 1983.

————. *Gesammelte Schriften und Dichtungen.* 10 vols. Leipzig: E. W. Fritzsch, 1898.

————. *Sämtliche Briefe.* Ed. Gertrud Strobel and Werner Wolf. Leipzig: Deutscher Verlag für Musik, 1979.

————. *Selected Letters of Richard Wagner.* Trans. and ed. Stewart Spencer and Barry Millington. London: Dent, 1987.

Wall, James M. "Philadelphia." *Christian Century* (16 March 1994): 268.

Weiner, Marc A. *Richard Wagner and the Anti-Semitic Imagination*. Lincoln: University of Nebraska Press, 1995.

———. *Undertones of Insurrection: Music, Politics, and the Social Sphere in the Modern German Narrative*. Lincoln: University of Nebraska Press, 1993.

Weininger, Otto. *Geschlecht und Charakter: Eine prinzipielle Untersuchung*. 25th ed. Vienna: Wilhelm Braumüller, 1923. 404.

Westernhagen, Curt von. *Richard Wagner: Sein Werk, sein Wesen, seine Welt*. Zürich: Atlantis, 1956. 527–29.

Whissen, Thomas Reed. *The Devil's Advocates: Decadence in Modern Literature*. Westport, Conn.: Greenwood, 1989.

Williams, Linda. *Hard Core: Power, Pleasure, and the "Frenzy of the Visible."* Berkeley: University of California Press, 1989.

Williams, Roger L. *The Horror of Life*. Chicago: University of Chicago Press, 1980.

Chapter 7
Spaces of the Demimonde/Subcultures of Decadence: 1890–1990

Emily Apter

Germans who ape Paris fashions, and apply *fin-de-siècle* almost exclusively to mean what is indecent and improper, misuse the word in their coarse ignorance as much as, in a previous generation, they vulgarized the expression *demi-monde*, misunderstanding its proper meaning, and giving it the sense of *fille de joie*, whereas its creator Dumas intended it to denote persons whose lives contained some dark period, for which they were excluded from the circle to which they belong by birth, education, or profession, but who do not by their manner betray, at least to the inexperienced, that they are no longer acknowledged as members of their own caste. . . .

One epoch of history is unmistakably in its decline, and another is announcing its approach. There is a sound of rending in every tradition, and it is as though the morrow would not link itself with to-day. . . .

Such is the spectacle presented by the doings of men in the reddened light of the Dusk of the Nations. Massed in the sky the clouds are aflame in the weirdly beautiful glow which was observed for the space of years after the eruption of Krakatoa. Over the earth the shadows creep with deepening gloom, wrapping all objects in a mysterious dimness, in which all certainty is destroyed and any guess seems plausible. Forms lose their outlines, and are dissolved in floating mist. The day is over, the night draws on. The old anxiously watch its approach, fearing they will not live to see the end. A few amongst the young and strong are conscious of the vigour of life in all their veins and nerves, and rejoice in the coming sunrise. Dreams, which fill up the hours of darkness till the breaking of the new day, bring to the former comfortless memories, to the latter high-souled hopes. And in the artistic products of the age we see the form in which these dreams become sensible.

Max Nordau, *Degeneration* (5–6)

The word *high-life* was invented by this period, the perfect type of a low-living period. There was a spaghetti style in morals corresponding to the style in architecture and literature. It is the moment of moral turpitude denounced by Balzac. The world had begun to live on its nerves. It was given up to drugs and women; never has the body been so insistent; there was a worship of sex, of the skin, of the hair; a fetishism of underclothing, boots and furs. The languor of Turkish baths, that renaissance of forbidden pleasures which appears whenever blood is about to flow; pity which is cowardice and a taste for crime. Novels, songs and stories celebrate the underworld of vagabonds and prostitutes and laugh at the bourgeois, from Aristide Bruant to

Mirbeau, passing by *Les Deux Gosses*, all extol the poetry of the wretch who lives on the immoral earnings of women. 1900 would like to appear dangerous. It hated being simply bourgeois.

Paul Morand, *1900 A.D.* (203–4)

In the Paris of 1930 (which was a rather provincial city compared to New York) [Henry] Miller re-found something of his fin-de-siècle youth, which had always had more in common with Europe than with America. Whenever I mentioned the Belle Epoque, or those famous cafés once frequented by the artists, Miller would tell me how much he regretted not having seen the prewar Paris, not having known Apollinaire, Max Jacob, Picasso, and Toulouse-Lautrec, not having haunted Montparnasse in its heyday. I once told him that when I was five, in 1904, I had spent a year in Paris, and pushed a little sailboat around the pool in the Luxembourg Gardens. He was immediately envious of my memory. "You knew the Paris of Marcel Proust! You saw the procession of vehicles in the Bois de Boulogne! You sauntered down the *grands boulevards*! You saw Paris at the imperial height of the Madeleine-Bastille horse-drawn omnibus!"

Georges Brassaï, *Henry Miller: The Paris Years* (22)

Life was bleak on the Lower East Side in the late 1970s, but it was a purposeful bleakness. We liked it that way. We were living a movie of youth in black-and-white that in order to be grand needed to be stark. We were scavengers, and the castoffs with which we dressed ourselves, our apartments, and our minds fortuitously matched our aesthetic. . . . The makeshift, the beleaguered, the militant, the paranoid, the outcast, the consumptive romantic, the dead-eyed post-everything — all the shifting and coinciding modes and poses played very well against a backdrop of ruins.

Luc Sante, "All Yesterday's Parties" (97)

My anger is more about the fact that WHEN I WAS TOLD THAT I'D CONTRACTED THIS VIRUS IT DIDN'T TAKE ME LONG TO REALIZE THAT I'D CONTRACTED A DISEASED SO-CIETY AS WELL.

David Wojnarowicz, "Postcards from America: X-rays from Hell" (375)

The purpose of juxtaposing Max Nordau's millennially hyperanxious "Man of the Dusk of Nations," Paul Morand's fetish culture of decadent modernity, Brassaï's evocation of Henry Miller's 1930s nostalgia for Belle Epoque Paris, and the testimonies of Nan Goldin's sick or strung-out friends in New York circa 1990 is to affirm the fluidity of decadent periodizations, catalyzing style, historicity, and social formation. Eminently recyclable, the twilight sensibility of decadent fin-de-sièclism, implanted in the modernist turn, is both historicist and abstractable from history; soldered to a specific Zeitgeist, yet transferable to new codifications of cosmopolitan life. In what follows, I want to take up the problem of the demimonde as a subcultural style that both relies on and is symptomatic of decadence as a gestalt of fin-de-siècle consciousness. Briefly comparing two paradigmatic photographic records of demimonde life — Nan Goldin's *Ballad of Sexual Dependency*, recently included in her controversial retrospective at the Whitney Museum of Modern Art, and Brassaï's *Le Paris secret des années trente* [The secret Paris of the thirties], originally conceived in the 1930s as part of a more comprehensive project entitled *Paris de nuit* [Paris by night], but censored until 1976 — I want to associate demimonde decadence with the representation of half-worlds: the shadowy visuality of nightworlds in extramural locations; the pathos of codependency (including the "queerly" familial spaces of sexuality-by-half: bisexed, third-sexed, cross, and transgendered); half-steps on the ladder of social hierarchy (blurred distinctions of race, ethnicity and class); and the poetics of psychosexual splitting. The issue of latency (historical and psychoanalytic) also emerges insofar as the demimonde functions as a temporal shifter, carrying the camp styles of fin-de-sièclism into the Belle Epoque, merging pre-World War I theatrical character types with the performative subjectivities of modernism and drag culture from the 1920s to the 1990s.

*   *   *

The demimonde, as social space, is proverbially associated with clichés of low-life and high-life bohemia circa 1870–1940. The aim here will be to activate the term in reference to a state of self-exile, or being "beside oneself" or "half-worlded" (to borrow phrases from Djuna Barnes's *Nightwood*). *Exile* is of course itself a term as fraught and tricky as *demimonde* or *decadence*; one that risks dubious parallels among subjects of markedly divergent legal, social, and material circumstances. Political refugees, economically disenfranchised citizens, legal aliens and illegal immigrants, privileged émigrés and expatriates, radicals, artists, dissidents, hoboes, global intellectuals, sick people, gender outlaws, quarantined racial and ethnic minorities, conscripts, convicts, boat people, *gastarbeiter*, tourists, bohemians, inhabitants of fashionable subcultures, hybrid postcolonial subjects, e-mail nationalists — all at some level may be accommodated under the rubric of exile, and so the question inevitably arises: what specific function does the category of exile perform? Is it simply a baggy, dehistoricized term for people on the move, some forcibly, others voluntarily? For whom is exile a redemptive or regenerative experience? Does it ignite a familiar bourgeois romance with otherness that many, particularly those working in the postcolonial field, have grown to distrust? Is it a shorthand appellation for exemplary modernists such as Natalie Clifford Barney, Gertrude Stein, Ernest Hemingway, James Joyce, Mina Loy, Henry Miller, Pablo Picasso, André Kertesz, Hannah Höch, Man Ray, and Brassaï, who gave modernism its internationalist cast, aesthetic agendas, and sartorial styles? Or is it simply a "lifestyle" rooted in estrangement from the *terre natale*? A mystificatory term, obscuring drastic civil, economic, and linguistic disparity?

While the term *exile, tout court*, surely invites criticism for its indiscriminate jumbling of materially privileged loners and involuntary vagrants, *self*-exile, or self-besidedness, might serve to refocus attention on differentials of marginality in a salutary way; adding impetus to rewriting the history of modernity so that it avoids the conceptual apartheid of sociologically reified categories. The aim is to cut across heuristic grooves, spurring investigation into the secret life of social interactions as they confound normative typologies. Terry Castle's recent study of "cross-homosexual friendship" in the case of Noël Coward and Radclyffe Hall comes to mind here as an example of "marginal-to-marginal" social exchange (109). In unearthing hitherto neglected bonds between same-sex communities of the opposite sex, Castle engages in a micro-history of modern subject formation that might equally well apply to larger communities of semi-exiles — say, the crossovers of race and class that took place in spaces of popular entertainment: bars, cafés, cabarets, dance halls, nightclubs, street fairs, brothels, artists' ateliers. I personally think self-exile can be an intellectually viable category when it is used in a qualified sense in relation to "decadent" subjects of late modernity: those represented as squatters in their own lives, denizens of subcultures or washed up souls whose nocturnal sensibilities exude loneliness and clannish loyalty to the habitus of the demimonde at one and the same time.

*   *   *

Nan Goldin's recycling of Brassaï's photogenic atmospherics, like Brassaï's borrowing of poses and photological effects from painters such as Manet and Degas, suggests that the demimonde, as an aesthetic package, lends itself to mimicry and appropriation. Offering a close fit between ethos and topos, between subject matter and style, the demimonde mystique can be traced to nineteenth-century fin-de-sièclism; to Nordau's technophobic vision of pathological overstimulation in the metropole; to sexological decadence, from Krafft-Ebing and Magnan to Mirbeau; to Baudelaire's "painter of modern life" dedicated to artifice and urban evanescence; to Des Esseintes's aboulia and oversaturated aestheticism in *A rebours*; to the opium and absinthe-induced physical wastage portrayed by Impressionist painting and late Naturalist fiction; to the backstage, boudoir private / public spheres of courtesans and clients; to *zutiste* songs and popular posters depicting "café-conc" society in 1880s Montmartre (Aristide Bruant's cabaret *Le Chat Noir*); to the sulfurously amorous partnership of Rimbaud and Verlaine; to the documentations of life in the "zone" by Atget and Apollinaire. This selective repository of nineteenth-century clichés (belonging to a vast source book), functions as an image archive of decadence upon which twentieth-century reimaginings of the demimonde would continually draw. The spring 1997 Guggenheim show entitled *Rrose is a Rrose is a Rrose: Gender Performance in Photography* (Spring 1997) offers ample evidence of this process of quotation and reuse; here, parallels are perhaps overdrawn between the sub rosa sociability of French gay and lesbian society in the twenties and thirties and contemporary gender masquerade in metropolitan America. Brassaï, Claude Cahun, and Pierre Molinier are set up on a demimonde continuum as the ancestors of Robert Mapplethorpe, Catherine Opie, Della Grace, and Goldin.

Claude Cahun (Lucy Renée Matilde Schwob, 1894–1954) was a French writer, artist, and photographer affiliated with the Surrealists. Her astonishing self-portraits, never exhibited in her lifetime, were discovered and exhibited in the 1980s. Alluring examples of lesbian chic, the portraits feature a "mannish" female subject either gazing frankly and frontally at the camera or experimentally montaged. The close-cropped hair, the cool black-and-white geometry of her clothing, and the self-conscious poses with mirrors and reflecting objects place Cahun's self-image at an aesthetic distance from itself (self-exiled), while projecting a totalizing aesthetic of modernist subculture that appears thoroughly "at home" in the same-sex ethos of the 1990s.

Like Claude Cahun, Pierre Molinier (1900–1976) was a Surrealism-influenced photographer who gained cult status as an avatar of the gay underground. Clad in corsets, leather masks, and stiletto heels, armed with whips and dildos, he used fetish regalia to problematize the bodily integrity of gender ideals and to explore a sphincteral eros. He is famous for photographing himself engaged in masochistic acts; indeed, as legend would have it, he expired as a result of repeated self-violation. Molinier's S/M allure, foreshadowing kinky eighties and nineties fashion (as in the dog-collar-and-leather look favored by the late Gianni Versace) makes his photos resemble stills from Nick Broomfield's 1996 clubland documentary *Fetishes*, itself an extended clin d'oeil at underground erotic practice. Mapplethorpe's sado-masochism redux, viewed in propinquity to Molinier, appears to be an eighties homage (in the key of gay classicism) to social contracts of bondage and dangerous pleasure.

Similarly committed to laying claim to what Max Nordau, in a fin-de-siècle context, stigmatized as "degeneracy" (a "morbid deviation from an original type" [16]), Catherine Opie is a contemporary photographer specializing in nonheteronormative bodies that have undergone the "art" of alteration. Not unlike Della Grace, who favors black-and-white shots of bald, jackboot-sporting female nudes, Opie portrays big, bulky anatomies and fleshy expanses that have been transformed into sites of reverential inscription. Biker tattoos, nipple-rings, branding and piercing, female facial hair — all shot close-up, in large format, and in brilliant color — chart an aesthetics of outsider identification and subcultural belonging.

In seeming to take the notion of the demimonde back to its nonvulgarized, "proper" meaning (its Nordauian denotation of "persons whose lives contained some dark period, for which they were excluded from the circle to which they belong by birth, education, or profession, but who do not by their manner betray, at least to the inexperienced, that they are no longer acknowledged as members of their own caste" [5]), *Rrose is a Rrose is a Rrose* attests to the way in which demimonde portrait galleries of gay outlaws, flesh-cutters, cross-dressers, sex workers, S/M communities, class pariahs, drag queens, artists, actors, liberated women, and transgender adventurers produce a frisson, a commodifiable buzz. The bourgeois public has always enjoyed a walk on the wild side as long as a safe house awaits at the end. But while the commercial return on a demimonde work of art may be reliable, the material contains interpretive pitfalls exceeding the usual problems of censorship and bad press. As a signifier of class dysfunction, drugged consciousness, and sexual addiction, the demimonde lends itself to content analysis, that is, to approaches privileging biography and social documentary over theory and/or formalist reading.

Criticism of Goldin's work in the art publications and mainstream media tends to fetishize her personal connection to the people in the pictures. Alhough discussion may branch out into questions of auto-ethnography and nonvoyeuristic intimism, it invariably emphasizes the work's social realism. Michael Kimmelman, in the *New York Times* review of her Whitney show, begins with a caveat against allowing fascination with content to supplant appreciation for technical virtuosity: "To say that Nan Goldin's subject for the past 25 years has been the urban demimonde, the world of drag queens and slum goddesses, of Lower East Side nightclubbers and Tokyo teenagers in black rubber, is to explain her current fashionable status but it doesn't say much about what makes her photographs good" (72) . Though he implies that "what makes her photographs good" has nothing to do with "fashion" or her demimonde subject matter, Kimmelman hardly wavers from such topologies. Praising the universalism of Goldin's subjects, Kimmelman assuages the fears of a public that might otherwise not choose to confront huge, frontal, cibachrome color prints of people fucking, beating each other up, masturbating, smoking crack, acting queer, or dying: "Her pictures combine trust, candor and vulnerability, which, after all, is the mix we look for in a friend" (74). Is Kimmelman's Sunday-papers humanism so different from the catalogue commentary of hip novelist Luc Sante, when he writes of Goldin, "She radiated interest and sympathy, but more than that, seemed to issue the challenge: *I dare you to be yourself*" (99)?

Even the best commentators on Goldin's work lapse into a language of humanist authenticity affirming an emotive-realist reading of her work. Joachim Sartorius remarks: "Nan often deliberately eschewed technical brilliance. She was always more interested in the intimate and the personal, which she observed with a detachment that was never voyeuristic" (320). Carol Squiers's review in *American Photo* begins: "Nan Goldin photographs only those people who are emotionally close to her. She intently tracks friends and lovers through a variety of activities and moods, from their angst-tinged travels to their unashamedly open love-making" (16). Here, as elsewhere, we find a curious pattern; it is as if Goldin's work, more than that of other chroniclers of risqué lifeworlds, gives license to suspend theoretical response. Many of the critics either are or want to be "Friends-of-Nan"; they provide anecdotes about Nan or reminiscences of their own lost days of debauchery and drugs. Goldin's social realism, for better or for worse, clearly triggers outflows of personal criticism.

It is easy to see why Goldin criticism has taken this turn. The current critical mood has turned "against theory," and, perhaps more importantly, there is in Goldin's images a sensitivity to violence, loss, eros, and survival that defies pompous theorizing. This said, why not try to work through the themes of sexual dependency and exilic *communitas* in more extensive relation to her inimitable photogeny—a mix of flashbulb radiation and blots of hard red; of nocturne blue and luminous bodily outline; of bathroom mises-en-abîme and magnified still lifes of purple-yellow bruises, stained teeth, and dirt-black feet? What do we make of this outré colorism of pain and bodily neglect (reminiscent of Nordau's identification of visual decadence with the retinal hysteria produced by "screaming yellows," "amblyopic" blues, and "dynamogenous" reds [28])? The stakes here involve questioning anew the habitual polarization between social realist approaches and formalist interpretation.

Like Djuna Barnes in a literary vein, Goldin invents a photology of loneliness and subjective splitting. Barnes's prose resonates uncannily with Goldin's kinetic choreography, featuring bony bodies propped up against each other, holding on to each other for dear life; separated from each other but together; clinging and embracing in advance of the death-drive. In *Nightwood*, originally published in 1936, Barnes wrote of a "life lying through her in ungainly luminous deteriorations," "a gap in 'world pain' through which the singular falls continually and forever; a body falling in observable space, deprived of the privacy of disappearance," of the "faintly luminous glow upon the upturned face of Robin, who had the smile of the 'only survivor,' a smile which fear had married to the bone," or "As if that light had power to bring what was dreaded into the zone of their catastrophe, Nora saw the body of another woman swim up into the statue's obscurity, with head hung down, that the added eyes might not augment the illumination; her arms about Robin's neck, her body pressed to Robin's, her legs slackened in the hang of the embrace" (34, 51, 62, 64).[1] Projecting homologies between half-life and half-light, Barnes and Goldin seem to have hit on a subjectivist formula whereby nocturnal photogeny translates the dark side of "being-beside oneself": the self "split" by virtue of its subjection to the will of another; the body semi-disappeared yet limning its absent outline.

In Goldin's *Ballad of Sexual Dependency*, the title of which is taken from a Brecht-Weill *Threepenny Opera* song played when the work is exhibited as a slide-show installation, the bodies seem to collaborate with the flashbulb in a relation of *anaclisis* or codependency. Goldin's photographs challenge nor-

Figure 7.1. Nan Goldin, *Philippe H. and Suzanne kissing at Euthanasia, New York City, 1981.*

mative boundaries between love and sexual addiction (sharply distinguished in the psychoanalytic literature, where love is defined as bonding
with an introjected object, whereas the "adhesive attachments" of addiction
are defined, at least in Joyce McDougall's scheme, as "sexual relations [that]
remain tied to an external object that is detached from essential introjects,
perhaps because they are missing, highly damaged, or too threatening in
the external world" [183]).[2] Blurring the categories of love and addiction,
there are no damaged goods vying with "good" introjectible objects. In her
image-repertoire, all the objects are willfully damaged or "bad"; whether
victim objects or predators, they are baroquely abject. Goldin's camera
revels in the way the epidermis, as the site that registers abuse, conflates the
traces of chemical and emotional dependency. Superimposed or artfully
mapped onto blotchy skin, needle tracks, pimples, black-and-blue marks,
and suppurating tattoos literalize "pathologies" that Goldin presents without apology with the help of an in-your-face format.

In the remainder of this essay, I want to draw some comparisons between
Goldin's *Ballad of Sexual Dependency* and Brassaï's *Secret Paris of the Thirties*.
This will be heresy for those sensitive to Brassaï's "greatness" as a photogra-

Figure 7.2. Nan Goldin, *Suzanne and Philippe on the Bench, Tompkins Square Park, New York City, 1983.*

pher, and receptive perhaps to the more scathing appraisals of Goldin's work as "hackish, overbearing, fake," and infused with "the bitter scent of fin-de-siècle fraudulence" (in the words of James Lewis in his "thumbs-down" rating of the year in *Artforum*'s "best and worst of exhibitions of 1996" issue [90]). Despite the asymmetry of their reputations as artists, there is a way in which they are equivalent as controversial chroniclers of a demimonde Zeitgeist. While Goldin works predominantly in color and Brassaï in black and white, and while Goldin prefers the rapid fire of Polaroids, snapshots, and slides and Brassaï was famous for bringing the concept of *longue durée* to photographic practice with his half-hour night shot, both photographers stage the demimonde as a pageant of seduction and nostalgia. Both have been accused of coaxing and posing their subjects to make them look more like "real life." Both have gained notoriety as "Atgets of the underworld," with pictures that perform a witnessing function, archiving vanished or endangered species of people and place. Both specialize in depicting "families" — that is, groups of rejects who support each other, having escaped dysfunctional homes.[3] Both capture loneliness within sociality, arranging their subjects side by side yet alone, heads penitentially bowed, backs to the viewer. Both eroticize sartorial and cosmetic detail; spit-curls, feather boas, sequins, and body-paint function as visual magnets or "holes in the real," igniting excitement and fascination. Both deal in social stereotypes grouped in narrative sequences, *romanesque* to the hilt: drag-balls, sadomasochistic couples, gay men, and dykes. (On this note, I should pass along Terry Castle's complaint, directed toward Brassaï's canonical portraits of butches: "What we need is something beyond the odd Brassaï-like set piece of Cinzano-sipping ladies in gentlemen's clothing" [72]).

Goldin and Brassaï excel in photographic techniques that, each for their own era, epitomize periodized, signature "looks" for the demimonde. In their periodicity, their images offer a marked contrast to the "timeless" appearance of Man Ray's experiments in solarization and rayography. Even when Man Ray couched his technicity in humanist, phenomenological language — as when he wrote, in the introduction to his 1934 album, *The Age of Light*, regarding "these images of oxidized residues, fixed by light and chemical elements, of living organisms," that "No plastic expression can ever be more than a residue of an experience" (qtd. in Penrose, 116) — his subjects seem to be more like scientific specimens of classic modernity than personifications of urban folklore in a given era.

The mythologies surrounding Brassaï and Goldin are, of course, quite different. Brassaï is cast, indeed self-cast, as a midnight stalker, roving through the dives, dockyards, urinals, and *quartiers chauds* of Paris with Paul Morand or Henry Miller by his side, bursting in on brothel parties or sleeping couples, yet keeping himself safely out of the picture. According to Michael Sand, an original version of Brassaï's *La toilette dans un hôtel de passe Rue Quimcampoix* (1932) reveals that in the "upper left hand corner one sees the trademark of the photographer's hand, holding a cigarette," which he dodges out of the final print (16–17). The late Craig Owens presents a similarly bloodless Brassaï, a producer of images in which "the social space is sucked out," "drained," sublimated into photography's depiction of photography itself, photography "en abyme."

Figure 7.3. Nan Goldin, *Nan as dominatrix, Boston, 1978.*

Brassaï's portrait of a group of young Parisians at the *Bal des Quatre Saisons* may at first appear, like most photographs, to be a straightforward description of an observed reality, as if the image had already existed in the world before it was suspended in the photograph. We might therefore be tempted to raid it for clues to the inner lives of its sitters or for memories of a long since vanished Parisian milieu. However, the longer we contemplate the image, the more remote that kind of information becomes. A complex web of internal duplications deflects attention away from that which, despite the status of photographs as imprints of the real, remains external to the image: the reality it depicts. Psychological and sociological details are displaced by the network of internal relationships between subject, mirror, and other, which structure the image (15).

In Rosalind Krauss's analysis of Brassaï's "situation of photography as a virtual image en abyme," formalist interpretation reinforces the sense of Brassaï as a coldly theoretical photographer. A shot of a bordello interior (*L'Armoire à glace* [1932]) is disengaged from the sociology of sex work (masterfully portrayed by Brassaï through his unromanticized behind-the-scenes shots of hygiene and postcoital indifference between partners). Krauss focuses on the semiotics of photographic self-reflexivity. Where some formalist accounts might take on Brassaï's ironic appropriation of the *scènes et types* genre — the tradition of tourist clichés featuring "ladies of the night" so dear to the folklore of Parisian culture — Krauss plots the indexicality, or rather "digitality" of gesticulation. In the famous portrait *La Fille au billard* (1932), she notes the right thumb's rigid grasp of the billiard cue and the left hand's splayed position, as if "in unconscious representation of opening flesh." This "extraordinary sign of sexuality" is then considered in relation to what is refracted in the mirrors that form a backdrop to the woman's figure (151). Krauss traces a deictic story, told by the reflection of a male customer's profile, as it links up visually with the reflected back view of the woman's neck, and then lines up with the erotically splayed hand. The ensemble, according to Krauss, "is a changing, multiple, beautiful sign, a sign that says: whore" (151). Here it seems that Krauss comes back to the social real, but it is a real that has been entirely transmogrified into a semiotic phantasmagoria.

While Brassaï's play with mirrors and reflections may suggest a formalist detachment from his subjects that Goldin's "I'll be your mirror" stance seeks to undercut, the differences between them may be exaggerated by traditional gender expectations; cold, techno-driven, masculine voyeur versus warm, empathic, self-implicating, female photographer. While it is true that Brassaï's subjects seem colder,, since many of them are sex workers travailing side-by-side rather than codependent couples bonded by common subcultural identifications, it may nonetheless be overly "friendly" to Nan if we exempt her work from the charge of icy visual interpellation. What about the cruelty of her camera toward bones, sticking out of drug-blasted, corpselike bodies? Doesn't the warm yellow glow suffusing a bedroom in which a woman has been or is about to be abused by her boyfriend act as a foil for the subjected, indeed *abjected,* condition of her subjects?

I will end by arguing that Goldin and Brassaï are more analogous than one might assume. Although the "influence" of roughly contemporary photographers such as Larry Clark and Diane Arbus is often cited, there may be

Figure 7.4. Brassaï, *La Fille au billard*.

a "suppressed origin" — Brassaï's photogeny of demimonde space and culture — that is all too frequently overlooked. Goldin begins her career with
retro-clad drag queens and punk streetwalkers who seem, hyperconsciously,
to be "acting out" portraits of Brassaï's famous *monstres sacrés* (Bijou, Bar-
bette, Colette, etc.). Like Brassaï, she has hit on a visual formula that typ-
ifies, for its era, a theatricalized, decadent, "end of history" sensibility.
Where Brassaï perfected the black-and-white version of "la vie en rose" in
his nostalgic depiction of "Paris as it looked at night; the windows that lit up

or hid misery, the dives packed with drunks and whores, from which shafts of light, familiar melodies, and streams of obscene epithets spilled out into the street" (26), Goldin masters the equally nostalgic "vie en rouge" as it appeared in Boston and New York in the late seventies and early eighties: a harsh-lit habitus of anaclitic bodies.

Notes

1. For a nuanced assessment of Barnes's gender politics and relationship to literary decadence, see Broe, *Silence and Power.*

2. McDougall wishes to underline the difference between the English word *addiction*, and the French word most often used for it, *toxicomanie*, meaning literally "a crazy desire for poison." While this makes sense in many contexts, McDougall's revision risks eliding the extent to which the craving for love, sex, and drugs may act as alternatives for each other within psychic economies of dependency.

3. Here I would venture that Goldin's queer families and menageries of misfits may be read against photography's historic institutionalization of the family. In Pierre Bourdieu's ascription, "if we bear in mind the fact that there is a very close correlation between the presence of children in the household and possession of a camera, and that the camera is often the common property of the family group, it becomes clear that photographic practice only exists and subsists for most of the time by virtue of its *family function* or rather by the function conferred upon it by the family group, namely, that of solemnizing and immortalizing the high points of family life, in short, of reinforcing the integration of the family group by reasserting the sense that it has both of itself and of its unity" (19).

Works Cited

Barnes, Djuna. *Nightwood.* 1936. New York: New Directions, 1961.

Bourdieu, Pierre, et al. *Photography: A Middle-brow Art.* 1965. Trans. Shaun Whiteside. Stanford: Stanford University Press, 1990.

Brassaï, Georges. *Henry Miller: The Paris Years.* Trans. Timothy Bent. New York: Arcade, 1975.

Broe, Mary Lynn, ed. *Silence and Power: A Reevaluation of Djuna Barnes.* Carbondale: Southern Illinois, 1991.

Castle, Terry. *Noël Coward and Radclyffe Hall: Kindred Spirits.* New York: Columbia University Press, 1996.

Goldin, Nan, David Armstrong, and Hans Werner Holtzwarth, eds. *Nan Goldin: I'll Be Your Mirror.* New York: Whitney Museum of American Art, 1996.

Kimmelman, Michael. "What Nan Goldin Saw This Summer." *New York Times Magazine* (22 September 1996), 72–74.

Krauss, Rosalind. *Le Photographique: Pour une Théorie des Ecarts.* Paris: Macula, 1990.

Lewis, James. "Fool's Goldin." *Artforum* (December 1996), 90.

McDougall, Joyce. *The Many Faces of Eros: A Psychoanalytic Exploration of Human Sexuality.* London: Free Association Books, 1995.

Morand, Paul. *1900 A.D.* Trans. Mrs. Romilly Fedden. New York: William Farquhar Payson, 1931.

Nordau, Max. *Degeneration.* 1892. Lincoln: University of Nebraska Press, 1993.

Owens, Craig. *Beyond Recognition: Representation, Power, and Culture.* Berkeley: University of California Press, 1992.

Penrose, Roland. *Man Ray*. London: Thames and Hudson, 1975.

Sand, Michael. " . . . et Lumiere." *Artforum* (February 1994): 16–17.

Sante, Luc. "All Yesterday's Parties." In *Nan Goldin: I'll Be Your Mirror*, ed. Nan Goldin et al., 97–103.

Sartorius, Joachim. "Deep Pictures of Us All." *Nan Goldin: I'll Be Your Mirror*. Ed. Nan Goldin, et al. 319–24.

Squiers, Carol. "Crossing Over." *American Photo* 4 (July-August 1993), 16.

Wojnarowicz, David. "Postcards from America: X-rays from Hell." 1989. In *Nan Goldin: I'll Be Your Mirror*, ed. Nan Goldin, et al., 374–84.

Identifications of Decadence and Decadent Identities

Chapter 8
"Comment Peut-on Être Homosexuel?"
Multinational (In)Corporation and the Frenchness of *Salomé*

Melanie C. Hawthorne

> Oscar Wilde was not American, but I feel nationalistic about him.
> Wayne Koestenbaum

Toward the end of World War I, a curious legal trial took place in Britain that once again placed the name of Oscar Wilde before the public in the context of libel. Although this case echoed and at times explicitly evoked the notorious 1895 trials in which Wilde had sued the Marquess of Queensberry for libel and in turn had been charged by the Crown with gross indecency and sodomy, when this trial began on 29 May 1918, Wilde was long since dead and was neither plaintiff nor defendant. Yet a cluster of associations he had helped to put into circulation clung to his work long after his death and helped to set the context for the 1918 court case.

The trial came about as a result of an announcement of a private performance of Wilde's play *Salomé* to be offered in April 1918. Following the advertisement, an Independent MP, Noel Pemberton Billing, published a deliberately provocative but cryptic article entitled "The Cult of the Clitoris" in his newspaper, the *Vigilante*. In the article (not written by Billing himself), it was implied that the actress who played the role of Salomé, Maud Allen, was a lesbian (Hyde *Annotated* 163).[1] The article may as well have accused Allen of "posing as a somdomite [*sic*]" as the Marquess of Queensberry had said of Wilde. Allen filed suit for libel, along with J. T. Grein, whose Independent Theater Society was to perform the play, and a curious reprise of the 1895 trials took place.

This time Alfred Douglas did take the witness stand, but as the star witness for the prosecution (as indeed in some senses he always had been), testifying that Wilde was "the greatest force of evil that has appeared in Europe during the last 350 years." Wilde's close friend and literary executor Robbie Ross was again drawn into a defense of Wilde. Just as the 1895 trial is thought to have led to Wilde's premature death, some have maintained that the 1918 trial, the last in a series of libel cases pitting Ross directly or indirectly against Douglas, precipitated Ross's demise shortly after. As Maureen Borland, Ross's biographer, points out, "Again it was Oscar Wilde who was really on trial," and she notes: "In the minds of the jury, the battle for public morality and the battle being fought against the German nation were one and the same thing" (279–80). In a word, the trial once again made Wilde's body (of work) the site of a debate between expressions of sexuality and the national interest.

Once again, repressive interests prevailed in the outcome of the trial. Besides the fact that Allen lost her case, a play that formerly seemed "only" immoral became, in the words of one critic, "not only immoral but also unpatriotic" (Bird 67). But how does immorality come to signify lack of patriotism? It is this connection between immorality — especially homosexuality — and nationality which I want to explore here.[2]

With historical hindsight, it is clear that Billing was merely using gay-baiting as a way to accuse a number of other prominent public figures of spying for the Germans. Moreover, as Michael Kettle has argued in *Salome's Last Veil*, Billing himself was also being used by government factions working behind the scenes to influence the way World War I was being conducted. (It was suspected that Prime Minister Lloyd George was preparing to meet in secret peace talks, and some in the military who opposed this move were conspiring to oust their leader.) In other words, Allen, Grein, and their associates were merely pawns in a much bigger game. But at the time the trial took place, the public was unaware of this larger context and became convinced that the issue of Allen's sexuality somehow was of national importance. It is the public's willingness to view sexual identity in terms of national identity that makes this trial of interest today.

Maud Allen (who, anyway, was Canadian) became Billing's target simply because her name appeared on the announcements for the play, but she was not the only target once the trial got under way. Ironically, the performance was intended to raise funds for the Red Cross (Kettle 201), but it came to be perceived as the opposite of a patriotic gesture. The reasons have been summarized as follows: "Wilde had been convicted of sodomy, and *Salomé* was banned on grounds of blasphemy; Grein was a foreigner, having been born a Dutchman; Allen was a reputed lesbian" (Tydeman 201). So deviant sexuality (Wilde and Allen), blasphemy (the play), and Dutch nationality (Grein) were the perceived crimes of this production, and these attributes were understood by the general public as reasonable grounds to suspect a form of treason. These attributes were grounds for Billing to introduce his accusations that the Germans had a "black book" listing the names of some

47,000 individuals who had been corrupted by German agents for purposes of blackmail and espionage. Being born in Holland (though Britain was ostensibly fighting the Germans, not the Dutch) was unpatriotic. Blasphemy was unpatriotic. Deviance was unpatriotic. All were part of the "foreigneering tendencies" perceived by the artist and stage designer Charles Ricketts in this particular production (qtd. in Tydeman 83). For Billing, identifying Allen as a German spy was merely a pretext to name others. But, for the general public, how do foreign birth, sexual deviance, and blasphemy all come to signify the same unpatriotic thing as they seem to do in this trial which, thanks to its wartime context, foregrounded questions of national identity?

The Love That Cannot Speak Its Name

To understand how sexuality and blasphemy become linked to issues of national identity, we must go back to the history of sexuality and reconsider the way sexual identities perceived as deviant have been constructed. We need to keep in mind the social constructionist perspective that sexual identity is not a given that transcends time and space, but is the product of a specific historical moment that selects and recombines various possible social signifiers according to the prevailing discursive practices of any particular moment. In this view, the elements of identity are not fixed in transhistorical categories, but are in a constant state of evolution according to shifting cultural patterns.

The possibility of tracing the broad movements of these social patterns enables Foucault — an early contributor to the history of sexual identity who established the dominant paradigm — to locate a major diachronic shift in perception in the latter half of the nineteenth century. According to Foucault, new attitudes toward sexualities (the plural is his) "entailed an *incorporation of perversions* and a new *specification of individuals*. As defined by the ancient civil or canonical codes, sodomy was a category of forbidden acts; their perpetrator was nothing more than the juridical subject of them. The nineteenth-century homosexual became a personage, a past, a case history, and a childhood, in addition to being a type of life, a life form, and a morphology, with an indiscreet anatomy and possibly a mysterious physiology" (42–43). Foucault zeroes in on the point at which certain adjectives cease to be applied to actions and begin to be applied to people; instead of "sodomy," an act, the focus shifts to the perpetrator of the act, the sodomite. An explanation of the action is sought in the person: the person's past, case history, childhood. The person and her or his behavior were, in a word, "consubstantial," a process Foucault calls "incorporation." He goes on to specify the date of this change in an aside: "Westphal's famous article of 1870 on 'contrary sexual sensations' can stand as its date of birth" (43).

Foucault's periodization is attractively neat. The year 1870 stands out in the French-trained mind as a date of capital importance, as the end of the repressive Second Empire and the foundation of the Third Republic with all its attendant connotations of reform, civic-mindedness, and republican ideals. That a new way of conceiving sexual identity should come into existence at the same time as such a major political shift makes for tidy history. History is considerably less tidy, however, when it is recalled that Westphal's article was published not in 1870 but in 1869 (Féray 246n.), and that it was not called "contrary sexual sensations" but "Die conträre Sexualempfindung," that is, that the article was written in German and not translated into French (or English) until later. Foucault's history is European, synthesizing the events of different nations from a twentieth-century perspective and overlooking the fact that these events have assumed their coherence through hindsight.[3] But to borrow a phrase from Vyvyan Holland, Wilde's son, "Frontiers seem to separate people far more than mere distances" (*Son* 104), and in the nineteenth century, national boundaries functioned at times like firewalls, insulating one country from another and preventing the spread of incendiary ideas (or "burning issues," as Rachilde would call them in an essay on Wilde). Add to this the additional "firewalls" that retarded the spread of Westphal's inflammatory work in France — the distractions of war and the Commune and the general Germanophobia that prevailed in the postwar period — and the spread of German sexology is further impeded.[4]

Thus, when Foucault narrates that "the homosexual was now [in 1870] a species" (43), we still need to ask where this species was recognized and by whom. Ed Cohen argues in *Talk on the Wilde Side*, for example, that in Britain it was not until Wilde's conviction on sodomy charges in 1895 that the concept of a "type" of person likely to commit certain acts crystallized in the mind of the general public.[5]

Foucault's synthetic historical view thus obscures the fact that, in the period from 1870 to 1895 (the quarter century separating the publication of Westphal's article in Germany from Wilde's trial in Britain), "homosexual" identity emerged unevenly. In both Britain and France, one obstacle to the recognition of the category Foucault invokes is the absence during this period of a single, unifying word to designate the type. The idea of "the homosexual" as a case history in either France or Britain in 1870 is anachronistic for the simple reason that the very word *homosexual* did not yet exist in either country.

Both English and French etymological dictionaries credit the invention of the word *homosexual* to an Austro-Hungarian writer named Karoly Maria Benkert von Kertbeny, who used the word in a pamphlet written in German and addressed as an open letter to the Prussian minister of justice.[6] The date of this composition — 1869 — fits Foucault's schema. However, the first attested usage of the word in French did not occur until 1891, when it appeared in an article by Dr. Chatelain in *Annales médico-psychologiques*.[7] Even so, the word remained restricted to the vocabulary of a few specialists, and it was not until the early twentieth century, when several trials in Germany involving homosexuality were widely reported and discussed in France, that the word entered common French parlance. Even then, as Jean-Claude Féray has shown, the word was perceived as a German loan word despite its classical etymology ("Une Histoire," 115–24). As late as 1889, as Marc Angenot writes in his study of French sexual discourse, "On trouve qu'à l'exception de quelques spécialistes, les sujets relatifs à la sexualité, normale ou pathologique, sont plutôt évités" (22). The first inclusion of the word in any French dictionary does not occur until the 1907 *Larousse*.

In English the pattern is scarcely different. According to the *OED*, the first attested English usage occurs in Charles Chaddock's 1892 translation of Krafft-Ebing's *Psychopathia Sexualis*, but even then, according to Cohen (9), the word was rarely found outside translations of obscure foreign medical works until the 1897 publication of Havelock Ellis's *Sexual Inversion*. It is only just after Wilde's trial in 1895, then, that the word begins to be disseminated in English.

Given this nominal "décalage," it seems necessary to ask, speaking of the fin-de-siècle period of the 1880s and early 1890s in France, "Comment peut-on être homosexuel?" It would appear that "the love that dare not speak its name" *could* not speak its (modern) name in either English or French at this time, even if it wanted to. How, then, did the identity that Foucault says took (corporeal) shape in 1870 but not named until the 1890s enter into discursive circulation?

"Do You Speak German?"

Although the word *homosexuel* was yet to be disseminated or accepted, there were numerous other euphemisms and expressions in use. Both church and state had long claimed an interest in regulating "sodomites," "pederasts," and "male prostitutes," hence the need to be able to label, refer to, and classify them. A linguistically informed version of social constructionism would recognize, however, that a perfect synonym is rare, because, although several related words may share the same referent, they have different connotations. The coining of a new word thus signals the delineation of a new concept. The new word *homosexual* comes into circulation precisely because preexisting words (such as "sodomite" and "pederast") do not carry all the desired connotations that the speaker wishes to express. As Foucault argues, the shift in perception in the late nineteenth century which leads to the coining of a new word involves the (new) belief that "the homosexual" is a "type" of person, not just the agent of certain actions. The label captures the belief in types of *people*, rather than in types of *behavior*.

A minor incident embedded in another sex scandal that emerged in England just before Wilde's case will serve to illustrate the perceived difference between, for example, the "sodomite" and the new category of the "homosexual." In 1889, a male prostitution ring came to light briefly, only to sink back into shadowy rumor thanks to a cover-up intended to protect the well-connected patrons of the establishment. The events have come to be known as the Cleveland Street Affair, after the location of the brothel. One of the male prostitutes charged by the police gave evidence, which has survived in police records. John Saul, also known to posterity as the author of "Recollections of a Mary-Anne" in the clandestinely published *Sins of the Cities of the Plain* (1882), described going to the Cleveland Street brothel with an aristocrat whom he described in the following terms: "He is not an actual Sodomite. He likes to play with you and then 'spend' himself on your belly" (qtd. in Simpson et al.51). At least for John Saul, then, who may be presumed to know a thing or two about the subculture of male-male erotic contacts, a form of homoerotic activity which today would be classified as "homosexual" is not sufficient for the person to be labeled as an "actual Sodomite" at approximately the time of Wilde's trial. Despite the undeniable degree of overlap in terms such as *sodomite, pederast,* and *homosexual,* they were not always perceived to be synonyms.

Before the word "homosexual" was available to denote the underlying essentialist assumption of type (as opposed to merely the agent of certain actions), how could such an emergent perception be conveyed? What other taxonomies were available? One common way of situating behaviors considered to be sexually deviant was to evoke (and indeed construct) the "otherness" implicit in such an identity by displacing it onto another (in Benedict Anderson's words) "imagined community." One such community which dominated the nineteenth-century imagination was that formed by nationality.

Many people are today familiar with the euphemism "Greek love," but the use of (foreign) nationality to figure deviance, particularly homosexual deviance, was not new in the nineteenth century. The trope already had a long history, in which sexual deviance was anything (to the French mind) but French. Already in the Middle Ages, the term *buggery* was used as a quasi-synonym for sodomy. The word represents a corruption of the adjective *bulgare,* Bulgaria being the reputed source of a heresy that spread into France from the tenth through twelfth centuries, culminating in the Albigensian heresy. This "Bulgarian" heresy opposed forms of sexuality that led to procreation on the grounds that human misery was the result of overattachment to the material world (Lever 43–47). Thanks to this heretical connection, *buggery* (originally a corruption of an adjective merely denoting national origin) then carried two meanings: it was used to designate any nonprocreative (e.g., anal) intercourse, both heterosexual and homosexual. At the same time, it could be used more generally as a catch-all for any heretical belief or practice. Practicing sodomy could lead to one being labeled a "heretic."

During the early Renaissance, homosexuality changed its geographical orientation to become "le vice italien" (Lever 75–76; see also Huas 45). Under the influence of Catherine de Medici, the French court Italianized itself, importing Italian art and culture, as well as a heavy dose of Neoplatonism. Leonardo da Vinci, the embodiment of Renaissance genius who would become an Italian expatriate at the French court, was accused of sodomy in an anonymous letter delivered to the Palazzo Vecchio in Florence in 1476 (Lever 71). Da Vinci, though but one emblematic example, illustrates the development of a popular association between Italian origin and sexual deviance in the French Renaissance mind.[8] The Italian connection also helped to make the Jesuits an especially suspect religious order. They drew hostile attention for many reasons, "d'abord l'origine étrangère de la compagnie, réputée 'italienne' de politique et de moeurs" (Lever 323). (Perhaps this was the connection Douglas was invoking when he claimed in 1918 that Wilde was the greatest force of evil to enter Europe since the midsixteenth century.) The perception that Italy harbored homosexuals remained active in the turn-of-the-century French imagination thanks to the bohemian reputation of the island of Capri. For example, when charged in connection with pederastic activities in 1903, the Baron Adelswärd-Fersen sought exile there. The island also serves as the inspiration and setting of Norman Douglas's campy novel *South Wind* (1917). Last, at the end of Lucien Binet-Valmer's novel *Lucien* (1910), the eponymous hero pretends to commit suicide but in fact escapes with his lover, Reggie, to start a new life in Italy.

But by the beginning of the twentieth century, the cultural geography of sexual orientation had shifted more toward a Teutonic pole. Thanks in large part to the Eulenburg affair, if sodomy was "le vice italien," homosexuality was "le vice allemand."[9] The Eulenburg affair was, however, only the most spectacular in a series of scandals involving homosexuality in Germany at the turn of the century. In the three years preceding the affair, reports James Steakley, "courts-martial had convicted some twenty [German] officers of homosexual conduct, and 1906–1907 witnessed six suicides by homosexual officers ruined by blackmail" (239).[10] This alone created a perception in France and elsewhere that homosexuality was widespread in Germany, but when Philipp Eulenburg, a close personal friend of Kaiser Wilhelm and an ambassador associated with the implementation of Wilhelm's political agenda, was denounced in 1907, the scandal took on an international dimension. (Some including Baumont even blame the affair for precipitating World War I.) It dragged on through a series of libel trials that captured press attention in France and cemented French perceptions of German vice. As Steakley notes, France "remains the only country to have produced monographs on the subject" (247). In particular, the French coined the term *Eulenbougre*, telescoping two markers of otherness into one (Huas 15), and "Do you speak German?" reputedly became a pick-up line for French gay men (Sedgwick 65).

While Germany was a favorite national stand-in for the homosexual type, no doubt for historical reasons, it was not the only one. Is it mere coincidence, for example, that the adolescent boy debauched by Huysmans's antihero Des Esseintes (in *A rebours*) is named "Langlois," a recognizable variant spelling of "l'anglais," the Englishman? My point is that whenever a way to designate the as-yet unnamed deviant type is sought, foreignness is consistently evoked. Metonymy is invoked as a pretext (it is where the vice comes from), either implicitly or explicitly, but my aim is to suggest that the trope is really based on metaphor, the perceived similarity between national identity and sexual identity both emerging at this time.

It was not only the French, moreover, who perceived homosexuality as a foreign affair. Just as, to the French, same-sex passion was German (or English or Greek or Italian or Bulgarian), to the English, it was French. This can be traced back at least as far as Dryden, who, in the epilogue to *The Duke of Guise*, refers to "a damned love-trick new brought o'er from France" (qtd. in Smith 1). In the late nineteenth century, Gilbert and Sullivan's parody of aestheticism, *Patience*, represented deviant sexuality by associating it with a French bean: "Then a sentimental passion of a vegetable fashion must excite your languid spleen, / An attachment *à la* Plato for a bashful young potato, or a not-too-French French bean" (qtd. in Sinfield 92). Although the bean is qualified as a "not-too-French French bean," the qualification permits a repetition that stands as an intensification: a French French bean, doubly French, doubly deviant. In addition to this, the attachment to the bean is introduced with the French expression "à la" (not to mention the reference to Platonic — i.e., Greek — love).

An even clearer example comes from the homoerotic sphere of the navy. A British naval officer in the early 1900s reported on his personal experiences of same-sex eroticism between men, claiming that "homosexuality was rife and one could see with his own eyes how it was going on between officers" and that "sodomy is a regular thing on ships that go on long cruises." Despite this firsthand experience of domestic vice, this same officer was persuaded that homosexuality was even more widespread among foreign forces: "I have been told that in some services (the Austrian and French for instance) nobody ever remarks about it, taking such a thing as a natural proceeding" (qtd. in Hyde, *Love* 159).[11] The peculiar thing about this testimony is that not only is no evidence necessary for this officer, but the very lack of evidence becomes proof of the charge. The very thing that proves the prevalence of homosexuality elsewhere is that no one mentions it! Such logic is beautifully irrefutable.

Although I am arguing that the tendency to view homosexuality as a foreign affair has its origins at the turn of the century, I do not mean to suggest that it has now disappeared. Indeed, anecdotes from our own fin de siècle would show the contrary, as a widely reported incident of the early

1990s illustrates. In one of the most recent manifestations of this figuration, the problem of homosexuality is construed this time as a British phenomenon by someone of no less a cultural standing than a future French prime minister. In a diplomatic faux pas picked up by the *New York Times*, Edith Cresson claimed in an interview in London's *Observer* that "25 percent of Englishmen — as well as Americans and Germans — are homosexual and that, in contrast to Frenchmen, 'Anglo-Saxon men are not interested in women.' "[12] The British popular press responded in kind, impugning the validity of the remark coming from "the leader of a country 'where men carry handbags and kiss each other on the cheek in public' " (qtd. in Riding).[13]

As this brief overview suggests, the association between the national type and the sexual "deviant" is persistent if protean. Pointing out the endurance of this figuration of "otherness" is not meant to promote belief in an underlying essentialism. The overview is intended, rather, to convey something of the different ways these associations were socially and historically structured, from the assimilation of theological deviance to sexual nonconformity and cultural colonization to political exploitation and the sometimes willful misprision of culturally specific gender role expectations. What is specific to the formation of these attributions in the late nineteenth century, however, is that sexual identity and national identity shared one important common feature: both were thought to be types of person, both were forms of "incorporation" where inner essence was thought to be manifested through the appearance and behavior of the outer body, a development facilitating their displacement from one to the other. While the use of nationality as a euphemism for sexuality can be traced throughout history, it takes on a special resonance in the late nineteenth century. One not only practices a foreign vice; one becomes, literally, a foreigner. The homosexual is viewed as "alien" in a particularly categorical, immutable, and saturated way.

Such metaphors of nationality were available, then, in the late nineteenth century as a way of alluding to same-sex male eroticism (national identity, too, being primarily a male attribute). Such networks of connotation allowed for considerable ambiguity: where the more literal-minded public might perceive nothing, a more knowing reader might perceive a coded allusion. The term *homosexual* itself originated in German, a connection played up in euphemisms such as "le vice allemand." Gradually, however, the German *practice* became a German *type*, the homosexual or "Eulenbougre." In the latter part of what Anderson calls "the age of nationalism in Europe" (67), 1820 to 1920, the use of nationality reflects a growing sense that national identity not only designates a point of origin but stands metonymically for a type of person, with "a past, a case history, a childhood" and now also a future.[14]

Switching Tracks

So far I have discussed primarily French and German contexts, but now I propose to turn to another writer who used foreignness, this time in a literary context. Oscar Wilde used equivocal metaphors of multinational embodiment skillfully in his work, playing particularly—though not exclusively—with the Anglo-French border. Wilde positioned himself in such a way as to invoke Frenchness in England and Englishness in France, using the foreign as a queer signifier to suggest the as-yet shadowy boundaries of an identity that was in the process of establishing fixed (corporeal) borders.[15]

Although Wilde appears today, in the words of Alan Sinfield, as "always already queer" (2), historians of sexuality have argued that this perception would not have been shared by Wilde's contemporaries. As already mentioned, Cohen has argued that it was not until Wilde's trial in 1895 that a cluster of characteristics loosely associated with aestheticism became so closely linked in public consciousness with homosexuality that today it is difficult to imagine they were ever separable. Similarly, while homosexuality is widely linked to effeminacy today, this may be seen as a result of the association between the perceived effeminacy of the Aesthetic Movement represented by Wilde and his subsequent conviction on charges of sodomy, as argued by Sinfield. Before that association was forged, it was not inconsistent for men to be portrayed as both feminine and vehemently heterosexual.

Before this new identity of "the homosexual" was consolidated, however, it was possible to use certain signifiers of what Eve Kosofsky Sedgwick terms textual "switchpoints." At such moments, some readers continue to read along one track, while, for others, the switchpoint makes a different reading possible. Thus, in the case of effeminacy, for example, some readers do not see the aesthete's sexuality as compromised by his effeminacy, but for others this signal is precisely what may trigger a different interpretation (Sedgwick 52–72).

In a culture used to thinking of sexual deviance as a matter of nationality, a new set of textual switchpoints becomes available. Sedgwick has described Wilde's incorporation of Germanness as one such important switchpoint in Wilde's play *The Importance of Being Earnest* (1895). She is careful to remind us that "in 1895 homosexuality is not yet referred to as *le vice allemand*" (65), but at least in France the association was becoming known, as a French novel by Armand Dubarry from 1896 entitled *Les invertis: Le vice allemand* suggests.[16] There was perhaps already enough awareness of the German origins of the discourse about same-sex desire to establish German as a code for those in the know in Britain, too.[17]

But while Sedgwick focuses on German switchpoints, my purpose is to focus on some examples of Wilde's incorporations of French. After all, even

Sedgwick's examples of Germanity depend upon French mediation: "le vice allemand" is named *in French*, and "Do you speak German?" was a pick-up line for *French* men. Another obvious example is Wilde's use of French decadent literature, in particular the novel *A rebours* (1884) by Huysmans, in *The Picture of Dorian Gray*. This "poisonous book" with its yellow cover is sent to Dorian by Lord Henry. When Dorian reads it (immediately after reading the account of Sibyl Vane's inquest), he is completely absorbed by it. "For years, Dorian Gray could not free himself from the influence of this book" (Wilde, *Complete*, Collins, 102). Dorian is thus "infected" by a foreign influence whose point of origin in France stands metonymically for the nationality of the vice to which allusion is being made.

The trope of a poisonous yellow book continues to be a switchpoint in cultural representations of Wilde. On 5 April 1895, Wilde left the Old Bailey after losing his case against the Marquess of Queensberry. Later that day, he was arrested at the Cadogan Hotel, an event witnessed and reported by the press, who made sure to mention that, under his arm, Wilde carried a yellow book. Some assumed the book in question was *The Yellow Book*, the review published by John Lane featuring the work of the aesthetes and the drawings of Aubrey Beardsley, but others have made different claims. Robbie Ross's biographer, for example, writes: "The association with Wilde's arrest killed the *Yellow Book*, even though, *in truth*, the book he carried was *Aphrodite* by Pierre Louÿs, which just happened to be bound in yellow" (Borland, 46; emphasis added).[18]

Yellowness had long been associated with the poisonous influence of French novels. As Kate Flint reports in *The Woman Reader*, the French novel, with its instantly recognizable yellow cover, was a "familiar nineteenth-century bugbear," and it rapidly became "an instant signifier of immorality" (87, 287). Yellow covers show up in texts both visual and literary to signify immorality throughout the nineteenth century. Virtually *anything* French was suspect, moreover, not just books. An anonymous correspondent to the *Daily Telegraph* complained about the pornography that was to be bought in the street, citing "French transparencies" as an example (Walkowitz 122). The adjective here serves less as an accurate description of origin than as a metonym for the sexual content. The substitution of a French book for an English one under Wilde's arm is thus overdetermined, but identifying the French book as being "in truth" *Aphrodite* adds yet another layer of myth, since *Aphrodite* would not be published until the following year (1896). The book would be the first successful publication of the Mercure de France press, an offshoot of the review closely associated with the decadent movement in France whose yellow covers with a caduceus were to become quite distinctive, and which would later publish Douglas's poems (Ellmann, *Oscar Wilde* 500–502).[19] It seems unlikely, then, that Wilde could have been carrying this novel when arrested, but the (ex post facto) identification of the poisonous yellow book as "in truth" a decadent French novel fulfills a cultural need: the supplanting of the native *Yellow Book* by a different yellow book that carries the marker of foreignness associated with deviant sexuality. The choice of author in this retroactive displacement was perhaps facilitated by the fact that what Louÿs *did* publish in 1895 was *Les Chansons de Bilitis*, a collection of poems celebrating lesbian love, one of the few French contributions to the debate over the merits of Greek love being waged primarily in England and Germany.[20]

The Frenchness of *Salomé*

One of Wilde's texts which seems to offer the most complex crossing of national boundaries is his play *Salomé*. The transnational history of this text — its composition, its plot, its publication history and reception, its illustrations, and its performance — underscore the importance of France in constituting homosexual identity in late nineteenth-century England.

Though engendered by an Anglo-Irish tradition, the "birth" of *Salomé* was decidedly French. Even the conception of the play was French: Wilde was influenced by, among other works, Flaubert's *Trois Contes*, which had been loaned to him by Walter Pater upon its publication in 1877 (Ellmann, *Oscar Wilde* 84); by the description of Moreau's *Salomé* in Huysmans's *A rebours*; and by Mallarmé's *Hérodiade* (Wilde met Mallarmé several times in Paris in 1891, as he began the composition of *Salomé*).[21]

Wilde was in France and had been thinking about the theme of Salome for some time. Richard Ellmann takes up the narrative: "One night [Wilde] told the Salome story to a group of young French writers, and returned to his lodgings in the boulevard des Capucines. A blank notebook lay on the table, and it occurred to him that he might as well write down what he had been telling them" (*Oscar Wilde* 343). After writing for a while, Wilde went out to a café where he heard some "wild and terrible music" that inspired him to go back and finish the play. Ellmann thus embeds the play in a French tradition, the product of interaction with French writers and French cafes, inspired by such wild music as is not heard in British drawing rooms and music halls. One of the writers who helped the most in its composition was the aforementioned Pierre Louÿs, to whom the French edition of *Salomé* was dedicated. That Louÿs should reputedly be the author of the book Wilde holds under his arm when he is arrested for sodomy in 1895, then, takes on additional significance.

Feminist critics have already noted that part of the subversive character of the play is its representation of the threat and punishment of the sexually aggressive New Woman,[22] but in a "straight" reading of the play, in which the principal romantic relationships are presumed to be heterosexual, the result is to make heterosexuality look pretty bad: Herod's infatuation with Salome is incestuous, while Salome's love proves fatal as well as vaguely necrophilic.[23]

In a queer reading of the play,[24] on the other hand, the euphemistic use of nationality in and around this play expands our understanding of queer textual switchpoints and illustrates how foreignness stands in for the yet-to-be-adopted category of the homosexual. To begin with, queer readings of the play sometimes rely on an identification of Wilde with the character of Salome, an identification cemented by Ellmann's publication in 1987 of a photograph allegedly of Wilde posing as Salome with the head of John the Baptist. As Merlin Holland, Wilde's grandson, states, "It seemed almost too good to be true," an answer to the prayers of critics frustrated by the lack of really overt queerness in Wilde, but also to the prayers of those who believe in the existence of a homosexual type, a person who cannot engage in homosexual acts without betraying the fact in campy cross-dressing. The photo exteriorized the inner type believed to exist in the body of Wilde. In this reading, Salome is not a woman who wants to kiss a john, but a man hiding behind a female mask in order to explore the fantasy of kissing the mouth of another man.[25]

This identification was complicated by the belated recognition that the photo was not of Wilde at all, but of a Hungarian opera singer — Alice Guszalewicz — in the role of Salomé, though the misattribution suggests how much, in the words of Elaine Showalter, we all wanted it to be true. We wanted to believe it was Wilde, even as it seemed too good to be true. What, besides the belief in "types," facilitated our rush to judgment? Could it have anything to do with the French sources of the photo, which was first published in *Le Monde* accompanying a review in 1987, and later reproduced in Ellmann's book with a French attribution (the caption identifies the photo as part of a French archive, "Collection Guillot de Saix, H. Roger Viollet, Paris")? It would seem, once again, that what comes from France is always already marked as sexually suspect.

The role of foreignness as coded reference also helps elucidate the question — one that has dogged the history of this play — of why Wilde wrote it in French in the first place.[26] There have been several theories: that Wilde *didn't* write it in French (which has been disproved by examination of the manuscripts); that it was written for Sarah Bernhardt, who didn't speak English; and that it was written in French to evade the strict controls of the English censors. Some question why Wilde wrote in French, given that his style would be impaired by writing in a language other than English. Wilde was not a native speaker of French, and while he expressed himself adequately, he did not write fluently; one critic even writes that Wilde "wrote French as he spoke it — that is, charmingly, but simply and somewhat in the manner of the phrasebook" (Bird 57). Others defend Wilde's French in *Salomé*, arguing that his simplistic but choppy style was meant to evoke the French and Belgian symbolists, especially Maeterlinck,[27] but why he could not have developed a symbolist style in English remains unclear.

The idea that Wilde wrote for Bernhardt has been consistently repudiated, though some (such as Kerry Powell) maintain that this may have been an unconscious intention on Wilde's part. Powell also argues that French was necessary in order to evade the censor, which would be a more convincing argument if Wilde had succeeded, but in fact the play was severely repressed. Permission was not granted for it to be performed publicly in Britain until 1931, long after other works had been allowed to slip by, such as Massenet's operatic version of the Salome story, *Hérodiade*, a license for which was granted as early as 1904. The official reason for the ban on Wilde's *Salomé* was not obscenity but a law forbidding the depiction on stage of biblical characters. As though to underscore the fact that Wilde's play was singled out for unusually strict scrutiny, however, in the English version of Massenet's opera, the characters of Herod and Herodias were merely transposed onto *other biblical characters* (Moreame and Mesotoade) and set in Ethiopia. Moreover, the title was changed from *Hérodiade* to *Salomé* (Bird 78)! The differential treatment of Massenet's opera shows that the censors could be very selective about the interpretations of the law. In the case of Wilde's *Salomé*, the censorship suggests that there was more at stake than merely proscribed biblical representation.

The invocation of the ban on biblical representation was clearly a mere pretext; the real reason for the ban lies elsewhere. In order to understand the possible coded meanings of writing a play in French for production in England and the threat that this posed, one can do worse than to defer to the words of the censor himself, Edward F. Smyth Pigott, who, testifying before the House of Commons shortly before he banned Wilde's play, stated: "With regard to *French* plays, my principle has always been to extend to them an *extra-territorial privilege*. People who go to see *French* plays, played by *French* companies and written for *French purposes*, know what they are going to see" (qtd. in Powell 37; emphasis added). Mr. Pigott attributed to audiences of French plays a special insider knowledge — "they know what they are going to see" — that is denied the average theatergoer, who must be protected by the censor from learning something he or she does not already know. Such unstated inside knowledge is precisely the kind activated by switchpoints. French plays (such as *Salomé*) are written for "French purposes," which are implicitly construed as somehow different from British purposes, though what these purposes are remains, so to speak, unspeakable. Wilde, however, no doubt knew something of "French purposes"; France is, after all, where he chose to spend his honeymoon, and it would be his home and final resting place after his release from prison. Like ambassadors with diplomatic immunity, French plays may receive extraterritorial privilege. If diplomatic immunity means not being subject to the same laws as national citizens, laws which in Britain included at this time the notorious and French-sounding Labouchere Amendment,[28] extraterritorial privilege means that French plays are exempt from the usual laws governing censorship. But *Salomé* was not granted such immunity, nor was its author exempt from prosecution under the Labouchere Amendment.

Though the censor declined to grant extraterritorial privilege, it seems obvious that in some ways *Salomé* was written in French precisely to be performed in French in England, presumably for the kind of people who go to French plays for French purposes. Wilde's play positioned itself, then, as something foreign, a yellow-covered French import into England like the decadent material that poisoned Dorian Gray. And although the play was banned and plans for its performance had to be dropped, it continued to circulate and to infect in print. One year, almost to the day, after the simultaneous publication of the French version in Paris and London, an English translation was published, and a new round of border crossings commenced.[29]

When the play "came out" in its English translation a century ago, in 1894, it was published with the illustrations by Aubrey Beardsley which have since become so intimately linked to it. Beardsley's first illustration of the play, showing the dripping head being held aloft by a triumphant Salome declaring, "J'ai baisé ta bouche Iokanaan," had appeared in the April 1893 issue of *The Studio*, leading to a commission to illustrate the English translation. For this, Beardsley added several more illustrations. In one of these, Salome holds aloft the head of John the Baptist, lying in a pool of blood on what Wilde's text describes as a silver shield. Beardsley's rendering manages also to evoke a halo, but in the fanciful image the shield-halo seems to form a sort of ruff around the head of John. One wonders whether Wilde and Beardsley were aware that in the memoirs of Pierre de l'Estoile, the "mignons" of Henri III are described in the following terms: "Ces beaux mignons portaient leurs cheveux longuets, frisés et refrisés par artifices, remontant par-dessus leurs petits bonnets de velours, comme font les putains du bordel, et leurs fraises de chemises de toile d'atour empesées et longues de demi pied, de façon qu'à voir leur tête dessus leur fraise, il semblait que ce fût le chef saint Jean dans un plat" (qtd. in Lever 82). That Wilde knew something of this history is evident from the reference to Anne de Joyeuse, one of the "mignons," in *The Picture of Dorian Gray* (*Complete*, Collins, 107). Perhaps Wilde or Beardsley had read Pierre de l'Estoile's work when it was republished in France in a twelve-volume edition between 1875 and 1896. Wilde might certainly have noticed that a ruff was the inevitable attribute of the ancestors of all French decadent heroes and heroines. Des Esseintes, hero of the "poisonous" *A rebours*, resembled, "par un singulier phénomène d'atavisme," the ancestor described as the "mignon" who linked the effeté des Esseintes to his robust forefathers: "une seule toile servait d'intermédiaire, mettait un point de suture entre le passé et le présent, une tête mystérieuse et rusée, aux traits morts et tirés, aux pommettes ponctuées d'une virgule de fard, aux cheveux gommés et enroulés de perles, au col tendu et peint, sortant des cannelures d'une rigide fraise" (47–48). Des Esseintes, himself a latter-day "mignon," thus had an ancestor whose morbid head with its "traits morts et tirés" evokes that of John the Baptist. The ancestor, moreover, served to "suture" the past and present, bringing together these representational codes "with a single stitch."

Similarly, Rachilde's Raoule de Vénérande, the heroine of *Monsieur Vénus* (a text which exerted considerable influence on Wilde during the composition of *Dorian Gray*), lives surrounded by portraits of "les aïeux en pourpoint, les aïeules en fraise Medicis," a costume she herself assumes in the drug-induced hallucinations of her would-be lover Raittolbe, who sees her "vêtue du pourpoint de Henri III, offrant une rose à Antinoüs" (158, 75). The evocation of a ruff was also the attribute of decadent Laurent Tailhade, who wore "un collier de barbe courte et soignée [qui] sembl[ait] appeler la fraise des Valois," according to Ernest Raynaud (118). While Tailhade himself was not known for homosexual behavior, the decadents in general were often perceived to affect "des goûts contre nature" (qtd. in Richard 98). The beruffled figure of John the Baptist thus offers yet another switchpoint that leads from *Salomé* to "le vice italien" in French and sutures together a tradition of sexually deviant identities.[30]

But let us return to Beardsley's illustration once again. It purports to illustrate the moment when the arm of the black executioner appears above the cistern bearing the head of John the Baptist, as requested by Salome. Beardsley depicts the shield/halo/ruff supported by a black column. The literal reading of this image is that of the arm of the executioner, with the muscles suggested by fine white lines and an arm band around his upper arm. But this arm is strangely elongated and detached from the rest of the body to which it belongs. The black arm thus becomes a kind of visual switchpoint, for the white details serve not only to delineate musculature but also to suggest a phallic quality, aptly illustrating the "superfluity of naughtiness" which, according to Robbie Ross, characterizes Beardsley's work (qtd. in Borland 108). (In the case of *Salomé*, some of the more obvious examples of genitalia were suppressed — on the title page, for example — but penises remain everywhere in this series, disguised as candlesticks in the "entrance of Herodias," for example, and as part of the musician in "The dance of the seven veils.") With the image of Salome reaching out for the head, Beardsley suggests the phallic power supporting this moment which marks Salome's possession of "Iokanaan" (as John is called in the play, evoking archaic and foreign versions of the French name *Jean* such as *Jehan* and *Johanne*), and which prepares the moment of consummation when she kisses his mouth. Perhaps this is why Wilde inscribed the copy of *Salomé* he gave to Beardsley with these words: "For the only artist who, besides myself, knows what the dance of the seven veils is, and can see that invisible dance" (qtd. in Bird 75).

The publication of the translation of *Salomé* completed a chain of events in which Wilde wrote the play in a language that was not his "national" tongue (French) and published it in Paris in 1893, the same year that Max Nordau's *Degeneration* appeared in French translation and named Paris as the capital of decadence and Wilde as one of its exponents. The translation "back" into English brings the text across a symbolic border and positions it as French within the anglophone context.

The English translation of *Salomé* is also remarkable for being attributed to none other than Lord Alfred Douglas. This was an unusual choice for a translator, for apparently Douglas's French was not all that good, and Wilde was extremely dissatisfied with the results. In Ellmann's words, "Wilde had not reckoned with his beloved's inadequate French" (*Oscar Wilde* 402), while, according to H. Montgomery Hyde, "Lord Alfred Douglas's translation of *Salomé* was in fact rejected by Wilde and is not the published version given [in Hyde's *Annotated Oscar Wilde*] *even though the text still bears his name as translator*" (305; emphasis added). In other words, most critics today concur that the translation owes very little to Douglas and is most likely the work mainly of Wilde himself (see also Bird 69). What is striking about this indeterminacy is that Douglas continued to be credited in print as translator regardless of his actual contributions, and this as recently as the 1989 Faber edition of the play. It is as though, in erasing the connotation of otherness conveyed by the use of French, the switchpoint had to be replaced with another sign, a trace of that queerness, which remains inscribed on the title page through the name of Douglas, the name that would continue to be the one most closely associated with Wilde and his nameless love. When Wilde's text crosses the national and linguistic boundary from French to English, Douglas's name replaces the foreignness of the text and embodies the unsettling sense of otherness latent in the play. Douglas's linguistic inadequacies stand for other inadequacies, not the least of which was the inadequacy of Victorian society's understanding of "the homosexual."

Even in recent editions of the collected works of Wilde, the play continues to bear the inscription "Translated from the French of Oscar Wilde by Lord Alfred Douglas," as in both the 1966 Collins edition and the 1994 Barnes and Noble edition. Both editions also reproduce on the cover Beardsley's drawing of Salome holding the head of John the Baptist aloft as the visual correlative to "collected works." (The Barnes and Noble edition even boasts a yellow cover, making Wilde, finally, the author of a yellow book a century after his trial.) Thus the play was not translated merely from French, but from "the French of Oscar Wilde," that is, an idiolect bearing some relationship to the language (or *langue*) called French but at the same time the unique property of an individual called Oscar Wilde. (In contrast, Ellmann's 1982 translation is simply "translated by Richard Ellmann.")[31]

By the time the play was first performed, in France in 1896, Wilde was serving his term in prison in England. Like John the Baptist, Wilde was in prison for heresy (thanks to the historical conflation of heresy and buggery), a foreign import like the play. Like John the Baptist, Wilde lost his head (a phrase he uses in *De Profundis*). Thanks to the Lord Chamberlain's ban, the play could not be performed publicly in England, but this did not mean the play could not be performed at all.[32] There were private representations (five from 1905 and 1931), but they continued to carry the stigma of both queer and foreign otherness with them, as the discussion of the 1918 performance I began with illustrates.

But, while *Salomé* stands at the center of a network of French connections that resonate with queerness, this play is not the only aspect of Wilde's work to invoke foreign identity as a switchpoint. As though in unconscious recognition of Wilde's incorporation of multinationalism, his son Vyvyan Holland begins his introduction to the *Complete Works of Oscar Wilde* by pointing out in the very first sentence: "Oscar Wilde's family is Dutch in origin." (Wilde thus has something in common with J. T. Grein, one of the plaintiffs in the 1918 case discussed at the beginning of this chapter who becomes associated with the unpatriotic immorality of *Salomé*.) In his memoir *Son of Oscar Wilde*, Holland goes into the family history in more detail, and emphatically rejects the idea that the Wilde family was from Durham, England, in favor of Dutch origins (14). When the family went into exile in Europe to avoid the unwanted publicity generated by the trial, they adopted the name "Holland." Vyvyan Holland claims this was a family name on his mother's side, thus the pseudonym would be unrelated to the Dutch origins of the Wildes (his father's side) (*Son* 76), yet the "Dutchness" of "Holland" obviously preserves, even embodies, the trace of the very criminal identity that the family wished to escape. Holland is home to Dutchmen, queer and unpatriotic men like Wilde and Grein; by taking their place of origin as his patronymic, Vyvyan preserves his affiliations in the very act of repudiating them.

But Holland's choices continued to make his father seem other, alien, foreign. When his memoir was republished in 1988, it included a foreword by Merlin Holland (Oscar's grandson), in which he quotes Alec Waugh describing Vyvyan's reluctance at first to write about Wilde: "No one could be more completely normal and he resented being pestered by homosexuals, *foreigners for the most part*, who wanted to pay their respects to the sacred memory of 'Oscar, the martyr' " (2; emphasis added). This reference to foreignness appears almost gratuitous, but is part of a pattern of associations where Wilde is concerned. In an appendix to the memoir, W. W. Laird adds a reminiscence of Wilde in which he opines: "There was something foreign to us, and inconsequential, in his modes of thought" (250). Such passages underscore the general impression of multinationalism that seems to have attached itself to cultural representations of Wilde's persona.

The trajectory through national otherness thus offers a partial answer to the question "Comment peut-on être homosexuel?" The zone of "otherness" created by national borders offers a way to name an identity that could not or dare not otherwise speak its name. The answer, then, to the question

"Comment peut-on être homosexuel?" may be "On peut être français." "Comment peut-on être français?" is, of course, another question.

Notes

1. See Michael Kettle, *Salome's Last Veil: The Libel Case of the Century*. See also Philip Hoare's *Oscar Wilde's Last Stand* and the fictionalized account of these events in Pat Barker, *The Eye in the Door*.

2. See Sylvia Molloy for information on how some of these issues played out in the context of a somewhat different process of national identity formation in Latin America.

3. For further discussion of Foucault, see Sinfield (11–17).

4. See Féray for further information about the role of Germanophobia in the French reception of "homosexualité."

5. Cohen seems, however, to be telescoping two moments. The reference to "posing" as a sodomite was relevant to the first trial, in which Wilde sued the Marquess of Queensberry for libel. To win his case, the Marquess had to prove not that Wilde *was* a sodomite, but that he posed as one (hence the concept of typing that Cohen evokes). Wilde lost his case and was then immediately sued for acts of gross indecency, a trial in which proof of action was required — and furnished. Wilde lost this case too, hence the sentence to Reading Gaol. The first trial supports Cohen's argument, but the second, with its focus on behavior, not appearance, seems to undo the conceptual work of the first by once again focusing attention on actions.

6. The dictionaries do not, however, provide this much detail on the subject. I owe these details to an unpublished article by Frederic Silverstolpe, who, drawing on recent scholarship in German, attempts to correct the distorted account created by Havelock Ellis that Benkert was a member of the medical profession. I am indebted to Martha Vicinus for helping me locate this article. See also Manfred Herzer, "Kertbeny and the Nameless Love"; and Jean-Claude Féray and Manfred Herzer, "Homosexual Studies and Politics in the Nineteenth Century: Karl Maria Kertbeny."

7. See *Trésor de la langue française: Dictionnaire de la langue du XIXe et du XXe siècle. Le Robert: dictionnaire de la langue française* (2d ed., 1985) further notes that this usage is as a substantive, and one must wait until 1894 for the first adjectival usage (underscoring Foucault's hypothesis that the word was perceived to refer to a person, an identity, rather than a quality of actions). See also Féray.

8. The use of the euphemism "le vice italien" was known in late nineteenth-century France and is recapitulated by John Grand-Carteret in *Derrière "Lui"* (13).

9. The Wilde trial may have contributed to a perception that homosexuality was also a British vice, but the association was not new. Maurice Lever reports that as early as the eighteenth century, Freemasons were targets of homosexual accusation because the order did not admit women. Hence the term served as something of a euphemism, but it was always used in English (rather than the French "franc maçon"), as in "Voulez-vous être *freemason*?" (323).

10. See also John Grand-Carteret, *Derrière "Lui."*

11. For further information about homosexuality in the British Navy, see Arthur Gilbert, "Buggery and the British Navy, 1700–1861."

12. Cresson's remarks are also credited with inspiring the republication of John Grand-Carteret's *Derrière "Lui"* by Patrick Cardon.

13. The tone of the *Times* article was one of detached amusement, but the United States has its own versions of these attributions. According to *The Joy of Gay Sex*, fellatio was dubbed by the French "le vice américain" (qtd. in *Contemporary French*

Civilization 16.2 [1992]: 201), and music critic Philip Brett reports that "gamelan is a gay marker in American music" (238). Joseph Litvak's essay about the eroticized space of the classroom, "Pedagogy and Sexuality," opens with an anecdote about a French teacher, which leads Litvak to muse parenthetically "Why . . . is it always a French teacher? If French teachers didn't exist, American culture would no doubt have to invent them. Come to think of it, it sort of *did* invent them" (19).

14. Anderson offers Hungary as one of his case studies of emergent nationalism; thus it seems appropriate that Benkert von Kertbeny, the inventor of the term *homosexual*, himself should have chosen this nationality for his imagined identity. It has long been assumed that "Kertbeny" was an anagrammatical pseudonym that he chose, but in fact it was a family name he was entitled to and which he adopted with full legal authority: "In almost all the literature on Kertbeny it is stated that his name is only a pseudonym made by a kind of Hungarianizing of his German family name, by exchanging syllables and adding the letter *y*" (Herzer 3). But Benkert liked to pose as a foreigner, specifically a Hungarian, a fact which fueled the myth of the Hungarian-sounding pseudonym. (See Manfred Herzer for a list of the people to whom Benkert introduced himself as a Hungarian.) Although born in Vienna and a native speaker of German, having grown up in Budapest, he claimed to be Hungarian and gained a reputation as a translator from Hungarian into German. Herzer theorizes that Kertbeny chose to represent himself this way because the widespread sympathy for persecuted and oppressed Hungarian patriots gave him an advantage in his social dealings (3), but it also positions him as a foreigner with respect to the sexual norms of mainstream Germanophone culture that he challenged. In addition, Kertbeny traveled extensively abroad, gathering information about those he would label "homosexuals." (His sources in France included Charles Baudelaire. This is not the only time the name of Baudelaire is linked to male homosexuality. Proust believed Baudelaire to have been a practicing homosexual, a claim discussed by Gide in his *Journal* of 14 May 1921.) His own biographical constructions thus enacted the multinational dimension of emergent homosexual identity.

15. On Wilde's reception in France, see Nancy Erber, "The French Trials of Oscar Wilde."

16. Féray, "Une Histoire" (326: 124, note 40). Oscar Méténier's *Vertus et vices allemands* (1904) is also useful in documenting the emergence of French perceptions.

17. According to Vyvyan Holland, while he was a schoolboy in Germany, Wilde's works "were already being used as textbooks of English in Germany" even though they were banned in England (87).

18. Borland's book is not one particularly sympathetic to Wilde: "Justice may have been served when Wilde was sent to prison, but he should not have been convicted on the perjured evidence of these young louts" (48). Wilde's biographer, Richard Ellmann, makes a less specific claim with regard to what Wilde was carrying when arrested; he says only that Wilde "groped . . . for a book with a yellow cover" (456).

19. *Aphrodite* was first published in serial form under the title *L'Esclavage* in the review *Mercure de France* 68–72 (Aug.-Dec. 1895). See Alfred Vallette, *Lettres à A.-Ferdinand Herold* (26).

20. See Christopher Robinson, *Scandal in the Ink* (17–18), and Linda Dowling, *Hellenism and Homosexuality in Victorian Oxford*.

21. For information on the sources and genesis of the play, see Bird (79–80) and Ellmann (339–45). For further information on representations of Salome, see Bram Dijkstra, *Idols of Perversity*; Françoise Meltzer, *Salome and the Dance of Writing*; and Helen Grace Zagona, *The Legend of Salome and the Principle of Art for Art's Sake*. For the biblical sources and an archetypal interpretation, see Bettina L. Knapp, *Women in*

Myth (87–110). For further details on Wilde's French sources, see Kelver Hartley, *Oscar Wilde: L'influence française dans son oeuvre.*

22. See, for example, Jane Marcus, "Salome: The Jewish Princess Was a New Woman."

23. The straight reading also sometimes erases the explicitly same-sex relationship that Wilde portrayed in the love of the page for the young Syrian. In some productions (and in Strauss's operatic version of Wilde's play), the role of the page is taken by a woman, yet the figure of the adolescent has often been the favorite site of projections or representations of same-sex desire. See, for example, Martha Vicinus, "The Adolescent Boy: Fin-de-Siècle Femme Fatale?"

24. In *Who Was That Man? A Present for Mr. Oscar Wilde*, Neil Bartlett comments on "the lament of a pageboy for his suicidal beloved" (40); that Salome is a "*daughter* of Sodom" and that Salome's desire for John the Baptist "is suddenly that of an adolescent boy" (42); and that, thanks to the symbolic use of flowers (particularly the infamous green carnation), "[t]he Princess reveals, when she promises her young man a little green flower, that she is part of an elaborate imagery and system of beliefs associated with homosexuality" (48). Bartlett is not the first, however. See also Kate Millet, *Sexual Politics*: "For all her exhibitionism and imperious clitoral command, Salome is not exclusively or even fundamentally female; she is Oscar Wilde too. The play is a drama of homosexual guilt and rejection followed by a double revenge. Salome repays the prophet's rebuttal by demanding his head, and then, in Wilde's uneasy vision of retribution, Salome is slain by Herod's guards" (153).

25. In "Overtures to *Salomé*," Ellmann has suggested that Wilde saw himself as Herod.

26. See Kerry Powell's *Oscar Wilde and the Theatre of the 1890s* (33–54). Powell writes, "the discussion of *Salomé* has not yielded final or even satisfying answers to some of the most obvious and pertinent questions which its strange career suggests. Why did Wilde write the play in French?" (33). There is no doubt, however, that it was written in French. Clyde de L. Ryals describes both the first draft and the fair copy manuscripts of the play, which sold at Sotheby's on 3 April 1950, as "both in French entirely in Wilde's own hand."

27. See Powell (46–47). It is curious to note, however, how closely the criticisms of Wilde's French echo those of Benkert's German. Some thought it strange that Benkert, a native speaker of Hungarian, should choose to invent the neologism "homosexualität" in German when his knowledge of the latter "n'est pas un modèle de correction, il lui échappe des fautes à faire frémir les moins délicats" (qtd. in French in Féray's "Une Histoire" 327: 177).

28. The radical MP Labouchere, responsible for the amendment, was indeed of French (Huguenot) origin. His name literally means "the butcher's wife" or "the butcher woman," and thus, for francophones, the name could add ironic or sinister associations to the amendment, which was sinister enough in its own right.

29. The French version was published on 22 February 1893 in an edition of 650 copies by the Librairie de l'Art Indépendent in Paris and Elkin Mathews and John Lane in London. The English translation was published on 9 February 1894 in an edition of 600 copies by Elkin Mathews and John Lane.

30. The trope of the sexually suspect, be-ruffed dandy survives in contemporary camp incarnations such as Tim Curry's portrayal of the transvestite transsexual from Transylvania, Dr. Frank N. Furter, in the cult film *The Rocky Horror Picture Show* (1975). In his first appearance, rising in an elevator as though evoking the elevation of John the Baptist from the cistern (as represented, for example, in Ken Russell's film *Salome's Last Dance*), the phallically named Dr. Frank N. Furter is wearing a

Draculaesque high-collared cape which forms a ruff framing his head. Just before Curry's appearance, Brad Majors, the "straight" male lead, attempts to explain the bizarre behavior of the "timewarping" Transylvanians by suggesting they might be "foreigners."

31. Wilde, *The Picture of Dorian Gray and Other Writings* (261–95). Also, the 1989 Faber edition states simply "Translated from the French by Lord Alfred Douglas" (iii).

32. The first public performance in England took place at the Savoy Theatre, London, in 1931. See Tydeman and Price for the most complete account of the history of the play in performance.

Works Cited

Anderson, Benedict. *Imagined Communities*. London: Verso, 1991.

Angenot, Marc. *Le cru et le faisandé: Sexe, littérature, et discours social à la Belle Epoque.* Brussels: Editions Labor, 1986.

Barker, Pat. *The Eye in the Door*. New York: Dutton, 1994.

Bartlett, Neil. *Who Was That Man? A Present for Mr. Oscar Wilde*. London: Serpent's Tail, 1988.

Baumont, Maurice. *L'Affaire Eulenburg et les origines de la guerre mondiale*. Paris: Payot, 1933.

Bird, Alan. *The Plays of Oscar Wilde*. London: Vision, 1977.

Borland, Maureen. *Wilde's Devoted Friend: A Life of Robert Ross*. Oxford: Lennard, 1990.

Brett, Philip. "Eros and Orientalism in Britten's Operas." In *Queering the Pitch: The New Gay and Lesbian Musicology*, ed. Philip Brett, et al. New York: Routledge, 1994.

Cohen, Ed. *Talk on the Wilde Side*. New York: Routledge, 1993.

Dijkstra, Bram. *Idols of Perversity*. New York: Oxford University Press, 1986.

Dowling, Linda. *Hellenism and Homosexuality in Victorian Oxford*. Ithaca: Cornell University Press, 1994.

Ellmann, Richard. *Oscar Wilde*. New York: Knopf, 1988.

———. "Overtures to *Salome*." In *Oscar Wilde: A Collection of Critical Essays*, ed. Richard Ellmann, 73–91. Englewood Cliffs, N.J.: Prentice-Hall, 1969.

Erber, Nancy. "The French Trials of Oscar Wilde." *Journal of the History of Sexuality* 6.4 (1996): 549–88.

Féray, Jean-Claude. "Une Histoire critique du mot homosexualité." *Arcadie* 325 (1981): 11–21.

———. "Une Histoire critique du mot homosexualité." *Arcadie* 326 (1981): 11–24.

———. "Une Histoire critique du mot homosexualité." *Arcadie* 327 (1981): 171–81.

———. "Une histoire critique du mot homosexualité." *Arcadie* 328 (1981): 246–58.

Féray, Jean-Claude, and Manfred Herzer, "Homosexual Studies and Politics in the Nineteenth Century: Karl Maria Kertbeny." *Journal of Homosexuality* 19.1 (1990): 23–47.

Flint, Kate. *The Woman Reader, 1837–1914*. New York: Oxford University Press, 1993.

Foucault, Michel. *The History of Sexuality*. Vol. 1: *An Introduction*. Trans. Robert Hurley. New York: Random House, 1990.

Gilbert, Arthur. "Buggery and the British Navy, 1700–1861." *Journal of Social History* 10 (1976): 72–98.

Grand-Carteret, John, ed. *Derrière "Lui."* 1907. Rpt. *Cahiers Gai-Kitsch-Camp* 16 (1992). Pref. Patrick Cardon.

Hartley, Kelver. *Oscar Wilde: L'influence française dans son oeuvre*. Paris: Librairie du Recueil Sirey, 1935.

Herzer, Manfred. "Kertbeny and the Nameless Love." *Journal of Homosexuality.* 12.1 (1985): 1–26.

Hoare, Philip. *Oscar Wilde's Last Stand: Decadence, Conspiracy, and the* Most *Outrageous Trial of the Century.* New York: Arcade Publishing, 1997.

Holland, Merlin. "Wilde as Salome?" *Times Literary Supplement* (22 July 1994): 14.

Holland, Vyvyan. *Son of Oscar Wilde.* 1954. Oxford: Oxford University Press, 1987.

Huas, Jeanine. *L'Homosexualité au temps de Proust.* Dinard: Editions Danclau, 1992.

Huysmans, Joris-Karl. *A rebours.* Paris: Union Générale d'Editions, 1975.

Hyde, H. Montgomery, ed. *The Annotated Oscar Wilde: Poems, Fiction, Plays, Lectures, Essays, and Letters.* New York: Clarkson N. Potter, 1982.

———. *The Love That Dared Not Speak Its Name.* Boston: Little, Brown, 1970.

Kettle, Michael. *Salome's Last Veil: The Libel Case of the Century.* London: Granada, 1977.

Knapp, Bettina L. *Women in Myth.* Albany: State University of New York Press, 1997.

Koestenbaum, Wayne. "Obscenity: A Celebration." *New York Times Magazine* (21 May 1995) 46–47.

Lever, Maurice. *Les Bûchers de Sodome: Histoire des "infâmes."* Paris: Fayard, 1985.

Litvak, Joseph. "Pedagogy and Sexuality." In *Professions of Desire: Lesbian and Gay Studies in Literature,* ed. George E. Haggerty and Bonnie Zimmerman. New York: MLA, 1995.

Marcus, Jane. "Salome: The Jewish Princess Was a New Woman." *Bulletin of the New York Public Library* 78 (1974): 95–113.

Meltzer, Françoise. *Salome and the Dance of Writing.* Chicago: University of Chicago Press, 1986.

Méténier, Oscar. *Vertus et vices allemands.* Paris: A. Michel, [1904].

Millet, Kate. *Sexual Politics.* Garden City, N.Y.: Doubleday, 1970.

Molloy, Sylvia. "Too Wilde for Comfort: Desire and Ideology in Fin-de-Siècle Spanish America." *Social Text* 31–32 (1992): 187–201.

Powell, Kerry. *Oscar Wilde and the Theatre of the 1890s.* Cambridge: Cambridge University Press, 1990.

Rachilde. *Monsieur Vénus.* Brussels: Brancart, 1884.

———. "Questions brûlantes." *La Revue Blanche* (1 September 1896): 193–200.

Raynaud, Ernest. *En Marge de la mêlée symboliste.* 3d ed. Paris: Mercure de France, 1936.

Richard, Noël. *Le Mouvement décadent: Dandys, esthètes et quintessants.* Paris: Nizet, 1968.

Riding, Alan. "Gallic Dart Distresses British Men." *New York Times* (20 June 1991): A3.

Robinson, Christopher. *Scandal in the Ink: Male and Female Homosexuality in Twentieth-Century French Literature.* London: Cassell, 1995.

Ryals, Clyde de L. "Oscar Wilde's *Salomé.*" *Notes and Queries* 6:2 (February 1959): 56–57.

Sedgwick, Eve Kosofsky. *Tendencies.* Durham: Duke University Press, 1993.

Showalter, Elaine. "It's Still Salome." *Times Literary Supplement* (2 September 1994): 13–14.

Simpson, Colin, Lewis Chester, and David Leitch. *The Cleveland Street Affair.* Boston: Little, Brown, 1976.

Sinfield, Alan. *The Wilde Century.* London: Cassell, 1994.

Smith, Timothy d'Arch. *Love in Earnest: Some Notes on the Lives and Writings of English "Uranian" Poets from 1889 to 1930.* London: Routledge and Kegan Paul, 1970.

Steakley, James D. "Iconography of a Scandal: Political Cartoons and the Eulenburg Affair in Wilhelmin Germany." In *Hidden From History: Reclaiming the Gay and*

Lesbian Past, ed. Martin Bauml Duberman et al., 233–63. New York: NAL, 1989.

Tydeman, William, and Steven Price. *Wilde: "Salomé."* Cambridge: Cambridge University Press, 1996.

Vallette, Alfred. *Lettres à A.-Ferdinand Herold*. Ed. Claire Lesage, Philippe Oriol, and Christian Soulignac. Paris: Editions du Fourneau, 1993.

Vicinus, Martha. "The Adolescent Boy: Fin-de-Siècle Femme Fatale?" *Journal of the History of Sexuality* 5.1 (1994): 90–114.

Walkowitz, Judith R. *City of Dreadful Delight: Narratives of Sexual Danger in Late-Victorian London*. Chicago: University of Chicago Press, 1992.

Wilde, Oscar. *Complete Works of Oscar Wilde*. London: Collins, 1948.

———. *Complete Works of Oscar Wilde*. New York: Barnes and Noble, 1994.

———. *The Picture of Dorian Gray and Other Writings*. Ed. Richard Ellmann. New York: Bantam, 1982.

———. *Salomé*. Intro. Steven Berkoff. London: Faber, 1989.

Zagona, Helen Grace. *The Legend of Salome and the Principle of Art for Art's Sake*. Geneva: Droz, 1960.

Chapter 9
The Politics of Posing
Translating Decadence in Fin-de-Siècle
Latin America

Sylvia Molloy

At a conference held a few years back in Brazil, I read a paper in which I reflected on the ambivalence and general disquiet awakened by Wilde in certain turn-of-the-century Latin American writers involved in the joint venture of constructing national identities and renewing literature. My paper attempted to capture the way in which José Martí's gaze, for one utopian moment, gathered Wilde the exemplary rebel and Wilde the problematic deviant (a *raro*, a *queer*, a fop) in one image — a conflictive one, to be sure, but still *one* image. I attempted to reconstruct the moment when both "sides" of Wilde could be thought of *together* before giving in to the pressure of ideology that would, first, tear them asunder and, second, retain one to the detriment of the other. Judging from the reaction of one of my respondents, the ambivalence and reader disquiet of the past century had carried onto this one. He proceeded to consider the relation between Wilde and Latin America as a "mere" case of imitation, mainly sartorial, a matter of fashion, an exercise in mimetic frivolity. Latin Americans had simply "played at" being Wilde, as one puts on a flashy costume that catches the eye, a green carnation on one's lapel. As such it was declared inconsequential and, moreover, insignificant. Decadence was, above all, a question of *pose*.

This reaction did not differ essentially from the way in which decadent Latin American literature had been read for years, that is, as frivolous and therefore reprehensible posturing. Indeed, when discussing the literary renewal effected by turn-of-the-century *modernismo* in Latin America, Max Henríquez Ureña wrote of Rubén Darío, "Rubén adopts a *pose*, not always in good taste; he flaunts his aristocratic attitudes and his nobleman's hands [*manos de marqués*]. . . . All this is a *pose* that he will overcome later, when he takes on the voice of the continent and becomes the interpreter of its anxieties and ideals" (97). Disdained for its levity or ridiculed for its effeteness and/or its extravagance, *posing* as a cultural gesture, whether in society or in literature, is considered by its critics a fleeting malady, a passing stage. A genteel fluttering of hands, an affected oddity, an *acting out*, it is reassuringly replaced by the authority of group ideology, the "voice of the continent." I want to think about *posing* in Latin America differently, not as the vapid posturing of some ghostly *fête galante*, a set of bodily or textual affectations at odds with national and continental discourses and concerns from which Latin America ultimately recovers, but as an oppositional practice within those very discourses and concerns, a decisive cultural statement whose political import and destabilizing energy I will try to recuperate and assess.

Posing in Latin America occurs (and becomes cause for concern) in a diversity of discourses—more precisely, in the intersection of those discourses, where the aesthetic, the political, the legal, and the medical converge. To trace the way in which posing constructs itself and to detect its points of tension, I shall look closely at a series of turn-of-the-century Latin American texts—articles, poems, social essays, case histories—and will consider them as they simultaneously converse and disagree with European constructions of posing.

Bodies on Display

Countries are read like bodies in the nineteenth century, in Latin America as well as elsewhere. Bodies, in turn, are read (and are offered up for reading) like cultural statements. To reflect on posing, I want to rescue that body, that posing body, in its intersection with nation and culture, stress its physical aspects even as it appears in texts, and consider its inevitable theatrical projections and its pictorial connotations. I want to consider what gestures accompany or, rather, determine the conduct of the Latin American *poseur*—how a field of visibility is constructed within which a pose is recognized as such and finds a coherent reading.

Exhibitions, as cultural forms, are the nineteenth century's genre of choice, scopophilia its guiding passion. Nationalities are displayed in world fairs, diseases in hospitals, art in museums, sex in *tableaux vivants*, goods in department stores, the quotidian as well as the exotic in photography, dioramas, panoramas. There are exhibitions; there is also exhibitionism. The latter word is first used to describe a pathology in 1866; the word for the individual—the exhibitionist—is coined in 1880. To exhibit is not only to show, of course; it is to make more visible. Charcot, that great exhibitionist of pathologized others, is described by Freud as "un visuel, un homme qui voit" (Didi-Huberman 30). When the resident photographers at the Salpetrière (resident because they had to be on hand to seize the "right" moment of pathology) photographed hysterics, they had to make sure that the disease would be seen. The touching up of photographs—cavernous eyes, darkened circles, grimacing mouths — was not uncommon. But, more important, the posing of patients themselves, eager to collaborate in the exhibition and repossess their disease, rendered the condition manifest (Didi-Huberman 46). I am particularly interested in that heightened visibility as it affects posing. Controlled by the poseur, exaggeration (i.e., the reinforcement of the visible) is a strategy of provocation, a challenge forcing a gaze, a reading, a framing. Posing is always an act of "being for" and, not infrequently, of "being against." Like Baudelaire's *maquillage*, "it should not hide nor should it avoid discovery; it must exhibit itself, if not with affectation, at least with a kind of innocence" (Baudelaire 914) — the very innocence that makes it threatening.

The fin de siècle reacts to the heightened visibility of the body, that is, to the *pose*, in different ways. The street, the clinic, and the text are three of its choice spaces of production; diagnostics, denunciation, and "private recognition scenes," as Wayne Koestenbaum has called them (45), are three of the responses it elicits. All three, from denunciation through identification, are intensely scopophilic. Excess always prompts what Uruguayan writer Felisberto Hernández would much later call the "lust of looking."

Playing the Ghost

On two occasions, when referring to a nineteenth-century poet of inordinate, even scandalous, visibility, Rubén Darío cites an epigraph from Villiers de L'Isle-Adam's *L'Eve future*: "Prends garde! En jouant au fantôme on le devient" (Villiers 103). In an essay on Lautréamont published in *Los raros* (a collection of literary portraits, in the manner of Gourmont's *Livres des masques*, which I can't help but translate as *The Queers*), Darío writes: "It would not be prudent for young minds to converse at any length with this spectral man, not even for the sake of literary curiosity or the pleasure of trying new delicacies. There is a judicious saying in the Kabbala: 'One should not play at being a ghost for one ends up being one' " (2:436). Then, in a second piece, "Purificaciones de la piedad" [Purifications of Pity], the notably ambivalent article on Oscar Wilde's death, Darío again writes: "Neglecting the advice of the Kabbala, that pitiful Wilde played at being a ghost and ended up one" (3:471). In both cases, the phrase is used in a cautionary way, to call attention to the extravagant character of both writers and to the dangers of "playing at" things in general. But Darío gives the phrase an odd interpretive twist. To play the ghost and end up being one, if taken literally, would seem to point to a loss of substance, of tangible appearance — in sum, to a disappearing act.[1] Yet Darío seems to point to the opposite as the end result of so much "playing," to an excess of visibility, of *presence*. The contradiction is only apparent, of course. Wilde's excessive visibility, Darío implies, is precisely what leads to his ruin: to play the ghost, to render it visible, is ultimately to play with death. Indeed, Darío calls Wilde a "martyr of his own eccentricity and of honorable England" (3:471), the order of the terms implying that he brought his end upon himself. Elaborating on the phrase, I propose that Darío's ghost be seen as the fantasmatic construct of what cannot be said, what lacks visibility because it lacks a name. In Darío's reading, Wilde plays at being something that is not named and by playing at it — by *posing* as that something — *is* that something. Posing is the representation of invisibility. The play's the thing — the rest, as Wilde might say, mere leather and prunella.

One should not forget the dense semantic texture acquired by the verb *to pose* in the context of Wilde's trials, closely followed in Latin America as, indeed, throughout the world. In a letter of 1 April 1894, the Marquess of Queensberry writes to his son: "I am not going to try and analyze this intimacy, and I make no charge; but to my mind to pose as a thing is as bad as to be it. With my own eyes I saw you both in the most loathsome and disgusting relationship, as expressed by your manner and expression. Never in my experience have I seen such a sight as that in your horrible features" (Hyde 71). A few weeks later, confronting Wilde in his own home, Queensberry says to him: "I do not say you are it but you look it, and you pose as it, which is just as bad" (Hyde 73). In a letter to his father-in-law, written a few months later, Queensberry again writes, "If I was quite certain of the thing, I would shoot the fellow at first sight, but I can only accuse him of posing." We know how the story ends: on 18 February 1895, Queensberry leaves a card for Wilde at his club, a card on which is written: "For Oscar Wilde, posing as a somdomite" (Hyde 76). The rest, as they say, is history.

The unnamed (the *thing*, the *it*) is, of course, Wilde-as-homosexual. It is what does not fit in words, cannot be formulated as a subjectivity, but is made manifest by Wilde's "manner," his "expression," his "horrible features," in a word, by a demeanor principally summed up in bodily attitudes and constituting an all-too-visible *pose*. As Moe Meyer writes, "It is important to remember that Wilde was initially entered into the legal process not for perverse sexual activity (sodomy), but for perverse signifying (*posing* as a sodomite). He was a semiotic criminal, not a sexual one" (98). Queensberry's cunning use of the verb *to pose*, calculated to avoid a countercharge of libel, ostensibly pointed to artifice, to deceit: Wilde was accused not of being a sodomite but of posing as one. Yet with equal cunning, and with a flair for paradox reminiscent of Wilde himself, Queensberry's accusation hints that *posing* and *being* may indeed be collapsed into each other, that one is what one poses as being. This hint, of course, was not lost on the prosecution. The fact that the crown moved on to a second trial, in which charges were brought against Wilde not for posing but for being, shows indeed the identifying power of posing. The pose opened a space in which the male homosexual was seen; he became a subject, was represented and named.[2]

This excursus is not immaterial if one bears in mind the intense curiosity awakened by Wilde — most specifically, by Wilde's body and dress — in Latin

American writers and, more generally, in writers of all the Spanish-speaking world. Wilde may well be cut down to mere particulars of fashion, but the impact of those particulars, as synechdoches for the individual, is undeniable. José Martí is obsessed by Wilde's hair, his clothing, his shoebuckles, his breeches, to the point that they threaten his wholehearted acceptance of Wilde's aesthetic message (Molloy, "Too Wilde" 187–89). Enrique Gómez Carrillo, who knew Wilde in Paris, is also struck by "the smooth shiny hair framing his huge face which disturbed me because of its feminine quality, or better said, because it was parted in an effeminate way" (*Bohemia* 190). Carrillo also memorably evokes Wilde at home "dressed only in a scoop-necked, red undershirt" (*Almas* 149), while, in Spain, Ramiro de Maeztu, who never laid eyes on Wilde, knew enough about him to imagine "a dandy who, even after death, would come before his Maker petulantly smoking a cigarette in a gold cigarette-holder and blowing out the smoke in rings" (Pérez de Ayala, 16). Darío, in the unforgettable article he writes on Wilde's death, compulsively brings up Wilde's dead body, the rot and decay of which he belabors, only to repress it, at the end of the piece, in favor of Wilde's everlasting work (Molloy, "Too Wilde" 189–91). Wilde is fetishized even before his work is read, recognized as standing in for that unnameable to which his posing points at every turn.

A Comedy of Mannerisms

Not all turn-of-the-century posing refers unequivocally to the homosexual, a subject yet to be defined and in whose formulation, both cultural and legal, Wilde's trials played such a large part. But I would argue that all turn-of-the-century posing does refer *equivocally* to the homosexual, for it refers to a theatricality, a dissipation, and a *manner* (the uncontrollable gesturing of excess) traditionally associated with the nonmasculine or, at the very least, with an increasingly *problematic* masculinity.[3] Posing makes evident the elusiveness of all constructions of identity, their fundamentally performative nature. It increasingly problematizes gender, its formulation and its divisions: it subverts categories, questions reproductive models, proposes new modes of identification based on recognition of desire more than on cultural pacts, offers (and plays at) new sexual identities. It also resorts to an exploitation of the public, in the form of self-advertisement and very visible self-fashioning, that appears to make the spectator very nervous about what goes on in private. Indeed, after Wilde, posing will become increasingly suspect, and will be read more and more as advertising sexual deviance.[4] In Latin America, this is particularly true in those cases when posing and decadence in general are considered in relation to hypervirile constructions of nationhood.[5] Posing invites new formulations of desire at once disturbing and attractive. That is why — in order to defuse its transgressive and, at the very least, homoerotic charge — it is usually reduced through caricature or dismissed as "mere imitation." It is accepted as a cultural detail, not as a practice, cut down to sissy proportions: "It is the gossip of snobs who go into our virgin jungles wearing spats, a monocle, and a chrysanthemum on their lapel" (Ulner 207).[6]

In the context of Latin American cultures, such disparaging remarks could be deadly. Indeed, in literature whose very foundational gesture is ironic mimicry and deviant citation — "Qui pourrai-je imiter pour être original?" writes Darío (in French, of course) — to dispatch posing, belittling it as a frivolous, copycat dressing-up, is a pernicious move. It reduces to slavish imitation what is surely Latin American *modernismo*'s most distinctive feature, its capacity to recognize decadence as a constructive, *critical* force[7] and to put that force to good use in the production of a complex, uneven, culturally dynamic Latin American modernity that goes well beyond sartorial or cosmetic emulation. In fact, one of the most striking scenes of posing (in that it gives rich new meaning precisely to the notion of "dressing up") is to be found in "Kakemono," an Orientalist piece by the Cuban poet Julián del Casal. In the poem, a voyeuristic narrator enumerates the very deliberate gestures of a female subject who, "Hastiada de reinar con la hermosura / Que te dio el cielo por nativo dote" [Weary of ruling with the beauty / which Heaven naturally bestowed on you] (173), ritually transforms herself into a Japanese empress. The near religious character imparted to the ceremony, in which every detail of dress signifies and every gesture constitutes a pose; the drastic erasure of "nature" and "self" that the transformation presupposes (so reminiscent, in fact, of a drag queen's routine); and, most important, the interpellative stance adopted by the text — in lieu of a third-person description, a voyeuristic "I" forcefully addresses a "you," becomes that "you" in the very act of reproducing each gesture, as would a mirror — all attest to an intensity of transformative *action* that goes far beyond the chrysanthemum on the lapel, the monocle and spats in the jungle. Casal's transformist knows, as did Wilde, that "a climax may depend on a crinoline" and that "attitude is everything" (Wilde 1065, 1078): in constructing her pose, s/he is the Japanese queen.

It is obvious that I am referring here more to the dynamics of posing than to the self-containment of isolated gestures. The latter can no doubt sum up, in one blow, the disruptive potential of posing, offering a bodily metaphor that will linger, uneasily, in memory: say Julián del Casal's Helen, stroking a lily as she gazes on the ruins of Troy, or his Petronius, calmly inhaling the smell of his blood, one last time, as it ebbs from his severed veins, or for that matter the proud drag queen "posing as an Honest Woman" that Jorge Salessi has rescued from turn-of-the-century police files (Salessi 346). Here I am interested in posing as narrative — a fitful narrative to be sure, of which one might say, as Arthur Symons did of Mallarmé's syntax, that it is "something irregular, unquiet, expressive, with sudden surprising felicities, with nervous starts and lapses, with new capacities for the exact noting of sensation" (Dowling 134). Only within a sequence does posing, either as a way of life or as a way of writing, *make sense.*

Few recognized the transgressive potential of posing as a way of writing better than the Uruguayan José Enrique Rodó in his essay on Rubén Darío. Rodó offers a remarkably sympathetic reading of Darío's poetry in which he literally takes on Darío's voice, incorporates his manner in an act of poetic ventriloquism, while at the same time attempting to curb the excess which he assimilates, once again significantly, to affectation in dress:

> Never has the rough cry of intense, devouring passion shot through the verses of this poetically calculating artist. One would say that his brain is steeped in perfumes and his heart enveloped in suede. The supreme preoccupation of art triumphs over personal feeling, masters that feeling by imitating it. Over the impetuous bursts of passion, over tragic attitudes, over movements that may disturb the elegant, untroubled purity of the line, [this poetry] prefers morbid and indolent obliqueness, serene idealizations, pensive languishing, all that makes the actor's robe drape over his supple body in ample, exquisite folds. (172)

This pensive languishing (akin to the "tender, caressing, voluptuous effects" that Leavis condemned in Shelley (Sinfield, *Cultural Politics* 34), and these ample, draping robes, are overt signs of artifice for Rodó. That they are perceived as noxious, evirating, and possibly homoerotic is shown by Rodó's caveat when referring concretely to Darío's poems: "Inviting verses, tempting and delicate verses, verses capable of making a Spartan legion swoon. . . . If there were an oncoming war, I would forbid them" (179). Indeed, early on, Rodó inscribes his attraction for and fear of the morbid, his preoccupation with virility and eviration, in a Latin American context that is defensively political. In that respect, the ideological framework of this essay on Darío is not insignificant. Over a period of several years, Rodó wrote a three-volume reflection on Latin American culture pointedly titled *La vida nueva.* The first volume, bearing the messianic title of "El que vendrá" [He who must come], was a call for a spiritual leader, a *revelador* (literally, he who reveals) for Latin America. The second volume, containing the long ambivalent essay on Darío from which I have quoted, answered the summons of the first book in the negative: Darío's poetry is a poetry of affectation, of pose; as Rodó famously asserts, "He is not the poet of America." The third volume of *La vida nueva* gave closure to the series, providing both the positive spiritual guidance that the first volume yearned for and a corrective to Darío's dangerous (yet attractive) posing, denounced in the second: an antidote to artifice, it contains Rodó's celebrated essay, *Ariel.* So in an ideological scenario of his own making, Rodó, the cultural diagnostician, first identified a need, then analyzed the "unsatisfactory" remedy — Darío's poetry of pose, which he simultaneously identified with and feared — and then, barely one year after his piece on Darío, triumphantly proposed his own solution.

Dedicated to "the youth of America," *Ariel* proposed a programmatic Latin American identity. It persuasively argued for self-improvement through renewed contact with Latin America's "strong" European forebears, Greece and early Christianity. A blend of evangelical *caritas* and Renanian Hellenism, whose sentimentalized virility would successfully glue together a male intellectual community for years to come, *Ariel* was the pedagogue's victory. Yet it would not be inappropriate to see this essay more connected to posing than it would at first seem. Indeed, I would argue that *Ariel* could be read as an act of posing *pro patria*, a model of homosociability that, while attempting to purify itself of the "morbid and indolent obliqueness" associated with posing, is no less an exercise in posing, and homoerotic posing at that, with its own brand of serene idealization and pensive languishing. The antidote to Darío's posing is itself a posing text, also indulging in mannerism or, as Rodó called it: "amaneramiento *voulu*" (172). Let me point to one telling example. This is an essay that shuns the visual with passion, an essay where only one voice is heard, that of the master Prospero, speaking for the last time to an undifferentiated group of male students. Not only do these students lack voice (thus deviating from the Socratic model that obviously inspires the scene) but they remarkably lack bodies, lack gestures — not to mention pensive languishing and draping robes. The only visual reference, the only physical detail contained in this essay is therefore all the more striking: gazing at his young disciples gathered one last time in his study, as if seeking inspiration before speaking, Prospero pauses to caress the winged statue of Ariel. That studied gesture, the only one in the whole book — the older man stroking the bronze ephebe — that *pose* on the brink, as it were, of an essay that sublimates physicality at every turn, contains Rodó's homoerotic *paideia* in its entirety. While Rodó may decry posing in Darío's poetry, the posing of his alter ego, Prospero, finds him out.

Pose and Pathology

I now want to think not of posing as a mannerism or as the expression of nonmasculinity but of mannerism and the visibilization of nonmasculinity — and, more concretely here, of homosexuality — as posing. What I propose is more than a mere reversal of terms: I want to argue that the terms are not equivalent to begin with and that this very noncoincidence complicates the work of posing in Latin America. The double movement would be as follows: (1) Posing refers to the unnamed, to the *it* or the *thing* the inscription of which, as Wilde's case made clear, is posing itself; thus posing *represents*, is a significant posture. But (2) the unnamed, once named and rendered visible may now be dismissed, in a specific Latin American context, as "just posing"; thus posing once again represents, but this time as a masquerade, as a significant *imposture*. To put it simply, posing points to a fleeting identity, states that one is something; but to state that one is that something is "to pose," that is, to pretend to be that something while not really being it.

It is in this context that I wish to take a look now at posing as pathology. As such, it appears in the complex, painstaking taxonomy devised by the Argentine psychiatrist, sociologist, and criminologist José Ingenieros at the turn of the century. A disciple of Nordau who also dabbled in poetry, Ingenieros seems not to have disliked posing himself. As Aníbal Ponce writes, "His costume, striking in its aesthetic refinement, his incredible epigrams, his unending taste for paradox, had turned him, in the frivolous opinion of other bohemians, into a strange dabbler in science and in art; an odd mixture of Charcot and D'Annunzio with Lombroso and Nietzsche" (Ponce 38).[8]

Like so many practitioners of forensic psychiatry at the turn of the century, wielding medical authority to force out "the truth" from their resisting patients, Ingenieros is interested in studying (i.e., exposing) pathologies and particularly concerned with simulation, which he follows from its purely biological manifestations (animal mimetism, for example) to those cases in which extreme altered states are simulated as compensatory strategies, for basically utilitarian, often criminal, purposes—as a "fraudulent means of succeeding in life" (*La simulación* 114). While the main goal of his study is the simulation of madness in criminals (the subject of his very popular doctoral dissertation), he strives to classify simulation of a more general kind, from the benign to the extreme, in an incredibly detailed system. Simulation, for Ingenieros, is born of a flaw, a maladjustment, a weakness. A strategy from the margins toward the center defined by the author as "pathomimicry," it allows the simulator to pretend to be what he or she is not in order to pass, in order to be successful, in order to achieve a goal. The criminal pretends to be mad in order to escape punishment; the fabricator pretends to be someone else in order to achieve prestige; the proletarian immigrant pretends to be middle-class in order to achieve acceptance. For Ingenieros, one cannot, like Oscar Wilde, simulate (pose as) what one is: to pose, for Ingenieros, is necessarily to lie.

To illustrate the pathology of simulation, that is, the pathology of posing, Ingenieros gives examples:

> The environment demands fraudulence: to live, for most human beings, is to submit to that demand, to adapt to it.
> Just imagine, for a moment, a wily speculator not simulating honesty in his financial dealings; a politician not simulating to uphold the interests of the people; a mediocre writer not simulating the qualities of those who succeed; a merchant not simulating concern for his clients; a student in an exam not simulating the knowledge he lacks and the professor not simulating infinite wisdom; . . . a trickster not simulating stupidity, a superior not simulating inferiority, according to the situation; a child not simulating sickness, a faggot [*maricón*] not simulating effeminacy [*afeminamiento*], a hack not simulating writerly passion, a cunning wife not simulating hysteria. (*La simulación* 185)

If I am not mistaken, Ingenieros's "faggot" (so much for the purported scientific nomenclature of these texts) marks a break in the series of "fraudulent simulations." For the "faggot," one might argue, does not pretend to be what he is not (like the wily speculator pretending to be honest, or the healthy child pretending to be sick) but what in a sense he is — effeminacy, *afeminamiento*, the exhibition of the feminine. Posing, in this case, is not a compensatory gesture (as in the case of the trickster simulating honesty). It is a way of highlighting a performance, rendering it more visible. The example disrupts Ingenieros's neat taxonomy unless a more drastic interpretive turn is effected. In that reading (which I venture is the one Ingenieros had in mind), a *man* poses as what he is not — a *woman* — because, Ingenieros tells us, he is *really* a man. This brutal reduction to an essentialist binarism would, of course, present a great advantage for the good doctor: it eliminates effeminacy from his equation — that is, a certain *performance* of gender — and it eliminates the problematic homosexual as subject.

Ingenieros is well aware of the manner in which simulation draws attention to itself with its excessive theatrical visibility. That he is concerned with its socially disruptive potential, as well as its creative possibilities, is obvious from his references to his mentor, José María Ramos Mejía, himself author of a treatise on simulation. For the author of *Los simuladores de talento*, a book whose "political projections" Ingenieros very much admires, simulators are guilty of "shameless histrionics." They rely on "all the elements of illusion and a theatrical constitution thanks to which, combining a few *blotches*, they achieve on canvas the impression of a whole" (*La simulación* 220). The mixed reference to the visual arts — simulation and, by extension, posing are simultaneously theatrics *and* depiction, embodiment and surface — is, I think, of interest here. Simulation and posing may be "pathomimicries" but they are also recognized as art forms.

Ingenieros's vigilant attitude toward poseurs, his self-described zeal at "unmasking" them, so reminiscent of Queensberry's epistemological tizzy (was Wilde or wasn't he), often leads, in the case of perceived sexual deviance, as in the case of the "faggot" simulating effeminacy, not to a pressing of charges but to a displacement in pathologies: "He's not really one (whatever *one* is). He's just pretending." This displacement, I suggest, produces something like a great cultural relief, similar to the "we don't have that here" of certain anxious constructions of nationality. Take the following case history of a "patient" whom Ingenieros "cures":

A young decadent writer, influenced by French *fumistes*, felt obliged to simulate the refinements and vices the latter pretended to have, believing them to be authentic. He pretended to be a passive pederast [a later version says *faggot*]; pretended to be addicted to hashish, to morphine, to alcohol; he wore bizarre clothes; he stayed up all night in cafés, pretending to be drunk, even when he felt a physical repulsion for alcohol. . . . This was all a product of his puerile imagination, resulting from the impostures of aesthetes and supermen whom he read avidly and who influenced his life [a later version adds: "*trying to adjust his actions and his ideas to the 'manual of the perfect decadent'*"]. ("Nuevos estudios" 707)[9]

In yet another version of the same case, worthy of being cited at length, Ingenieros gives additional details about the case and, more generally, about the process of posing:

> In one of our intellectual circles, we met an intelligent, cultivated young man who was quite suggestible. Devoted to literature, endowed with uncommon talents and a certain refinement of the artistic sensibility, and influenced by clever *fumistes*, he fell sick with decadent aestheticism . . .
>
> Inspired by those masters — and possibly by other local *fumistes* — the young man believed that, in order to emulate them, it was necessary *to have or to simulate their psychopathic symptoms* [emphasis added]. A purely physiological reason, his youth, contributed to determine the particular aspects of his simulated perversions.
>
> He began by simulating digestive problems, attributed to the abuse of alcohol; he described pre-hypnotic hallucinations, typical of alcoholics, and terrible nightmares that could have no other origin; he carefully studied the clinical phenomena that he strived to simulate.
>
> Then, in private conversations, he started a campaign against normal love relations. The interests of the individual were, to his mind, opposed to those of reproduction . . . That is why the aesthete should find in himself his own voluptuousness, removed from all notions of procreation.
>
> From this apotheosis of onanism he went on, later, to other perversions . . . After a time, he displayed a deep and total aversion for the female sex, extolling the conduct of Oscar Wilde, the English poet who had just been found guilty in London and was paying the consequences of his homosexual relations with Lord Douglas in Reading Gaol. He wrote and published an "Ode to Masculine Beauty," and went so far as to declare that he only found pleasure in male intimacy.
>
> Some people believed these simulations to be true, and prudently avoided his company. Fortunately, his friends made him understand that if these simulations might serve to enhance him from a literary point of view in the eyes of his *modernista* colleagues, they would harm him after a while when he gave up his youthful aestheticism.
>
> The simulator protested that no one had the right to censure his inclinations, even if others thought them feigned. However, understanding that in the long run no one would believe those inclinations to be true, he renounced his feigned psychopathies. (*Locura* 24–25)

That the possibility of being considered queer in any form (either as a "passive pederast" or as a "faggot") should be deemed desirable, indeed considered a sign of literary prestige, is hard to imagine. *Modernismo* — the literary movement where, according to Ingenieros, such a reputation would be considered a plus — was already defending itself anxiously (perhaps too anxiously) from intimations of sexual dissidence and avoiding implications of nonmanliness. Rodó distanced himself from Darío's *mollitia*, Darío castigated Wilde for his excesses, censured Rachilde's gender-bending, and informed his readers that Verlaine's homosexuality was (again!) "mere" posing.[10] Martí busied himself with the task of heterosexualizing Whitman

(Molloy, "His America"). It is difficult to imagine that, in such an atmosphere, a simulation of passive pederasty should add distinction, or even enviable notoriety, to anyone's position. To anyone's *literary* position, that is, since it is clear that the appearance of sexual dissidence outside literature, in whatever form, had adverse effects not only on reputations but on personal lives. Thanks in part to the dogged investigative efforts of Ingenieros himself, these appearances, detected by the diagnostician's sharp eye and eagerly constructed as narratives of deviance, usually landed suspects in jail, in psychiatric wards, in police files, or in medical literature.[11]

The tenacity and the resourcefulness with which Ingenieros's medical narratives strive to establish the mendacious nature of posing is striking. In this particular case, he peppers the case history with such words as *simulate, feign, emulate, fumiste*. Additionally, in order to confirm the ultimately illusory and therefore inconsequential qualities of posing, he strips the poseur of full responsibility: the young writer is puerile, easily suggestible, naive, too "refined." He affects poses he has read in books (the topos of the "poisonous book" is revived here) and is gullible enough to think that his models are "true" when, in fact, Ingenieros authoritatively tells us, they are all "false." In other words, the pathological poseur is modeling his conduct on models, taken either from literature or from life, that are already impostures, models that should not be taken seriously. D'Annunzio, Ingenieros observes elsewhere, is "an Italian who has suffered French psychological contagion [and] has pretended to be in favor of sororal love and homosexuality: it is fitting to consider those 'refinements' of the sexual instinct as simulations. It is obvious that . . . he did not copulate with his sisters or with other men" (*Psicología* 477).[12] In the case history I have cited, the defensive zeal, the need to establish lack of authenticity is only compounded by the fact that the young man is not a more or less distant European aesthete but "ours"; he belongs to "one of our intellectual circles," threatens the very fabric of "our" culture.

This case history leaves unanswered questions that may be unanswerable; their very unanswerability makes them crucial to a reflection on turn-of-the-century posing. For example, in what manner does one simulate being a passive pederast? What are the words, the declarations, the conduct—surely nongenital—that allow for such a reading? What are the gestures, the bodily metaphors, the artifices that would express an unformulated (but nonetheless visible) identity? Additionally, where is the locus of simulation? Where, but in the panicked discursive reiteration of the diagnostician, that is, in ideology, is it detected? What is the pose or series of poses that would, on the one hand, allow the diagnostician to detect a pathology, this particular pathology (he *is* a passive pederast) and, on the other hand, exhibit that pathology as a simulation (he *is posing* as a passive pederast). The disquieting last paragraph of Ingenieros's narrative abounds in hiatus. The poseur "protests" the censuring of his inclinations, then "understands," then "renounces." Although the verb, with its echoes of more formal recantations or abjurations of belief, is strong, what it is that the young man renounces remains unclear. For Ingenieros, it is a simulation. For the poseur, it is "his inclinations," inclinations to which he believes he has every right "even if others think them feigned." Note that even Ingenieros (in a rare moment of professional caution?) does not have him say, "because they are feigned." For the poseur, as for the modern reader of this scene of repression, the difference matters little. For Latin American culture, torn between the powerful aesthetics of artifice in which it found its measure and the fear that that very artifice might have disquieting implications in terms of gender, it seems to have mattered a lot. It too "renounced" its poses, those poses which, during the briefest of moments, *signified* beyond their own simulation. Emptied out of meaning, emptied out of bodies, those Latin American poses hang in the closet of representation, not to mention the closet of criticism. It is time to return to them, if only ephemerally, the dashing visibility they once had.

Notes

1. For a provocative approach to ghosting and spectral metaphors in connection with homosexuality, specifically with lesbianism, see Terry Castle.

2. As Jeffrey Weeks writes, "The Wilde trials were not only the most dramatic, but also the most significant events, for they created a public image for the homosexual" (21).

3. On the complex readings of effeminacy at the turn of the century, see Alan Sinfield's *Wilde Century* (esp. 25–51).

4. What Alan Sinfield writes of the dandy might be extended, synechdochically, to the pose: "The dandy figure served Wilde's project because he had a secure cross-sex image, yet might anticipate, on occasion and in the main implicitly, an emergent same-sex identity. . . . Wilde is exploiting the capacity of the image of the dandy to commute, without explicit commitment, between diverse sexualities" (*Wilde Century* 73).

5. There are a few notable exceptions. Lisa E. Davis interprets Puerto Rican Miguel Guerra Mondragón's late translation of *Salomé* in 1914 (at a time when there were already three Spanish translations available) as a sign of political resistance. Wilde's play had been performed to mixed reviews and repeatedly banned from theaters in Spain and Latin America. Davis contends that Mondragón's new translation of Wilde's play, to a point superfluous, should be read as a revolutionary gesture. By translating *Salomé*, she argues, Guerra Mondragón, "a statesman on the eve of a long, distinguished career in his country's service," reinscribed the defiance of "a minority of politically resistant aesthetes [against] a new social class influenced by United States pragmatism" ("Traducción" 36–37).

6. Recourse to metaphors of dress to deride poetry and poets persists well into the twentieth century. When comparing Darío's poetry to that of his Spanish predecessor, Bécquer, José Bergamín writes: "Chaste nudity is proof of virility: witness the poetry of Bécquer. Sensuality of attire is proof of effeminacy: witness the poetry of Rubén Darío" (Rodríguez Monegal 12).

7. "Ces époques de décadence sont fortes en critique, souvent même plus fortes que les grands siècles" (Renan 112). Renan's decisive mark on Latin American fin-de-siècle culture has yet to be studied in depth.

8. For a discussion on the role of literature in Ingenieros's medical diagnoses and for further analysis of the intersection of art and science in Ingenieros's writing and in his clinical diagnoses, see Molloy, "Diagnósticos de fin de siglo."

9. I quote from the first version of the case published in an *Archivos* article. The second version, enabling one to measure the progress from "scientific" description to slur (from "passive pederast" to "maricón"), appears in *La simulación en la lucha por la vida* (241).

10. When reviewing Edmond Lepelletier's biography of Verlaine for his Latin American readers, Darío dismisses Verlaine's homosexuality as malicious gossip: "Those enamored of twisted matters will be disappointed to learn that the famous Rimbaud question is documented here [in Lepelletier] in a way to dismiss all malicious fabrication, and it is ultimately proved that such and such declarations or allusions in verse or prose are mere aspects of simulation, so proficiently studied, from a clinical point of view, by Ingegnieros" [*sic*] (2:718).

11. For an excellent overview of the obsession, on the part of the medico-legal establishment in Argentina, to classify homosexuals, and the prurient curiosity that guided that classification, see Jorge Salessi.

12. In a later version of this paragraph, all reference to homosexuality disappears and D'Annunzio simulates only incest—presumably, by then, a safer affectation (*Simulación* 232).

Works Cited

Baudelaire, Charles. *Oeuvres complètes*. Paris: Gallimard, 1954.

Casal, Julián del. *Obra poética*. Havana: Editorial de Letras Cubanas, 1982.

Castle, Terry. *The Apparitional Lesbian: Female Homosexuality and Modern Culture*. New York: Columbia University Press, 1993.

Darío, Rubén. *Obras completas*. 5 vols. Madrid: Afrodisio Aguado, 1955.

Davis, Lisa. "Oscar Wilde in Spain." *Comparative Literature* 25 (1973): 136–52.

———. "La traducción de *Salomé* de Guerra Mondragón." *Sin Nombre* (Puerto Rico), 10.4 (1981): 26–39.

Didi-Huberman, Georges. *Invention de l'hysterie: Charcot et l'iconographie photographique de la Salpêtrière*. Paris: Macula, 1982.

Dowling, Linda. *Language and Decadence in the Victorian Fin de Siècle*. Princeton: Princeton University Press, 1986.

Gómez Carrillo, Enrique. *Almas y cerebros*. Paris: Garnier, n.d.

———. *En plena bohemia*. Madrid: Mundo Latino, n.d.

Henríquez Ureña, Max. *Breve historia del modernismo*. Mexico: Fondo de Cultura Económica, 1962.

Hyde, H. Montgomery. *The Trials of Oscar Wilde*. New York: Dover, 1962.

Ingenieros, José. "Psicología de los simuladores." *Archivos de Psiquiatría, Criminología y Ciencias Afines* 2 (1903): 449–87.

———. "Nuevos estudios sobre la psicología de los simuladores." *Archivos de Psiquiatría, Criminología y Ciencias Afines* 3 (1904): 647–709.

———. *La simulación en la lucha por la vida*. Vol. 1 of *Obras completas*. Buenos Aires: Ediciones L.J. Rosso, 1933.

———. *Simulación de la locura*. Vol. 2 of *Obras completas*. Buenos Aires: Ediciones L. J. Rosso, 1933.

Koestenbaum, Wayne. *Double Talk: The Erotics of Male Literary Collaboration*. New York: Routledge, 1989.

Meyer, Moe, ed. *The Politics and Poetics of Camp*. New York: Routledge, 1994.

Molloy, Sylvia. "Decadentismo e Ideologia: Economias de Desejo na América Hispánica Finissecular." In *Literatura e História na América Latina*, ed. Ligia Chiappini and Flávio Wolf de Aguiar, 13–26. Sao Paulo: Editora da Universidade de Sao Paulo, 1993.

——. "Too Wilde for Comfort: Desire and Ideology in Fin-de-siècle Latin America." *Social Text* 31–32 (1992): 187–201.

——. "His America, Our America: José Martí Reads Walt Whitman." In *Breaking Bounds: Whitman and American Cultural Studies*, ed. Betsy Erkkila and Jay Grossman, 83–91. Oxford: Oxford University Press, 1995.

——. "Diagnósticos de fin de siglo." *Cultura y tercer mundo*. Vol. 2, *Cambios de identidades y ciudadanías*. Ed. Beatriz González Stephan. Caracas: Ediciones Nueva Sociedad, 1996.

Pérez de Ayala, Ramón. *Las máscaras*. Vol. 2. Madrid: Renacimiento, 1924.

Ponce, Aníbal. Prologue. *La simulación en la lucha por la vida*, by José Ingenieros. Vol. 1 of *Obras completas*. Buenos Aires: Ediciones L. J. Rosso, 1933.

Ramos Mejía, José María. *Los simuladores de talento*. 1904. New ed. Buenos Aires: Editorial Tor, 1955.

Renan, Ernest. *Cahiers de jeunesse*. 1845–46. Paris: Calmann-Lévy, 1906.

Rodó, José Enrique. *Ariel*. Cambridge: Cambridge University Press, 1967.

——. *Ariel*. Trans. Margaret Sayers Peden. Austin: University of Texas Press, 1988.

——. "Rubén Darío. Su personalidad literaria. Su última obra." *Obras completas*. Madrid: Aguilar, 1967.

Rodríguez Monegal, Emir. "Encuentros con Rubén Darío." *Mundo nuevo* 7 (1967): 5–21.

Salessi, Jorge. *Médicos, maleantes y maricas*. Rosario, Argentina: Beatriz Viterbo, 1995.

Sinfield, Alan. *Cultural Politics — Queer Readings*. Philadelphia: University of Pennsylvania Press, 1994.

——. *The Wilde Century: Effeminacy, Oscar Wilde and the Queer Moment*. New York: Columbia University Press, 1994.

Ulner, Arnold L. "Enrique Gómez Carrillo en el modernismo, 1889–1896." Ph.D diss., University of Missouri, 1972.

Villiers de L'Isle Adam, Auguste. *L'Eve future*. Vol. 1 of *Oeuvres complètes*. Genève: Slatkine Reprints, 1970.

Weeks, Jeffrey. *Coming Out: Homosexual Politics in Britain from the Nineteenth Century to the Present*. London: Quartet, 1977.

Wilde, Oscar. *The Complete Works of Oscar Wilde*. New York: Harper and Row, 1989.

Chapter 10
Improper Names
Pseudonyms and Transvestites in
Decadent Prose

Leonard R. Koos

In 1898 an article appeared in *La Revue scientifique* entitled "La découverte rapide de l'identité littéraire du Répertoire Bibliographique *onomastique* des Anonymes." Its author Marcel Badouin, a librarian and self-styled "journaliste scientifique et surtout médical" [scientific and especially medical journalist] (648), proposed the construction of a system, in his own words "une police scientifique" [a scientific police] (651), that would be able to determine the identity of an author whose work had been published anonymously or under a pseudonym.[1] In a vocabulary characteristic of late nineteenth-century criminal anthropology, Badouin contended, "L'Anthropomètre classe des *corps* d'homme; Le Bibliographe, qui s'occupe des anonymes, classe non pas des *cerveaux* d'homme mais des sortes de tracés photographiques du fonctionnement de ces cerveaux, c'est-à-dire les *productions de leur intelligence*. Et, qui plus est, grâce à elles, il peut souvent arriver à dépister le corps et le cerveau qui les a enfantées, c'est-à-dire leur véritable personnalité" [The Anthropometer classes men's bodies; The Bibliographer, who deals with anonymous writers, does not class the minds of men but kinds of photographic traces of the functioning of the brain, that is to say, the productions of their intelligence. And, moreover, due to them, he can often arrive at tracking down the body and the mind that gave birth to them, that is to say their true personality] (655–56). Badouin's proposed catalog sought to amass and classify a myriad of details regarding genre, subject, theme, and style in the totality of contemporary literary production in France, its completion leading to the indisputable detection of the proper name of the author of the text in question. Although this enormous literary onomasticon was obviously never realized, its theoretical formulation represents perhaps the most extreme position of an ongoing nineteenth-century cultural concern that expresses itself in the proliferation and circulation of dictionaries of anonyms and pseudonyms.

As early as 1835, Charles Nodier would remark: "Le temps seroit donc favorable à la publication d'une *clef* des pseudonomies si multipliées alors" [The time would seem therefore favorable for the publication of a key to pseudonomies so manifold in these days] (4). These dictionaries, whose very existence announces the potential exercise of discursive authority as do all systems of ordering and regulating individuals, often cite practical justifications, as in the preface of Jean-Marie Quérard's *Les Auteurs déguisés de la littérature française du XIXe siècle*: "pour écrire avec exactitude l'histoire littéraire" [in order to write with exactitude literary history] (10). While precision and truth seem laudable enough as motives, elements of the discursive underside of Quérard's gesture surface and betray an undercurrent of fear and potential censure of or violence toward those who "renoncent de parti délibré aux splendeurs du nom propre . . . si bien qu'on serait tenté de prendre ces écrivains pour des faussaires, non pour des pseudonymes" [intentionally renounce the splendors of the proper name . . . such that one would be tempted to mistake these authors for falsifiers rather than pseudonymous writers] (7). Indeed, many of the titles of these compilations — Quérard's *Les Supercheries littéraires dévoilées*, Nodier's *Des artifices que certains auteurs ont employés pour déguiser leurs noms*, Reboul's *Anonymes, pseudonymes, et supercheries littéraires*, and so forth[2] — reveal a similar perspective that treats any departure from the original proper name as shameful aberration bordering on the criminal. Badouin goes so far as to consistently compare the method of his "Répertoire" to that of the police detective and the judicial process, forcefully figuring the erasure or the changing of the given proper name as an act akin to criminal transgression that must be identified, prosecuted, and obliterated if order is to be maintained.

The proper name is conceived of by these texts as a privileged and distinctive category in the linguistic hierarchies of nineteenth-century discursive culture. From John Stuart Mill's famous assertion in *A System of Logic* (1843) that proper names denote but do not connote, merely imposing their function without signifying, to Michel Bréal's refutation of that theory in his *Essai de sémantique* (1897) where he contends, echoing a number of thinkers of classical antiquity, that the proper name is the richest of signifying structures because it is the most individual,[3] the nineteenth century valorized the proper noun as the crowning element of its construction of selfhood, a given linguistic form that should remain unaltered as a testament to the authority of the past. But, as the prefaces of the aforementioned dictionaries imply, the counter-discursive threat presented by the invented name, the pseudonym, the fictitious name born outside of patriarchal authority yet indistinguishable from the true name, becomes increasingly viewed as a dangerous abnormality that, in the atmosphere of fin-de-siècle medical theory and its cultural expansion into other disciplines, reflects moral degeneracy. The pseudonym, then, challenges turn-of-the-century discursive formations as the literary equivalent of the socially suspect and morally deviant gesture, that of renaming.

Staged Names

> Chez moi, il n'y a pas d'art d'écrire. La littérature fut mon infirmité dès mon plus bas âge. Je m'en suis cachée, dès son début, comme j'ai essayé de dissimuler que j'avais une jambe plus courte que l'autre. (101–2)

> [With me, there is no art of writing. Literature was my infirmity from my earliest age. I hid myself in it, from its beginning, just as I tried to conceal that I had one leg shorter than the other.]
> — Rachilde, *Dans le puits ou la vie inférieure, 1915–1917*

The mutilation and erasure of the traditional proper name by the writers of the Decadent Movement in France establishes a simulacrum of the name that is inscribed in the generalized oppositionality of their aesthetic program, paratextually with the extensive and particular use of the pseudonym and textually with the figure of the decadent transvestite. Pseudonyms and transvestites both participate in a linguistic reconstruction of the self whose agency challenges the limitations of a passive acceptance of the received, while nonetheless depending on and profiting from the inherent ambiguity in textual or textile systems of signification.

Pseudonyms, of course, existed long before the emergence of the Decadent Movement of the 1880s. In the nineteenth century, they were consistently used (although not always within the limits of the law) by four groups: writers, journalists, actors, and prostitutes. Most of the writers involved in the Decadent Movement employed a pseudonym.[4] One of the major contributors to the journal and then the review *Le Décadent* (10 April-4 December 1886; December 1887–15 May 1889), Ernest Raynaud, later wrote about the excessive and playful use of invented monikers in the composition of that periodical:

Lorsqu'à la veille de paraître, la copie manquait, nous devions y suppléer mais pour faire illusion, nous étions obligés de multiplier les pseudonymes. . . . D'autres fois, on faisait collaborer, à leur insu, des personnalités fameuses, tel Coppée, tel Sully Prudhomme, tel le général Boulanger, tel Sarcey, dont nous annoncions, avec une joie feinte, la conversion au décadisme. Et le plus admirable, c'est qu'à ce propos nous recevions des lettres de félicitations. (75)

[When on the eve of its appearance, the copy was lacking, we had to add to it, but in order to create an illusion, we were required to multiply the pseudonyms. . . . Other times, famous personalities, without their knowledge, were made to collaborate, like Coppée, like Sully Prudhomme, like General Boulanger, like Sarcey, whose conversion to decadentism we would announce. And the most admirable in this respect was that we would receive letters of congratulations.][5]

Beyond the excessive and parodic use of invented names on the part of the contributors of *Le Décadent*, a certain number of cases can be identified involving the writers of decadent prose in which the impropriety of pseudonymous activity and the disruption of the boundaries of nineteenth-century self-fashioning that it implies are pursued, developed, and amplified. The first of these onomastic manipulations came about in the following way: in 1886 Paul Adam and Jean Moréas (the pseudonym Jean Pappadiamantapoulos chose to erase his Greek ancestry and appear to be nominally French) published a novel entitled *Les Demoiselles Goubert*, which told the story of two sisters in the Parisian metropolis, very much on the model of Huysmans's *Les Soeurs Vatard*. Near the end of the novel, Marthe, the morally pure sibling, is asked by her employer to consider a marriage proposal from an acquaintance of his, Jacques Plowert. The latter, described from a photograph, seems to be "un garçon robuste aux traits féminins où se devinait une peau lisse, où s'arrondissaient des yeux clairs" [a robust boy with feminine traits betraying a smooth skin, and round limpid eyes] (211). His only drawback and the characteristic that ultimately causes Marthe to reject his offer is that he had lost his left hand while testing a cannon in a military exercise. The mutilated Jacques Plowert disappears from the novel which ends with the heroine still unmarried. But the novel's final page does not mark an end for the name of Jacques Plowert. It appears in a small volume published in 1887 entitled *Petit glossaire pour servir à l'intelligence des auteurs décadents et symbolistes*, a compilation of neologisms coined in selected decadent and symbolist texts. This time, however, Jacques Plowert appears not in the text but on the book's title page as the name of the author. That the name Jacques Plowert was employed as the pseudonym of one of its creators, Paul Adam, thus establishes the paratext as a possible site at which to problematize the border between fiction and reality. In this instance, the title page functions as a multidirectional threshold through which the proper name, textual or extratextual, can be transmitted without any of its linguistic privilege. Although the volume's preface attempts to justify the compilation as an aid to understanding the subtleties of decadent and symbolist prose, the onomastic mystification on the title page ultimately destabilizes authorial agency and identity.

Another problematic proper name surfacing in decadent circles and circulating outside of them that relies on a similar manipulation of the conventional distinctions between the fictional and the extrafictional involves the most renown of decadent, *A rebours* by Joris-Karl Huysmans. In this instance, the readers of the work play a greater role in the nomination of a fictional character to the status of a living being.[6] In an influential article that a number of critics have identified as one of the major instigating forces behind the conceptualization of the Decadent Movement in the 1880s, a young Maurice Barrès writes that "le héros d'*A rebours* nous intéresse comme type au même titre documentaire que Mallarmé ou Rollinat" [the hero of *A rebours* interests us as a type in the same documentary way as Mallarmé or Rollinat] (440). Mallarmé dedicated a poem to the protagonist of *A rebours*, "Prose pour Des Esseintes." In addition, an article appeared in *Le Décadent*'s thirty-second issue entitled "Le Moderniste" and signed with the name "Des Esseintes." Literary representation operates in such a way that proper names from the extrafictional realm can be included in the fictional universe in an entirely acceptable and nondiscontinuous manner (as in the historical novel), but any movement in the opposite direction — the fictional proper name circulating without its frame of fiction — normally requires a transformation of the referential function of the name in question. Most often, when this "false" movement does occur, the proper name passes from the fictive context to the real only to be stripped of its "properness": when one speaks of a "tartuffe" or an "Archie Bunker," the referential origin of the fictional character has been erased and the proper name becomes a common noun that describes, much like a nickname, the characteristics of a repeatable, general type.

The treatment of the character of Des Esseintes on the part of fin-de-siècle critics, confronted with the unconventional nature of the novel that includes large portions of what would be considered "nonfiction" in another context as well as by the free circulation of the name of the main character outside of the novel, most often took the form of biographical explanation. Des Esseintes, in this sort of defictionalizing commentary, stands as the nearly transparent pseudonym of the writer Huysmans. The reduction of the fictional work to the life and times of its author, a traditional way of interpreting decadent prose (examples of this type abound in Max Nordau's *Degeneration* wherein any work is seen as a documentary barometer of the mental health of its creator), performs an exercise of control that seeks to defuse the danger of seductively transgressive fictions and attempts to reinstitute by way of an insistence on the unequivocal proper name the notions of identity and accountability in the pseudonymous scenario.

The inception and subsequent spectacle of the circulation of Marguerite Eymery's pseudonym provides another example and dimension of the onomastic project of the decadent proper name in the late nineteenth century. In the provincial setting of her youth, Marguerite claimed to have attended several séances in the course of which she pretended to have been in contact with a sixteenth-century Swedish courtier named Rachilde. She narrated at length the life of this completely imaginary figure, his successes in the royal court, his amorous exploits, and frequent debaucheries. So shockingly detailed was her account that Marguerite's mother came to believe that her daughter's stories were in fact being dictated by the communicative spirit. When she began to publish in the 1880s, Marguerite took the name Rachilde as her pseudonym, thus creating the illusion of a nonarbitrary (the fantastic basis of spiritualism notwithstanding) onomastic origin which would replace that of her actual, patronymic past. Later, when Rachilde became a Parisian celebrity in the wake of the banning of *Monsieur Vénus*, she carried the implications of her supposedly male pseudonym to their logical extreme by carrying a *carte de visite* that read "Rachilde, homme de lettres." She also requested permission from the local police to appear in public in male attire.[7] Rachilde's staging of her own name and the ensuing travesty of its development, a practice evident throughout her long and prolific career,[8] reveal the decadent writer's penchant for thwarting social conventions of identity by reestablishing nominal origin and for theatricalizing the proper name in ways that blur traditional boundaries of selfhood.

In the circumstances surrounding the invention and eventual circulation of the names of Jacques Plowert, Des Esseintes, and Rachilde, the fictionalization of the proper name goes beyond the initial act of renaming and exploits the onomastic conventions of reception in the creation of a counterfeit genealogy that ambiguates the distinction between the fictional and the extrafictional. Such a program attempts to manipulate and destroy the meaning and propriety of onomastic reference. The decadent pseudonym, contrary to the panoptically driven critics' claims of simple mystification or hoax, seeks to write the final chapter in the rise and fall of the proper name and therefore destabilize dominant conceptions of self and meaning in the late nineteenth century.

Corpus Delicti

> Tous les masques sont assassineurs. (213)
>
> [All masks are murderers.]
> — Jean Lorrain, *Le Crime des riches*

The proper name in the fictional world referentially functions and circulates in the same linguistic role as it does in the realm of the extrafictional. Moreover, that which represents the pseudonym or locus of pseudonymity in the decadent novel can be found in the figure of the transvestite. His/her proper name, the nominal property that heritage has provided, has become improper because of the act of impropriety, transvestism. The transvestite, then, needs a new name, a name as improper as the impropriety, a false name to correspond to the "falseness" of the transvestite, a pseudonym. The originality of the transvestite can be located as much in the act of renaming as in the simulation of a gender-opposite body. By this re-creation, the transvestite proposes and controls the illusion of his/her origin by disrupting the continuity of the inherited name and the genealogy of sex. The pseudonym consequently forms the basis of the particular linguistic orientation that the transvestite must employ in order to begin and complete the gesture of transvestism. Emanating from the transvestite's linguistic dilemma is the radical inversion of sartorial codes that must now be made to correspond to the revised referentiality of the new name.

The transvestite appeared as a literary figure long before the advent of the nineteenth century. In previous representations, however, fundamental differences can be noted. The conditions of representing transvestism in earlier periods were often reduced to the dictates of a "situational" necessity: to escape a danger, to find out a secret, for comic effect, etc. There was another type of cross-dresser who chose to wear the clothes of the opposite sex as a more permanent and more narratively problematic "aesthetic" choice. In the seventeenth century there were the exploits of the celebrated Abbé Choissy, recounted in detail in his memoirs published in the following century. In the eighteenth century the adventures of the Chevalier d'Eon were well known (his memoirs were published in 1836) as well as the libertine novel *Les Amours du Chevalier Faublas* by Jean Baptiste Louvet de Couvray, which involved the transvestism of its protagonist. This type of character became increasingly frequent in nineteenth-century French literature judging from the profusion of works involving cross-dressing: Charles Nodier's *Thérèse Aubert* (1816), several episodes in Casanova's *Mémoires* (published in 1826), Théophile Gautier's *Mademoiselle de Maupin* (1829), Henri de Latouche's *Fragoletta* (1829), Honoré de Balzac's *La Fille aux yeux d'or* (1834) and *Sarrasine* (1835), Auguste de Villiers de L'Isle-Adam's *Isis* (1862), Victor Cherbuliez's *Le Comte Kostia* (1865), as well as the numerous examples in late nineteenth-century decadent prose. It can be noted as well that in most pre-nineteenth-century versions of the transvestite (particularly those involving "situational" necessity), the reader was often alerted to the gesture of transvestism from the outset such that any surprise or confusion at the revelation of the character's true sexual identity is limited to the level of the story. In a number of the nineteenth-century texts involving cross-dressing characters, the narrative participates in the secret and its unmasking.

While the decadent transvestite may not qualitatively differ from a number of nineteenth-century French literary cross-dressers, his/her profusion in decadent prose betrays yet another facet of the counter-discursivity of an aesthetic that sought to attack outrageously, scandalously, and very nearly anarchistically at its very roots the dominant culture's modes and habits of signification. Rarely relinquishing the system of transvestism at the text's point of resolution, the figure of the transvestite in decadent prose is clearly cultivated for its ability to disrupt and problematize the notion of discourse, economically expressed in his/her power to construct a new self.[9] By examining several texts, it can be shown how the transvestite's signifying reconstruction of the self and, by extension, the world affects the form and function of language and narration in decadent textuality.

In the short stories of Jean Lorrain (the pseudonym of Paul Duval) collected in *Histoires de masques* (1900), the transvestite most often appears as a participant of the *bal masqué* or of the carnival.[10] In the story "L'un d'eux," the narrator begins by considering the essential and seductive nature of the mask: "Le mystère attirant et répulsif du masque, qui pourra jamais en donner la technique, en expliquer les motifs et démontrer logiquement l'impérieux besoin auquel cèdent, à des jours déterminés, certains êtres, de se grimer, de se déguiser, de cesser d'être ce qu'ils sont, en un mot, de s'évader d'eux mêmes?" [The attractive and repulsive mystery of the mask, who will ever be able to yield its technique, to explain its motives and logically show the imperious need to which surrender, on specific days, certain beings, to make up one's face, to disguise oneself, to cease being what they are, in a word, to escape from themselves] (3). The mask invites the dissolution of the established, signified self by erasing the two prominent exterior components of identity: the face and gender. The mask, then, embodies the "face trouble et troublante de l'inconnu, c'est le sourire du mensonge" [the turbid and troubling face of the unknown, it is the smile of the lie] (5).

In the skeletal story that follows Lorrain's brief articulation of a theory of the mask, it is indeed the persistent and resistant alterity of the mask's surface that haunts the narrator's memory and narrative authority. The short story's plot can be easily summarized: an unnamed narrator, kept late in Paris one evening on business, is forced to wait for a late train to his suburban home. In the street on his way to the train station, he sees a masked figure whom he presumes is walking to the Eden Theater's masked ball. Shortly thereafter in the train station, the masked figure reappears and boards the same train as the narrator. The disguised character wears a costume that is half masculine and half feminine, thus creating the "trouble équivoque d'un sexe incertain" [the equivocal confusion of an uncertain sex] (11). The masked passenger's only action involves looking at his/her reflection in a small hand mirror. At the fourth stop, the *travesti* gets off the train and disappears into the early morning. Throughout the story, the masked figure creates an inviolable, hermeticized circuit to and from his /her image which is directly related to the covering up of the body and the transformation of the resulting image into an impenetrable surface, an opacity that even resists narrative authority. The mask in "L'un d'eux" does not allow, by gestures or by words, its story to be told. The narrator, faced with the absence of an unequivocal signifying body and encouraged by his paranoid curiosity, is unable to successfully narrate a plot that could correspond to the masked figure's presence, to provide an acceptable interiority for the ambiguous, unacceptable exteriority of the stranger. In the end, the "sourire du mensonge" triumphs as the masked figure not only eludes narrative control but also presents an insurmountable obstacle to it. Left in the wake of the mystery of the mask is a series of attempts at narration that result in an aborted plot.

In another story from *Histoires de masques* entitled "Un crime inconnu," the narrator begins with an implied questioning of his own authority as observer, recounting how he recently had been cured of ether addiction and yet retained the paranoid fear of "une présence effrayante et sans nom" [a fearful, nameless presence] (60). In the story that follows, the narrator watches two men check in to the third-class hotel where he resides. From the outset, he regards them suspiciously as they do not look like the provincial butchers they claimed to be, "[b]ien élégante d'allure et de vêtements, malgré leurs chapeaux melons et leurs pardessus de voyage" [very elegant bearing and clothes despite their bowlers and travel coats] (64). The confusion of signs, in the language of gestures and of clothes, that these two represent for the narrator fuels his heightened curiosity. Later, while spying on them through the keyhole of an adjoining room, he watches one of the men dress himself in a carnival mask and costume and commit the horrific crime of rendering his companion a raving drug addict by tying an ether-filled glass mask without airholes to his face. The first man commits the crime only after he has donned his own disguise. The account of the scene parallels the action as the narrator admits "Je ne reconnaissais plus mon homme" [I no longer recognized my man] (68) and the disguised man becomes in the text "une forme verte" [a green form], "un larve" [a mask], and simply "un masque" [a mask] (69). The man who voluntarily put on the mask loses his identity in the story to the extent that the desubjectifying, generalizing surface of the mask alone is recognizable and available to narrative agency. In addition, the mask filled with ether serves as the instrument of the crime (which consists of stripping another of his reason and his identity) such that, in the text, the duplicitous nature of the word *masque* ultimately can refer to both the author and the instrument of the crime. The mask has the considerable power of depersonalizing and removing the wearer from the contextual scene of the crime (as the title suggests, underlining the impotence of the narrator as witness, the crime was never detected), whether its wearer be criminal or victim. Textually, it influences and ultimately determines the narrator's response — in words and in actions — which initially could have reestablished the context of the crime and the identities of the two men. The story ends with the narrator's submissive assertion that the crime went undiscovered and the identity of the victim who became a resident of the asylum at Villejuif was never ascertained. Once again the mask tells no stories, leaving the narrator, based on equivocal fragments of a possible story, with his failed speculations.

In the third of Lorrain's stories from *Histoires de masques*, "L'homme au bracelet," the setting is the lurid landscape of suburban prostitution, specifically that of a *fenestrière*, a prostitute who attracts clients from the window of a house or apartment. The story begins in a typically voyeuristic position of exteriority, a common vantage point for Lorrain's narrators. As seen from the street, a woman's arm emerges from an upper window: "un bras très blanc et d'un galbe très pur sortait de derrière un rideau de soie rouge, se déployait comme un cou de cygne et démeurait là des heures, réplié, de façon de montrer la tache duvetée de l'aisselle, ou bien pendre au dehors, dans la rue, langoureux et fluide, écharpe dénuée lancée vers le désir. Le bras et jamais plus" [a very white arm with pure curves would come out from behind a red silk curtain, would stretch out like a swan's neck and then would remain there for hours, turned back, in order to show the downy spot of the armpit, or rather to hang outside, in the street, languorous and fluid, stripped scarf cast toward desire. The arm and never more] (128). The arm, the text recounts, is powdered, seductively feminine in gesture, and wears a gold bracelet that dangles from the wrist. In reality, the arm belongs to a man posing as a female prostitute in order to rob or blackmail prospective clients taken in by the trick. It is the narrative, however, of "L'homme au bracelet" which is the most deceitful. The narrator asserts the existence of a woman with correspondingly feminine gestures while, in truth, as the narrator knows all along, the woman is a man posing as a woman. The readers of Lorrain's stories, like the embarrassed clients of "L'homme au bracelet," have been tricked by the surface value of meaning, by the travestied combination of signs written on the page that correspond to those deceitful ones written on the body. The referential "crime" of an irreconcilable doubleness, dominant in Lorrain's stories as well as throughout decadent prose, emanates from the false body and obliterates the possibility of determining or fixing identity.[11] The scene of the crime, the transvestite's body, creates in Lorrain's stories a repetitive obstacle to narrative precision and closure in which the duplicitous character impedes the telling of its story and all that can be produced is a text whose duplicity resists readerly expectations of a referential and narrative resolution.

Oral Delinquency

> Fixed tightly in her left eye was a single eyeglass; she wore a high stiff collar, a white necktie, an open waistcoat, a little black coat of masculine cut and a gardenia in her buttonhole. She affected the manners of a dandy and spoke in a deep husky voice. And just therein lay the secret of her attraction — in this imprint of vice, of depravity, of abnormality in her appearance, her attitudes and her words. (186)
> — Gabriele D'Annunzio, *The Child of Pleasure*

The paralyzation of narrative in the telling of the story of the transvestite that is proposed variously by the "mask" stories of Jean Lorrain receives its fullest articulation in one of the most scandalously renowned of decadent novels, *Monsieur Vénus* by Rachilde. While Rachilde enjoyed a certain vogue during her long, prolific career and *Monsieur Vénus,* upon its publication and subsequent banning in 1884 and republication in 1889 with a preface by Maurice Barrès, was the "succès de scandale" that greatly determined the author's reputation in the late nineteenth century, Rachilde, more than any other writer of the decadent group, lay in virtual obscurity until quite recently. The dramatic and effective recuperation of Rachilde and *Monsieur Vénus* has been due to a generalized interest in questions of gender expressed in the novel's complicated representations and potential critique of late nineteenth-century gender constructs emanating from the actions and antics of its cross-dressing heroine. Another dimension of *Monsieur Vénus*'s gender politics regards the ways by which the transvestism of its main character affects the textual habits of narration and referentiality, one of Rachilde's significant contributions to the array of representational strategies of decadent prose of the 1880s.

Monsieur Vénus's complicated plot centers on the character Raoule de Vénérande (a name whose venereal echoes are entirely consistent with her status as a decadent femme fatale) and the two men in her life, the baron Raittolbe, a lifelong yet continually rejected suitor, and her chosen paramour, Jacques Silvert, a mediocre artist of working-class origins whose androgynous beauty initially attracts her interest. Raoule de Vénérande embodies the most clichéd characteristics of decadent portraiture: she is, like Des Esseintes, the last member of an ancient, noble family, a child "né de la mort" [born of death] (36). Her father, who blushes at the works of the marquis de Sade, " mais pour une autre raison que celle de la pudeur" [but for a reason other than that of a sense of decency] (39), used up his vitality in excesses of debauchery. She owns an inherited library of shameful books that she keeps safely locked, and her present hysteria had its origin in the reading of an illustrated, pornographic novel. Hysteric, sadist, transvestite, emasculating femme fatale, female dandy, reader of scandalous fiction, the character of Raoule de Vénérande belongs to and at times seems to parody an extensive body of literature produced in the late nineteenth century in which traditional gender-specific elements of representation were disintegrating, reversing, and polarizing. Significant in the portrait of Raoule de Vénérande (and in that of the latently homosexual baron Raittolbe, who dreams of exotically ending his days hunting lions in Africa) is the recognizable figuration of the aristocracy's inevitable degeneration into perversion. Raoule's transvestism and sadism as well as Raittolbe's eventual homosexuality participate in the formation of a growing compendium of decadent themes and figures that announce a domain of transgression if not inversion of commonly held discursive values.

From the outset, *Monsieur Vénus* proposes a thematic problematization of the notion of identity through gender reversals. In the opening passages of the novel, Raoule arrives at Marie Silvert's hovel. When she asks Jacques if she may speak to the florist, he replies: "Pour le moment, Marie Silvert, c'est moi" [for the moment, I am Marie Silvert] (24). This willful, verbal travesty of reference, which takes the form of the usurpation of the other's name, sex, and identity, is merely the first in a series that will mark the novel's plot at every stage. In order to extract money from the obviously smitten Raoule, Marie Silvert pens a letter to the slumming aristocrat, signs Jacques's name, and later goes to see her on the fictive behalf of her brother. Raoule, pretending to the world to be the patroness to Jacques's unreasonable artistic aspirations (his major work up to that point is a pastoral landscape in which a sheep appears to have five legs), attempts to orchestrate a Pygmalion-like education of her so-called protégé in order to enact the social travesty of rendering him more acceptable in appearance and demeanor to the aristocratic and fashionable circles through which she circulates. *Monsieur Vénus* illustrates, as Dorothy Kelly has remarked, that "gender is so superficial, so artificial that one can assume and discard it at will" (151). Significant in these gender reversals and social travesties, nonetheless, is the parodic if not anarchical valency of Raoule's gestures.

In the private theater of Raoule de Vénérande's existence, she keeps the effeminate Jacques as a "mistress." She dresses him in women's negligées, and forces him to submit to her sadistic desires and whims when she arrives in male dress at the apartment where she keeps him. A delirious example of this social and linguistic ventriloquism occurs near the end of the novel when Raoule discovers Jacques dressed as a woman in Raittolbe's rooms. She demands that her honor be defended, exchanges her male costume for Jacques's female clothing, and forces Jacques to play the role of the outraged husband seeking revenge. At the duel the next morning, Jacques, who believes the scene to be yet another episode of the elaborate farce staged by Raoule's theater of cruelty, dies from a single shot of the baron's gun. Raoule then descends into pseudo-necrophilia as she worships a wax mannequin that she has made in Jacques's likeness with real hair and fingernails. Still in control, she is able to operate a hidden spring and animate the figure's mouth. In all of these examples, from Marie and Jacques's mutual usurpation of the other's name and voice to Raoule's institution of transvestism and her animated mannequin, the lines of referential authority which, when functioning authentically and efficiently, allow for a clear distinction between reality and fiction, truth and falsehood, real voice and usurped voice, upper and lower class, life and death, become blurred in *Monsieur Vénus*'s narrative. This situation proves fatal for Jacques, whose downfall results from misreading these false signs. Voice and identity, then, become the wherewithal of the transvestite's plot to challenge narrative culture.

One of the novelties of Rachilde's *Monsieur Vénus* is that its protagonist, Raoule de Vénérande, is a female transvestite who establishes a language that corresponds to the nature of her transvestism. She describes herself as an "honnête homme" [man of honor] (70) and declares with a masculine adjectival form, "je suis amoureux" [I am in love] (88). She says to Jacques at one point "Tu es une petite femme capricieuse qui a le droit, *chez elle*, de me torturer" [You are a capricious little woman who has the right, in her own home, to torture me] (103–4) and eventually refers to him as Madame de Vénérande (194). She exercises the power of renaming herself in order to correct the discontinuity of socially constituted linguistic signs in conflict with her imposed transvestism. Such a linguistic reversal resonates through the novel—in pronouns and adjectives—requiring readerly attention in following the equivocal traces of textual reference.[12] The proper noun, at the head of the narrative chain that is ultimately replaced by corresponding pronominal forms, is manipulated and ultimately subverted in Rachilde's novel. The transvestite's inversion of language is a temporary albeit radical disruption of the referential marks and conventions that link the various elements and make narrative comprehensible. For example, after having finished the novel, the reader can reasonably ask to whom the "Monsieur Vénus" of the title refers: is it the seductive Jacques in women's clothes, or is it the seducer Raoule dressed as a man? This sort of ambiguity and confusion is at the heart of the linguistic condition of the transvestite itself.

The most fantasmagorical example of this radical perversion of signifying systems instituted by the transvestite can be found in the novel's last chapter: "La nuit, une femme vêtue de deuil, quelquefois un jeune homme en habit noir, ouvrent cette porte. / Ils viennent s'agenouiller près du lit, et lorsqu'ils ont longtemps contemplé les formes merveilleuses de la statue de cire, ils l'enlacent, la baisent aux lèvres" [At night, a woman in mourning, sometimes a young man in a black suit, open that door. / They come to kneel down near the bed, and when they have contemplated at length the marvelous forms of the wax statue, they hug it, kissing it on the lips] (227–28). If the narrator is to be believed, there is only one remaining character to play the role of the man and woman in this passage: Raoule de Vénérande. The doubling of character, in hallucinatory, seeming simultaneity, the mask and the face unmasked on the stage at the same time, can only exist on the printed page, a duplicity permitted by the grammatical construction of the sentences in which the plural forms of the subject require a continued plural in the verbs that follow. In the final sentences of *Monsieur Vénus*, Raoule, as Melanie Hawthorne has remarked, "is herself no more than a pronoun" (177), and the transvestite triumphs in language and narration as its simulated self attains a linguistic and referential status as indistinguishable in its signifying authority as that of the real self.

The terminus of the onomastic problematic in and around decadent prose approaches the boundary of meaning and nonsense, chaos and coherence. The writing of the name in decadent prose, which begins with the fictionalization and manipulation of the paratextual proper name in the form of the pseudonym, enters the text with the figure of the transvestite. The narration of the transvestite's crime against nature and the crime produced by the transvestite's language, which originates in a false name necessitated by the scandalous impropriety of transvestism, seek to proclaim the twilight of the proper name. The false genealogies created by the decadent pseudonym, the narrative impotence instigated by Lorrain's maskers, and Rachilde's triumphant march of the falsettos all lead to the same result: the attenuation of referential authority and stability in the process of signification. The linguistic impropriety of the decadent name put into service by the figure of the transvestite has as its goal the emptying of the real from reality by replacing so-called traditional and true value with a false and dissimulated one, a counterfeited alternative that inverts all conventional values of society and selfhood and establishes a semiological labyrinth to which a definitive escape becomes impossible short of renouncing the readerly act. On its own terms, however, decadent prose functions like a textual funhouse whose simulations and parodies mockingly distort for a time their models and whose falseness encourages confusion with and oppositional subversion to those very values.

Notes

1. All translations, unless otherwise indicated, are my own.

2. For a history and survey of anonym and pseudonym dictionaries, see Archer Taylor and Frederic J. Mosher. For more on the discursive formations and implications of these compilations, particularly in the nineteenth century, see Maurice Laugaa.

3. For a discussion of the details of nineteenth-century works on the linguistic value of the proper name, see Holger Steen Sørensen.

4. Pseudonyms of the prominent members of the Decadent Movement include Rachilde, Jean de Chilra (Marguerite Eymery Vallette); Jean Lorrain (Paul Duval); C. Valerius (Catulle Mendès); Jacques Plowert (Paul Adam); la princesse Minska (Joséphin Péladan); A. Meunier (Joris-Karl Huysmans); Raoule Vague, Louis Villatte, Pombino (Anatole Baju). For a list of the presumed pseudonyms of less well known contributors to *Le Décadent*, see Richard (261–64). In addition, several writers of this group modified their given names: Joris-Karl Huysmans was christened Charles-Marie-George Huysmans. Joséphin Péladan, beyond his use of the ancient Assyrian religious title "Sâr," was originally named the decidedly less rarefied Joseph Péladan. Anatole Baju, the editor of *Le Décadent*, was named by his parents Adrien Bajut, but he took his brother's first name and changed the spelling of his surname.

5. The review *Le Décadent*, in addition to its free and playful use of the pseudonym, was also the center of a controversy concerning the authenticity of certain poems by Rimbaud. Having been the first Parisian journal to publish Rimbaud's poems (obtained through Verlaine, an early contributor to *Le Décadent*), the editors soon followed suit with several additional works in some of its later editions which were soon recognized to be "forged" pastiches. This created, as was perhaps the intent of the perpetrators of this hoax, a lively scandal that consequently required a retraction in print. For more on *Le Décadent*'s Rimbaud forgeries as well as other Rimbaud pastiches in the late nineteenth century, see Bruce Morrissette (11–45).

6. There is an amusing example of Huysmans's playful use of the pseudonym. In 1885, the publisher Vanier included an "interview" in his series *Hommes d'aujourd'hui* with the author of *A rebours* and a fairly hostile critic named A. Meunier. A. Meunier, however, was a pseudonym of Huysmans (borrowed from the name of his friend Anna Meunier), and the so-called interview was rather a carefully scripted parody of that genre that nonetheless reveals important details about the parodically disruptive strategies of presentation of the decadent pseudonym and the decadent aesthetic in general.

7. According to nineteenth-century French penal codes, transvestism was a punishable offense. Claude Dauphiné reports that Rachilde was accorded authorization to appear in public in male dress (25–26), as were other turn-of-the-century celebrities including Sarah Bernhardt, the archaeologist Madame Dieulafoy, and the writer

Marc de Montifaut. Significant, however, in these examples is the "professional" justification behind those requests.

8. In a volume of her memoirs, *Face à la peur*, Rachilde recounts a comical albeit dubiously autobiographical episode that illustrates this particular proclivity throughout her career. She tells of her frustration in attempting to obtain money from a bank in a provincial town where she found herself after fleeing the approaching German army during World War II. Having lost her purse and all her means of identification in transit, she was forced to buy a copy of one of her books—most likely *Monsieur Vénus*, her biggest success—and present it at the bank in order to establish her identity. As if on cue, the bank clerk did not initially believe her and replied, "Madame . . . Ah! oui, je connais ce nom et je pensais qu'il s'agissait d'un homme. (Sourire) C'est vous l'auteur?" [Madame . . . Why yes, I know that name and I thought that it was a man's. (Smile) You are the author?] (70).

9. An important distinction should be made between the figure of the androgyne, popular throughout the nineteenth century, and the transvestite. The former, with its mythical echos of a being before a primordial separation of the sexes, mixes masculine and feminine signs but disrupts signifying conventions only by way of a perceptual ambiguity on the part of the viewer. The transvestite, in contradistinction to the androgyne, redraws the parameters of agency by constructing the signs that correspond to the opposite sex, thus tricking the viewer into reading those signs as a part of an authentic version of referentiality. It can be noted, however, that many decadent transvestites are also androgynous, thus facilitating the successfully received simulated self.

10. While the masked ball and carnival contexts provide a disruptive semiological indeterminacy entirely consistent with the sexually, socially, and criminally transgressive nature of the maskers in Lorrain's stories, Philippe Jullian suggests another reason for the author's obsessive interest in masks: "Lorrain adorait le masque pour dissimuler le visage qui le navrait; le domino pour lui donner l'illusion de porter une robe. Depuis des charades de son enfance, il se déguisait au moindre prétexte" [Lorrain loved the mask in order to dissimulate the face that greatly pained him; the domino in order to give him the illusion of wearing a dress. From the charades of his childhood, he would disguise himself at the slightest excuse] (190). Gender reversal, then, would seem to be an essential element behind Lorrain's masked ball and carnival costumes.

11. In "Le Dernier Masque" from *Le Crime des riches*, the tenuous nature and ultimate unreliability of the body as a signifying structure relate to the ease with which the mask is donned and the referential dangers that masking invites, which verge on the fantastic. For more on the relationship of the decadent aesthetic to the fantastic, particularly in Lorrain's work, see Koos (121–26). In the story a group of men have spent the evening telling each other morbid accounts of masks and the crimes that seem to emanate from them. The group, planning to stop off at one of their members' homes before definitively dispersing, arrive at a darkened entryway. One of them trips over something and accuses their friend Quinsonnes of having left a wax mannequin there as a prank to frighten them on their return. The mannequin feels cold to the touch, "on dirait un cadavre" [one would say a cadaver] (260). Despite Quinsonnes's continued denials, the others harangue him further, claiming that the prankster even had come up with the ghoulish idea of removing the mannequin's head. The mannequin's description emphasizes the supreme artistry employed to make this object successfully imitate the form of the human body. Vergy, who has examined the figure while the others attempt to find out where Quinsonnes had procured such a lifelike "pseudo-cadaver," announces that the mannequin is in fact the headless corpse of a young woman. In the ensuing police investigation the

only verifiable bit of information regarding the corpse was the approximate time of its appearance at Quinsonnes's doorstep. According to the traces left on the body by its previous existence (the mark of a ring and of a garter, manicured toenails and fingernails), the police investigators like Lorrain's narrators unsuccessfully attempt to reconstruct the story of the young woman's demise and her identity. The body, as perhaps the end of this story as well as a number of Lorrain's others in their lack of closure attest, once masked loses forever its fixedness as a signifying entity thus potentially submerging all identity in the irresistibly counterdiscursive sway of indeterminacy.

12. In the 1884 edition of *Monsieur Vénus*, published by Brancart in Belgium, one typographical style was employed throughout the text. In Brossier's 1889 Parisian edition of the novel, ostensibly in order to curb any referential confusion on the part of the reader when confronted with these passages, the "inverted" sections of the text were italicized, a practice adopted by all subsequent French editions of *Monsieur Vénus* as well as by foreign translations of the novel. It is not clear, however, whether the decision to distinguish these words came from the author or the publisher. For more on the changes made between the 1884 and 1889 editions of the novel, see the anonymously published 1995 pamphlet *Monsieur Vénus par Francis Talman*.

Works Cited

Adam, Paul, and Jean Moréas. *Les Demoiselles Goubert*. Paris: Stock, 1888.

Badouin, Marcel. "La Découverte rapide de l'identité littéraire à l'aide du Répertoire Bibliographique *onomastique* des Anonymes." *La Revue scientifique*. 4th Series. 9:19 (1898): 648–56.

Barrès, Maurice. *L'Oeuvre de Maurice Barrès*. Vol. 1. Paris: Club de l'Honnête Homme, 1965.

D'Annunzio, Gabriele. *The Child of Pleasure*. Trans. Georgina Harding. London: Dedalus, 1991.

Dauphiné, Claude. *Rachilde, femme de lettres 1900*. Paris: Pierre Fanlac, 1985.

Hawthorne, Melanie. "*Monsieur Vénus*: A Critique of Gender Roles." *Nineteenth-Century French Studies* 16 (1987–88): 162–79.

Jullian, Philippe. *Jean Lorrain ou le Satiricon 1900*. Paris: Fayard, 1974.

Kelly, Dorothy. *Fictional Genders: Role and Representation in Nineteenth-Century Narrative*. Lincoln: University of Nebraska Press, 1989.

Koos, Leonard R. "Fictitious History: From Decadence to Modernism." In *The Turn of the Century: Modernism and Modernity in Literature and the Arts*, ed. Christian Berg, Frank Durieux, and Geert Lernout. Berlin: de Gruyter, 1995. 119–31.

Laugaa, Maurice. *La Pensée du pseudonyme*. Paris: Presses Universitaires de France, 1986.

Lorrain, Jean. *Le Crime des riches*. Paris: Pierre Douville, 1905.

———. *Histoires de masques*. Paris: Ollendorff, 1900.

Monsieur Vénus par Francis Talman. Paris: Le Fourneau, 1995.

Morrissette, Bruce. *La Bataille Rimbaud; L'Affaire de la Chasse spirituelle*. Trans. Jean Barré. Paris: Nizet, 1959.

Nodier, Charles. *Des artifices que certains auteurs ont employés pour déguiser leurs noms*. Paris: Techener, 1835.

Plowert, Jacques [Paul Adam]. *Petit glossaire pour servir à l'intelligence des auteurs décadents et symbolistes*. Paris: Vanier, 1887.

Quérard, Jean-Marie. *Les Auteurs déguisés de la littérature française du XIXe siècle*. Paris: Au Bureau du Bibliothécaire, 1845.

Rachilde. *Dans le puits ou la vie inférieure, 1915–1917*. Paris: Mercure de France, 1918.

———. *Face à la peur*. Paris: Mercure de France, 1942.

———. *Monsieur Vénus*. Paris: Flammarion, 1977.

Raynaud, Ernest. *La Mêlée symboliste (1870–1890)*. Vol. 1. Paris: La Renaissance du Livre, 1918.

Richard, Noël. *Le Mouvement Décadent: Dandys, Esthètes et Quintessents*. Paris: Nizet, 1968.

Sørensen, Holger Steen. *The Meaning of Proper Names*. Copenhagen: G. E. C. Gad, 1963.

Taylor, Archer and Frederic J. Mosher. *The Bibliographical History of Anonyma and Pseudonyma*. Chicago: University of Chicago Press, 1951.

Chapter 11
Imperial Dependency, Addiction, and the Decadent Body

Hema Chari

[I]n 1856 . . . the Anglo-Indian Government drew a revenue of £25,000,000, just the sixth part of its total state income, from the opium monopoly . . . [I]n its Indian capacity, it forces the opium cultivation upon Bengal, to the great damage of the productive resources of that country; compels one part of the Indian ryots to engage in the poppy culture; entices another part into the same by dint of money advances, keeps the wholesale manufacture of the deleterious drug a close monopoly in its hands; watches by a whole army of official spies its growth, its delivery. . . . The Indian finances of the British Government have, in fact, been made to depend not only on the opium trade with China, but on the contraband character of that trade.
— Karl Marx (219)

The economic dependency that Marx ascribes to India, with respect to the opium cultivation and trade there by the East India Company, is a reflection on several levels of the country's total addiction to, and dependency on, the imperial British rule. In the late eighteenth century and the early nineteenth century, the cultural significance of opium, and of opiate India, had a great impact on English literature. At this time, India was barely recovering from the repercussions of the Sepoy Mutiny, and the depictions of India in English literature were attributing cannibalistic traits to Indian culture. Colonizers were convinced that Indian culture itself was in need of refinement, and the British rule in India—through its discursive apparatus—successfully constructed the discourse of opiate dependency and, in turn, of India as the colonial toxin that the imperial self delineated, and disposed of, as the "other." The construction of the discourses of opium, dependency, and Indian culture as the junkyard of western imperialism subsequently gave rise to a paradigmatic equation of decadence with the colonized. We find such depictions of dependency, degeneracy, and decadence in Wilkie Collins's novel *The Moonstone* and its portrayals of an opiate India and an addicted race. The novel portrays how the characterization of the colonized culture as decadent became necessary to justify the colonial processes, and it demonstrates the ways in which colonial discourses use the rhetoric of decadence to create paradigms of race, class, gender, ethnicity, and sexuality that sustain colonial knowledge and power structures. The discourse of colonial decadence becomes a site of interaction with, and alienation from, the colonized other and, within the literary context, decadence as a cultural construct is always a double articulation, revealing simultaneously the colonizer's deep fascination with, and paranoid anxiety about, the other.

It is no surprise that the discourse of decadence in colonialism is invariably associated with Orientalist ideology. These two terms—*decadence* and *Orientalism*—have become interchangeable signifiers, defining and decoding each other in literary and critical theories. Decadence is a powerful ideological construction in colonial discourse, one that profoundly dislocates the political, epistemological, and ontological conditions of colonial identity and subjectivity. It is grounded on notions of contamination and contagion that are considered prevalent in distant frontier outposts and that invariably are presented as calling for colonial intervention. Colonial centers are haunted by the paranoiac fear and threat of infection, of inside/outside boundaries disrupting and defiling colonial centers. Sander Gilman writes, "Degeneracy is the label for the Other, specifically the Other as the essence of pathology" (209). Similarly, Edward Said discusses how Orientalist theories not only circulated racial stereotypes in their representations of the colonial other but promoted rigid dichotomies and binary oppositions that constantly emphasized the issue of racial/ethnic difference and of the East/West binarisms (*Orientalism* 3, 20). The fear of the unknown prompted a complex set of fabricated representations which for the West figured the "Orient." These representations of the East determined the West's understanding of the Orient and provided the basis for the understanding of its subsequent self-appointed imperialist rule.

In *Orientalism*, Said comments that the Orient "was routinely described as feminine, its riches as fertile, its main symbols the sensual woman, the harem, and the despotic—but curiously attractive—ruler" (225). Sexuality is a loaded metaphor for domination, and sexual images illustrate the iconography of the rule. Said examines the ways in which the sexual and political are imbricated within the dynamics of race, and investigates how the feminization of the Oriental cultures, in turn, delineated these races as decadent.[1] However, although Said's analysis of Orientalism is crucial to the point of departure of my paper, my analysis of decadence is not based on a neat division of accepted discourses of domination and excluded discourses of antagonism. Instead, this paper concentrates on those liminal cultural spaces that constantly expose colonial identities and subjectivities as ambivalent and contradictory.

The discursive sites of colonial decadence are complicated by the representation of homosexual identity in colonialism. Foucault's analysis of sexuality is crucial in examining the performative subjectivity of colonial decadence and the ways in which the discourse of colonial decadence was formed, interpreted, consolidated, and circulated ("Deployment" 105–6). Indeed, the construction of sexuality and of homosexual identity in nineteenth-century discourse is closely allied to the colonial project, for the colonial other was initially articulated through a set of differences that were also categorized as deviancies. Bhabha argues that, in order to understand the production of the colonial other, "it is crucial to construct its regime of 'truth,' not to subject its representations to a normalizing judgement. Only then does it become possible to understand the *productive* ambivalence of the object of colonial discourse — that 'otherness' which is at once the object of desire and derision, an articulation of difference contained within the fantasy of origin and identity" (19). The decadent other is sustained by abjecting negative aspects of the self in order to form an other.

An investigation of the ways in which the self and the other in any culture are different aspects of the same entity and how every culture constitutes the other to the self becomes vital to uncovering the contradictions and ambivalences inherent in colonial discourses of decadence. Foucault points out that though the other has never been an object of reflection, yet all that was unwanted, negative, and cancerous in culture was transferred to and unloaded on the other. The other became the junkyard where all the toxic materials of modern civilization were dumped. Eventually, established and reinforced through power and knowledge as the poison of the self, the other was finally constructed as different from the self: "For though this double may be close, it is alien, and the role, the true undertaking, of unthought will be to bring it as close to itself as possible" (Foucault, *Order* 327). Although Foucault attributes the historical time frame of the nineteenth century to the constitution of the discourse of the other, a period when the self was systematically and distinctly constituted in western discourses as different from the other, he never mentions the colonial project or colonial rule.[2] Similarly, Foucault shows how gay sexuality was constituted around the same time in the nineteenth century, but he never alludes to colonization. However, one cannot deny that, on a geopolitical level, Victorian Britain was the major world imperial power, and the West was legitimating the colonizing status of the Third World others by establishing the colonies as being culturally and racially flawed. Even categories of "colonizer" and "colonized" were secured through forms of sexual control. Gender-specific sexual sanctions and prohibitions demarcated positions of power and prescribed the personal and public boundaries of race.

The exotic tropics provided a site of European pornographic fantasies, emphasizing the sexual license, perversions, and gynecological anomalies of the Orient. For example, Sander Gilman claims that the Hottentots, especially the black female, prevailed as the essence of the black in the nineteenth century. Gilman also argues that the sexuality of the black becomes an icon for deviant sexuality during the colonial period, and "anomalous sexuality" is one of the most salient marker of decadence and of "otherness" (89). The colonies functioned as sites of sexual fantasies for the imperial voyeur, especially in their colonial project of the subordination of *men by men*. However, during colonization, one of the defiling aspects of the colonized cultures, according to the empire, was their proclivity toward homosexuality. Eve Kosofsky Sedgwick points out that some of the assumptions about male homosexuality connected them exclusively to the colonies: "Running eastward the Sotadic Zone narrows, embracing Asia Minor, Mesopotamia and Chaldea, Afganistan, Sind, the Punjab and Kashmir." She concludes that "the most exploratory of Victorians drew the borders of male homosexual culture to include exclusively, the Mediterranean and the economically exploitable Third World" (183).

One cannot ignore the fact that questions of sexual orientation, of female impersonation, and of androgyny are consistently associated with the Orient or the East, especially in English literature of the eighteenth century onward. Similarly, the narratives of Anglo-Indian literature are haunted by a persistent but disembodied insinuation of homoeroticism. Even in the Romantic period of De Quincey's opium eaters, the underbelly of culture — addiction and addicts — is associated with the East. It is the artistic inspiration of opium, that purer ideal self refined by the muse, that is reserved for the English masculinized romantic imagination. Concurrently, even in a Victorian novel as early as Wilkie Collins's *Moonstone* (1868), the negative and repulsive aspects of culture, sexuality, and gender indeterminacy are situated within an eastern context of the Orient.

The Moonstone points to a series of discursive and ideological displacements or splits that allow for mediations between the Orient and the Occident but only to reappropriate and to reestablish colonial power. Its portrayal of colonialism initiated and articulated a literary legacy of representing the Orient as a nebulous site for the production of a colonial discourse of Oriental decadence. Therefore, to understand the production and circulation of decadence, one must consider the complex, ambiguous, and often contradictory interplay of representations of decadence in colonial discourse and its connections with complicated power structures and relations. *The Moonstone* exemplifies the contradictions of imperialist, Orientalist discourse, its repressed ambiguities, and ideological splits. The novel uncannily unmasks the paranoid anxiety and panic of the political and epistemological status of the Empire.

The adventure and suspense of Collins's novel are structured around the discovery and possession of the enormous and unusual yellow diamond that was stolen from the holy city of Somnauth in India by John Herncastle. Collins begins *The Moonstone* with the siege of Seringapatam under General

David Baird in 1799, when Tipu Sultan, who vehemently opposed the British occupation of India, was killed:

A cry inside hurried me into the room, which appeared to serve as an armoury. A third Indian, mortally wounded, was sinking by the feet of a man whose back was towards me. The man turned . . . and I saw John Herncastle, with a torch in one hand, and a dagger dripping in blood in the other. A stone set like a pommel, in the end of the dagger's handle, flashed in the torchlight, as he turned to me. . . . The dying Indian sank to his knees, pointed to the dagger in Herncastle's hand, and said, in his native language: "The Moonstone will have its vengeance yet on you and yours!" He spoke those words, and fell dead on the floor. (5)

The novel's sensational dramatization of the fall of Tipu Sultan is aligned with the expansionist and imperialist ideology of the empire, and it significantly underlines the rapacious character of the Indian whose curse will plague the English home and colonies.[3] In fact, the narrator, an unnamed cousin, in the prologue attests to the fact that the only reason he recollects that night at Seringapatam is because he carries the burden of a "moral evidence" (6). By appealing to the English cultural rubrics of rationality and sensibility, he hopes to appease his family by explaining his motives for ending his friendship with Herncastle. In the process, the narrative casts doubts on the facts of the incident: "I have not only no proof that he killed the two men at the door; I cannot even declare that he killed the third man inside — for I cannot say that my own eyes saw the deed committed. It is true that I heard the dying Indian's words; but if those words were pronounced to be *the ravings of delirium,* how could I contradict the assertion from my own knowledge?" (6, emphasis added). Although the novel accentuates gaps, slippages, and narrative inconsistencies, it still underlines some of the deep anxieties of the English: the probability of an Englishman such as Herncastle "going native" in a bizarre land and of the strength of the occult power of an Indian's malevolent curse. In this scandal, Herncastle has done a deed that dissolves him of his English identity and entraps him in a horrifying sequence of decadent "Oriental" activities: murder, plunder, and brutality. The apprehension that Herncastle has "gone native" is confirmed after he returns to England and adopts a lifestyle similar to the ways of the "savage." He isolates himself, acquires exotic pets, leads a "solitary, vicious, underground life," and is "given up to smoking opium" (34). In fact, as Ashish Roy points out, the "novel brings together a semiotic repertoire that demonstrates the structural cohesion the imperial imagination aimed at, but could never quite achieve, when challenged on issues of morality and reason." The narrative echoes "the imperialist project's vigilance against the native hindsight that would pit the rapacious foreign exploiter cast as self against the innocent other" (Roy 657). In the process, the opening narrative also rationalizes the moral compulsion on the empire to bolster its surveillance and vigilance over India, particularly after the 1857 rebellion.

While explaining Herncastle's "usurpation" of the pernicious diamond, the narrator carefully documents the history of India's colonization by conquerors other than the British. The story of the "yellow diamond" chronicles in turn an interminable history of continued usurpation and pillage. The subtext in this particular narrative reinforces the commonly acknowledged beliefs of the empire that the decadence of Indians and their culture incapacitates them for self-rule and presents the Christian rule of the British administration as more civilized than India's earlier conquerors:

> At that age the Mohammedan conqueror, Mahmoud of Ghizni, crossed India; seized the holy city of Somnauth; and stripped of its treasures the famous temple. . . . One age followed another — and still, generation after generation, the successors watched their priceless Moonstone, night and day. One age followed another until the first years of the eighteenth Christian century saw the reign of Aurangzebe, Emperor of the Moguls. At his command havoc and rapine were let loose once more among the temples of the worship of Brahmah. . . . The generations succeeded each other; the warrior who had committed the sacrilege perished miserably; the Moonstone passed (carrying its curse with it) from one lawless Mohammedan hand to another. . . . Time rolled on from the first to the last years of the eighteenth Christian century. The Diamond fell into the possession of Tipoo, Sultan of Seringapatam. (2–3)

All this time, of course, the Hindu priests guard their treasure by lying in wait. "Powerless to recover their lost treasure by open force, the three guardian priests followed and watch it in disguise" (3). The Hindu population of India is portrayed as passive, caught in an endless ahistorical and pagan convention, waiting interminably, and prophesying a series of disasters on the accursed. In addition, from the imperial viewpoint, by putting an end to Tipu Sultan's dissolute regime, the British liberated India from the brutality of contemporary despots. As a matter of fact, the British administration believed that they had salvaged India from its long history of decadent Oriental despotisms.[4]

The prologue invokes both the Sepoy Mutiny of 1857 and the presentation to Queen Victoria of the legendary Koh-i-noor diamond, which had been captured in the Anglo-Sikh wars of 1848–49.[5] In Britain, there was an uproar over the revolt, and writers virulently attacked the "monstrous" rebellion.[6] Collins dramatizes the decadent elements of the Sepoy Mutiny in the novel, even though he does not refer to it directly.[7]

With the arrival of the Moonstone in England, every strata of British class and society is infected by its vicious, occult power, which spreads calamity and grief wherever it goes and infects whomever it touches. The fundamental concern of the narrative is not the diamond's recovery by the three disguised Indians but its violation of an "English" home and its women: "Who would have thought that horrible Diamond could have laid such a hold on her in such a short time?" (91). "The cursed Moonstone had turned us all upside down" (91). The moonstone defiles the sanctity of the

English home, tarnishes the purity of the English character, and threatens to violate the innocence of English women:

Here was our quiet English house suddenly invaded by a devilish Indian diamond — bringing after it a conspiracy of living rogues, set loose on us by the vengeance of a dead man. . . . Who ever heard of the like of it — in the nineteenth century, mind; in an age of progress, and in a country which rejoices in the blessings of the British constitution? Nobody ever heard the like of it, and, consequently, nobody can be expected to believe it. (67)

In contrast to this portrayal of English culture as rational, scientific, and orderly, the Indian priests disguised as magicians and jugglers resort to pagan rituals of sorcery and black magic. For instance, when Betteredge finds one of the articles left by the Indian jugglers, he shows it to Franklin Blake, who remarks that the Indians are "foolish enough to believe in their own magic — meaning thereby the signs on a boy's head, and the pouring of ink into a boy's hand, and then expecting to see persons and things beyond the reach of human vision" (54). At certain points in the novel, the skepticism voiced by Betteredge and Blake regarding the magical powers of the three Indians is undercut by the narrative's intolerance toward scientific reasoning. However, the instances of magic and mystery are invested with plot significance, and as the Indians are fixated on repossessing the diamond, they endanger the innocence of an English woman, Miss Rachel, for "there she stood, innocent of all knowledge and truth, showing the Indians the Diamond in the bosom of her dress!" (78).

The otherness of the Indian jugglers is reinforced by the mystical and magical qualities of the diamond. In addition, the significance of the diamond for English culture is a double-articulation exemplifying the ambivalence of colonial rule in India. On one level, it is a beautiful and priceless jewel, just as the country is a "Jewel in the Crown," but, on another level, it is malevolent, spiteful, and decadent:

Lord bless us! it *was* a Diamond! As large, or nearly, as a plover's egg! The light that streamed from it was like the light of the harvest moon. When you looked down into the stone, you looked into a yellow deep that drew your eyes into it so that they saw nothing else. It seemed unfathomable; this jewel, that you could hold between your finger and thumb, seemed unfathomable as the heavens themselves. We set it in the sun, and then shut the light out of the room, and it shone awfully out of the depths of its own brightness, with a moony gleam, in the dark. (68–69)

However, like the country of its origin, the jewel, in spite of its splendor, is "flawed." The value of the jewel and of India is always questionable and ambivalent, and these paradoxical ruptures are not merely discursive but contribute to the empire's enigmatic fascination with, and abhorrence of, the other: "The question of accurately valuing it presented some serious difficulties. Its size made it a phenomenon in the diamond market; its colour placed it in a category by itself; and, to add to these elements of uncertainty, there was a *defect*, in the shape of a *flaw*, in the very *heart* of the stone" (41, emphasis added). Not only does the color of the diamond resemble the yellow of poppies, but in this sense it resembles opium itself and becomes the signifier for opium.

The gem is also precious and diabolical, and its recovery is attempted by the three dark and mysterious Brahmin priests who prowl around the English neighborhoods and homes in search of it. In their quest to restore the jewel from the British crown to the forehead of the Indian goddess — which also represents the pagan third eye common to the Indian deities — the three are reconstituted from their priestly profession to that of jugglers and magicians. With this slip from priesthood to sorcery and performance, the stereotypes of those aspects of cultural forms that are closely allied with magic and barbarism — hocus-pocus occultism — are constantly reinforced and identified with Indian cultural practices. Even though the diamond was stolen from the Indian goddess and the temple was desecrated by the British, the discourse of the uncivilized, violent, and irrational is carefully constructed through the Indian race. The Brahmins will not hesitate to commit murder to accomplish their avowed purpose, and their barbaric incivility is further established by tracing Gothic elements of darkness to the cultural heritage and belief systems of the Indian culture, a culture which has been studied and documented by English scholars, including Murthwaite: "A Hindoo diamond is sometimes part of a Hindoo religion. I know a certain city, and a certain temple in that city, where, dressed as you are now, your life would not be worth five minutes' purchase.' Miss Rachel, safe in England, was quite delighted to hear of her danger in India" (73). The cultural values and practices of the three Indians are supported by their fierce and medievalistic religion in which blood and vengeance are demanded by a pantheon of unforgiving gods and goddesses:

"In the country those came from, they care just as much about killing a man, as you care about emptying the ashes of your pipe. If a thousand lives stood between them and the getting back of their Diamond — and if they thought they could destroy those lives without discovery — they would take them all. The sacrifice of caste is a serious thing in India, if you like. The sacrifice of life is nothing at all." (81)

In a Christian world of order, peace, and rationality, of course, these darker aspects of civilization are toxins that require disposal.

Significantly, it is the women who become addicted to the diamond and inherit the narcotic wealth. The curse of the Indian goddess is transferred to another woman, Rachel Verinder. As she is drawn into the sinking sands of the Moonstone, the erotics of desire is played out on two levels: first, through the three dark Indian jugglers on the secular level, and, second, through the Hindu goddess of the Moonstone on the sacred level. Later, these two levels are metamorphosed and displaced through the gendered bodies of race and sexuality, a theme which is developed in the interaction between Rachel Verinder and the opium addict, Ezra Jennings.

Still further, the complexities of gender and class are unfolded through the conflicted narrative of Rosanna Spearman's desire and through her neurotic obsession with Franklin Blake, which culminates with her inevitable suicide in the sinking sands. These sands become the crucial site of dependency, addiction, and enslavement. Issues of gender, race, class, sexuality, and the colonized other merge and submerge, and the quivering sands of colonization rupture the gendered space of opium, the gendered covetousness for the diamond/wealth, and the feminized dependency of the colonies on imperial administration. The sinking sands are the chief nexus in the novel to symbolize the symbiotic but decadent relationship between colonial dependency and colonial sovereignty. The gendered bodies of race, class, and sexuality, dislocated from colonial to imperial centers, threaten to violate the boundaries of the home and the center and to infect the numerous signifiers of the center, which are successively represented as empire/England/home/boudoir/cabinet.[8]

The diamond is relocated from the narratives of precolonial plunders prior to Nāder Shāh's 1739 invasion of India, to Tipu Sultan's reign, and ends up in Seringapatam during the colonial rule of Britain. Once in the hands of the British officer, Herncastle, the diamond moves to the boudoir of a quiet English household whose mistress, Rachel Verinder, stores it in her Indian cabinet: "She bethought herself of an Indian cabinet which stood in her sitting-room; and instantly made up her mind to put the Indian diamond in the Indian cabinet, for the purpose of permitting two beautiful native productions to admire each other" (85). To some extent, the geographical spaces and locales of London as the colonial center and of India as the peripheral colony are made liminal. These global shifts are conspicuous when the Moonstone moves from India to England and the three Indian priests wander into English homes. Yet, throughout these geographical relocations, the novel sustains the paranoia of the colony contaminating these English spaces, as well as the colonial fascination with and desire for the other.[9] The greater the degree of possession, irrespective of whether these possessions are trivial or precious Indian goods, the more imminent is the fear of pollution that could invade English homes and assail English women.[10] Therefore, the civilizing mission of colonization is, in its double duty, obligated to protect its own women from colonial contamination and to civilize the decadent culture of the colonies.

Jennings is the only person to whom Rachel agrees to talk about the Moonstone, even though his character and racial lineage are cast in doubt by his Gypsy complexion, his opium addiction, and his questionable sexuality. He is portrayed in the novel as lonely and secretive; he is an outcast who is associated with either criminal or socially offensive behavior. He is

also considered by the other characters in the novel to be physically repulsive:

> "Why is he so unpopular?"
> "Well, Mr. Franklin, his appearance is against him, to begin with. And then there's
> a story that Mr. Candy took him with a very doubtful character. Nobody knows who
> he is — and he hasn't a friend in the place. How can you expect one to like him, after
> that?" (359)

When Blake meets with Jennings, he too finds him unattractive. Jennings's
racially hybrid origins make him physically repugnant to the other characters, an abhorrence that is repeatedly underscored in the novel: "I was born,
and partly brought up, in one of the colonies," Jennings tells Blake. "My
father was an Englishman; but my mother — we are straying away from our
subject, Mr. Blake; and it is my fault." Subsequently, Blake concludes that
Jennings "had suffered as few men suffer; and there was the mixture of some
foreign race in his English blood" (411). Because he is racially flawed,
Jennings is unacceptable to English society. He is a product of colonial
miscegenation, a painful consequence of imperialism's covert desire for and
abhorrence of the other. At the same time, he is also a needling reminder of
imperialism's shameful secrets and lies:

> His complexion was of a gipsy darkness; his fleshless cheeks had fallen into deep
> hollows, over which the bone projected like a penthouse. . . . And to add to this a
> quantity of thick closely-curling hair, which, by some freak of Nature, had lost its
> colour in the most startlingly partial and capricious manner. Over the top of his head
> it was still of the deep black which was its natural colour. Round the sides of his
> head — without the slightest gradation of grey to break the force of the ordinary
> contrast — it had turned completely white. The line between the two colours pre-
> served no sort of regularity. At one place, the white hair ran into the black; at
> another, the black hair ran down into the white. (358–59)

The man with the piebald hair and dark complexion becomes the emblem
of the repressed other inexhaustibly haunting the psyche of the empire with
irrepressible anxiety, guilt, desire, fascination, and repulsion. Consequently,
Jennings's repressed Eurasian origins recall the perilous expanse of the
Indian subcontinent as a decadent site of a regressive culture.[11] Jennings's
hybrid racial and ethnic nationalities threaten the purity of English nationalism and racial pride.[12]

Jennings is also carefully portrayed as being burdened with the effeminacy that deprived colonized men of self-governance: "I . . . burst out crying.
An hysterical relief, Mr. Blake — nothing more! Physiology says, and says that
some men are born with female constitutions — and I am one of them!"
(414). Given the enormous gaps in Jennings's narrative, together with the
repeated references to his femininity, his own confession to Blake of an
unspeakable "disgrace" (420) suggests another possible blemish in his char-

acter besides that of opium addiction. As readers, we are aware that femininity in men was extremely problematic in Victorian England.[13] In Jennings's
portrayal, opium addiction seems to function as a signifier for the Oriental
"secret vice" of homosexuality (Sedgwick, 180–200). Native men were considered unable to govern themselves for several reasons, their greatest im-
pairments being effeminacy and sexual perversion. Jennings's dark secret,
along with his Eurasian origins, recall the depraved, enigmatic, and iniq-
uitous expanse of the perverted subcontinent, and India's decadence consequently necessitated the "civilizing mission" of cleansing the degenerate
culture through colonial rule.

Jennings is also an opium addict:

For ten years past I have suffered from an incurable internal complaint. I don't
disguise from you that I should have let the agony of it kill me long since. . . . The one
effectual palliative in my case, is — opium. To that all-potent and all-merciful drug I
am indebted for a respite of many years from my sentence of death. . . . The progress
of the disease has gradually forced me from the use of opium to the abuse of it.
(421–22)

Opium, the noxious Oriental commodity, reinforces the double articulation and slippage characteristic of colonial discourse.[14] In the hands of the
natives, opium is abusive and decadent, but when possessed by the colonizers and utilized in a western scientific and rational manner, it can become a healing agent. Of course, Jennings, the other, is allowed to play a
pivotal role in solving the mystery. In this instance, however, the novel yields
once again to the incursion into the English home by the racially mixed
Jennings, the native/alien, insider/outsider. In addition, as Roy explains,
"the episode has about it a hint of superstition or a primitive touch of
exorcism. . . . That this crucial event is entrusted to . . . the figure of the
other graphically registers the homeopathic cure as crisis of reason, almost a
case of sympathetic magical ritual" (673–74). Moreover, inasmuch as Jennings represents imperialism's secrets and lies, the onus of the colonial guilt
is projected onto the scapegoat figure of this hybrid Eurasian. Subsequently,
the burden of cleansing himself of his decadent origins weighs on him. He
expiates this burden by solving the mystery and showing that Blake stole the
diamond under the influence of opium, a pernicious Oriental drug. The
novel, however, clearly indicates that the only resolution for Jennings's degenerate lifestyle and conduct is death.

Nevertheless, the novel carefully establishes that part of his racial heritage
is Anglo-Saxon; after all, he does maintain in his confession that his father
was an Englishman (411). Accordingly, the toxic opium holds the clue to
resolving the mysterious disappearance of the Moonstone. Opium in Jennings's hands is no longer diabolic; he is able to extract its healing elements,
and opium becomes the cure.[15] As Roy argues, "Poison and cure, at once
harmful and beneficent, the opium detaches the Moonstone's synecdochic

reference from its accidental obtrusion in the schemes of reason" (672). In Jennings's scientific experiment, opium constitutes a western scientific discourse of medicine opposed to the hocus-pocus occultism of the native poison of the Orient.

While Jennings embodies the conflicts of race and sexuality in colonial discourse, Rosanna Spearman accentuates the perplexing predicaments of gender and class within British culture, especially when they confront the discursive contradictions of colonial domination. Although Rosanna is just a maid and represents the working class, her role is significant. Her knowledge of Blake's theft of the Moonstone and her subsequent actions of burying the incriminating piece of evidence (his paint-stained nightshirt), entombing her letter expressing her desire for him, and drowning herself in the sinking sands bring together several strands of the ambivalent epistemological and ideological conflicts of the novel, particularly as these aspects reinforce associations of colonial decadence with perversion. As is the case with Jennings, the novel underscores Rosanna's physical deformity and alludes to her moral depravity. Rosanna, convicted of thievery, was rescued from the reformatory by Rachel, who employed her as her maid; Rachel's magnanimity sustains the pretense of benevolence of the British upper classes towards the less fortunate. According to Betteredge, Rosanna was not attractive. "She was the plainest woman in the house, with the additional misfortune of having one shoulder bigger than the other" (24).

Similarly, Rosanna's closest friend, Limping Lucy, expresses her intense erotic attraction to Rosanna and censures heterosexuality and class discrimination in British culture: "If she had only thought of men as I think, she might have been living now!" (206). While her passionate declaration reinforces the aberrant qualities of unconventional sexuality, it also becomes a foil to the dominant heterosexual romantic plot (206). The "most horrible quicksand" (24) is Rosanna's grave and, besides being a "gothic site" (Heller 149), is also the predominant symbol of decadence pulling together its constitutive elements of race, class, and sexuality.

The sand-hills here run down to the sea, and end in two spits of rock jutting out opposite each other, till you lose sight of them in the water. . . . Between the two, shifting backwards and forwards at certain seasons of the year, lies the most horrible quicksand shivering and trembling in a manner most remarkable to see, and which has given to it, among the people in our parts, the name of the Shivering Sand. (24)

As Tamar Heller suggests, the "sinking sands" are "an image of the female body" and a "female sexual symbol" (149). In addition, Heller claims that Rosanna links the metaphoric associations of the sands to the subjugated condition not only of women in general, but of all colonized Indians when she visualizes the "broad brown faces" (28) in the sands. With the reference to Indians, the novel, according to Heller, implies "an analogy between sexual and imperial domination" (145). I suggest, however, that equating issues of race, class, and gender domination or subordination within colonial discourse, as Heller does, is problematic within the context of colonial decadence.

For instance, Blake and Rosanna are both hypnotized and horrified by the Gothic elements of the sinking sands. Their interaction with the sands replays the analogous double articulation of colonialist discourse of decadence and of imperialist panic: Rosanna frequently visits the sands while languishing for Blake. She also stumbles over the buried racial and gendered secrets of colonial repression and resistance.

Nonetheless, from these muted epistemological gaps and suppressions emerge the double articulation of colonial decadence and the nightmare of a devilish India. These silenced murmurs illustrate once again the menacing, duplicitous, and traitorous characteristics attributed to Indians. Consequently, the British were ethically and morally coerced into administering their civilizing mission, besides responding to the native desire for British knowledge and power. Rosanna tells Betteredge of the horrible choked faces she perceives and the throttled voices she hears from the depths of the sands:

"Look! . . . Isn't it wonderful? isn't it terrible? I have seen it dozens of times, and it's always new to me as if I had never seen it before!"
I looked where she pointed. The tide was on the turn, and the horrid sand began to shiver. The broad brown face of it heaved slowly, and then dimpled and quivered all over. "Do you know what it looks to *me*?" says Rosanna, catching me by the shoulder again. "It looks as if it had hundreds of suffocating people under it—all struggling to get to the surface, and all sinking lower and lower in the dreadful deeps!" (28)

Rosanna's description of these buried faces and throttled voices in the "ugliest little bay" (24) are the "broad brown face" of the depraved colonial other.

Similarly, the "dreadful deeps" recapitulates the fatal and dark origins of the other. Rosanna's hallucinations allude to several political and violent events of 1848–49—uprisings in Europe, wars in the Indian colonies, especially in the Punjab–that concurrent with the main action of the novel. *The Moonstone* recalls the storming of Tipu Sultan's palace at Seringapatam in 1799 by General David Baird. The temporal structure of the novel, written in 1868 and set in 1848, elides the Sepoy Mutiny of 1857–58, one of the most violent and crucial events in the history of British India. However, as contemporary revolts—the 1857–58 rebellion and other Anglo-Indian wars—haunt the national and cultural psyche of Britain, the specter of the Sepoy Mutiny stalks the novel even in its absence.[16] British fear that the repressed other will return is not merely an imperialist panic but also a cultural paranoia that afflicts all classes of the imperial culture. Rosanna's, and later Blake's, reaction to the phantasms in the sinking sands echo the hysteria of the British Raj when the colonies resisted foreign rule. On one level, Rosanna's Gothic vision of the sands reverberates with the violent events of 1865 at Morant Bay. General Edward Eyre's powerful retaliation in the face of that Jamaican rebellion was supposed to have far exceeded the original violence (Brantlinger 28–29, 37–38; Lanoff 178–79; Mehta 622–623). On another level, Rosanna's tormenting visions of "suffocating people . . . struggling to get to the surface, and all sinking lower and lower in the dreadful deeps" evoke and revise the two most notorious episodes of the British Raj in India: the Black Hole of Calcutta (1756) and the Well of Cawnpore (1857–58). Of all the fables of the dissolute and despotic barbarians of the Indian colony, these two incidents reinforce the ambivalent, contradictory, and nebulous discursive sites for the production and dissemination of colonial decadence. The key figures in these incidents, Suraja Dowlah and Nana Sahib, are prototypes for Oriental despots who are depicted as notorious for their barbarism and treachery. Blake visualizes similar fears in the quicksand when he tries to exhume the inculpating clues that Rosanna has concealed: "The bared wet surface of the quicksand . . . hid the horror of its false brown face under a smiling face" (342). The "brown face" and casualties of the uprising (quivering, trembling, and smiling fraudulently) resurface constantly on the quicksand for Rosanna, Betteredge, and Blake (28, 136, 342). These images recapitulate the stealthy movements and reappearances of the sly, fraudulent Indians roaming the streets of London (Heller 149, Mehta 625), extending the phobic representations of the imperialist panic not merely to Nana Sahib, Suraja Dowlah, and Tipu Sultan but ultimately to all Indians.[17] In the aftermath of the Black Hole of Calcutta and the Well of Cawnpore, the colonial administration maneuvered its domination by shifting its strategies of power and control away from expansionist policies toward an altruistic civilizing mission and a martyred/sacrificial rule.

The significance of the sinking sand is crucial for the paradigmatic embodiment of decadence in colonized discourse. The quicksand, a prototype for the decadent colony, is situated on the outskirts and is frequented by the lower classes who perform menial jobs. The quicksand is also the site of vulnerability and resistance and ties together an economy of decadent signifiers — opium, visionary ink, the Moonstone. Earlier, the "chief Indian" poured black ink into the notch of the English boy's hand and hypnotized him, reinstating the occult powers of the deceptive East: "The boy became quite stiff, and stood like a statue, looking into the ink" (19). Later, Betteredge's description of this scene connected the visionary ink to the vial of opium that plays a crucial role in the plot as a signifier of colonial decadence. Issues of dependency, addiction, mesmerism, violence, and colonial decadence are linked through this chain of signifiers, portraying in turn the conflicting predicaments of race, gender, class, and sexuality in colonial discursive constructions of decadence. And yet this discourse of colonial decadence is not behind us.

Today, the commercialization and marketing of opium by colonial Britain continues on a more subtle level. With the advent of immigration and the influx of a large foreign-born population to the metropolis of London, the opium trade retains its lucrative and alluring appeal, and for migrants it can seem their only hope for survival. So, in Hanif Kureishi's film *My Beautiful Laundrette*, the only option for immigrants is to deal drugs. In the postmodern world of enterprise culture, Kureishi shows the laundrette becoming a viable site for transferring contraband goods and for laundering drug money. However, even here the representational options are limited, and the discourse of opium, drugs, and colonial decadence is still reinforced through recycling stereotypes of the addicted body of imperial dependency.

Notes

My sincere gratitude to Elizabeth Constable and Dennis Denisoff, whose suggested revisions and editorial changes contributed positively to the final form of this essay.

1. Much as Said's discussions are useful in deconstructing the racial stereotypes in colonial discourse, they completely ignore the question of gender, of women's positions in these portrayals of harems and female fantasies, even while discussing the exoticism of the East. Said describes the sexual images as an archetype of colonial asymmetries and does not comment on the relationships of men and women in colonialism or the impact of these decadent sexual tropes on the identity of women.

2. Accordingly, it is astonishing that Foucault, in *The Order of Things*, mentions that the "other" was constituted during the beginning of the nineteenth century and how the "other" became the dumping ground for the negative aspects of western culture, but he does not refer to the discourse of colonization.

3. Several scholars on *The Moonstone*, especially with regard to the incident in question, comment that Collins has portrayed the unnaturally irrational and barbaric quality of Herncastle's behavior and claim that it is an anti-imperialist novel. See John Reed; Sue Lanoff (174–83, 213–35); Patricia Miller Frick. See also T. S. Eliot's eulogy in his 1934 introduction to the novel and his claim that it is a "classic detective tale" (426). Similarly, Eliot emphasizes the ominous "fatality" that besets the diamond. But he also asserts, "This fatality of the diamond puts no strain on the credulity; we are not expected to accept the occult powers" (427). The novel does put pressure on the credulity of the Indian characters and their potency to use mystic powers and magic. In addition, by drawing attention to the Indian's curse, the rest of the novel is burdened by it and the curse begins to *contaminate* English society. For a detailed analysis of the expansionist policies of the British in India, see Musselwhite (79–82).

4. In Denys Forrest's *Tiger of Mysore: The Life and Death of Tipu Sultan*, the events of Seringapatam resulted in one of the largest booty of arms and treasures and substantially increased the British coffers. Karl Marx expresses similar sentiments about India when he writes about the Sepoy Mutiny: "How came it that English supremacy was established in India? . . . A country not only divided between Mohammedan and Hindu, but between tribe and tribe. . . . Such a country and such a society, were they not the predestined prey of conquest? . . . India, then, could not escape the fate of being conquered, and the whole of her past history, if it be anything, is the history of the successive conquests she has undergone. *Indian society has no history at all, at least no known history.* What we call its history, is but the history of the successive intruders

who founded their empires on the passive basis of that unresisting and *unchanging society*. The question . . . is not whether the English had a right to conquer India, but whether we are to prefer India to be conquered by a Turk, by the Persian . . . to India conquered by the Briton" (81; emphasis added).

5. For details about the history of the diamond, see Roy (658–60). Collins wrote twice about the revolt, and both articles were published in Charles Dickens's weekly magazine *Household Words*. One of his articles, "The Perils of Certain English Prisoners," he co-authored with Dickens, and it appeared in November 1857. The second article, "A Sermon for Sepoys," was published on 27 February 1858 (244–47). For an account of the revolt from a British perspective, see Hibbert and Metcalf.

6. Dickens called for the "extermination" of the Indian race and applauded the "mutilation" of the wretched Hindoo who were punished by being "blown from . . . English gun[s]" ("Speech" 284). In a letter to Angela Burdett-Coutts on 4 October 1857, Dickens wrote: "The first thing I would do to strike that Oriental race with amazement . . . should be to proclaim to them, in their language, that I should do utmost to exterminate the Race upon whom the stain of the late cruelties rested" (*Letters* 350).

7. See Jaya Mehta, "English Romance: Indian Violence." Mehta elaborates on the fact that Collins carefully avoided a direct reference to the Sepoy Mutiny: "Written in 1868 and set in 1848, [*Moonstone*] neatly oversteps the most significant and horrific event in the history of British India, which took place almost precisely at the mean of those two dates. The utter elision of the 'Sepoy Mutiny' of 1857–58 in Collins's novel is all the more striking as newspapers were drawing attention to the tenth anniversary of the Mutiny" (617).

8. See Jaya Mehta's argument that this "nesting structure turns itself inside out. . . . Interior involutes into exterior; outside folds into inside" (621). See also Tamar Heller (145).

9. Several readings of the novel claim that geographical locations such as center and periphery are blurred. See Duncan (302); Heller (617).

10. The frenzy of colonial administrators after the Sepoy Rebellion embellished the immoral and heinous aspects in Indian men who unscrupulously attacked and raped English women. See Jenny Sharpe for a comprehensive analysis of rape in post-mutiny fiction; see Paxton for rape as justifying imperial violence according to renovated chivalric conventions.

11. Ronald Inden analyzes nineteenth-century British depictions of India as archaic, ahistorical, timeless, epitomized by Hinduism's pagan rituals of image-worship and oriental despotism (12–21, 49–74, 86–89, 109–15, 165–72).

12. Gauri Viswanathan argues that British national culture was formed as a result of imperial establishment, rather than vice versa (47–64). See also Suleri (10, 22).

13. See also Sedgwick; Mrinalini Sinha; and Ashis Nandy. In the nineteenth century, doctors and ethnographers besides Freud associated Orientals with degenerate and feminine traits; see Sandra Siegel (119, 219); Elaine Showalter (1–18).

14. The opium trade conducted by the East India Company was extremely successful not only in generating huge profits and revenues for the company but also in clinching the political grasp necessary to completely colonize India and China. The opium trade was the most successful business venture of the East India Company, and opium trade gave the company complete monopoly over the Indian/Chinese markets. See Mehta (630).

15. See also Ashish Roy, who maintains that Jennings is "alien and native at once" (674). To a large extent, Jennings is redeemed from his native genealogy because his father was English, and the male Anglo-Saxon heritage redeems Jennings and privileges him to be entrusted with the solution to the mystery.

16. See Jaya Mehta for a discussion of the European and Indian revolutions that are suggested by Collins's novel (621–22). See also Ashish Roy (665–67). John Reed points out that the British newspapers in 1868 were drawing attention to the tenth anniversary of the mutiny (290n), and Brantlinger claims that even a decade later the uprising stories of rebel monstrosities flourished in Britain (220–22).

17. The imperial phobia and panic caused by the Sepoy Mutiny filters down to all classes of the British culture. It is interesting that Rosanna, a lower-class maid, alludes to both the paranoic horror of the Black Hole of Calcutta and to the Sepoy Mutiny and empathizes with the upper-class British women who were affected by the insurgence. Similarly, Betteredge, who is also of the lower class but on a higher status than Rosanna, and Blake, from the wealthy class, echo their anxieties about India and Indians.

Works Cited

Bhabha, Homi. "Remembering Fanon: Self, Psyche, and the Colonial Condition." In *Remaking History*, ed. Barbara Kruger and Phil Mariani. Seattle: Bay, 1989.

———. *The Location of Culture*. London: Routledge, 1994.

Brantlinger, Patrick. *Rule of Darkness: British Literature and Imperialism, 1830–1914*. Ithaca: Cornell University Press, 1988.

Collins, Wilkie. *The Moonstone*. 1868. New York: Oxford University Press, 1991.

Collins, Wilkie, and Charles Dickens. "The Perils of Certain English Prisoners." In *The Lazy Tour of Two Idle Apprentices and Other Stories*, 237–327. London: Chapman and Hall, 1890.

Dickens, Charles. *Letters from Charles Dickens to Angela Burdett-Coutts*. Ed. Edgar Johnson. London: Jonathan Cape, 1953.

———. *The Speeches of Charles Dickens*. Ed. K. J. Fielding. Oxford: Clarendon Press, 1960.

Duncan, Ian. "The Moonstone: The Victorian Novel and Imperial Panic." *Modern Language Quarterly* 55.3 (September 1994): 297–319.

Eliot, T. S. "Wilkie Collins and Dickens." In *Selected Essays*. 2d ed. London: Faber & Faber, 1934.

Forrest, Denys. *The Tiger of Mysore: The Life and Death of Tipu Sultan*. London: Oxford, 1970.

Foucault, Michel. "The Deployment of Sexuality." *The History of Sexuality*. Vol. 1: *An Introduction*. New York: Random House, 1980.

———. *The Order of Things: An Archaeology of the Human Sciences*. New York: Vintage, 1973.

Frick, Patricia Miller. "Wilkie Collins' 'Little Jewel': The Meaning of the Moonstone." *Philological Quarterly* 63 (1984): 313–21.

Gilman, Sander L. "Black Bodies, White Bodies: Toward an Iconography of Female Sexuality in Late Nineteenth-Century Art, Medicine, and Literature." *"Race," Writing, and Difference*. Ed. Henry Louis Gates, Jr. Chicago: University of Chicago Press, 1986.

Heller, Tamar. *Dead Secrets: Wilkie Collins and the Female Gothic*. New Haven: Yale University Press, 1989.

Hibbert, Christopher. *The Great Mutiny: India 1857*. New York: Penguin, 1980.

Inden, Ronald. *Imagining India*. Oxford: Oxford University Press, 1990.

Lanoff, Sue. *Wilkie Collins and His Victorian Readers: A Study in the Rhetoric of Authorship*. New York: AMS, 1982.

Marx, Karl. *On Colonialism: Articles from the New York Tribune and other Writings by Karl Marx and Frederick Engels*. New York: International, 1972.

Mehta, Jaya. "English Romance: Indian Violence." *Centennial Review* 39.3 (Fall 1995): 611–57.

Metcalf, Thomas. *The Aftermath of Revolt: India, 1857–1870*. Princeton: University Press, 1964.

Musselwhite, David. "The Trial of Warren Hastings." In *Literature, Politics and Theory: Papers from the Essex Conference, 1976–84*, ed. Francis Barker, Peter Hulme, Margaret Iversen, and Diana Loxley. London: Methuen, 1986.

Nandy, Ashis. *The Intimate Enemy: Loss and Recovery of Self Under Colonialism*. Delhi, London, and Oxford: Oxford University Press, 1983.

Paxton, Nancy L. "Mobilizing Chivalry: Rape in British Novels About the Indian Uprising of 1857." *Victorian Studies* 36 (1992): 5–30.

Reed, John. "English Imperialism and the Unacknowledged Crime of *The Moonstone*." *Clio* 2 (June 1973): 281–90.

Roy, Ashish. "The Fabulous Imperialist Semiotic of Wilkie Collins's *The Moonstone*." *New Literary History* 24 (1993): 657–81.

Said, Edward. *Orientalism*. New York: Vintage, 1978.

——. "Orientalism Reconsidered." In *Literature, Politics and Theory: Papers from the Essex Conference, 1976–84*, ed. Francis Barker, Peter Hulme, Margaret Iversen, and Diana Loxley. London: Methuen, 1986.

Sedgwick, Eve Kosofsky. *Between Men: English Literature and Male Homosocial Desire*. New York: Columbia University Press, 1985.

Sharpe, Jenny. *Allegories of Empire: The Figure of Woman in the Colonial Text*. Minneapolis: University of Minnesota Press, 1993.

Showalter, Elaine. *Sexual Anarchy: Gender and Culture at the Fin de Siècle*. New York: Viking. 1991.

Siegel, Sandra. "Art and Degeneration: The Representation of 'Decadence.' " In *Degeneration: the Dark Side of Progress*, ed. J. Edward Chamberlain and Sander Gilman. New York: Columbia University Press, 1995.

Sinha, Mrinalini. *Colonial Masculinity: The "Manly Englishman" and the "Effeminate Bengali" in the Late Nineteenth Century*. Manchester: Manchester University Press, 1995.

Spivak, Gayatri Chakravorty. "Three Women's Texts and a Critique of Imperialism." In *"Race," Writing, and Difference*, ed. Henry Louis Gates, Jr. Chicago: University of Chicago Press, 1986.

Suleri, Sara. *The Rhetoric of English India*. Chicago: University of Chicago Press, 1992.

Teltscher, Kate. " 'The Fearfu! Name of the Black Hole': Fashioning an Imperial Myth." In *Writing India: 1757–1900*, ed. Bart Moore-Gilbert. Manchester: Manchester University Press, 1996.

Viswanathan, Gauri. *Masks of Conquest: Literary Study and British Rule in India*. New York: Columbia University Press, 1989.

Decadence, History, and the Politics of Language

Chapter 12
Pale Imitations
Walter Pater's Decadent Historiography

Matthew Potolsky

> In the acceptance of depravity the sense of the past is most fully captured.
> Djuna Barnes, *Nightwood* (118)

It is a long-standing critical commonplace to characterize literary decadence — usually disparagingly — in terms of imitation. "In the final analysis," writes Remy de Gourmont, "the idea of decadence is identical with the idea of imitation" (116). G. L. Van Roosbroeck remarks, "The notion of decadence includes esthetically, the notion of imitation" (19). And James M. Smith writes that decadence relies on a "sterile imitation" of more "vigorous" literary forms (650). This dismissal of imitation, so widely imitated, as it were, in critical approaches to decadent writing, assumes that all imitation is somehow the sign of creative deficiency, the dying fall of exhausted intellects. Devoid of original ideas, the argument goes, the decadents turned feebly to a past they could only ransack but never equal. Their writings were inevitably pale imitations of great classics. Désiré Nisard, who introduced the term *decadence* into modern aesthetic discourse, accordingly dismisses decadent writers as "poets without invention, without genius," who must as a result imitate others rather than create for themselves (164). Max Nordau, pushing the metaphor of sterility to an absurdly literal extreme, sees the tendency toward imitation as a clear index of the degenerative hysteria gripping decadent writers, whom he characterizes as criminal mimes: "Clever in discerning externals, unscrupulous copyists and plagiarists, they crowd around every original phenomenon, be it healthy or unhealthy, and without loss of time set about disseminating counterfeit copies of it" (32).

To criticize decadent writing in this way is, of course, to miss both the forest and the trees. Imitation — in the varied forms of allusion, citation, parody, translation, and tribute — is the very stuff of decadent writing, its basic narrative and structural principle. Decadent texts make no secret of their penchant for literary imitation and often read more like bibliographies than fiction or poetry. They draw pervasively on both classical and contemporary models, to such an extent, indeed, that as Jean Pierrot claims, at no other period in western literature has there been "such a ferment of legendary and mythic references" (191). Decadent texts, moreover, do not merely practice imitation, they explicitly thematize it. The valorization of artifice, which responds to conventional valorizations of artistic mimesis, is only the most obvious example of this thematization. Other examples occur on the narrative level as well. Thus, for instance, decadent works often detail relationships of education and discipleship, which turn crucially upon a student's imitation of the teacher. Oscar Wilde's novel *The Picture of Dorian Gray* (1891) is perhaps the most prominent instance, but these relationships are very common. Similarly, the thematic and stylistic prominence of ekphrasis in decadent writing — the extended descriptions of paintings and sculpture, as well as the many retellings of the Narcissus and Pygmalion stories — explicitly foregrounds the unstable relationship between copy and original, art and life.

All of this goes to suggest that decadent imitation is far more than the mark of exhaustion that its critics have understood it to be. Or rather, the sense of exhaustion that critics discern is an *effect* of imitation, not its *cause*. Indeed, imitation constitutes a pivotal concern of decadent writing, perhaps its founding problematic. As such, readers must attend not simply to the "presence" of imitation in a text — as if this were somehow avoidable in any work — but to the way the text makes use of it and to the interpretive valences that arise from this use.[1] In what follows, I shall examine the uses of imitation in Walter Pater's final fictional narrative, "Apollo in Picardy" (1893). This story is made up almost entirely of imitations: allusions to, and translations of, both ancient and more modern works, as well as near-citations from Pater's own earlier texts. It is also a story about a medieval prior's unwitting — and fatal — imitation of the classical past. Pater's story, I will argue, plays this prior's imitation against those of the text itself, and in so doing indicates the potential political implications of decadent imitation.

*   *   *

Pater's writings in many ways constitute an extended meditation on the problem of imitation. All cultural development, for Pater, is achieved not by invention *ex nihilo*, but by imitation and reincorporation, by "a reawakening of the forces of earlier work" (Wallen 17). No aspect of culture is truly original. Instead, cultural change arises out of a complex interplay of influences from the past, which are selected and organized according to the specific vision of an artist, a movement, or an entire society. Pater's major critical subject is the nature and pathways of cultural history, and in particular those moments of historical recovery that generate change through the imitation of an earlier age. "The supreme artistic products of succeeding generations," Pater writes, "form a series of elevated points, taking each from each the reflection of a strange light, the source of which is not in the atmosphere around them, but in a stage of society remote from ours" (*Renaissance* 159). The Renaissance is the paradigmatic case for Pater of such cultural imitation, but he interprets other historical periods and other cultural projects according to the same model. For example, in his novel *Marius the Epicurean* (1885), he describes the early Christian liturgy as a recapitulation of several previous but contradictory forms of worship: "In a generous eclecticism, within the bounds of her liberty, and as by some providential power within her, she gathers and serviceably adopts, as in other matters so in ritual, one thing here, another there, from various sources, Gnostic, Jewish, Pagan, to adorn and beautify the greatest act of worship the world has seen" (2:126–27). The "originality" of the Christian liturgy is really an imitation, a process of what Linda Dowling calls the "ceaseless recombination of cultural materials" that Pater notes across history (*Hellenism* 98). In all cultural change, as Pater writes in *Plato and Platonism* (1893), the "seemingly new is old also, a palimpsest, a tapestry of which the actual threads have served before" (8). Even in the writings of Plato, which stand at the origin of western metaphysics, there is "nothing absolutely new" (8).[2]

As Pater's cultural model implies, imitation is a fundamentally historical gesture, for it necessarily looks back, whatever its larger purpose, to a prior model. It seeks to revive or rearticulate something in the past by repeating it in the present. This historical orientation corresponds to the conventional understanding of mimesis, which defines imitation by its temporal and ontological remove from the real. The conventional notion of imitation informs the characterization of decadence as a "pale" imitation of some prior literary form: decadence is the false copy living off some real original. But imitation, the decadents recognized, is also a practice of resignification, a repetition with a difference. It necessarily alters the "original" meaning of that model; or, to put it another way, it renders the model a model, "creates" it as an original. To this extent, the imitation is both effect and cause, both temporally subsequent to the original and simultaneous with it.[3] This double status renders imitation epistemologically problematic and makes it difficult to ascertain its interpretive or political resonances. While, for example, the historical orientation of imitation is often deeply conservative, indicating the cultural authority of the past, it can just as easily challenge that authority. Epic and parodic imitation are for all intents and purposes formally indistinguishable. Both modes are based on extended imitation of the style, subject matter, and even specific incidents of a prior text or body of texts. No textual marker can indicate the distinction between a serious and a comic imitation; they "look" exactly the same. Only an interpretation of context or authorial intent can account (unreliably) for their notably different effects.[4] Imitation thus highlights the possibility that the same text, the same event, the same material trace, can serve radically different aims in radically different artistic, political, or cultural contexts.

"Apollo in Picardy" is on many levels a story about just this inherently ambiguous quality of imitation. This narrative concerns the final days of a medieval French monk, Prior Saint-Jean, and his novice Hyacinth. The Prior has been sent, "for the benefit of his body's health," from the monastery in which he grew up to a grange in the Picardy countryside (*Miscellaneous* 146). He is to finish there his long scholastic treatise on mathematics and to oversee, as part of his convalescence, the construction of a monastic barn.[5] But both projects are soon disrupted by the influence of a strange transient peasant, known among the villagers by the name of "a malignant one in Scripture, Apollyon," who turns out to be the exiled god Apollo (152). This "hyperborean" Apollo, who figuratively enacts the *translatio* of classical cultures into the "northern" realms of Europe, brings with him the knowledge of ancient civilization and the music of his lyre. Apollyon's physical beauty and artistic gifts dazzle the repressed Prior and lead him into a madness that allegorically anticipates the full flowering of the Renaissance. But along with his classical attributes, Apollyon also carries with him the ancient narrative of Apollo and Hyacinthus, which he reenacts with the Prior's companion, leaving the Prior himself confined and under suspicion of murder.

Apollyon's influence seems at first to be salutary, prompting a kind of revival among the residents of the town in which he resides. Having been raised wholly within the "narrow compass" of his monastery, the Prior is both intrigued and disturbed by Apollyon's presence (145). Apollyon heals the Prior's illness, and his music aids him in his tasks. Hyacinth becomes under his tutelage "really a boy at last," shedding his monastic garb to join his new companion in ancient games (155). Even the natural world seems affected by Apollyon, as his presence transforms the late November landscape into "a veritable paradise" (150). He brings to the vale animals unknown to the Prior or Hyacinth. Even the streams "babbled as they leapt," raised to a higher pitch by Apollyon's presence (159). Yet Apollyon is also the source of various suspicions. He comes to seem both a "pagan outlaw" and an emblematic "shepherd," who cured the sheep and carried them back to the fold "if they strayed afar" (158). "Monastic persons," the narrator notes, "would have seen that image many times before. . . . over the low doorway of their place of penitence at home" (158). Although he had "a just discernible tonsure," the townspeople sense about him "an air of unfathomable evil as from a distant but ineffaceable past" (152). He is rumored to have been the source of a recent plague and is "suspected of murder" (158). Prior Saint-Jean, too, worries about Apollyon's spiritual purity, fearing his connection with the "irredeemable natural world" (158), and becoming disturbed at the strong homoerotic feelings and the "inexplicable misgivings" that the stranger inspires in him (149).[6] Hyacinth also becomes fearful of "his late beloved playmate" and of the effect he has upon the Prior, but finds that Apollyon will not let them leave the vale (166).

It is important to note that Apollyon's influence on the Prior and Hyacinth is not inherently dangerous. Although he is suspected of crimes, he causes no physical harm to either of his wary students, at least until his ill-fated discus throw. Nor is his knowledge, however unfamiliar to the medieval context, threatening in and of itself. What drives the Prior into madness is an effect of imitation: the new significance that Apollyon's presence gives to seemingly familiar ideas. When, for example, the Prior and Hyacinth turn "once more to their neglected studies somewhat sadly" in the interest of completing the Prior's manuscript, they are followed by Apollyon, who dons "a much-worn monk's frock, drawn forth from a dark corner" and takes on the deceptive aspect of a student (162). As the Prior "makes an effort to recover the last thought of his long suspended work," Apollyon listens "with the manner of a mere suppliant for the crumbs of their higher studies" (162–63). Soon, however, he displays an intuitive knowledge of everything his "teacher" labors to understand, "racing forward incredibly on the road to facts, and from facts to luminous doctrine" (162–63). The "student" Apollyon becomes a teacher of sorts, for his knowledge of the Prior's own materials far outstrips that of the Prior himself.

The new "light" that Apollyon's teaching casts upon the Prior's work proves excessive, a "beam of insight" that the Prior seeks in vain to "arrest" within the limits of his own knowledge. This inability to grasp Apollyon's lessons disrupts the Prior's attempt to conclude his work, to "draw tight together the threads" (143) of his argument, and sends him into madness: "If he set hand to the page, the firm halo, here a moment since, was gone, had flitted capriciously to the wall; passed next through the window, to the wall of the garden; was dancing back in another moment upon the innermost walls of one's own miserable brain, to swell there—that astounding white light!—rising steadily in the cup, the mental receptacle, till it overflowed, and he lay faint and drowning in it. Or he rose above it, as above a great liquid surface, and hung giddily over it—light, simple and absolute—ere he fell" (164–65).

Apollyon's teaching overwhelms the unprepared monastic student, leading him to insights he can neither control nor fully understand. Tellingly, however, Apollyon's "light" here emanates not from the teacher himself but from the Prior's own "page." In his attempt to write, the Prior finds that the ideas that make up his treatise have taken on a new life apart from—and incompatible with—their initial function in the context of his argument. They "swell," and "dance," and "rise" like "liquid" within his own brain, elevating him but at the same time leading him toward a "fall." The Prior's attempt to capture this overflowing and uncontrollable light in the end produces only monsters, "winged flowers, or stars with human limbs and faces," rather than any cogent truth (165).

Apollyon's baleful influence on the Prior thus comes across not as the threat of a dangerous idea but as a threat associated with resignification. The Prior's madness is stirred by an additional meaning that Apollyon's influence elicits from the ancient textbooks and not by anything he adds to them. The light of Apollyon's teaching, that is, does not simply offer a collection of radical new ideas. Instead, it casts a radical light upon the past from which the Prior draws his authority:

> He can but wonder at this strange scholar's knowledge of a distant past, evidenced in his familiarity (it was as if he might once have spoken them) with the dead languages in which their text-books are written. There was more surely than the utmost merely natural acuteness in his guesses as to the words intended by those crabbed contractions, of their meaning, in his sense of allusion and the like. An ineffaceable memory it might rather seem of the entire world of which those languages had been the living speech, once more vividly awake under the Prior's cross-questioning, and now more than supplementing his own laborious search. (163)

These textbooks, however pagan their origin, had posed no immediate threat within the Prior's argument, and their apparently dead letters served as the basis for his strict logical system. Apollyon's influence "revives" these books, returning them to their ancient context, restoring their pagan associations, and thus altering the Prior's confident understanding of their teachings. In being reread, they come to gain a different, even opposed, significance. The "hard and abstract laws" that the Prior had originally extracted take on, under the influence of "this extraordinary pupil," a "very different guise or attitude" (163–64). No longer simply matters of reason, they become matters of sense, "to be seen rather, to be looked at and heard" (164). The lessons that the Prior had habitually learned from his ancient readings show themselves to be but one possible lesson inherent in them. The Prior is exposed under Apollyon's influence not to dangerous ideas but to a dangerous interpretation of familiar ideas, an interpretation that imitates their ancient associations rather than their medieval associations. The ideas he seemed to control, the "dead" letters upon which he confidently built his system, come to "life" when read within a different context.

Apollyon's teaching lends a similarly complicating interpretation to Prior Saint-Jean's other project: the completion of a monastic barn at the grange. Under Apollyon's influence, this Gothic structure takes on "a sort of classical harmony." Although the barn appears to the visitor to be a desecrated church, it displays the architectural trappings of a pagan temple (152). Much as Apollyon's effect on the Prior's treatise arises less from new ideas than from new interpretations of old ideas, so his effect on the monastic barn marks a change "not so much of style as of temper, of management, in the application of acknowledged rules" (153). Nearly everything about the barn is open to this kind of multiple interpretation. The narrator, for example, provides at least four glosses on a "decorative touch" on the north gable, suggesting in turn that it may be the "idle singer" Apollyon playing his harp, or an angel, or King David, or, as he offers in a footnote, a sundial "turned from the south." Similarly, some lettering below the decoration turns out to be "the relics of a familiar verse from a Latin psalm . . . inscribed as well as may be in Greek characters." Like the decoration, and like the barn itself, this lettering figures the presence of potentially conflicting interpretations arising from a single material trace. And both the decoration and the lettering are, according to the narrator, further evidence of the Prior's increasing madness in his "last days" (154).

* * *

Nearly every aspect of Pater's story points to the uneasy coexistence of interpretations that can arise from a single trace. The resignifications that the Prior confronts in his manuscript and in the monastic barn not only lead him into madness but define his madness. Take, for example, the narrator's account of the Prior's definitively "mad" vision just before his death in prison: "Gazing thither daily for many hours," the narrator states, "he would mistake mere blue distance, when that was visible, for blue flowers, for hyacinths, and wept at the sight; though blue, as he observed, was the colour of Holy Mary's gown on the illuminated page, the colour of hope, of merciful omnipresent deity" (170–71). This "mistaken" movement from the blue sky to the conventional significance of the color blue suggests the kind of proliferation of interpretive possibilities that marks the Prior's unwitting imitation of the past. The Prior "sees" the sky from his chamber, but spins a complex interpretive chain out of this initial impression. From the blue of the sky, he passes to the blue of a flower, to the specific blue flowers that replace Hyacinthus in Ovid's tale, to the blue pigment of an illumination, to the allegorical connection between the color blue and the theological notion of hope, and then from this notion to the existence of a "merciful omnipresent deity." Literal and figurative, natural and conventional, classical and medieval, pagan and Christian all coexist, albeit uneasily, in the Prior's interpretation of his vision.

This process of resignification, moreover, is not confined to the Prior's experience. It also pervades Pater's narrative. The resignification that reawakens Prior Saint-Jean's ancient textbooks and defines his madness, for example, also comes across in the narrator's peculiar literary style. M. F. Moran points to the narrator's excessive equivocations, contradictory evaluations of characters, rhetorical questions, and constant attribution of opinions to others, all of which prevent one from concluding on the meaning or even the "reality" of any aspect of the story (186–87). J. Hillis Miller, similarly, notes the narrator's seemingly ironic doubleness with regard to the story he tells, in particular his repeated references to anonymous or uniden-tifiable prior sources ("Apollyon" 33–35). Every event is subject to some degree of uncertainty, and nearly every account of Apollyon's origin and power is conspicuously based on rumor or speculation. Thus the portrait opens with a long quotation from a "writer of Teutonic proclivities" (*Miscellaneous* 142), which offers a mythographical interpretation of the story; and everything the tale reports about Apollyon comes from a series of hedging speculations offered by the "silent tonsured porter" who lives at the grange (151).

One might further note, in this regard, the effect created by one of the narrator's most characteristic gestures: his repeated use of the word *veritable*. This word has two distinct effects in the narrative. It ironically distances the narrator from the action by allowing him to avoid deciding upon the "truth" of his story. Like the other equivocations that characterize his telling, it emphasizes the uncertainty of his account. But insofar as the word *veritable* is often used to stress the aptness of a metaphor ("he was a veritable giant"), it also functions as a kind of microcosmic enactment of the Prior's madness, allowing the coexistence of a figurative and a literal reading of the image to which it is appended. To say that the Prior, for example, has been disturbed by a "veritable 'solar storm,'" has the effect of introducing a metaphor (thought as a storm) and at the same time denying it (by means of the word *veritable*).

The same process of imitative resignification that defines the Prior's literal madness as well as the narrator's stylistic madness also governs the constitution of the story itself. For just as the Prior's old textbooks take on a "very different guise" under Apollyon's influence, so "Apollo in Picardy" is almost wholly constructed out of images and ideas — presented under a changed aspect — that marked previous stages of Pater's own career.[7] One finds, for example, a virtual prospectus for the story in one of Pater's earliest essays, an anonymous review article entitled "Poems by William Morris" (1868). Writing of the impossibility of any true Hellenic revival in modern art, Pater expresses his admiration in this essay for the strange and grasping Hellenism of the Middle Ages: "But the choice life of the human spirit is always under mixed lights, and in mixed situations; when it is not too sure of itself, is still expectant, girt up to leap forward to the promise. Such a situation there was in that earliest return from the overwrought spiritualities of the middle age to the earlier, more ancient life of the senses; and for us the most attractive form of classical story is the monk's conception of it, when he escapes from the sombre legend of his cloister to that true light" (307).

Almost every element of Pater's final story may be found in this early statement, from the monk's "escape" from his cloister, to the "light" that comes to be associated with Apollyon. Similar versions of Pater's early interests may be found throughout the story. For example, Pater's fascination with the possibility of a medieval French foreshadowing of the Renaissance dates to the early 1870s, and his concern with mythography is first developed in two articles, on Dionysus, and on Demeter, written later in the same decade. Precisely the mixing of classical stories and contemporary perceptions that Pater finds in medieval mythography shapes the portrait that comes to narrate this mixing.

In addition to these concerns from the distant past, "Apollo in Picardy" also incorporates some of Pater's contemporary concerns, often in near-citations from recently published books and articles. Pater's depiction of Apollyon, for example, draws heavily on his discussion of Pythagoras from *Plato and Platonism*. In this discussion, Pater alludes to legends regarding the Greek philosopher that, "like some antique fable," describe him as "the twilight, attempered, Hyperborean Apollo," and claim that "he had been, in the secondary sense, various persons in the course of ages" (53–54). Pater alludes throughout "Apollo in Picardy" to these legends, as Monsman notes, by repeatedly associating Apollyon with music and artistic harmony and the imagery of circles (*Pater's Portraits* 187–88). Pater also alludes in the portrait to an essay entitled "The Age of Athletic Prizemen" (1894), probably written within a few months of "Apollo in Picardy." Here, Pater lingers over the "contagious pleasantness" (*Greek Studies* 281) of Myron's *Discobolus*, and raises the possibility that it may depict "some legendary quoit-player . . . Apollo with Hyacinthus, as Ovid describes him in a work of poetic *genre*" (290).

Pater's final portrait also marks the return of one of his favorite literary conceits. As readers of "Apollo in Picardy" have long noted, the story in many ways constitutes an extended allusion to Heinrich Heine's tale "The Gods in Exile" (1853). Heine imagines "the poor ancient gods" of Greece, cast out of their temples by the victorious Christians, and finding their way north to Europe. Forced underground, they live in secret, disguised in manners that bear "the greatest analogy" with events from their previous lives (401). Thus Apollo repeats his service to Admetos by working as a shepherd in Lower Austria; Dionysus, disguised as a monk, leads his displaced revelers in a hidden forest glade in Tyrol; Zeus shivers in rabbit skins in the frozen north; and Hermes guides souls to Hades on the shore of East Friesland. For Heine, this story of the gods' disgrace offers an ironic indictment of modern Philistinism. Pater, however, refigures it throughout his career as an allegory of classical influences in western culture and specifically of the classical revival of the Renaissance.[8] The conceit appears first in Pater's essay, "Leonardo da Vinci" (1869), where it suggestively explains the similarities between the painter's depictions of John the Baptist and Bacchus (*Renaissance* 93). It later serves, in the essays "Two Early French Stories" (1872) and "Pico della Mirandola" (1871) to characterize the movement of pagan sensuality and of classical myth into European culture. In addition to its use in "Apollo in Picardy," the story forms the basis for two other imaginary portraits— "Deny L'Auxerrois" (1886) and "Duke Carl of Rosenmold"

(1887) — both of which similarly figure the "return of a golden or poetically-gilded age" as a literal return of a Greek god (*Imaginary Portraits* 47). Heine's theme reappears, shortly before the publication of "Apollo in Picardy," in Pater's essay on "Raphael" (1892), where it helps to explain a painting of Apollo and Marsyas, both of whom are depicted wearing "semi-medieval habits" (*Miscellaneous* 47).

Even the figure of Apollyon himself is, on this level, an imitation. As Billie Andrew Inman notes, "There is not a detail in Pater's characterization of Apollo . . . which cannot be traced to a classical source" (*Reading* 145). Each of his actions, each of his implements, each of his apparently contradictory aspects may be found among the writings of Homer, various Greek and Roman mythographers, or later authors.[9] For example, Apollyon's service as a farm laborer alludes to his servitude to Admetos; the rumors that he "greatly needed purification" refer to his slaying of Python when founding the Delphic oracle (156); and his association with music recalls not only his legendary relationship with Pythagoras but also his slaying of the flute player Marsyas. John Smith Harrison points out that almost all of the plants, animals, and incidental objects mentioned in the portrait (such as the laurel, the swan, the moon, and even the "conical . . . stones" that Apollyon and Hyacinth use in their game) were conventionally associated with Apollo (676–85). Apollyon is, to this extent, as much a classical allusion as an "actual" classical deity. And his return alludes as much to the mythical *translatio* of ancient works into Europe during the Renaissance as it does to any movement of Apollyon in the portrait.

This uncanny return of so many of Pater's early and contemporary interests in "Apollo in Picardy" might, of course, be explained as evidence of his unwavering intellectual focus, and would thus mark a self-confident culmination of his life's work. In his reading of the story, for example, Gerald Monsman cites "Poems by William Morris" as "undeniable proof of the life-long consistency" of Pater's thought (*Pater's Portraits* 193). Similarly, Robert and Janice Keefe suggest that the story as a whole has "a valedictory quality . . . a sense of finality," and thus constitutes Pater's glance back at his intellectual career (133). Yet all of these revived interests take on a significantly darker quality in their new context. They are associated here not with renewal, as in their original versions in Pater's work, but with danger. The "outbreak of the human spirit" that Pater had earlier found in the classical revival of the Renaissance here becomes the image of Apollyon "scattering the seeds of disease" on his way north, and of the Prior's confusion and self-division (*Miscellaneous* 156); the return of the pagan gods narrated by Heine's tale is less satirical than tragic (*Renaissance* xxii). Apollyon's light is no longer, as it was in the Morris essay, simply "true," and the Prior's "leap forward" turns into an emblematic fall. This process of incorporation and reinterpretation of the past shapes Pater's text to such an extent that the story about a dangerous imitation of the past cannot be distinguished from the imitations of the (literary) past out of which it is largely constructed. Pater's text, that is, stages the Prior's madness both thematically (in the narrative itself, and in the narrator's telling) and intertextually (in Pater's use of material from his own and from the literary past). The same danger attending imitative resignification that drives the Prior insane and marks the narrator's equivocations also governs the production of the story.

*   *   *

The most resonant example of the threatening imitation that fells Prior Saint-Jean, however, arises from Pater's own imitation of the Apollo and Hyacinthus story from Ovid's *Metamorphoses*. Pater's rewriting of Ovid's story, like his incorporations of fragments from his own career and from his reading, lends to the story a more ominous significance. Much as the imitation inherent in the Prior's ancient textbooks yields grave consequences, so Pater's imitation of Ovid's ancient text leads to Hyacinth's literally "pale" imitation of Ovid's Hyacinthus. Ovid's version of the story, narrated by Orpheus, tells the tale of Apollo's abandonment of Olympus for the love of a young Spartan boy. Just as Apollyon labors as a shepherd and servant in Picardy, so the enamored Apollo does menial chores for the Spartan Hyacinthus. When Hyacinthus is killed by a discus that bounces from the ground and strikes him in the face, Apollo decides to immortalize his companion as a flower.

In the context of Pater's portrait, however, Ovid's story about Apollo's transformation of his "fallen" companion is itself transformed into a threat. The hyperborean Apollyon, in contrast to his ancient alter ego, seems unmoved by his part in Hyacinth's death. He leaves his companion untransformed and lays all responsibility at the feet of the "speechless" Prior Saint-Jean (169). Apollyon's grim reenactment of Ovid's story is prompted, as is common in Pater's imaginary portraits, by the rediscovery of an ancient artifact—in this case a discus, brought from the earth by men digging a grave. Apollyon knows intuitively how to use the "strange thing," and he and Hyacinth set themselves to restoring it (166). Soon Apollyon is teaching his companion how to play, in imitation of his fateful game with the Spartan Hyacinthus. Unmindful of an approaching storm, they continue to play until it becomes dark. The darkness that cloaks this scene figures the danger shadowing the game itself. For the "grave of unusual depth" from which the discus has been drawn was opened specifically for a victim of the "fiery plaguesome weather" brought on by Apollyon's presence (166).

The Prior's madness begins when the words of his treatise take on a life of their own, when the "light" of Apollyon's insight becomes a "firm halo" that moves from the page and into the Prior's unprepared brain. A similar caprice also marks the progress of Apollyon's game. When, for example, the discs that Apollyon and Hyacinth have discovered are sufficiently restored, they seem to take on an independent life, flying "as if they had a proper motion of their own in them" (167). The entire game of quoits, like the Prior's very treatise, seems to develop as if beyond the control of the players. Whereas in Ovid's story the discus Apollo throws bounces from the ground and accidentally strikes Hyacinthus as he runs to it, in Pater's version the discus is carried too far by a gust of wind: "Under the overcast sky it is in darkness they are playing, by guess and touch chiefly; and suddenly an icy blast of wind has lifted the roof from the old chapel, the trees are moaning in wild circular motion, and their devil's penny-piece, when Apollyon throws it for the last time, is itself but a twirling leaf in the wind, till it sinks edgewise, sawing through the boy's face, uplifted in the dark to trace it, crushing in the tender skull upon the brain" (168).

The uncontrolled and impersonal quality of Apollyon's act suggested in this passage is underscored by the persistent attribution throughout the episode of human emotions to inanimate things. The church bell, for example, "cries out harshly" (167), the trees are "moaning," and the storm moves "tearfully" through the woods (168). The story's introduction of the wind's intervention in the proceedings has precedent in other versions of the Apollo and Hyacinthus story, where the jealous Zephyrus is responsible for the boy's death. But here the name that would tie the act to a personified, rather than a wholly impersonal, force is significantly suppressed.[10] Conversely, Apollyon's grief, which ironically seems to revive "that half-extinguished deity," restoring for a time "its proper immensity, its old greatness and power," sounds to the villagers like "some natural catastrophe" rather than an expression of emotion (168).

Like Apollyon himself, the discus becomes in Pater's story a figure for the threatening effects of imitation. Just as Apollyon returns from the past in a newly threatening form, so the discus, recovered from an uncertain past, becomes a direct threat to Hyacinth. And while the discus embodies the dangers of imitation on the thematic level, it also indicates the effects of a threat that works intertextually. This threat comes across in Pater's erasure of a crucial aspect of Ovid's version of the story. Like many of his stories involving Apollo, Ovid's myth of Apollo and Hyacinthus is an allegory of artistic creation, specifically of writing.[11] Ovid is quite explicit, for example, in emphasizing the "literary" quality of Apollo's grief. Apollo memorializes his companion in two ways: by producing from his blood a blue flower, and by inscribing on this flower's petals an "imitation" of his grief as a supplement to his initial creation: "Phoebus . . . himself inscribed his grieving words [*gemitus*] upon the leaves [*foliis*], and the flower bore the marks [*inscriptum*], AI AI, letters of lamentation [*funestaque littera*] drawn thereon" (Ovid *Metamorphoses* 2.79, 10.214–16). Hyacinthus's transformation serves to memorialize Apollo's grief scripturally, to replace the absent boy with a "text." To underscore this literary aspect of Apollo's creation, Ovid twice describes the god as an *auctor*, a word that in the Latin of Ovid's time could mean both originator and writer: Apollo is the "author" of the boy's death [*ego sum tibi funeris auctor*], as well as of his miraculous metamorphosis [*is enim fuit auctor honoris*] (Ovid 2.79; 10.199, 214).

In Ovid's story the meaning of Apollo's writing is tied directly to the emotions of its author. Any faithful reading of the "text" depends on an account of its origins, of the "original" to which the "copy" must be compared. In the absence of this account, the letters and the flower itself no longer bear Apollo's signature and might come to mean anything at all. Such, indeed, is the fate of Apollo's writing in the *Metamorphoses* itself. For in his account of the debate between Ulysses and Ajax for the honor of receiving the arms of the slain Achilles, Ovid attributes another significance to the "letters" on the hyacinth's petals. The rustic Ajax, as the story goes, is unable to compete with Ulysses's greater rhetorical skill. Following his defeat, Ajax stabs himself in frustration and shame. The blood from his wound spills on the ground and, in Ovid's account, forms a flower: "The ensanguined ground produced from the green sod a purple flower which in old time had sprung from Hyacinthus' blood. The petals are inscribed with letters, serving alike for hero and for boy [littera communis mediis pueroque viroque inscripta est foliis]: this one a name [ΑΙΑΣ], and that, a cry of woe [ΑΙΑΙ]" (Ovid 2.257; 13.394–98). Thus in Ovid's work Apollo's text serves "alike" to memorialize two figures. In one case, the letters stand for the expression of grief; in the other, they are like a signature memorializing Ajax's suicide. Ovid's own intratextual reference underscores the extent to which even (indeed, especially) the most personal literary expressions may be subject to differing or additional interpretations. The flower that signifies Apollo's mourning also stands for Ajax's disgrace. Apollo's expressive utterance — letters meaningless as articulate language — can also function as a name, as a simulacrum for the missing hero. The material inscriptions upon the flower are identical, but the meaning attributed to them changes within a different context.

The fate of Apollo's inscription within the *Metamorphoses*, I would argue, epitomizes precisely the danger of excessive signification that arises throughout Pater's story. The inscriptions on the hyacinth, like those on the Prior's manuscript, carry the potential for multiple and incompatible significations. In Ovid's work, however, this potential is not explicitly threatening. Apollo, indeed, predicts the fate of his inscription: "the time will come when a most valiant hero shall be linked with this flower, and by the same markings shall he be known" [in hunc florem folioque legatur eodem] (Ovid 2.79; 10.207–8). But in the context of Pater's story, Apollo's ancient inscription, like the Prior's own ancient texts, becomes a distinct threat. And as with the threats faced by the Prior, this threat is intimated both thematically and intertextually. The manner of Hyacinth's death, that is, subtly indicates the problematic underlying Pater's incorporation of Ovid's story into his own portrait.

Hyacinth's uncovering and restoration of the discus parallels Pater's use of Ovid's story. Like the discus, Ovid's story is an ancient artifact uncovered, restored, and put back into use. This implicit analogy between the fatal discus and the fate of Ovid's text becomes explicit in a metaphor that Pater includes in his staging of Hyacinth's death. In his description of the fatal game of quoits, Pater compares the falling discus to "a twirling leaf in the wind" (168). The wind's effect on the discus, of course, contributes directly to Hyacinth's death, as it sends it beyond the arc presumably intended by Apollyon's throw. But the particular movement of the discus in the wind also traces its intertextual course. For the word *leaf* can refer both to a plant and to paper. Precisely this double sense of the image is exploited by Ovid in his repeated use of the Latin word *folium*, which can carry similar resonances to its English counterpart, when describing Apollo's mournful writing: "Phoebus . . . himself inscribed his grieving marks upon the leaves" [Phoebo . . . ipse suos gemitus foliis inscribit] (Ovid 2.79; 10.214–15). The flying discus thus becomes the very leaf upon which Apollo writes his mourning. It is at once a thematic element of the story and an allegorical intimation of the intertextual relationship that its uncovering produces. As such, Pater's "leaf" twirling in the wind describes the uncontrolled "movement" of both the thematic discus and the Ovidian intertext. Like the discus, Apollo's writing in Ovid's story is here carried beyond its apparently intended arc. And precisely in being so carried, it becomes a threat. The game of "quoits" is at the same time a game of "quotes." Just as the falling quoit "fells" Hyacinth, so the "falling" quote figures on an intertextual level the potential danger that attends any imitation.

The analogy between the discus and the Ovidian intertext also governs the unhappy results of Apollyon's fatal throw. On the day following Hyacinth's death, after Apollyon has departed from the grange, the Prior gazes from his window to find the landscape transformed: "Prior Saint-Jean arose, and looked forth — with wonder. A brief spell of sunshine amid the rain had clothed the vale with a marvel of blue flowers, if it were not rather with remnants of the blue sky itself, fallen among the woods there" (169). Although Hyacinth himself remains untransformed, blue flowers do grow. They arise, however, not from the devotion of a repentant Apollyon but seemingly apart from any intention. Unlike the single flower that Apollo cultivates from the blood of Hyacinthus and inscribes with his grief, these flowers spread uncontrolled, seeming to "fall" from the sky and covering the entire valley. From the single flower of Ovid's story come the multiple flowers of Pater's portrait, much as the single argument of the Prior's treatise takes on multiple meanings under the harsh glare of Apollyon's light, and the Prior's story becomes multiple in the hands of the equivocating narrator.

*   *   *

The falling flowers that the Prior observes before his death offer an apt figure for the problem of imitation in "Apollo in Picardy." The Prior's unwitting imitation of antiquity is but one of an entire series of imitations in the narrative. These imitations, it is worth noting, seem to confirm the prevailing critical interpretation of decadent imitation. Every act of imitation in the story leads to ruin: the Prior goes mad, and Hyacinth dies like his Ovidian namesake. These tragic imitations on the level of the plot are enacted as well on the level of narration and composition.

But before concluding that Pater's tale merely confirms the suspicions of those who treat decadence as a pale imitation of stronger works, one must attend to an often overlooked detail in Pater's portrait. For the story of Prior Saint-Jean's madness does not constitute the diegetic present of Pater's narrative, nor does the tale report events that could even be verified. Instead, this story emerges from the narrator's interpretation of the Prior's mad scribblings. These scribblings are fortuitously preserved in a recovered historical document, "a certain manuscript volume taken from an old monastic library in France at the Revolution" (143). The manuscript, a product of the Prior's final days, tells its story by means of the literal traces of Apollyon's presence that seem to mark its pages. The narrator interprets these traces as a pictorial gloss on the Prior's breakdown, an image of his divided mental "kingdom" (143): "And whereas in earlier volumes you found by way of illustration no more than the simplest indispensable diagrams, the scribe's hand had strayed here into mazy borders, long spaces of hieroglyphic, and as it were veritable pictures of the theoretic elements of his subject. Soft wintry auroras seemed to play behind whole pages of crabbed textual writing, line and figure bending, breathing, flaming, into lovely "arrangements" that were like music made visible" (144–45).

The Prior's division comes across in the "invasion" of his logical discourse by the overwhelming "light" of Apollyon's presence, the "veritable 'solar storm'" of images that disrupts the rational order of his "long and intricate argument" (144). This second discourse seems to infect the Prior's reason, breaking out between the lines of his "crabbed textual writing" and in the margins of his treatise. Apollyon's influence subjects the Prior's text to competing discourses that occupy the very same "page." Despite their conflict, these discourses, in fact, refer to the same subject. The pictures illustrate the "theoretic elements" of the Prior's argument. They constitute a kind of figurative supplement to the logical argument, picture against word, an alternative scenario produced from the same material trace.

To this extent, Pater's framing device in and of itself repeats the logic of the Prior's madness. The act of reading the manuscript imitates Apollyon's invasion of medieval Picardy. Or so it would seem. Indeed, the frame foregrounds the narrator's interpretive intervention and thus emphasizes the ideological effect of his account. If, in other words, the story presented by the narrator explicitly concerns the multiple interpretive effects of a single material trace, then the material traces that underlie this story should themselves be open to other interpretations as well. The narrator's own imitation (the narrative itself) closes off the process of resignification by telling a single story in which imitation leads to madness and death. The effect of this closure, I would argue, comes across in the threatening quality of imitation itself. Rather than treating imitation as potentially a matter of choice and innovation — a characterization that the composition of the story explicitly leaves open — the narrator characterizes it as a matter of fate. It becomes something involuntary and uncanny, the cause of both the Prior's insanity and Hyacinth's demise. The course of history becomes a series of inevitable repetitions that mere mortals (indeed even immortals) can neither control nor alter.

Yet Pater's remark in the introduction to the portrait that the Prior's manuscript was discovered during the French Revolution offers another perspective on the narrator's story. For the Revolution explicitly cast itself as a voluntary imitation of ancient political ideals, a classical revival akin to the revival inspired by Apollyon's presence in Picardy. It thus poses a subtle counterexample to the interpretation of history elaborated by the narrator. In his "Theses on the Philosophy of History" (1940), Walter Benjamin notes the way in which the revolutionaries transformed an image that has traditionally epitomized imperial power into a model for political subversion:

History is the subject of a structure whose site is not homogeneous, empty time but time filled with now-time. Thus to Robespierre, ancient Rome was a past charged with now-time which he blasts out of the continuum of history. The French Revolution understood itself as a Rome returned. It cited [*zitierte*] ancient Rome exactly the way fashion cites attire of the past. This jump, however, takes place in an arena where the ruling class gives the commands. The same leap in the open air of history is the dialectical one, which is how Marx understood the revolution. (261; trans. modified)

As Benjamin points out, the revolution looked to the past not as a bastion of authority (the normal aim of a citation), or as a teleological series of inevitable events, but as an alternative to contemporary power structures. The past here provides a model for the present, and so gains a potential significance — a resignificance — wholly apart from the mechanistic cause and effect relationships of historical change across "empty time." This "tiger's leap into the past," for Benjamin, made history in the French Revolution a radical force, a potential threat to the ruling class, and not a reliable source of its authority (261).[12] Benjamin's point here is that the significance of the past is never fixed, that it is always open to reinterpretation in the light of subsequent events. "In every era," Benjamin writes, "the attempt must be made anew to wrest tradition from the conformism which is about to overpower it" (255). To characterize history as a grand and fateful — or a fearful and unwitting — march toward the present constitutes but one interpretation among others; but it is the interpretation most comforting to the conformism that Benjamin wants to challenge.

Decadent writing, I would argue, adumbrates a similar lesson to Benjamin's. "The phrase 'literature of the decadence,'" writes Charles Baudelaire in his essay "Further Notes on Edgar Allan Poe" (1857), "implies a scale of literatures, one infantile, one childish, one adolescent, etc. etc. The term, I mean, presupposes something fatal and foreordained, like an ineluctable decree" (93). The critics who condemn decadence as a pale imitation of the past, Baudelaire's complaint suggests, treat literary history in much the same manner as Pater's narrator treats the history of Prior Saint-Jean's manuscript. They interpret decadent imitation as a sign of some "fatal and foreordained" decline: cultural, artistic, or even physiological. "Apollo in Picardy," like almost all decadent texts, seems initially to confirm this critical judgment. Its account of the Prior's doomed imitations echoes the critics' association of imitation with sterility and exhaustion. Pater's reference to the French Revolution, however, implicitly undermines the narrator's account, suggesting that his interpretation of imitation is only one among many others that the story allows. Much as Baudelaire questions the fatalistic metaphors that blind contemporary literary judgment to the value of new writers, so Pater questions the fatalistic historiography that would find only madness and death where it might also find anticipations of a revival.

Notes

1. Tellingly, the critics who condemn decadence for its imitations necessarily overlook the importance of imitation to nearly all Roman and early-modern literature. In many ways, it might be said that decadence returns not simply to past literatures but also to an earlier model of literary *imitatio*. On imitation as a literary doctrine in the Renaissance, see Thomas Greene.

2. For further accounts of Pater's models of and metaphors for historical development, see J. Hillis Miller ("Walter Pater"), William F. Shuter, and Carolyn Williams. On the problem of origins and originality in Pater, see Jay Fellows (esp. 23–39).

3. On this paradox of imitation, see Derrida's discussion of Plato and Mallarmé in "The Double Session."

4. For a discussion of parody and its relationship to the idea of decadence, see Michele Hannoosh.

5. On convalescence as a topos in decadent writing, see Barbara Spackman.

6. On the homoerotic resonances of Apollyon's influence, see the recent readings of Richard Dellamora (186–92) and Linda Dowling (138–40).

7. Pater's penchant for freely reworking texts–both his own and those of other writers — is the premise for Christopher Ricks's well-known condemnation of his

critical method. According to Ricks, Pater's common misquotations "rewrite" the authors in question "so that they say special Paterian things," and in a broader sense reflect his general conflation of criticism with creation (408).

8. The persistence of the gods-in-exile theme in Pater's work is nicely documented by Harrison. Harrison further notes the significance of Pater's interest in such mythological figures as Dionysus and Demeter, both of whom spend part of the year in exile. For an account of Pater's tendency to reuse his own imagery and arguments, see Shuter (109–24).

9. On Pater's sources, see Inman (132–48).

10. Pater was well aware of this variant. In his description of the Spartan *Hyacinthia* in *Plato and Platonism*, he notes that "Boreas (the north-wind) had maliciously miscarried the discus" (229).

11. The pivotal example of such an allegory is the story of Daphne. The Pygmalion story, which follows shortly after the story of Apollo and Hyacinthus in the *Metamorphoses* and is likewise told by Orpheus, is another famous artistic allegory.

12. For an account of some major British literary responses to the French Revolution, see Friedman. On the importance if ancient Rome to the French Revolution see Parker and Outram (chapter 5 and 6).

Works Cited

Barnes, Djuna. *Nightwood*. New York: New Directions, 1961.

Baudelaire, Charles. "Further Notes on Edgar Allan Poe." In *"The Painter of Modern Life" and Other Essays*, ed. and trans. Jonathan Mayne. New York: Da Capo, 1964.

Benjamin, Walter. "Theses on the Philosophy of History." *Illuminations*. Ed. Hannah Arendt. Trans. Harry Zohn. New York: Schocken, 1969.

Dellamora, Richard. *Masculine Desire: The Sexual Politics of Victorian Aestheticism*. Chapel Hill: University of North Carolina Press, 1990.

Derrida, Jacques. "The Double Session." *Dissemination*. Trans. Barbara Johnson. Chicago: University of Chicago Press, 1981.

Dowling, Linda. *Hellenism and Homosexuality in Victorian Oxford*. Ithaca: Cornell University Press, 1994.

Fellows, Jay. *Tombs, Despoiled and Haunted*. Stanford: Stanford University Press, 1991.

Friedman, Barton R. *Fabricating History: English Writers and the French Revolution*. Princeton: Princeton University Press, 1988.

Gourmont, Remy de. "Stéphane Mallarmé et l'idée de décadence." *La culture des idées*. Paris: Mercure de France, 1926.

Greene, Thomas M. *The Light in Troy: Imitation and Discovery in Renaissance Poetry*. New Haven: Yale University Press, 1982.

Hannoosh, Michele. *Parody and Decadence: Laforgue's Moralités légendaires*. Columbus: Ohio State University Press, 1989.

Harrison, John Smith. "Pater, Heine, and the Old Gods of Greece." *PMLA* 39 (1924): 655–86.

Heine, Heinrich. "Die Götter im Exil." *Sämtliche Schriften*. Vol. 6, Pt. 1. Munich: Hanser, 1975.

Inman, Billie Andrew. *Walter Pater and His Reading, 1874–1877: With a Bibliography of His Library Borrowings, 1878–1894*. New York: Garland, 1990.

Keefe, Robert, and Janice A. Keefe. *Walter Pater and the Gods of Disorder*. Athens: Ohio University Press, 1988.

Miller, J. Hillis. "Walter Pater: A Partial Portrait." *Daedalus* 105 (1976): 97–113.

——. "Example: Apollyon in Cranford." Unpublished essay, 1992.

Monsman, Gerald Cornelius. *Pater's Portraits: Mythic Pattern in the Fiction of Walter Pater*. Baltimore: Johns Hopkins University Press, 1967.

Moran, M. F. "Pater's Mythic Fiction: Gods in a Gilded Age." In *Pater in the 1990s*, ed. Laurel Brake and Ian Small. Greensboro, N.C.: ELT, 1991.

Nisard, Désiré. *Etudes de critique et de moeurs sur les poèts latins de la Décadence*. 2d ed. Paris: Hachette, 1849.

Nordau, Max. *Degeneration*. Lincoln: University of Nebraska Press, 1993.

Outram, Dorinda. *The Body and the French Revolution*. New Haven: Yale University Press, 1989.

Ovid. *Metamorphoses*. 2 vols. Trans. Frank Justus Miller. Rev. G. P. Goold. Cambridge: Harvard University Press, 1984.

Parker, Harold T. *The Cult of Antiquity and the French Revolution*. Chicago: University of Chicago Press, 1937.

Pater, Walter. *Greek Studies: A Series of Essays*. London: Macmillan, 1910.

———. *Imaginary Portraits*. London: Macmillan, 1910.

———. *Marius the Epicurean: His Sensations and Ideas*. 2 vols. London: Macmillan, 1910.

———. *Miscellaneous Studies*. London: Macmillan, 1910.

———. *Plato and Platonism: A Series of Lectures*. London: Macmillan, 1910.

———. "Poems by William Morris." *Westminster Review* 90 (Oct. 1868): 300–11.

———. *The Renaissance: Studies in Art and Poetry*. Ed. Donald Hill. Berkeley: University of California Press, 1980.

Pierrot, Jean. *The Decadent Imagination, 1880–1900*. Trans. Derek Coltman. Chicago: University of Chicago Press, 1981.

Ricks, Christopher. *The Force of Poetry*. Oxford: Clarendon, 1984.

Shuter, William F. *Rereading Walter Pater*. Cambridge: Cambridge University Press, 1997.

Smith, James M. "Concepts of Decadence in Nineteenth-Century French Literature." *Studies in Philology* 50 (1953): 640–51.

Spackman, Barbara. *Decadent Genealogies: The Rhetoric of Sickness from Baudelaire to D'Annunzio*. Ithaca: Cornell University Press, 1989.

Van Roosbroeck, G. L. *The Legend of the Decadents*. New York: Institut des Etudes Françaises, 1927.

Wallen, Jeffrey. "On Pater's Use and Abuse of Quotation." *Arnoldian* 14 (1986–87): 1–20.

Williams, Carolyn. *Transfigured World: Walter Pater's Aesthetic Historicism*. Ithaca: Cornell University Press, 1989.

Chapter 13
"Golden Mediocrity"
Pater's Marcus Aurelius and the
Making of Decadence

Sharon Bassett

There is some accidental irony in including in a study of decadence a text—
Marius the Epicurean: His Sensations and Ideas—that was proclaimed by its
author as an antidote to the implied decadence of Pater's earlier *Studies in
the History of the Renaissance*. The apparent irony is deepened when the
modern student of decadence observes Pater's specifically targeted audience within Oxford attack as a moral and aesthetic threat his carefully
crafted tribute to the rebirth of classical culture in Europe. There were
appreciative and discerning reviews of *Studies in the History of the Renaissance*.[1]
But the misgivings expressed (both publicly and privately) by the Oxford
world would have been troubling to Pater.

An anonymous writer in the *London Quarterly Review* describes the volume
as "pure selfishness." Mrs. Oliphant (in a *Blackwood's Monthly* review), after
describing Pater's work as "rococo," is relieved to conclude, "We are not
afraid that this elegant materialism will strike many minds as an admirable
view of life." Presumably Pater was unaware that George Eliot had written to
the editor of *Blackwood's* in support of Mrs. Oliphant's position. Eliot writes:
"I agree very warmly with the remarks made by your contributor this month
on Mr. Pater's book, which seems to me quite poisonous in its false principles of criticism and false conceptions of life" (qtd. in Hill 446). Pater's close
friend, Jonathan Wordsworth, grandson of the poet, wrote privately to Pater
deploring what he had read, especially the conclusion. He understood Pater
to have been saying that "no fixed principles either of religion or morality
can be regarded as certain, that the only thing worth living for is momentary
enjoyment and that probably or certainly the soul dissolves at death into
elements which are destined never to reunite" (qtd. in Evans 13).

Mrs. Humphry Ward, Pater's Oxford neighbor, knew him well when *Studies in the History of the Renaissance* was published. In her 1918 memoir she

remembered "very clearly the effect of that book, and of the strange and poignant sense of beauty expressed in it; of its entire aloofness also from the Christian tradition of Oxford, its glorification of the higher and intenser forms of esthetic pleasure, of 'passion' in the intellectual sense — as against the Christian doctrine of self-denial and renunciation. It was a doctrine that both stirred and scandalized Oxford . . . There was a cry of Neo-paganism, and various attempts at persecution" (qtd. in Hill 446–47). Mrs. Ward's memory is confirmed by the sermon preached by Pater's former tutor, W. W. Capes, in Oxford in November 1873. His sermon is addressed to clergy, and after mentioning Pater by name, Capes takes aim at "any philosophy of life that shrinks into a system of mere personal culture, and narrows all our enthusiasm for progress to an effort at individual perfection" (qtd. in Hill 447). Selfish, rococo, poisonous, advocating momentary enjoyment over the immortality of the soul, a theology of neopaganism, and cautionary threats of persecution: this inventory of transgressions sets out the conceptual and rhetorical boundaries that largely define the environment in which the phenomenon of Victorian decadence was produced.

Why would Pater think that a historical study of the rebirth of the classical spirit in Europe would be construed by contemporary readers as "decadent," while a fictional account by a naive witness (i.e., Marius) of the process of the collapse of the classical world could be offered to the same audience as a corrective? *Marius the Epicurean* was written after a period of intense inner struggle and intellectual repositioning and it was offered by Pater to his readers as a very specific kind of amendment. In his note to the restored text of the much condemned conclusion to *The Renaissance: Studies in Art and Poetry*, Pater explained that he was republishing the material at this time (despite, by implication, all the criticism) because he was able to direct his readers to the text of his novel, *Marius the Epicurean*. The reading of *Marius* is prescribed as an antidote for the possibly poisonous or neopagan misreadings: "This brief 'Conclusion' was omitted in the second edition of this book, as I conceived it might possibly mislead some of those young men into whose hands it might fall. On the whole, I have thought it best to reprint it here, with some slight changes which bring it closer to my original meaning. I have dealt more fully in *Marius the Epicurean* with the thoughts suggested by it" (qtd. in Hill 186).

Marcus Aurelius: Proximity and Mediocrity

This highly qualified defiant demurer (note the phrase "might possibly mislead some of those young men into whose hands it might fall") indicates much more the kind of uncertainty and misapprehension that Pater expected to find among his readers than it indicates any doubt or uncertainty in Pater about the significance or value of what he had written. Among the small number of "young men" who "might" read the text, there would be an even smaller number who "might" be misled by their reading. It is to this elite within an elite that Pater directs the force of *Marius*: young men who might be misled, young men who might misread. But this corrective does not correct. Indeed, we find that in *Marius the Epicurean* Pater compounds rather than simplifies the reading/misreading, leading/misleading potential for its susceptible young male readers. In this old world of Roman hegemony coming to its lumbering end, the most charismatic and alluring character is Marcus Aurelius, the philosopher king/emperor. It is toward this imperial figure that Marius's early pilgrimage takes him, and it is away from this dubious *pater familias* that Marius's journey toward his own death takes its trajectory.

Remembering that, while the criticism of *Studies in the History of the Renaissance* came from Pater's *old* readers, the corrective in the form of the novel is addressed to young readers. *Marius the Epicurean* is concerned with the making of decadence in the specific sense that it teaches Pater's young readers how to "read" their (philosophical and aesthetic) fathers. It teaches (or could teach) them how to interpret the near canonization of Marcus Aurelius in the Victorian pantheon, and it could further teach the young readers to question the process of canonization itself. Marcus Aurelius is central in Pater's project of rereading not only for his presence at the point of transition from Latin pagan to vulgar Christian culture but also for the role he plays in the Victorian consciousness, particularly the role he plays in Arnold's staging of classical culture. As Frank M. Turner explains in "Why the Greeks and Not the Romans in Victorian Britain?" the philosophy of Plato and Aristotle became the pedagogical vehicle for inculcating in the British ruling class the image of the "ideal state" governed by a union of freedom and order. However, as Turner goes on to explain, "no Roman philosopher could serve that same function. All were too close to the life and events of early Christianity to serve as prescriptive models. It was, after all, the paganism of the Roman world that Christianity had displaced and eventually conquered. This was why the very discontinuity between Greek and Victorian culture was so important. Only one Roman writer could even possibly seem useful: Marcus Aurelius" (79). In singling out Marcus Aurelius, Turner makes the following observation about Arnold's use of the philosophic emperor: "The great charm of Marcus Aurelius was not that he was a Roman but rather that he might have been a Christian." It is clear that in characterizing Marcus Aurelius in this way, Turner is thinking of Arnold's version rather than of the version that the reader of *Marius the Epicurean* would have encountered. In Arnold's 1863 essay "Marcus Aurelius," not only might he have been a Christian, but he might also have been a Victorian. Arnold emphasizes the ways in which he is an imitable philosopher king:

Marcus Aurelius has, for us moderns, this great superiority over Saint Louis or Alfred [both Christian], that he lived and acted in a state of society modern by its essential characteristics, in an epoch akin to our own, in a brilliant centre of civilisation. Trajan talks of our "enlightened age" just as glibly as the *Times* talks of it. Marcus Aurelius thus becomes for us a man like ourselves, a man in all things tempted as we are. Saint Louis inhabits an atmosphere of mediaeval Catholicism, which the man of the nineteenth century may admire, indeed may even passionately wish to inhabit, but which, strive as he will, he cannot really inhabit. Alfred belongs to a state of society (I say it with all deference to the *Saturday Review* critic who keeps such jealous watch over the honour of our Saxon ancestors) half barbarous. Neither Alfred nor Saint Louis can be morally and intellectually as near to us as Marcus Aurelius. (140–41)

Pater's Marcus Aurelius is not the proto-Christian *manqué* he appears to be in Arnold's essay. He is close enough to this prototype to make his appearance in *Marius* into a distinct and nuanced critique of the values this prototype stands for. One sees only a trace of antagonism as Pater recasts the philosophic emperor. In particular Pater makes use of all the ways in which Marcus Aurelius could be understood to be "a man like ourselves, a man in all things tempted as we are" by writing a narrative in which the identities thought to be "modern" by Pater's contemporary culture (the particular voices that could be heard calling *Studies in the History of the Renaissance* decadent) were the very identities that in another historical context were themselves (and by Arnold's own values) associated with both poisonous beliefs and, quite literally, a neopagan theology. These are, of course, the same terms flung at the conclusion to *The Renaissance* by its critics and go to make up the "decadent" ethos that Pater had been accused (inaccurately, as we see from reading the novel) of having engendered.

The Marcus Aurelius who forms a central and magnetic pole in the narrative of *Marius the Epicurean* displays all the idealized Victorian features that Arnold holds up for emulation. But he is found, wanting by Pater and within the perspective of his novel, wanting not simply because he causes (by allowing) the persecution and deaths of large numbers of the early Christians, but because his words and actions reveal a *mediocrity* of thought. And it is mediocrity, golden though it be, that undermines critics who had denounced *Studies in the History of the Renaissance* while at the same time providing the "young men" reading any of Pater's work with a means of equipping them with the rhetorical means of answering their adversaries.

Arnold's Marcus Aurelius is very much like Arnold himself. He is a figure caught between two worlds, one dead and the other powerless to be born, like his own disavowed ancient doppleganger Empedocles, condemned to cast his philosophical stoical pearls to the swine. We can imagine Arnold's Marcus Aurelius taking on the role of Moses, whose devotion to the often unworthy Israelites is repaid with disobedience, lasciviousness, idolatry, and (possibly) decadence and who will not be allowed to triumphantly enter the promised land. Arnold's Marcus Aurelius makes himself available to the nineteenth-century reader by way of his almost wholly decontextualized words. Arnold's essay gives us a figure who is primarily a generator of "touchstones" (the textual equivalences of "the best that has been thought and said"). Arnold quotes Marcus Aurelius's words since, as he claims, "the record of him on which his fame chiefly rests is the record of this inward life, — his *Journal,* or *Commentaries,* or *Meditations,* or *Thoughts,* for by all these names has the work been called" (141).

Pater's Marcus Aurelius is not so much a refutation of Arnold's portrayal — Pater never engages in strenuous debate — as it is a contextualization, even a historicization of the philosophical emperor. He appears in Pater's narrative in the context of a rather intense self-examination on the part of Marius in which he scrutinizes his own "Epicurean style," a style that is a problem not only because it is style (i.e., concerned only with superficial formalities), but also because it is a style that is associated in the Victorian mind with a (non-Greek-speaking) form of hedonism comparable to decadence. Pater is diligent in making sure that the readers of his novel are aware that Marius himself is conscious of being someone quite open to the charge of hedonism. He is, in fact, criticized and defended for being someone for whom "pleasure — pleasure, as they so poorly conceived it — [was] the sole motive of life; and they precluded any exacter estimate of the situation by covering it with a high-sounding general term, through the vagueness of which they were enabled to see the severe and laborious youth in the vulgar company of Lais" (1:50). Pleasure and the subsequent reference to words like *hedonism* evoke the ethos of decadence that Pater attempts to disconnect from the rhetoric of denunciation and to reinsert into a broader philosophical realm of discourse. As an Epicurean or New Cyrenaicist, Pater places Marius in the midst of a philosophical practice (hedonism) for which Pater himself had been pilloried. Marius is a technical example of Victorian "decadence." However, as Marius draws near to and experiences what seems to be an altruistic martyrdom, his much vilified hedonism seems to call forth actions of the sort that Pater's critics believed themselves to be advocating. The very word *hedonism* is, for Pater, a term "of large and vague comprehension — above all when used for a purpose avowedly controversial, [one of several terms which] have ever been the worst examples of what are called 'question-begging terms' " (I, 151).[2] So where Pater's critics and the susceptible readers whom he is addressing would see a simple opposition between a healthy stoicism represented (but at the same time undercut) by Marcus Aurelius and a decadent epicureanism/hedonism represented (but at the same time undercut) by Marius himself, Pater's rhetorical focus is designed to confound and question this reductive polarity. If we project this configuration of ideas and agents forward onto Pater's contemporary context, we have yet another perspective from which to interpret the text, one where Pater's readers can see the dark side of philosophical (Victorian as well as Roman) stoicism.

The fictional strategy by which the young Marius and the austere emperor are brought together is remarkably slight. The transition, like many of Pater's narrative moves, is prompted more by the needs of his argument than by the exigencies of character. The move from the rural countryside to the Roman court takes place within a paragraph, almost as an accident of the slight plot: "The emperor Marcus Aurelius, to whose service Marius had now been called, was himself more or less openly a 'lecturer' . . . and it was with no vulgar egotism that Marius, at the age of nineteen, determined, like many another young man of parts, to enter as a student of rhetoric in Rome" (1:159). The character of Marcus Aurelius and Marius's vocation as a rhetorician having been established, the motive and agency that make his move to Rome possible is gradually unfolded in the next chapter: "That summons to the emperor's circle in Rome had come from one of the former friends of his father in the capital, who had kept himself acquainted with the lad's progress, and assured of his parts, his courtly way, above all of his beautiful penmanship, now offered him a place, virtually that of an *amanuensis*, near the person of the philosophic emperor" (1:158). As apprentice rhetorician and *amanuensis*, Marius is completely identified with the (presumably) "superficial" aspects of language: the rhetorician skilled in shaping and delivering oral arguments and the amanuensis whose artful hand makes written communication effective and appealing. Once again we observe Marius practicing the sorts of "superficial" skills that are associated with decadence, a reduction of matters of "essence" to matters of "style." But Pater would want his reader to see Marius as (to use John Henry Newman's language) "a master of the two fold Logos" in which the personality of the individual is the decisive expressive medium that binds the complementary "folds" of the logos into a single signification.[3]

It is precisely the lack of this "binding" of the logos that is missing in the character of Marcus Aurelius. One of Marius's first sightings of the emperor occurs when Marcus is summoned to make birthday offerings to his household gods: "A heavy curtain of tapestry was drawn back; and beyond it Marius gazed for a few moments into the *Lararium* or imperial chapel" (1:228). Here is Marcus Aurelius at his most "Christian," devotedly honoring his past teachers: "On richly carved *consoles*, or side boards, around this narrow chamber, were arranged the rich apparatus of worship and the golden or gilded images, adorned to-day with fresh flowers, among them the image of Fortune from the apartment of Antonius Pius, and such of the emperor's own teachers as were gone to their rest" (1:229). As he ascended into the chapel the emperor paused, "and with a grave but friendly look at his young visitor, delivered a parting sentence, audible to him alone: *Imitation is the most acceptable part of worship: the gods had much rather mankind should resemble than flatter them: — Make sure that those to whom you come nearest be the happier by your presence!*" (1:229; Pater's emphasis).

Marius meets Marcus Aurelius at a moment of intense piety on the part of the emperor. His piety is addressed to the teachers of his past. The emperor is about to take (or seems about to take) the part of Marius's teacher. The first lesson Marcus Aurelius teaches his new pupil is the lesson of *imitation*, that is to say, Marcus urges Marius to imitate *him*. Hearing this, Marius exclaims, "How temperate! how tranquillising! what humanity!" Marius has found the innermost sanctuary of Roman imperial power and culture presided over by virtually the only figure from Latin culture (apart perhaps for Virgil) with whom Pater's Oxford readers could allow themselves to be identified. And in this very sacred place in the presence of one of the few philosopher-kings, Marius expresses (or does Pater express? or should we imitate Marius expressing?) some striking doubts: "Yet, as he left the eminent company concerning whose ways of life at home he had been so youthfully curious, and sought, after his manner, to determine the main trait in all this, *he had to confess that it was a sentiment of mediocrity, though of a mediocrity, for once really golden*" (1:229; emphasis added).

Readers of *Marius the Epicurean* are already acquainted with the trait or quality or color that the adjective *golden* evokes. An earlier chapter is, after all, called "The Golden Book," and it narrates a rapturous joint reading of Apuleius's *Golden Ass* by Marius and his (now dead) pagan friend Flavian. Flavian was, like Marcus Aurelius, the paradigmatic embodiment of what it is possible to achieve in pagan self-development. In Flavian's case the development had been an aesthetic one (he was working on his poetic style and developed an ornate form of euphuistic writing from Apuleius), while Pater emphasizes a philosophical/ethical development for Marcus Aurelius. But both Apuleius and Marcus Aurelius are Marius's teachers, and both initiate their pedagogy under a gilded or golden patina. The "golden book" of the *Golden Ass* is read—or consumed—in an old granary that is bathed in and constituted by golden light:

How like a picture! and it was precisely the scene described in what they were reading, with just that added poetic touch in the book which made it delightful and select, and, in the actual place, the ray of sunlight transforming the rough grain among the cool brown shadows into heaps of gold. What they were intent on was, indeed, the book of books, the golden book of that day, a gift to Flavian, as was shown by the purple writing on the handsome yellow wrapper, following the title *Flaviane!* (1:55)

The splendid contents of the book are equal to its imposing wrapping:

And the inside was something not less dainty and fine, full of the archaisms and curious felicities in which that generation delighted, quaint terms and images picked fresh from the early dramatists, the lifelike phrases of some lost poet preserved by an old grammarian, racy morsels of the vernacular and studied prettinesses:—all alike, mere playthings for the genuine power and natural eloquence of the erudite artist, unsuppressed by his erudition which, however, made some people angry, chiefly less well "got-up" people, and especially those who were untidy from indolence. (1:56)

It is very often difficult to determine, at any given moment, whether the lavish details belong to the text as fetishized commodity or text as bearer of signification (or what one naively thinks of as reading for the "meaning"): "What words he had found for conveying, with a single touch, the sense of textures, colours, incidents! 'Like jewelers' work! Like a myrrhine vase!' — admirers said of his writing. 'The golden fibre in the hair, the gold thread-work in the gown mark her as the mistress' — *aurum in comis et in tunicis, ibi inflexum hic intextum, matronam profecto confitebatur*— he writes of one of his heroines" (1:57). What one can see clearly is the extent to which the material object (what is associated with the superficial, utilitarian, and accidental aspects of the text) and the signification or meaning of the text (its essential readerly aspect) are synesthetically linked. The linkage of style and content established in this early stage of Marius's moral journey is revisited, as we have seen, when Marius graduates from the tutelage of Flavian to that of Aurelius. In the court setting, Marius is the specialist in rhetoric and penmanship (epicurean, i.e., hedonistic), while the emperor specializes in the (stoic) essentials of philosophy. Pater subtly but continually calls into question the classical valorizing of the ideal over the representation, of content over style, of stoic self-sacrifice over epicurean self-indulgence. This questioning is implied in Pater's decision to offer a historical fiction (*Marius the Epicurean*) to "amend" a fictional history (*Studies in the History of the Renaissance*).

But the connection between the "The Golden Book" and "The 'Mistress and Mother' of Palaces" (the name of the chapter wherein Marius first meets Aurelius) is underscored by the faintly discernible (and faintly disapproved of) presence of the emperor himself in this "golden" moment: "*Aurum intestum*: gold fibre: — gold fibre: well! there was something of that kind in his [Apuleius's] own work. And then, in an age when people, from the emperor Aurelius downwards, prided themselves unwisely on writing in Greek. [Apuleius] had written for Latin people in their own tongue; though still, in truth with all the care of a learned language" (1:57). Marcus Aurelius is associated with the unwise, prideful, and, in Pater's terms, affected use of the Greek language, indicating another dimension of the emperor's character that is not itself to be an object of imitation. Pater is also making the point that Greek (which, as we have seen from Turner's work, the Victorians valorized over Latin) is not the only language in which it is possible to be "learned." Moreover, Apuleius is "learned" in a text that not only is composed in Latin but also mingles under its narrative umbrella a variety of fictional genres, and operates on a number of levels of seriousness from the asinine (the frame story is about someone who is accidentally turned into an ass) to the sublime (the account of Cupid and Psyche — a metamorphosis, from mortal to divine, of an entirely different nature).

The world of decadence is frequently associated with a particularly intense kind of reading. Decadence, in fact, can be seen as the epitome of logocentrism, as a bravura display, in the last quarter of the nineteenth century, of classical learning whose brilliance and daring was such that it dared to live its bookish education. What had been the escapist fictional phantasms of young manhood, to be put aside for the sake of patriarchal sobriety, are instead, under the aegis of decadence, reconstituted as viable and possible ways of life.

The readerly ethos that Pater creates — with its scrolls, paintings, books, inscriptions, languages, translations among languages, and the fervent emotional environment in which the textual scenery is consumed — seems to demand further analysis. Linda Dowling claims that there is something specifically English about the centrality of language (and reading) in the work of decadence and that Pater had a particularly striking part to play in the phenomenon: "[The] displacement of cultural ideas and cultural anxiety onto language explains why we . . . glimpse in the background of Victorian Decadence no lurid tales of sin and sensation and forbidden experience but a range of stylistic effects, of quiet disruptions and insistent subversions in the prose of Walter Pater. . . . Pater's writing . . . is best understood as an attempt to rescue from the assaults of scientific philology and linguistic relativism an ideal, however diminished and fugitive, of literature and literary culture" (104).

Although neither Newman nor Arnold could be thought of as participating in what Dowling calls "Victorian Decadence," it is nevertheless the case that both of them, like Pater, undertook strenuous and extensive defenses of "literature and literary culture." The telling difference is that, while Newman and Arnold defended literary culture against science, Pater had an openness to science and the philosophical implications of a scientific view of language that made it unnecessary for him to construe science as the featureless antithesis of sweetness and light.[4] In fact, Pater's style, as well as his manner of conceptualizing historical process within an unbounded time frame, owes a great deal to his receptivity of Charles Darwin's ingenious merging of the "struggle for existence" with the fundamental "interdependence" of all living forms.[5]

Pater's ecological equity, his efforts to construe "struggle" as "interdependence" (rather than a resigned acceptance of aggression as a trait built into nature) lead us back to the golden granary with Marius and Flavian reading their "golden book" — golden in the sense of mature, rich, and immensely valuable, and (because of its archaic, learned style, its miscellany of genres, and, less important, its "yellow" cover) linked to the "fatal book" of decadent lore.[6] But the "golden" (and perhaps fatal) book of the early stage of Marius's paidaeia is both augmented and modified by the "golden" (and certainly fatal) mediocrity of Marcus Aurelius.

If there is nothing mediocre in the sublime reading experience of the golden granary that Marius and Flavian enjoy together, there is everything mediocre (in the several senses of the word with which we will be concerned) in Marius's encounter with, and extensive experience of, the household of Marcus Aurelius. If Marius's textual experience with Apuleius's *Golden Ass* confirms him in his commitment to Latin literary culture as the medium of his own personal development, his life at court brings home to him, and to the reader, specific systemic inadequacies that mark that very highly esteemed civilization. The mediocrity that Marius encounters (like the qualifying adjective *golden*) cuts two ways. The first, obvious way to understand it is to note that mediocrity usually means common, ordinary, barely adequate. The second significance that the reader of Pater's novel grasps — and this is one of the "quiet disruptions" that for Dowling characterizes Pater's participation in the formation of literary decadence — is that *mediocrity* is, according to the *OED*, a "quasi-technical term" for the "mean" part of Aristotle's "golden mean." Moreover, the phrase "golden mediocrity" comes immediately after Aurelius's sotto voce advice to Marius that he should become adept in "imitation," another term with elaborate Aristotelian associations.

It is not until the next chapter, with the provocatively suggestive and — as we shall see — deeply ambivalent title of "Manly Amusement" that the implications of Pater's semiotic "disruptions" become clear. "Manly" and "amusement" both come in for their share of semiotic dismantling, but this turns out to rest on the patterning already in place as a result of the analysis of "golden mediocrity." And just as the golden mediocrity of Marcus Aurelius was anticipated in the rapturous reading that Marius shares with Flavian of the "golden book" when the narrator reminds us of the emperor's affected habit of composing in Greek, so here, when Pater is about to open up the brutal subtext that sustains and, even further, complicates Aurelius's philosophic serenity, Marius's earlier companion, Flavian, returns to his mind. Marius thinks of him in contrast to his current companion, Cornelius:

The discretion of Cornelius, his energetic clearness and purity, were a charm, rather physical than moral: his exquisite correctness of spirit, at all events, accorded so perfectly with the regular beauty of his person, as to seem to depend upon it. And wholly different as was this later friendship, with its exigency, its warnings, its restraints, from the feverish attachment to Flavian, which had made him at times like an uneasy slave, still, like that, it was a reconciliation to the world of sense, the visible world. . . . It was as if his bodily eyes had been indeed mystically washed, renewed, strengthened. (1:234–35)

But the connection between Flavian and Aurelius is colored for Marius by the suggestion that he (Marius) could take the role vis-à-vis his friend of the "uneasy slave," just as, presumably, it is in fact what his relation to Aurelius must be. Part of the attraction that had inclined Marius toward willing (if uneasy) slavery to Flavian is the fact that Flavian himself would have been willing to join the audience about to witness the spectacle of the martyrdom of a large number of Christians along with other wild animals: "And how eagerly, with what a light heart, would Flavian have taken his place in the amphitheatre, among the youth of his own age! With what an appetite for every detail of the entertainment, and its various accessories: — the sunshine, filtered into soft gold by the *vela*, with their serpentine patterning spread over the more select part of the company" (1:235). This filtered golden light, coming through slats, embellishing and adorning a scene, transforming an ordinary moment, is the same light that Marius and Flavian encountered in the profoundly transforming experience of reading *The Golden Ass*. But what can that idyllic interlude of bibliolatry have to do with the orgiastic carnage that readers of *Marius the Epicurean* know is coming? What does reading a book have to do with wholesale killing? What is public about the intimate act of reading? What is intimate about the ego-melting melodrama of being part of an audience undergoing a hugely transgressive (though socially sanctioned) experience of witnessing a spectacle of slaughter? What is the point of having Marius, at this juncture in his self-fashioning, minutely scrutinize Marcus Aurelius as he (the emperor) conspicuously does not scrutinize in any sense the "manly amusement" he has orchestrated for his subjects?

The one-sentence paragraph that begins with Marius's mixed memories of Flavian, and reintroduces the golden light, moves from gold through white and finally to red. As we look at this array of color, in what is otherwise a predominantly monochromatic novel, we notice that the progression is not arbitrary. After the "select company" are bathed in the golden light already noticed, the narrator's attention is drawn to "the Vestal virgins taking their privilege of seats near the empress Faustina, who sat there in a maze of double-coloured gems, changing, as she moved like the waves of the sea." We are not told what color the "double-coloured gems" are whose reflections create the coruscating marine impression, and the narrative moves from Faustina to the

cool circle of shadow [where, one presumes, other privileged spectators are seated] in which the wonderful toilets of the fashionable told so effectively around the blazing arena [again a series of unspecified colors which are intensified by their contrast] with clean sand for the absorption of certain *great red patches* there, by troops of white-shirted boys, for whom the good-natured audience provided a scramble of nuts and small coin, flung to them over a trellis-work of silver-gilt and amber, precious gift of Nero, while a rain of flowers and perfume fell over themselves, as they paused between the parts of their long feast *upon the spectacle of animal suffering.* (1:235, emphasis added)

We should remember that we are still looking at the last part of a long sentence/paragraph, and that the beginning of the passage imagines the (by now long dead) Flavian to be in the audience in the Roman amphitheatre where Marius now finds himself. And when we recall that the part formerly taken by Flavian in Marius's *wanderjahr* has now been assumed by Aurelius and his court, we come to understand that the presence of the words indicating colors (in this case gold, white, red, and Faustina's "double-coloured gems") are not to be understood, in any sense, as part of a visual/spatial experience.

If this exemplary installation of color is not to be taken mimetically, if it is not to be understood as representing some kind of historical or psychological "reality," then how is one to take it? Readers of Pater who return to his oeuvre regularly cannot help but be struck by his singular reluctance to use color as a routine aspect of developing ideas, characterizing a physical scene or setting, or even (and this from a writer whose texts form part of the aesthetic theoretical canon) in analyzing a work of art. There is a certain "statuesque" quality in his fictional characters. As we have seen, they appear in situ, and we do not quite grasp how Marius got from his Tuscan family home to the imperial heart of Rome. Pater's verbal palette is both atonal and monochromatic. His avoidance of color is perhaps another aspect of both his ability to fabricate a decadent aesthetic and a mark of his logocentrism. The black-and-white steel engravings of Italian paintings and French churches must have seemed contiguous with, and participating in, the same interpretive universe as the black marks on white paper he was continually writing and reading, making and interpreting.[7]

But when color does appear in the text, as it does in the scene of the Roman amphitheatre, attention must be paid. Pater's application of color in the text is important not only because of its relative rarity but also because the colors he uses in this single paragraph are intensely contrastive: the gold of the light, the white of the young men's shirts, and the red of the bloodied sand. Each stands out distinctly. However, it is not the case that color in Pater's text is either allegorical or figurative; gold can be construed, neither here nor in any other part of the text, to mean or stand for nobility, value, wealth, or riches; nor does any other color open up any systematic reference or meaning.

In a text as unmodulated, as uninflected, and finally as logocentric as Pater's, I would suggest that his use of color can be understood to indicate a moment of "truth" that points to, and in fact capitalizes on, the limitations of language. Of course, this is a distinctly colorless moment of truth for Pater, although it serves him well in the double project I have been outlining here. Pater's project sets out to both vindicate Marius, the alleged decadent (rococo, poisonous, neopagan, etc.) and to indict (in very subtle, nuanced ways) that model of Roman/Victorian propriety, Marcus Aurelius. But this criss-crossing of praise and blame is not sufficient to accomplish the second part of Pater's project in writing *Marius the Epicurean*; he needs to present an alternative to an oversimplified decadent/proper antinomy. The alternative is one that takes seriously the quality for which Pater is renowned both as a writer and as a theorist: style. How can there be a moment of truth in terms of style? Derrida's meditation on Kantian aesthetics, *The Truth in Painting*, suggests one approach to the written presence of color in a text. "As pure forms," Derrida writes, "sound and color can give rise to a universal appreciation, in conformity with the quantity of a judgment of taste; they can procure a disinterested pleasure, conforming to the quality of a judgment of taste" (76–77). Charles Riley, in his wide-ranging study *Color Codes*, gives the following overview of Derrida's take on color, which is analogous with what I understand Pater to be striving for in his work. Derrida, Riley indicates,

confers on color an originary potency that is both timeless and boundless. Derrida is suggesting that "the truth in painting" is embodied by color in its pure and direct application, not as a supplement (as Ingres would have it) but like a voice breaking the silence with a pregrammatical, prerhetorical cry of presence and irreducible meaning. The finished work in line, by comparison, is closed and somehow impotent next to the "open, viable" drawing in color. There is such a theory as a fertile trace, as opposed to a sterile one, and the implication is that the "inaugural voyage" of color is the fertile one. (68–69)

There is only a trace of color in Pater's text, but that trace is extremely fertile. With its "pregrammatical, prerhetorical cry of presence and irreducible meaning," color and the "styled" aesthetic landscape of modernism that it anticipates makes the misreading of misleading texts an antidote to mediocrity — golden or leaden.

Notes

1. For an excellent overview of the textual and critical reception of *Studies in the History of the Renaissance*, see the "Critical and Explanatory Notes" in Hill's edition.

2. Under its entry for "hedonism," the *OED* gives as an example a remark by Pater as quoted by Edmund Gosse. Pater exclaimed that he wished "they would not call me a hedonist; it produces such a bad effect in the minds of people who do not know Greek."

3. Newman's "Literature," which had a formative impact on the composition of Pater's essay on "Style," emphasizes the extent to which the role of the intermediary, interpreter, or (in Arnold's parlance) "critic" is as essential in the sustaining and transmission of culture as the "work" itself. The "master of the two fold Logos" is the very kind of learned hermeneuticist that Marius fashions himself (and is fashioned by circumstances) to be. Newman had written that "speech, and therefore literature, which is its permanent record, is essentially a personal work. It is not some production or result, attained by the partnership of several personas, or by machinery, or by any natural process, but in its very idea it proceeds, and must proceed, from some one given individual. . . . [S]cience uses words merely as symbols, but literature uses language in its full compass, as including phraseology, idiom, style, composition, rhythm, eloquence, and whatever other properties are included in it" (qtd. in Tennyson, 315–16).

4. I am thinking here of Newman and Arnold's concern that scientific pedagogy

would eclipse the power that literary culture or humane letters had in shaping the ethical intelligence. See in particular Matthew Arnold's "Literature and Science" (1882) and John Henry Newman's *The Idea of a University* (1852).

5. Like Darwin, Pater viewed his own painterly and writerly version of the "tangled bank" with the affirmative sense that, regardless of its immediate ideological ramifications, "there is [in Darwin's words] grandeur in this view of life" (452).

6. For a provocative exploration of the role played by "yellow" in the work of some women writers of this period, see Liz Constable.

7. Pater makes this question a very real one when he writes, in the same chapter, that "the long shows of the amphitheatre were, so to speak, the novel-reading of that age — a current help provided for sluggish imaginations, in regard, for instance, to grisly accidents, such as might happen to one's self or every one's self but with every facility for comfortable inspection" (1:239).

Works Cited

Arnold, Matthew. *Lectures and Essays in Criticism*. Ed. Robert H. Super. Ann Arbor: University of Michigan Press, 1962.

Constable, Liz. "Fin-de-Siècle Yellow Fevers: Women Writers, Decadence, and Discourses of Degeneracy." *L'Esprit Créateur* 37.3 (1997): 25–37.

Derrida, Jacques. *The Truth in Painting*. Trans. Geoff Bennington and Ian McLeod. Chicago: University of Chicago Press, 1987.

Dowling, Linda. *Language and Decadence in the Victorian Fin de Siècle*. Princeton: Princeton University Press, 1986.

Pater, Walter. *Letters of Walter Pater*. Ed. Lawrence Evans. Oxford: Clarendon, 1970.

———. *Marius the Epicurean: His Sensations and Ideas*. 2 vols. London: Macmillan, 1913.

———. *The Renaissance: Studies in Art and Poetry*. Ed. Donald L. Hill. Berkeley: University of California Press, 1980.

Riley, Charles A. *Color Codes: Modern Theories of Color in Philosophy, Painting and Architecture, Literature, Music and Psychology*. Hanover: University Press of New England, 1995.

Tennyson, G. B., and Donald J. Gray, eds. *Victorian Literature: Prose*. New York: Macmillan, 1978.

Turner, Frank M. "Why the Greeks and Not the Romans in Victorian Britain?" In *Rediscovering Hellenism*, ed. G. W. Clarke, 61–81. Cambridge: Cambridge University Press, 1989.

Chapter 14
Fetishizing Writing
The Politics of Fictional Form in the
Work of Remy de Gourmont and
Joséphin Péladan

Jennifer Birkett

One of the most entertaining — and, politically speaking, most instructive —
parts of writing cultural history is the chance it gives to revisit the great
ideological battlegrounds. Every such terrain has its own irreducible identity, formed out of the original negotiations its inhabitants conducted with
each other and with the forces of their own past. But each generation of
historians and critics who walks the ground comes bearing fresh information and perspectives and, not least, different vested interests, all of which
together can produce renewed understandings of the energies locked into
that particular form. Lines that traditionally defined opposing forces, apparently so absolute, suddenly become permeable. New dimensions open
up, through which can be seen the provisional nature of apparently solid
alliances and connections, and affinities can be identified between positions
that once seemed poles apart. In the contemporary critical moment, fin de
siècle is one of those landscapes to which new scholarly and theoretical
perspectives, and the clash of shifting political imperatives and interests, are
now bringing fresh relief.

Out of the turmoil of the 1880s, literary tradition brought a kind of order
with the clear and simple distinction between the progressive and the retrograde: the realists, scientific and objective, advancing with the Third Republic, and the dreamers, drowning in the tide of progress, retreating into
fantasies of private desire. The distinction created the discursive category of
decadence, identifying a certain set of creative writers and a particular kind
of production centered on the stylish exhibition of contemporary neuroses.
Decadents are self-centered Idealists devoted to the representation of perverse pleasures in common forms and images drawn from what by now is a

well-thumbed catalog. From Mario Praz (1930) to Bram Dijkstra (1986), the names on the register are well established, and nobody would argue against the broad-brush distinction that sets them all, as a group, in opposition to their creative counterparts working in the Realist mode.

On closer inspection, however, the differences between individual decadents begin to seem at least as marked as the family resemblances. A hundred years on, in a culture that, thanks to the pioneering work of the fin-de-siècle generation, has developed new insights into the workings of dream, the exchanges of politics and desire, and the operations of writing, it is possible to recognize that writers may find themselves using the same discourse and expressing common personal and political fears and resentments, and yet still be speaking from vastly different hinterlands of experience, feeling, and commitment. Restoring these different hinterlands to the analysis of decadent form can lead to radically different assessments of the role played by the work of individual writers in their own cultural moment, and the inheritance they have left to our own. Borrowing the language of Remy de Gourmont, the imperative must always be to dissociate familiar presumptions. The present essay, then, will seek to consider what sharp political differences, in every sense, can be veiled by surface similarities of discursive form.

This essay focuses on the writings of Joséphin Péladan and Remy de Gourmont, particularly on the importance in their writing of the fetish — the decadent motif par excellence. In the first volume of *Histoire de la sexualité* (1976), Foucault characterizes the fetish as the model perversion around which fin-de-siècle psychoanalysis organized its discussion of all the others. Each writer, I hope to show, gives a different construction of the fetish, in very different operations of image and syntax. These internal differences in the construction of what, in outline, is the same form of desire, represent different degrees of awareness of the role the fetish plays in their thought and feeling. They are associated with substantially different degrees of openness to the possibilities that their historical moment offers for political and personal change.

The socio-historical context of decadent writing, the subject of a number of recent scholarly accounts by political and cultural historians (see, for example, Magraw, Silverman, and Teich and Porter), is now a familiar one and can be summarized briefly. The authors classified as decadent fantasists were, as a group, men who were committed to the hierarchies of capital but were unable to accept the internal transformations of those hierarchies associated with the development of the mass market and its politics. As writers, they depended on that market, and actively benefited from the expansion it brought to the publishing sector. In its turn, the market depended on them for the production of images that could act as safety valves and reinforcements of late-capitalist order. They continue the relationship between writer and "hypocrite lecteur" identified by Baudelaire thirty years earlier: the producer and consumer of erotic fantasies of introjected revolt locked together in collusion with the repressive forces that regulate modern life. Like Baudelaire, though they attack the particular manifestations of capital in their times, they are unwilling to embrace alternative options (from the 1870s to the 1890s, socialism and feminism), which would put an end to familiar hierarchy. In their own terms, they are elitists, egoists, and individualists. They remain attached to and dependent on hierarchical power while struggling with the frustrating awareness of the marginal state to which it consigns them.

It is not as easy to characterize the nature of the connection that can be made between the sociopolitical structures of a society and the forms of the texts it generates: in what terms a literary-critical analysis can most usefully draw together its discussion of the representation of private desire in decadent style and a decadent's fantasy relationship to the society and the politics of his day. The present essay is built on the propositions offered in Deleuze and Guattari's *L'Anti-Oedipe* (1972), which argues that an identical dynamic characterizes the discourses produced in a given historical moment, which are all re-presentations of the contemporary order of desire. Deleuze and Guattari define Freudian psychoanalysis not as the transhistorical account of human nature that it has claimed to be but, like all discourses and more transparently than most, the child of its moment. They make comparisons between the functioning of capitalism, the rhythms of its basic structures and the form of its basic concepts, and the rhythms and forms that Freudian psychoanalysis identifies in the structures of individual desire. Deleuze and Guattari see Freud's work—which was developed within the fin de siècle—as a key descriptor of subjects within a specific moment of capitalism, providing a fresh set of myths to articulate contemporary experience for Freud's period and our own. The myth of the Oedipal family, a production of capitalist culture, is a very particular re-presentation of capitalist order, reenacting the way in which it generates, blocks, and recuperates the challenges of individual desire. In the economic order, the fetishizing of private property acts as a block and a focus for economic and social energies; in the realm of private desire, the sexual fetish performs the same function. The possessive individual, sexual and economic, is articulated of a piece. And of course—the polemic thrust of their text—the Oedipal myth has served, since Freud, as a politically significant instrument bringing to public consciousness the patterns it articulates and reinforcing them.

Extending the thesis put forward by Deleuze and Guattari, it can be argued that Joséphin Péladan and Remy de Gourmont, contemporaries of Freud, are bound by similar conditions in seeking an appropriate language to express the distinctive contemporary form of desire. Like Freud, they are concerned to rework existing myth (in their case, the whole gamut from Christian to pagan) to represent the conscious and unconscious exchanges of individual subjectivity with its structuring forms. In the process, they also help reinforce unarticulated social assumptions about how subjectivity and its structuring forms are to be defined. They too contribute to the construction of subjects-in-capitalism, plotting personal and, especially, sexual desire in terms of the terrors and seductions of the Oedipal romance. At the center of their sensibility they place the fetish, which, following the logic of Freud's analyses, may be seen as serving both to perpetuate and to resolve the Oedipal antagonisms.[1] The mechanism of the fetish, repeatedly invoking and displacing the fear of castration, constantly reenacts the rebellion against and submission to the order of the Father in which decadent identity is grounded.

Deleuze's study, in *Présentation de Sacher-Masoch*, of the hinterland of Sacher-Masoch's work and the nationalist ambitions and populist nostalgias, as well as the personal traumas, from which it springs suggests interesting insights into the nature of the political attitudes with which the fetishistic sensibility is associated in the Paris of the 1880s and 1890s. I have pointed out elsewhere the welcome given to Sacher-Masoch by the cultural establishment in 1886, which remained constant through to the early 1890s (Birkett, 31–33). The stylistic and thematic features (disavowal, suspense, waiting, and phantasy) which, in Deleuze's analysis, combine with fetishism to generate the specific constellation of masochism correspond readily to the distinctive mixture of sporadic revolt and quiet desperation by which that period is marked. Elites and populace vented their frustration and insecurities in nationalistic slogans, hid from the challenges of the present in nostalgic evasions, and allowed themselves, in the process, to be led quietly to market. It is in this context that the importance of making distinctions between the bearers of decadent fetishism emerges. The backward-looking frenzy of nationalist insecurity, and all it connotes, matches the preoccupations of Péladan, deeply and unreflectively embedded in both the contemporary order of desire and the language of religious traditions in which he represents it. Gourmont, from the beginning, kept a healthier distance. His starting point was the same discourse — indeed, some of his most striking fetishistic constructions work with the symbols of the Catholic revival that accompanied the post-1870 nationalist *revanche*. (*Sixtine*, for example, discussed below, returns obsessively to the iconography of the Virgin Mary and the thematics of suffering with which the Marian figure is associated.) But Gourmont, distinctively, refuses to be trapped by icons of his own or others' invention. He writes in increasing awareness of the prisonhouse of language and the constructed nature of desire, and in the process he points to different horizons.

Recent criticism has already made significant inroads into investigating the fetish's role in the decadent moment, emphasizing the historical status of Freudian discourse and drawing, on that basis, useful conclusions about the nature of contemporary political attitudes on various levels. Emily Apter's *Feminizing the Fetish: Psychoanalysis and Narrative Obsession in Turn-of-the-*

Century France (1991) is a key source book, especially for its introductory overview of the place occupied by the fetish in sociocultural theory, from Marx, Binet, and Freud to Benjamin and Baudrillard. In the collection edited by Apter and Pietz (*Fetishism as Cultural Discourse*, 1993), two essays are especially appropriate for mention here. Charles Bernheimer, in "Fetishism and Decadence: Salome's Severed Heads," meditates on the extent to which Freud's theory of fetishism "participates" in the ideology of decadence and "corresponds to" decadent aesthetics, which, like its Baudelairean avatar, valorizes artifice over nature and encodes that valorization by gender. Bernheimer's assessment of the significance of the decadent approach to female sexuality, like my own, emphasizes the decadent's repulsion and terror before the recognition of difference it imposes and the threat of supersession that difference brings with it. His formulations go straight to the heart of the matter. What is denied in decadent art is its origins in nature; what is denied in the decadent image of woman is that she is castrated—or rather, more telling, that she is *not* castrated, for such a denial takes thought outside the Oedipal limits. Bernheimer characterizes this as the "phallocentric deceit" that Freud's theory enshrines: "When psychoanalysis attributes to woman a sexual nature that is lacking, wounded, incomplete, it is duplicating the revelation that Wilde attributes to Art: 'Nature's lack of design . . . her absolutely unfinished condition' (65). Castration, I am arguing, is as decadent an interpretation of sexual difference as is the defense mechanism it motivates, fetishism."[2]

The study which to date has offered the most comprehensive account of fetishism in the fin de siècle, pulling together the strands of sexual politics, the politics of class (inseparable, in decadent demonography, from the Woman Question), nationalism, and the politics of writing is still Julia Kristeva's forceful *La Révolution du langage poétique* (1974). With due acknowledgment to Deleuze and Guattari, Kristeva characterizes the fundamental structure of fin-de-siècle French society as fetishistic, and fixes the source of its perversion in the link between family and state. France in the 1880s and 1890s, she says, fetishized the family and fetishized Order, and this process was reproduced in the writing of the period.[3] Her analysis differs from that offered in the present essay in its foregrounding of the most subversive writers of the time, Mallarmé and Lautréamont, who were least complicitous, she argues, in the collective Oedipal delusion, and whose work produced anarchic gestures that challenged head-on the repressive pull to Order. They were, she notes, far from the only challengers to Order, but for lack of an appropriate language (that of the unconscious), most of the challenges raised by others were displaced and lost as alternative fetishizations of Art or Religion. In this context, she mentions Gourmont approvingly, if briefly, as a stylist, a fetishist of Art, who comes close to opening up his writing to produce a revolutionary version of the subject. She refers appreciatively to his overt challenge to hierarchy, unique among the Symbolists, and points out that it was picked up by the anarchist journal *La Révolte*.[4] She makes no reference to Péladan, but as a fetishist of Religion who constantly attacked the values of the secular State, he fits her second category admirably.

For those who stopped short of the break with authority, linguistic, moral or political, more was at issue than the underdevelopment of psychoanalysis. A Péladan or Gourmont might rebel against certain features of the established order, but still have interests vested in it that would prevent any radical break. This, perhaps, is the defining characteristic of the decadents: that they go as far as they can go in gestures of rebellion and resistance, while still remaining subjects of their own time. They would rather, with the fetish, embrace the Oedipal symbolic, the familiar source of terror and pain, than contemplate the Mallarméan alternative: the voyage to the frontiers where the relinquishing of conventional orders of logic, syntax, and power throws all familiar order back into the melting pot.

Within the conforming group, as Kristeva indicates, there are significant differences of commitment and awareness, and these are the ones that interest me here. In *Sixtine*, Gourmont's hero Hubert, walking the Paris streets, puzzling over the image of the dead mistress that invades his imagination whenever he makes love, is accosted by a literary acquaintance, a man of the occult who, mysteriously, knows his fantasy and says it is also his own. The occultist walks away, leaving Hubert to wonder briefly what it signifies to share such an obsession and then, characteristically, to dismiss the problem and carry on his own way. But the incident is crucial. Two writers can be, in a sense, of one mind: they walk the same streets of the same city, make their living in the same circles, their sensibility feeds on the same parts of the collective imagination. But they can be coming from different quarters and traveling in different directions. In both Péladan and Gourmont, writing is marked with the stylistic counterparts of Freudian fetishistic practice: the predilection for foreplay, fragmentation, reconstruction of the body of desire, and the cult of violence. But the difference is absolute between the stance taken by the positivist, Péladan, fixated on the content of traditional symbolic forms, and that of the materialist, Gourmont, far more interested in the processes that bring forms to being.

The rest of this essay will seek to characterize the difference. Péladan, I shall argue, writes in mystified and mystificatory terms, making visible Oedipal structures of desire and its frustrations in an alienated form that seems to confirm that there is no alternative to their reinscription. Gourmont, in contrast, achieves a relative measure of openness, evoking a subjectivity caught in similar blocks and flows but foregrounding in his writing his awareness of being so caught. His writing demands a different and more modern kind of reader, for he builds into the way he writes his recognition of the constraints exerted on imagination of the materiality of discourse, and of the way subjectivity is constructed and reinscribed by the exchanges in any given historical moment of sensibility and form.

Joséphin Péladan: The Limits of Magic

In the annals of literary history, Joséphin Péladan has slipped into an obscurity illuminated only by sporadic studies (most recently, the excellent biography by Christophe Beaufils, *Joséphin Péladan: Essai sur une maladie du lyrisme* [1993]). In his own period, he had a certain dubious celebrity. Often ridiculed and marginalized for the poseur and fantasist he undoubtedly was, he nevertheless made his own mark on the contemporary scene, as art critic and founder in 1892 of the Symbolist Salons de la Rose+Croix Catholique, author of a twenty-one-volume cycle charting *La Décadence latine* (1886–1925), and playwright whose dramas, refused by mainstream Paris theaters, could, for just one night, fire equally the imaginations of the crowd gathered in the arena in Nîmes or the intimate circle in Lady Caithness's drawingroom.[5]

Joséphin's father, Adrien, was an active propagandist in the cause of traditionalist Catholic revival in Nîmes in the middle of the nineteenth century. He became important again in the early 1870s, after the defeat by Prussia, as the author of nationalist pamphlets on the apocalyptic prophecies associated with the supernatural appearances of the Virgin Mary. Joséphin inherited his crusading mantle. His brother, another Adrien, initiated him into the occult and shared with him his investigations into magnetism and medicine. Adrien's unsuccessful medical thesis, submitted in 1878 ("Le traitement homéopathique de la spermatorrhée, de la prostatorrhée et de l'hypersécrétion des glandes vulvovaginales"), explored the links between sexual libido and the intellect. Adrien identified a connection between sperm and nervous fluid, which he saw as a modification of electricity, and characterized the cerebral and genital systems as opposite polarities. He proposed that unused sperm, transformed into vital fluid, was used to irrigate the brain; in consequence, intellectual creativity and sexual activity must be seen as mutually exclusive activities. His theses, combined with the ascetic commitment of traditionalist Catholicism, provided the basis for Joséphin's own theories of the Magical vocation. The Magus, who learns to repress, concentrate, and direct his sexual desires to strengthen his intellect and will, becomes a powerhouse of energies that can be put to work in the service of the Ideal. The fetishized female finds her place in this system as both source and channel of sexual desire, feeding the Magical force and enabling it to win back the masses to tradition and theocracy.

Péladan's novel cycle, written as the conflict between Church and State unfolded in the 1880s and 1890s, tracked against its key historical and political manifestations the efforts of the heroes of the Ideal to turn the tide of democratic politics and culture. In 1884, when the first novel (*Le Vice suprême*) was published to general acclaim, a monarchist revival still seemed a possibility. But, by the time the final volumes appeared, the Pope had rallied to democracy and the Republic and Catholic legitimist groups had abandoned the struggle. Hope dwindles and present-day patriarchs abandon their charges, but the Magus perseveres in his determination to maintain the ultimate authority of the true Father, to preserve old hierarchies, and to maintain traditional symbols. At the end of the epic, the Magus Mérodack stands alone, unique representative of a defeated world, still refusing to surrender and preparing to carry the Cross of his allegiance into exile.

Up to the last, Péladan's fictions chart an unflagging determination to transform politics by the assertion of his heroes' unlimited phallic power. Paradoxically, he shows that power as expressing itself most fully in abstention (a neat formulation, which justifies a hero's failure in advance). Sexual repression is the basis on which he proposes to create new private and political subjects; and within the heterosexual couple on which his thought is focused, the greatest repression is reserved for the female. Péladan's erotic politics start and end with the subordination and fetishization of women. Three theoretical texts — *Comment on devient mage: Ethique* (1892), *Comment on devient fée: Erotique* (1893), and *La Science de l'amour* (1911) — are devoted to its exposition. Briefly, the role of the Fairy is to mirror the Ideal of her Magus and lend her sexual energies to further it — and her money and social connections, which for Péladan are an integral part of the tribute that woman owes to masculine genius. Love is only to be found in luxury, without which it degenerates into mere sexual frenzy and loses its political and metaphysical power.[6]

Three volumes of his novel cycle — *Curieuse!* (1886), *L'Initiation sentimentale* (1887), and *A coeur perdu* (1888) — dramatize the Magus's attempt to reform a Russian princess into the perfect androgyne, idiosyncratically defined by Péladan as one in whom sexual libido has been both fully aroused and fully repressed. The androgyne fetish is to be used as an emblem to fascinate the mob, to fix their disorderly libidinal energies, and to turn them to rebuilding theocracy. The ploy fails because the woman, as in most of Péladan's scenarios, rebels. Péladan frequently complains that the resistance of the should-be fetish to the divine right of masculine authority is both mirror and source of the central problem in modern French politics: the insurgency of women and the masses, in the name of democratic rights.

Political ambition, a high degree of personal libido, wild imagination, and a strong sense of the market value of the erotic come together to create an epic cycle of narratives without parallel in Péladan's own time, though the mode is familiar in our own. Training the fetish in the knowledge and repression of desire involves a number of semipornographic scenarios, which tended not to damage Péladan's sales while being, in his terms, entirely justi-fied by his political and moral intentions. The supreme confrontation of Magus and Fairy-fetish in the third volume of the sequence is written to catch the popular (masculine) erotic imagination, in order to confront it with the spiritual challenge. The process, an extended one, is an exemplary model of the investment of masochistic desire in the fetishistic act. Most striking is the attachment to the conventional scenarios, images, and syntax of erotic dis-course, with the penetration of the "mystery" of the unknown expressed in terms of a rigid adherence to a carefully controlled rite. A theatrically staged ritual is conducted by the artist-priest in a temple ostentatiously lined with phallic symbols. Péladan exploits the images and rhythms of a very conven-tional Romantic rhetoric to create an icon where the threat of sexuality is displayed only to be safely displaced, with metonymic focus on gauzy veils, jewels, and breasts.[7] But the effort cannot be sustained. Péladan lacks both the will and the stylistic resources to present untrammeled desire, and his vocabulary and syntax remain locked in the limits of rationalist logic. The best he can do is ironically acknowledge his own failure, as the smoke and flames of passion die down and the clear voice of the fetish attacks her would-be Lord: "O pontife, c'est tout ce qui t'inspire l'idole?" [O Pontiff, is that all the idol inspires in you?].

La Décadence latine perpetually recycles fetishistic scenarios: countless fe-male bodies fixed in tableaux, framed in artificial decors, motionless, meto-nymically fragmented, often to grotesque effect (for example, the exhibi-tionist displays of breast fetishism in L'Androgyne [1891], or, outside the cycle, the text of 1895, Mélusine, which takes foot-fetishism to ludicrous extremes). These fragmented bodies are the center of textual spaces marked by stillness and masochistic waiting, scenes of the prolonged fore-play that Freud censures in fetishism as a diversion of sexuality from pro-creation. (Children are altogether absent from his narratives, as from most decadent texts: the fetishistic sensibility puts the future on hold in order to eternalize a present of frustrated desire.) Péladan writes up such immobility in regular, incantatory rhythms which, he spells out, represent the harmo-nious, stately condition of ideal subjects in the ideal state. The violence that accompanies such repressions is an acknowledged part of the scenario, but is confined by various devices to the edge of the action. Artistic imagination works overtime to maintain calm in the ambit of the fetish.

Péladan is caught in a contradictory relationship to the patriarchal and capitalist hierarchy that regulates contemporary order. On the one hand, he is committed to the principle; on the other, he is equally committed to rejecting institutions and figures in which it is currently embodied. This is one explanation, perhaps, for the plethora of strong female figures in his work who resist the Magus's attempts to work them over into his own image —displacement of his own revolt into the feminine. Whatever the case, in the last analysis, his commitment to the principle of hierarchical authority is paramount. There is no representation of desire in his work, including the desire for difference, that is not in thrall to the Oedipal symbolic, submissive to the law of the Father, marked equally by phallic ambition and fear of castration.

The overwhelming place given to the power of the Father in Péladan's work is best illustrated in his most successful—that is, most pliant—fetish-istic creation, Bélit, the mother-mistress who comes closest to total submis-sion to the Magus. *Un coeur en peine*, read and admired by August Strindberg during his stay in Paris in 1896, at the height of his own mystical crisis,[8] is an account of her initiation into service. Yearning, like Alexandre Séon's Chi-mera, to be consumed by the unknown lover, Bélit is the center around which Péladan constructs the scenario of his own dreamworld. In a symbolic landscape of sea and cliffs, untamed natural forces—the storms and winds of desire—meet and clash, waiting for the mediator who will place them at the Magus's feet. The "raw" wildness is all carefully ordered, within the limits of familiar representational conventions. The narrative structure, ap-parently discrete fragments of lyrical prose, modeling the leaps of inchoate desire, follows Wagnerian form: the fragments are clearly and symphonic-ally linked by leitmotifs of imagery and rhythm and by calculated counter-pointing and juxtaposition, and all carry the same message of nature's long-ing to submit to Order. The site of the narrative action, the sea tossed by storms, is the epitome of energy that lacks adequate form; and in the con-ventional Romantic metaphor, the sea doubles as mirror-image of feminine desire, giving birth to Bélit, who swims to shore in the first pages of the text to stand on a promontory, screaming her desire into the void.

But neither formlessness nor void bears close inspection. Péladan's land-scape sets strict limits. The tossing sea is contained by high surrounding cliffs, and the direction of Bélit's yearning is magnetically fixed. The Castle of the Rosicrucian Maguses delineates her horizon. The substance of the text—the sequences of memories and fantasies that come "unbidden" to drift across her mind—is fixed throughout in the same strict binary, limit-ing the forms her desire can take: rebellion or service. In the dark, the sea brings to her the figure of her alter ego, the emancipated, self-serving Rose de Faventine; to become Rose or Bélit, man's tyrant or man's slave, is the single option for feminine desire. Over the length of the novel, Péladan alternately invokes and veils the threat of castration that constitutes the center of his fetish. The Echo who denies Narcissus his mirror, then con-cedes it again, is an inexhaustible source of masochistic pleasure. Bélit's reward, in the final pages, is to be incorporated into the rituals of the Rosicrucian Tower. But in Péladan's discourse, she has never been out of it. In this Oedipal text, feminine difference is never other than repressed; the rules and hierarchy of paternal Order are always dominant.

Remy de Gourmont: Subject to Style

While Péladan was driving himself ever deeper into the sand of symbolic discourse, Gourmont was applying his own critical intellect not so much to the content of discursive forms as to the processes by which they are produced. Grounding his exploration of the relation between ideas and the senses in a practical, materialist investigation of the way language works, he gained what Péladan always lacked: an insight into the way his own sensibility was constructed, within the constraints of the contemporary moment. His sensibility remains locked, he acknowledged, within inherited imaginative forms; but space is made, however tentatively, in his work for other kinds of language and other hierarchies.

Gourmont's role as a mediator of Nietzschean and Schopenhauerean ideologies of the role of the will and the imagination in determining the relation of subject and world is well known. Less so, perhaps, is his interest in the more empirically based investigations of contemporary psychologists such as Théodule Ribot, author of *L'Imagination créatrice* (1900),[9] and Paul Chabaneix, author of *Physiologie cérébrale: le subconscient chez les artistes, les savants et les écrivains*, both of which he drew on for his own inquiry into "La Création subconsciente" (in *La Culture des idées* [1900]), which emphasizes the role of sensation, immediate or recollected, in artistic creativity (Burne 48).[10] Their influence also informs the thinking of *Le Problème du style* (1902), particularly important for disclosing his understanding of the historical and material base of style. In his preface, he wrote: "Le véritable problème du style est une question de physiologie. . . . Nous écrivons, comme nous sentons, comme nous pensons, avec notre corps tout entier. L'intelligence n'est qu'une des manières d'être de la sensibilité, et non pas la plus stable, encore moins la plus volontaire" [The real problem of style is a question of physiology. . . . We write, just as we feel, and as we think, with our whole bodies. Intelligence is only one of the modes of sensibility, not the most stable, even less the most voluntary]. Gourmont is not just the idealist he is usually labeled. In English-speaking countries particularly, we owe that interpretation of his work to its enthusiastic dissemination by Richard Aldington, the novelist, poet, and critic who worked with Ezra Pound on the *New Freewoman* (later the *Egoist*) and helped place there translations of chapters from Gourmont's novel *Les Chevaux de Diomède* (*New Freewoman*, September-December 1913; *Egoist* January-March 1914). Aldington's own stylistic and political partialities (and, be it said, the middling nature of his own talents) colored his perceptions of the nature and importance of Gourmont's work. His selection of extracts from Gourmont's work, still to be found on the shelves of libraries and secondhand bookshops, gives minimal space to the French writer's investigation of questions of language and style. It concentrates rather on presenting the dreamer, the individualist, the elitist, advocate of liberties and denouncer of herds and mediocrities, the Nietzschean man of passion and the great writer of the erotic.[11]

Gourmont is also a materialist (in Pound's words, "un cérébral sensuel") in his approach to discourse, engrossed in the reality of language: how rhetorics come out of and link into the historical continuum, what nerves you touch when you finger a particular metaphor, how assonance and alliteration can be worked to ground semantics in the senses. It is a matter of debate how much the technical aspects of his work influenced directly and permanently the poetic practice of Pound, who, along with Eliot, was his most celebrated admirer and advocate in the Anglo-American cultural circles of the 1910s and 1920s. But certainly, the early Pound picked out for comment his theories of writing and his practice, and saw them as at least as important as his sensitive evocations of erotic psychology, his advocacy of liberty and individualism, and his recovery and defense of European cultural tradition. Through Gourmont's collection of neo-Latin poetry, *Le Latin mystique* (1892), Pound acquired his own interest in the assonantal and rhythmic innovations of the neo-Latin poet Gotteschalk Notker; and, as Glenn Burne has argued, he was impressed by Gourmont's notion of an "absolute rhythm" for emotion, whose cadences correspond to the movements of the breathing body, and which Pound appreciated in the poems in Gourmont's *Litanies de la Rose* (1892) (Burne 125).[12] These are the rhythms we shall shortly see at work, more subtly and with greater significance, in Gourmont's prose.

The Oedipal subject is as much to the forefront in Gourmont's work as in Péladan's, but in Gourmont it is framed for the serious pleasure of intellectual play, and the writing draws attention to the conditions and the processes of its constitution. Its center of interest is the relationship between libidinal drives and the formations in which they appear to the intellect; in this, Gourmont picks out the central place given to the feminine in the masculine imagination, and how that imagination invests the feminine with meaning — or, rather, meanings, since in Gourmont's writing, almost alone among fin-de-siècle authors, this investment involves a contract whose terms can and do change.

A close consideration of two prose texts will show how Gourmont evokes the process of investment. Between them, they also show that changing of subject positions in operation. The novel *Sixtine: roman de la vie cérébrale* (1890) and the tale "Stratagèmes" (from the short story collection, *Histoires magiques* [1894]) play variants on the same autobiographical source material, Gourmont's affair with Berthe Courrière.[13]

Investigating the fetish is the central preoccupation of *Sixtine*. Hubert des Entragues is, as he reflects, incurably smitten with "la folie des yeux," and intrigued by the mystery of "cette constante union de deux sensations aussi différentes que la sensation visuelle et le spasme" (275). Exploring how the process of "seeing" the fetish take form relates to the spasm of pleasure is for him, he says, the purpose of writing: "La fin d'une vie intelligente ce n'est pas de coucher avec la princesse de Trébizonde, mais de s'expliquer soi-même en ses motifs d'action par des faits ou par des gestes. L'écriture est révélatrice de l'acte intérieur; il est bien moins important de sentir que de connaître l'ordonnance des sensations, et c'est la revanche de l'esprit sur le corps: rien n'existe que par le Verbe" (276–77) [The goal of an intelligent life is not to sleep with the princess of Trébizonde, but to make sense of one's motivations through deeds or gestures. Writing reveals inner acts; it is much less important to feel than to know the order of feelings, and therein lies the revenge of the mind over the body: nothing exists other than through the Word].

Hubert's idealist declaration of faith, with which he begins his lovemaking, is often quoted, to the effect that I can know no world outside myself, except the one I create through my senses (51).[14] But at least as important is the account that precedes it of his attempts to develop a language of the senses, rejecting conventional rhetoric for rhythms drawn directly from body experience: "Je ne suis pas poète, je ne sais pas bien couper ma pensée en petits morceaux égaux ou inégaux, selon le hasard du hachoir: ma prose n'est rythmée que par mon souffle; les coups d'épingle de la sensation, seuls, en marquent les accents et la puérilité royale de la rime riche dépasse mon entendement" (50) [I am not a poet, I don't really know how to cut up my thoughts into even and uneven sized little pieces according to the way the blade falls: my prose finds its rhythm through my breath; the pinpricks of sensation, they alone, mark its accents, and the royal puerility of rime riche lies beyond my comprehension]. The novel models these individual body rhythms of feeling and the pinpricks of sensation and their production within inherited collective symbolic forms. The perceived world, the narrative indicates, is structured out of structures, and the variations to be played within them. Hubert watches his consciousness flicker to and fro through serialized sequences of fantasies, travel notes, tales he tells himself, and poems and stories he writes for himself and others. All these tales have a doubling structure that stands them up internally, and each one doubles some aspect of Hubert's dialogue with Sixtine, his fetish personified. That dialogue, his long negotiation with the form of his desire, constitutes the central narrative flow with which the other tales he tells criss-cross, punctuate, block, and, in blocking, turn into significance. Doubling, Hubert muses, is the psychic base of his experience and literally constitutes it.[15] Modestly, he declines to say his is a representative subjectivity, but it clearly is a mirror — a critical one — held up to contemporary narcissism.

As the doubled subject observes the flow effortlessly turning into forms, disruptive elements emerge, unexpectedly, signaling undercurrents, points of absolute resistance where imagination has no transforming powers. Two formative traumas are disclosed that explain Hubert's fetishization of eyes and of Art. Both are instances when desire was first realized — in the double form of sexual pleasure and the pleasure of writing — and in both, desire is immediately joined to humiliation and constraint. From puberty, there is a memory of his first experience of sexual pleasure, stimulated by the eyes of the Madonna of Masolino da Panicale seen in a book of sacred pictures. The memory is overlaid with violent resentment and humiliation at being sent to bed early that day by an old aunt, as though he were a child (140ff). Then, as a young adult, there is another humiliation, that of being forced by poverty brought about by the loss of his aristocratic inheritance to write for the marketplace (190).

These two moments bring together in their modeling of the origins of his fetishes the confrontations of desire with power in the family and power in the public sphere — the power of the market. Hubert prides himself on his autonomy, but Gourmont's narrative knows better and positions him in history. It takes him through a sequence of public places that ultimately are the determiners of his dreams: publishers' offices, house parties, and salons (gathering the elite of business, high society, literature), and the streets and bridges of Paris, filled with the populace and its screaming children. His own library, that private place of retreat, has also its public dimension as the space of a material cultural history to which he is also subject. He can and does choose who he reads (Origen, Gotteschalk, Dante, or, among contemporaries, Villiers, Mallarmé, Huysmans, Whitman). But whether he chooses him or not, the narrative notes, Zola is still there, dominating the present.

The interplay of discourses that constitutes Hubert's subjectivity comes to coherence in the process of fetishization. The fetish performs the same function as the collection mania that entrances Hubert when he reads about it in Ribot; both are obsessions that hold a personality together. The important thing, he notes, is for the obsession to be "inépuisable" (158).

Sixtine (or, rather, what she can be made to represent) is indeed inexhaustible. Her eyes are those of his Madonna, with their perpetual reminder of the association of pleasure and frustration, potency and humiliation, and his imagination proliferates their image in a series of dream scenarios all through the text. She is inexhaustible also because she resists fetishization. She deconstructs the fetishizing project, spelling out that Hubert worships not her but the dream he has incarnated in her. This resistance is welcomed by Hubert as a mirror of his own desire for autonomy and self-knowledge (306). So, in the end, she does not destroy him when she leaves him for a Russian playwright. He lets her go, in an experiment in switching subject positions, deciding, with the narrative, that it would be generous to let the woman have the happy ending (238).

In Gourmont, the fetishizing process is seen to offer scope for interpreting, reading, and negotiating subject positions. There is, he establishes, no room to change libidinal patterns by the time the subject can understand what they are. There is, however, room to stylize them (not a trivializing word, as Foucault showed in the third volume of his history of sexuality, *Le*

Souci de soi [1984]), and, by taking care with style, the subject survives. With Sixtine gone, Hubert retreats to his library, folding back on himself, reaching out for the consoling rhythms and images of Origen. But what he has just experienced is not castration; articulating that ever-present threat as a stylish joke defuses it. He slips now into the resting period—"repos" (327) —of a healthy subject-in-process ready to enter another story at the next throb of desire.

A short analysis of a segment of the chapter "Figure de rêve" shows the skill with which Gourmont composes textually his reenactment of the fetishizing process, and illustrates particularly his awareness of sexuality and subjectivity as linked elements of a reading. Here, Gourmont takes up the familiar rhythms seen already in Péladan and turns significant sensuous detail (the "pinpricks of sensation") into metonymic image —pulls, in fact, all the familiar triggers of fetishistic stimulus. But he does so to disrupt them, sweeping them up, without denying them, into changed configurations that produce not just the reenactment of erotic desire but also a more powerful intellectual sensation of sheer delight in the workings of signifying form.

The sequence plunges straight into fantasy, suppressing any framing placing of Hubert in his "real" world, and sets up a protracted hallucination of Sixtine's presence, on a walk that lasts the whole afternoon ("the," not "a": the whole passage is in the language of immediate presence and real time). Against this continuing backdrop, the leaps of dream and the slow rhythmic build-up of desire are staged in precisely modulated rhythms: "elle apparaissait," flickering, the tense suggests, in and out; the sound of her voice breaks, with "positive" emphasis, the silence of three carefully produced phrases; a sunshade bursts open, interrupting the flow: and suddenly, Sixtine has life and volition of her own, has changed position, is reading. Significant details build metonymically what begins as an equally flickering image and ends in clear, single focus, foregrounding the workings of art and interpretation. From specular images—Sixtine's dress (shot green silk, standing in for her eyes, which, interestingly, are not referred to), her boots, her smile–the text moves to the sound of her voice, offering to tell a story, and then back to sight, to construct a precisely-noted interplay of color, line, light, and shade (all refracted through the sunshade) that evokes Sixtine's shoulders; and finally, unexpectedly, her head, bent to her book. From Sixtine and "elle," the movement is to "la lecture"–a considerable reworking of the motif of fetishized femininity and, in its mode, more Impressionist than Symbolist, with all that that implies.

"Stratagèmes" is less an experiment in stylized (self-)control and more an attempt to recuperate repressed sensual experience, using its female object as an instrument to enter that unknown territory. There are far more instances in this text of the syntactic disruptions, changing subject-positions, and blurring of categories that mark, in Kristevan language, a would-be revolutionary subject. Correspondingly, the moves to recuperation, reestablishing self-control, are cruder and more violent. Structurally, the narrative works, as in *Sixtine*, on a collage of tales, snatches of dialogue, anecdotes, memories, poems, songs — without, however, the narrative continuity provided by the self-distancing, rationalizing Hubert. The "I" of the short story presents himself much more as a receiver of impressions: a screen on which dream is projected.

The tale opens in the kaleidoscope of memory, in glimpses of the formative scenarios that have shaped the (unidentified male) narrative voice. The eyes, tears, disembodied voices, silences of successive women fade in and out and flow together, hard to distinguish at times from the dominant narrative voice of whom they are now part, as subject pronouns and subject positions disappear in the delirium of erotic dream. The repetitive rhythms of the train of desire — "Ah! ce train qui va, qui va! Ah! ma vie qui va, qui va!" (182) — and the brief flickering images caught in its windows, threaten to carry sexual experience into unpunctuated, inarticulate darkness — "L'ombre est violette. Le roulis roule le fugace enlacis . . ." (182). That blurring is given significant form by being countered and cut by sharp-edged images and repeated motifs that characterize precisely the nature of his sexual experience: sometimes a mutual consuming, but most often a competitive exchange marked by violence, coldness, cruelty. Equally precise is the underlying recognition that, so far, he has only known desire clothed in its learned, rationalized, cultural forms. What he knows best about himself, it emerges from these memories, is his fetish for eyes.

The narrative focuses on the narrator's determination to turn his latest mistress into fetish. This time, the project contains the consciously sadistic choice to deny her both autonomy and sexual satisfaction. The conventional mechanisms are skillfully worked, and the pair conclude in traditional roles: he Pygmalion, she Galatea; he Apollo, she Daphne. But within that movement, other processes are also at work, of which the most interesting is the narrator's effort to break out of the eye-fetish around which his subjectivity coheres, and to find something different in "le jeu des sensations élémentaires" (185). Of taste, touch, sight, scent, he only knows sight and he wants to know the others. He wants to bring his masculine modes of perceiving (vision and intellect) into the domains of sensation that culture has allocated to the feminine: "Mettre de l'esprit dans la saveur, de l'âme dans le parfum, du sentiment dans le toucher . . ." (183) [To bring mind into taste, soul into scent, feeling into touch].

The segment chosen for analysis, the penultimate phase of their relationship, goes to the heart of this operation. Set "Chez elle," it is the key experiment he must complete before he can enter the final stage, with its parallel opening "Chez moi" — a triumphant entry into self-possession. In her domain, the narrator first establishes himself as controlling subject ("Je la trouve"), and then steps right into the disconnected, contradictory, sensuous delirium which women inhabit (she remains invisible among her crowding silks, "l'air tres amusé, sérieuse" [looking very amused, serious]). Under her guidance, he practices touching silk, velvet, embroideries, knowing by feeling ("le pouce . . . voit" [the thumb . . . sees]). Mimicking her abandonment to sensation, he finds himself infected: "la contagieuse névrose me gagne" [contagious neurosis is overwhelming me]. The syntax enacts a movement in which "je" abandons the initiative to objects and finds intellectually discriminated sense-categories blurred into synaesthesia, abstracts and concretes falling together ("voici un pourpre brûlé d'où s'émancipe une tiédeur charnelle" [here is a burnt purple which is giving off a bodily warmth]). He recovers control by invoking the censorious voice he attributes to his fetishized female: "Vous embrassez mes chiffons maintenant!" [You're kissing my clothes now]. But he loses it again in the flow of desire, as colors become personified, populating and dominating the narrative landscape. He saves himself from the flow by throwing himself a metaphor, a banal one, but a lifeline: desire is a "water journey" in which, whenever I want to, "je reprends pied" [I can regain my footing]. The visual image, metaphor or metonymy, is the mode of control, and with it "I" restores familiar order, subject reining in its objects: "je te retrouve" [I find you again]. The foray into the terrain of repression ends in panic, and controlled retreat. With brutal honesty, the text maneuvers the now self-mystifying narrator into spelling out the consequences of refusing the chance of letting go. In the end, both of them are left incomplete, fantasy figures, *both* fetishized. In fetishizing her, the passage shows, he fetishizes himself: he's nothing but a "je" and a hand — or in one instance, a punning finger, modeling her into his required shape, his statue, Galatea.

There can be no claiming that these texts produce that degree of immediate contact with libidinal drive, in radically disruptive rhythms, that Kristeva sought and found in such writers as Lautréamont and Mallarmé (or, even more tellingly, that great disruptor of Oedipal family and state, James Joyce). Gourmont's writing, compared to these, takes only tremulous steps toward either *jouissance* or revolution. But it retains its interest as a still insufficiently appreciated attempt to move toward a new threshold of understanding. Gourmont pushes the representational capacity of the language of his time not, certainly, to its limits but as far as it could go while still remaining within its moment. And, as such, it represents the epitome of decadent writing, reenacting with futile lucidity the deadly reinvestment of self in the constraining fetishes of its own invention.

Notes

1. See Freud's "Fetishism" (1927); and also his "Unsuitable Substitutes for the Sexual Object-Fetishism" (65–68) in *Three Essays on the Theory of Sexuality: I. The*

Sexual Aberrations (1905–20). Freud defines fetishism as an abnormal sexual practice that refuses to acknowledge that the primary sexual object is conjugation, that embodies a simultaneous fascination and horror for the female genitalia (said to stir fears of castration), and that works to displace desire into substitute forms. Assumed in his work, but not particularly spelled out, are also the anthropological origins of the term: the fetish as an object of worship, which the worshipper invests with symbolic power.

2. While Bernheimer's argument, by and large, stays on the terrain of gender politics, Jeffrey Mehlman, in "Remy de Gourmont with Freud: Fetishism and Patriotism," follows a different line. Mehlman investigates the link between fin-de-siècle nationalism and the Freudian fetish with reference to Gourmont's celebrated attack on revanchism, "Le Joujou patriotisme," published in the *Mercure de France*, where Gourmont declared his generation's unwillingness to die for their fathers' fetish of Alsace-Lorraine. The knot of interests that Mehlman identifies is not completely untangled, and one major strand remains undeveloped. The loss of the Franco-Prussian War and the loss of Alsace-Lorraine (1871) are associated, in the decadent imagination, with the far more traumatic episode of the Commune (March-May 1871), the most significant warning of supersession that French capitalism and its dependents could have received. The combined pressure of "barbarians" without and within — the politics of nation and of class — stimulates a flurry of images of collapsing empires — Babylon, Rome, and Byzantium — in which decadent fantasy is staged.

3. "Le texte, qui explore la position et la dissolution du fétiche dans la mesure où il se constitue autour de la castration subie et fuie, se trouve en outre contraint — par les institutions sociales où se projette et se modèle le désir du sujet — de reproduire leur mécanisme fétichiste, le terme désignant cette fois ce qui oblitère les rapports de production" (Kristeva 363). All page references are to the edition published in Seuil's Collection Points; the original edition was published in Seuil's collection *Tel Quel* in the same year. The English version of Kristeva's text (*Revolution in Poetic Language*, trans. Margaret Waller and intro. Leon S. Roudiez [New York: Columbia University Press, 1984]) leaves out the two-thirds of the book containing Kristeva's actual discussion of texts (and the overt political thrust of the work) and retains only the theoretical elements.

4. "Remy de Gourmont est l'un des rares participants au mouvement symboliste qui aient dénoncé la 'voie hiérarchique' suivie par ses confrères comme par l'idéologie plus ou moins spiritualiste de son époque: '*Mais parlez-lui de Hiérarchie: M. Dupuy se redresse, sourit, ou s'encolère, mais ce sujet ne le laisse pas indifférent. Les fibres de son coeur sont des fibres hiérarchiques; la substance de son âme est une substance hiérarchique; sa chair est hiérarchique et son sang; il est hiérarchique de la tête aux pieds; bref, on ne saurait nommer une partie, même des plus secrètes, de la personne de M. Dupuy, qui ne soit faite de la plus pure essence hiérarchique,*' écrit-il; et on comprend que ce texte ait pu être reproduit par *la Révolte*, No. 21, 5–11 fév. 1893" (Kristeva, 427–28n).

5. Péladan's six plays for the Théâtre de la Rose+Croix were published between 1895 and 1897. The background detail of this section draws on the chapter on Péladan in my book. For a recent excellent full-length account of his life and work, see Beaufils.

6. "*Elle*: Elle dans le luxe, lui dans la gloire: voilà un théorème où la grandeur d'âme arrivera en troisième. — *Lui*: Pour jouer Polyeucte, le chef-d'oeuvre de l'art français, notre Parsifal, comme pour les ignominies d'un Palais-Royal, il faut d'abord un théâtre. Ainsi de l'amour; il ne peut pas être mal mis, mal logé, mal nourri; la main qu'on baise, laver la vaisselle, est-il admissible? Vous n'ignorez pas qu'il faut avoir des rentes pour habiter une chaumière. Certes, on peut toujours faire de la

passion, c'est-à-dire entrer dans un vertige et aller au bout; mais on ne fait de l'amour qu'avec de rares et divers ingrédients. L'attrait sexuel étant la base érotide, vous savez qu'il s'augmente et se continue par le cadre et l'accessoire' (*Un coeur en peine*, 1984 edition, 186).

7. I discuss this passage in detail in my essay on Péladan in *The Decadent Reader* (Zone Books).

8. See Beaufils (408–9), who describes Strindberg's interest, during his mystical crisis, in *Comment on devient mage* and in the novel, and quotes his description in the diary he kept in French of his first confrontation with Péladan's work: "Le Sâr Péladan, jusqu'alors un inconnu pour moi, se présente comme un orage, une révélation de l'homme supérieur, de l'*Übermensch* de Nietzsche, et avec lui le catholicisme fait son entrée triomphale dans ma vie." Thereafter, the two regularly promoted each other's work.

9. "Ribot represented the fusion of two streams of psychological investigation — psychiatric practice and mechanistic theory — and saw brain physiology as the basis of personality. Ribot, along with William James, Alfred Binet, Féré, and others, emphasized physiological functions as important clues of psychological functions, and developed a new psychology dependent on the findings of physiological research" (Burne, 48).

10. "Les imaginatifs sont aussi des sensitifs . . . [ils ont] une sensibilité très vive et une capacité de sentir incessamment renouvelée. Cette sensibilité appartient encore en grande partie au domaine du subconscient" (Gourmont, "La Création subconsciente," *La Culture des Idées*, 1916 edition, 63). See Burne (45–47) for a discussion of Gourmont's ideas on the exchanges of intellect and the subconscious within the creative process.

11. See Burne and Doyle for further details on Aldington's interest in Gourmont.

12. For further discussion of the connections between Gourmont, Pound, and Eliot, see Burne's excellent chapter on "Gourmont and the Anglo-Americans"; see also Sieburth. Pound's main essay on Gourmont, "Remy de Gourmont: A Distinction," first published in *Instigations* (1920), is collected in the edition of his essays published by T. S. Eliot. See also Paige's edition of Pound's letters. At a later stage in his career, Pound produced an important translation of Gourmont's *Physique de l'amour. Essai sur l'instinct sexuel* (1903), expressing considerable enthusiasm for the attempt to discuss human sexual behavior in the light of observations of the animal kingdom, and developing especially Gourmont's comments on the link between sexual activity and intellectual creativity.

13. Hubert Juin's preface to the edition of *Histoires magiques* published in the Collection 10:18 in 1982 gives a useful account of Gourmont's relationship with Berthe Courrière, his mistress from 1886, famous in literary history for her fascination with occultism and the Cabbala. See also Gourmont's own sketch in *Portraits du prochain siècle* (1894), Baldick (1955), and Shattuck (1969).

14. "Y a-t-il un monde de vie extérieure à moi-même? C'est possible, mais je ne le connais pas. Le monde, c'est moi, il me doit l'existence, je l'ai créé avec mes sens, il est mon esclave et nul sur lui n'a de pouvoir."

15. "Quand un fait s'est produit, il se reproduit toujours une seconde fois. — C'est l'axiome. Il est évident que, pour le démontrer, il faudrait se munir d'une multiplicité d'anecdotes historiques, et je ne sais si cela serait possible. Pour ce qui est de moi et de ma vie écoulée, il est d'une surprenante et d'une effrayante exactitude, si bien que je pourrais, je crois, prédire la moitié de ce qui m'arrivera d'ici le sommeil final. Au reste, cet axiome m'est peut-être tout personnel, spécial à mon organisme" (236).

Works Cited

Aldington, Richard. *Remy de Gourmont: Selections from All His Works*. 2 vols. New York: Covici Friede, 1929.

———. *Remy de Gourmont: Selections*. London: Chatto and Windus, 1932.

Apter, Emily. *Feminizing the Fetish: Psychoanalysis and Narrative Obsession in Turn-of-the-Century France*. Ithaca: Cornell University Press, 1991.

Apter, Emily, and William Pietz, eds. *Fetishism as Cultural Discourse*. Ithaca: Cornell University Press, 1993.

Baldick, Robert. *The Life of J.-K. Huysmans*. Oxford: Clarendon, 1955.

Beaufils, Christophe. *Joséphin Péladan: Essai sur une maladie du lyrisme*. Grenoble: Jérôme Millon, 1993.

Bernheimer, Charles. "Fetishism and Decadence: Salome's Severed Heads." In *Feminizing the Fetish*, ed. Apter and Pietz, 62–83.

Birkett, Jennifer. *The Sins of the Fathers: Decadence in France, 1870–1914*. London: Quartet Books, 1986.

Burne, Glenn S. *Remy de Gourmont: His Ideas and Influence in England and America*. Carbondale: Southern Illinois University Press, 1963.

The Decadent Reader. New York: Zone Books, 1998.

Deleuze, Gilles. *Présentation de Sacher-Masoch*. Paris: Minuit, 1967.

Deleuze, Gilles, and Félix Guattari. *L'Anti-Oedipe: Capitalisme et schizophrénie*. Paris: Minuit, 1972.

Dijkstra, Bram. *Idols of Perversity*. New York: Oxford University Press, 1986.

Doyle, Charles. *Richard Aldington: A Biography*. London: Macmillan, 1989.

Foucault, Michel. *Histoire de la sexualité*. Vol. 1: *La Volonté de savoir*. Paris: Gallimard, 1976.

———. *Histoire de la sexualité*. Vol. 3: *Le Souci de soi*. Paris: Gallimard, 1984.

Freud, Sigmund. "Fetishism." 1927. *Penguin Freud Library*. Vol. 7: *On Sexuality*. Ed. Angela Richards. Harmondsworth: Penguin, 1981. 351–57.

———. *Three Essays on the Theory of Sexuality: I. The Sexual Aberrations (1905–20)*. *Penguin Freud Library*, vol. 7: *On Sexuality*. Ed. Angela Richards. Harmondsworth: Penguin, 1981.

Gourmont, Remy de. *Les Chevaux de Diomède*. Paris: Mercure de France, 1897.

———. "La Création subconsciente." *La Culture des Idées*. Paris: Mercure de France, 1916.

———. *La Culture des idées*. Paris: Mercure de France, 1900.

———. *Histoires magiques*. 1894. *Histoires magiques et autres récits*. Collection 10:18. Paris: Union Générale d'Editions, 1982.

———. *Le Latin mystique*. Paris: Mercure de France, 1892.

———. *Litanies de la rose*. Paris: Mercure de France, 1892.

———. *Physique de l'amour. Essai sur l'instinct sexuel*. Paris: Mercure de France, 1903.

———. *Le Problème du style*. Paris: Mercure de France, 1902.

———. *Portraits du prochain siècle*. Paris: Girard, 1894.

———. *Sixtine, roman de la vie cérébrale*. 1890. Collection 10:18. Paris: Union Générale d'Editions, 1982.

Kristeva, Julia. *La Révolution du langage poétique: l'avant-garde à la fin du XIXe siècle: Lautréamont et Mallarmé*. Paris: Seuil, 1974.

Magraw, Roger. *France, 1814–1915: The Bourgeois Century*. Oxford: Fontana, 1983.

Mehlman, Jeffrey. "Remy de Gourmont with Freud: Fetishism and Patriotism." In *Feminizing the Fetish*, ed. Apter and Pietz, 84–91.

Péladan, Joséphin. *A coeur perdu*. Paris: Edinger, 1888.

————. *L'Androgyne*. Paris: Dentu, 1891.

————. *Comment on devient mage: Ethique*. Paris: Chamuel, 1892.

————. *Comment on devient fée: Erotique*. Paris: Chamuel, 1893.

————. *Un coeur en peine*. 1890. Paris: Union Générale d'Editions, 1984.

————. *Curieuse!* Paris: A. Laurens, 1886.

————. *Diathèse de décadence. Psychiatrie. Le Septénaire des Fées. Mélusine*. Paris: Ollendorff, 1895.

————. *L'Initiation sentimentale*. Paris: Edinger, 1887.

————. *La Science de l'amour*. Paris: Albert Messein, 1911.

————. *Le Vice suprême*. Paris: Librairie des Auteurs Modernes, 1884.

Pound, Ezra. "Remy de Gourmont: A Distinction." 1920. *Literary Essays of Ezra Pound*. Ed. T. S. Eliot. London: Faber and Faber, 1954.

————. *The Selected Letters of Ezra Pound (1907–41)*. Ed. D. D. Paige. London: Faber, 1982.

————. *The Natural Philosophy of Love*. Trans. of Gourmont 1903. London: Casanova Society, 1926.

Praz, Mario. *La carne, la morte e il diavolo nella litteratura romantica*. Milan-Rome: La Cultura, 1930. 2d ed. Trans. A. Davidson. *The Romantic Agony*. London: Oxford University Press, 1970.

Shattuck, Roger. *The Banquet Years: The Origins of the Avant-Garde in France: 1885 to World War I*. London: Jonathan Cape, 1969.

Sieburth, Richard. *Instigations: Ezra Pound and Remy de Gourmont*. Cambridge: Harvard University Press, 1978.

Silverman, Deborah. *Art Nouveau in Fin-de-Siècle France: Politics, Psychology and Style*. Berkeley: University of California Press, 1989.

Teich, Mikuláš, and Roy Porter, eds. *Fin de Siècle and Its Legacy*. Cambridge: Cambridge University Press, 1990.

Chapter 15
"Ce Bazar Intellectuel"
Maurice Barrès, Decadent Masters, and
Nationalist Pupils

Liz Constable

Decadent Masters

When we consider our encounters with the term *decadence*, in both nine-
teenth- and twentieth-century contexts, we are inevitably struck by the
term's volatility across disciplinary boundaries, its nebulous character, and
its omnivorous capacity, in the hands of those who deploy it, to designate
any phenomena — aesthetic, social, political–that are deemed threatening,
potentially contaminating, or nihilistic in the face of a tacit consensus about
cultural norms and values. The very slipperiness of the term means that it
effectively eludes responses to the question "What is decadence?" It doesn't
offer itself to unambiguous interpretation, but instead seems to exist by dint
of filling, and naming, the places where uncertainty abounds.[1] And yet, if
decadence dodges definitional integrity and referential stability, as many
critics have noted, one can nevertheless ask how this name functions in the
hands of a given individual or group. When, where, and by whom is it
adopted as a term to identify oneself? With the exception of a small group of
late nineteenth-century writers, isn't it instead, almost invariably, a term
used by one's critics, a term proffered as part of an attack or denunciation,
what Richard Gilman refers to as "an onlooker's term" (19)?

If decadence were to function as a unifying sign, one with which subjects
could identify and name themselves, and through which they could articulate a position — aesthetic, social, political — not only would its periodic
waves of discursive volatility likely ebb away, but the questions implicit in the
expression "the politics of decadence" might yield some equally unifying
responses. By "the politics of decadence," I am raising the questions posed
by the political or cultural interventions that accompany, seem implicit in, or
follow from the literary strategies we associate with nineteenth-century deca-

dents. Maurice Barrès, French aesthete (or decadent?) of the 1880s, and subsequently an extreme right-wing, anti-Semitic nationalist in the 1890s, offers an interesting case to explore in terms of the politics of decadence. For it is the questions raised by the *articulation* of such crossovers, or *passerelles*, from fiction to history, art to life, aesthetics to politics, as opposed to their existence per se, that I am making the site of my interrogations and analysis.

These are vast and challenging questions, and to approach them globally would be to encounter exactly the frustrating slipperiness of the term *decadence* itself; our critical claws would slide over the surface of the issues like those of a cat trying to scratch an old, leathery armchair, waxy and resistant through generations of wear. However, one can offer local responses, which is what my analysis undertakes here. Critics generally treat the aesthetic dimensions of Barrès's work and the political dimensions as chronologically and ideologically distinct. Decadence is usually invoked in relation to the ostensibly aestheticist themes of his early writings[2] and also, to a certain extent, in the context of his explicitly Orientalist texts.[3] However, critics generally analyze Barrès's politics through a different set of texts, through his subsequent articulation of an extreme nationalist position marked by the shift from the individual to the social as the framing context, from an early emphasis on the cultivation of the *Moi-Individu* in the first *Le Culte du moi* trilogy (1888–91), to an emphasis on the *Moi-Nation* in the second trilogy, *Le Roman de l'énergie nationale* (1897–1902), which marks the switch to nationalism.[4] This is not to say that the interdependence of the aesthetic and political in Barrès's writings has been overlooked; on the contrary, David Carroll, in *French Literary Fascism: Nationalism, Anti-Semitism and the Ideology of Culture* (1994), undertakes a rigorous exploration of the aestheticizing of politics in Barrès's nationalist phase.[5]

However, in looking again at the commonly accepted critical boundary separating a supposedly decadent early Barrès from a later nationalist Barrès, my analysis focuses on rhetorical continuities and discontinuities to ask what happens to the aesthete, and to the aestheticist strategies, of the early "decadent" phase of Barrès's writings.[6] In his nonfiction essays *Scènes et doctrines du nationalisme* (1902), referring to his early novel *Un Homme libre* (1889), part of the first trilogy which had earned him the title "prince de la jeunesse," he comments on the readers who remain faithful to him, "les purs," the "diehard Barrèsians":

> They recognize that I have only ever written one book, *Un Homme libre*, and that at twenty-four, I outlined, in that text, everything that I have subsequently developed, and that in *Les Déracinés*, in *La Terre et les morts*, and in this *Vallée de la Moselle* (where perhaps I'm at my best), all I have done is to add greater complexity to my original, and unchanged, opinions. . . . And it's not we who have changed, it's the "Affair" [*sic*] that has repositioned many minds. . . .
> As I sought to do in *Sous l'oeil des barbares*, and in *Un Homme libre*, I created a discipline for myself, all the while preserving my independence. (14–15)

While resisting the position of compliant reader, which would be to take Barrès at his word here, it is nevertheless significant that his writings should advance two apparently contradictory positions. It is striking, first, that in his nationalist phase he should claim his earlier fiction, replete with themes and strategies of decadent fiction (and read as such by literary critics), in fact lays the foundations for his later nationalist fictions and political writings, and *yet*, in those same later texts, that he should isolate the threats to his nationalist project by naming specific cultural, philosophical, and political phenomena as decadent. Decadence is never quite *what* it seems to be, nor *where* it seems to be, in Barrès's trajectory, one might suggest. Or rather, I will suggest that a more productive point of departure would be to analyze the processes governing the naming, or not naming, of decadence in Barrès's work. As a preliminary step, we can note that the earlier texts teem with rhetorical strategies, themes, and topoi that we associate with decadence, and yet Barrès does not *name* them as such. The term is quite noticeably absent from those supposedly decadent texts. Conversely, the later texts, those which *appear* to display very few rhetorical or thematic affinities with decadence, are those where Barrès resorts to that very term, albeit now in a denunciatory way, as the dark menace to his nationalism.

In the early *Culte du moi* trilogy, Barrès's textual credentials as a decadent writer are undeniable and unmistakeable. For a reader familiar with Huysmans's *A rebours* (1884), for example, the parallels between Barrès's narrator, Philippe, in *Un Homme libre* (1889) and Huysmans's Des Esseintes are overwhelming. Barrès's narrator, rejecting the mediocrity and vulgarity of the values of his bourgeois world, retires to a meticulously orchestrated provincial life of contradictory extremes where he becomes a living oxymoron: monastic deprivation and rarefied self-indulgence; rigorous discipline and artificial stimulation; a search for ever greater sources of stimulation [surexcitation] and an accompanying exhausted aching to insulate the self from the world [lassitude]; an insatiable appetite for immaterial realities matched by a renunciation of nourishment and a longing for corporeal immateriality. When Barrès's narrator travels to Venice only to retreat rapidly into the seclusion of his hotel room, preferring the imaginative, idealized evocation of memories of the city "which laid itself out before my closed eyes, outside of time and space" (234), we are reminded of Des Esseintes's substitution for a planned trip to London of the pleasures of armchair tourism: travels of the mind, evocations of Dickens, and the pleasure of inhabiting "a fictive London" (242). Likewise, when Barrès's narrator yearns to stimulate sensations and feelings at will, and to systematize them by transforming his soul into a mechanical organ capable of playing different (affective) melodies at the press of a button (276), we recall Des Esseintes's experimentations with an "orgue à bouche," serving a range of liqueurs whose various combinations modulate synesthetically into musical harmonies (135). In sum, when Barrès's narrator exclaims, "I've sampled vulgar humanity. It's made me suffer. Let's flee, let's take refuge in artificiality" (274), the words could be Des Esseintes's own.

Although *Un Homme libre* traces a similar endeavor to that of Des Esseintes in such marked ways—a decadent bildungsroman in reverse, or a Baudelairian quest to be "Any where out of the world" — Huysmans himself is not among the potential aesthetic masters most frequently cited by Barrès. Instead, it is Baudelaire whom he consistently identifies as one of his decadent masters. In a long essay, *La Folie de Charles Baudelaire* (1884), Barrès enumerates his own lessons in "the life of the senses" (25) gleaned from a "Baudelairian education" (7). And then, in a short obituary written for his schoolfriend Stanislas De Guaita, Barrès signals his discovery of the poet as "the moment from which I date my birth" (*Amori* 129). Situating his own literary education in this essay, he returns to his time as *lycéen* in Nancy to identify the specific textual sources of his covert literary pedagogy. As a boarder at the *lycée*, Barrès presents the initiation as a scene of schoolboys reading racy soft porn under cover of the dormitory darkness: "In 1878, he [De Guaita] was seventeen, and I was sixteen. He was a day-boy; in secret, he brought me [Gautier's] *Emaux et camées*, [Baudelaire's] *Les Fleurs du mal*, [Flaubert's] *Salammbô*. All these years later, I am still in the thrall of these texts, which suddenly gave form to an entire sensibility previously unknown to me. . . . What an impact books can have on a delicate, and voracious, young organism!" (123–24).[7]

In place of a conventional opposition between education and seduction—the maieutic drawing out of mental and physical aptitudes (L. *educere*) versus the leading astray or derailing of such potential (L. *seducere*) — here, education in the school dorms takes place *through* seduction. Against the backdrop of an unenticing institutional pedagogy, the delicate yet desirous, rarefied yet robust young Barrès finds a more seductively appealing and edifying "turn-on" in the pages of Gautier, Baudelaire, and Flaubert. Indeed, education and seduction in turn also constitute the main structuring axes in Barrès's own explicitly pedagogic literary production In extra- and intra-diegetic contexts, Barrès's literary pedagogy progressively defines itself as a natio*list* corrective, or fin-de-siècle *éducation sentimentale*, for a defective national state education. *L'éducation nationale*—its grounding in the principles of 1789, Parliamentary democracy, German philosophy, notably Kantianism, are all associated for Barrès with an undesirable rationality, logic, and abstraction. In 1892, when Barrès adds the "Examen des trois romans idéologiques" to the second edition of his first book, *Sous l'oeil des barbares*, he redefines didacticism as "an impassioned ideology" (174), merging the appeals of sensual seduction and indoctrination:

These monographs are *teachings*. Whatever risk I take in owning up to rather lofty aims, if I weren't to acknowledge them, I would be letting the reader get hopelessly lost [s'égarer infiniment]. I have never given up on the ambition expressed by a foreign poet: All great poetry undertakes a commitment. I want to be thought of as a master or not at all. (175)

From Baudelaire, as Barrès's decadent *maître*, to Barrès in turn, as nationalist *maître* of his readership, the surreptitious reading of Baudelaire in the dorms nevertheless seems an unlikely departure point to reconcile with Barrès's later aims at initiation into nationalism through seductive literary exemplification. The Barrèsian Baudelaire is primarily a poet whose poetic sensuality combines virtually contradictory inward and outward directed desires, blending the capacity of refined *receptivity* to intensified and nuanced sensations with the *appetitive* immediacy of the conventionally unpoetic aspects of the body—touch, smell: "Not only does his poetry display a delicate nervous sensibility, it exhibits instinctual bodily desires" (*La Folie* 24). Together with this topos which we have seen Barrès recycle in *Un Homme libre*, the theory of synesthesia underlying Baudelaire's aesthetics provides Barrès with the materials for constructing him as master of an intuitive, sensory poetics of suggestiveness. At this stage, no surprises. We find features of a Baudelaire we recognize. However, when the profile of a more distinctly Barrèsian Baudelaire comes into focus, recognition fades, for Barrès isolates the value of such a poetics as its ability to rigorously minimize the very medium of its existence—i.e., language. He describes Baudelaire's poetry as "not wordy, nor full of apostrophizing, it flows through the nervous system with an almost physical acuity. A line of *Les Fleurs du mal* is a phrase of music which is cut short, which ends within us, against our will, a fragrant droplet redolent with sensations, enigmatic thoughts, and silence" (*La Folie* 16–17). This is a poetry which almost erases its very medium of existence, yet which depends on that medium of existence to elicit bodily sensations—an abstracting of a Baudelairian model from its very constitutive materiality in language: by interpreting and making a model of Baudelairian aesthetics in this way, Barrès finds a ready aesthetic recruit for enlistment in his nationalist pedagogy, since he considers the "new [Baudelairian] means of feeling" (*La Folie* 101) to be a form of spirituality rivaled only in its intensity by the writings of orthodox Catholic writers.

Spirituality, defined as the expression of a national unconscious, the intuiting of voices of past generations that connect each individual to "the land and the dead," forms the core of Barrèsian nationalism. In 1896, at a stage when a nationalist intensity has infused his writings, he republishes, in the June issue of the journal *L'Aube*, passages earlier omitted from *Un Homme libre*, where he describes Baudelaire as a poet who "more than any other, possessed the gift of spirituality" (Carter, *Baudelaire* 153). Barrès's focus on nationalist spirituality—to be sensed, rather than articulated verbally—joins forces with his political denunciation of the governing principles of the Third Republic, whose abstraction and rational logic Barrès deems incompatible with the spirituality of a nationalist unconscious. Barrès borrows

from his objections to what he considers the *goals* of Republican education—a congeries of *conceptual abstractions* culpable of a distancing from,
and distorting of, a desired spontaneous immediacy of nationalist feeling—
the tools for his condemnations of the *means* of that same education, *verbal
or rhetorical abstractions*: "A *verbalism* which *distances* children from all realities, a *Kantianism* which *uproots* children from the land and the ancestors"
(*Scènes* 60–61, emphasis added). The parallelism of syntax here, and the
deliberate alignment of double cause-and-effect relationships through the
rhetorical figure of isocolon make any distinctions between the two terms
verbalism and *Kantianism* recede as his rhetoric emphasizes the aspects that
constitute the terms' common ground, from Barrès's perspective: that is, a
conceptual *and* rhetorical remoteness rendering them ominously inaus-
picious elements for an education in nationalist sensibility.[8] Feeling uprooted, experiencing disorientation, and then getting lost in one's reading,
or not knowing how to read: all these threaten Barrès's nationalist aspirations and give shape to his perspective on decadence.

From Rerouting Decadence to Rerooting Language

Barrès effectively pursues the rerouting of *his model* of Baudelairian aesthetics toward a nationalist education by gradual infusions of cultural determinism, a Barrèsian Baudelaire who emerges clearly through their positions
on the role of the imagination. Baudelaire's formulation enthrones the
artist's subjectivity as the only pertinent "nature" in question, and, consequently, fidelity to that perspective, rather than to any external referent,
becomes the "realism" at stake. However, in 1888, the traces of Barrès's
reworking of Baudelaire appear in his first novel, *Sous l'oeil des barbares*:
"Reality varies with each one of us since it is constituted by the entirety of
our habitual ways of seeing, feeling and reasoning" (51). The introduction
of "habitual ways" lays the ground for the later emergence of cultural determinism as the primary explanatory element relating the individual to the
collectivity. And yet it is not only through *conceptually* rerouting and rerooting Baudelairian aesthetics that Barrès finds nationalist potential; his texts
also undertake a gradual rhetorical and semantic rerouting of Baudelairian
aesthetics through rerooting the latter's reliance on the rhetorical device of
the oxymoron.

In *Sous l'oeil des barbares*, the narrator defines the barbarians of the title as
"the not-I, all that can harm or resist the Self," which in turn finds expression as a rejection of limits on the self, an impulse to dissolve and overturn
society's definitions of the self: "What! To be just like others! To define
myself, that's to say, to limit myself! To end up reflected in those minds that
will deform me in ways that correspond to their own minds!" (241). While
this early individualist refusal of the influence of social environment seems
at odds with Barrès's subsequent cultural determinism, in fact both the

quests of the early aesthete protagonist, as well as those of the later nationalist pupils, aim at demarcating the self—individual or collective—from contamination by the mediocrity and banality perceived in the existing models of the self.[9]

In resisting definition, or containment, by the words of others, and in thwarting stabilization of the self through language, Barrès instrumentalizes oxymoronic structures in his early writings; as demonstrated by Jean Foyard's study of the decadent self of Barrès's early fiction, this self is characterized by simultaneous yet opposing euphoric and dysphoric impulses, *surexcitation* and *lassitude*, *délire* and *dégoût*, *enthousiasme* and *écoeurement*. The recourse to a dynamic nondialectical maintenance of contradictions through oxymorons is not specific to Barrès; indeed, it is one which Christine Buci-Glucksmann presents as the workings of a "baroque" aesthetic of alterity originating with Baudelaire and Benjamin, and then providing a rhetorical matrix for decadent writers and artists in the fin de siècle, a theatricalized space of *figuration* rather than *representation*.

Not only do Barrès's early texts deploy oxymoronic structures in order to destabilize fixed notions of the self; they also fissure and split terms from within, most consistently figuring a decadent self through actualizing the seemingly contradictory connotations of the term *feverish* [fiévreux]. *Fiévreux* figures both the intensity of an individual's passion, fervor, or enthusiasm—that is, the appetites of a presumably vigorous body and mind—*and* the agitated yearnings of a sickly body and mind, one tormented by existence, ailing, in a society hostile to its aspirations. Straddling the semantic boundaries that would separate its devitalizing from its invigorating connotations, its literal from its figurative connotations, Barrès makes of sickness the site of a spiritual vitality, developing the Baudelairian topos of convalescence as the site of aesthetic renewal, recovery from illness as the catalyst for imaginative re-envisioning, a form of aesthetic life from death.

However, even in 1884, in *La Folie de Charles Baudelaire*, Barrès points to the shortcomings of his Baudelairian lessons when it comes to collective, rather than individual, goals of self-renewal: "This vague mysticism which enshrouds them [the generation influenced by Baudelaire] doesn't take on any form, doesn't go anywhere [ne prend pas corps]; it allows them to desecrate others, but not to orient themselves. That is why, however feverishly fervent [tumultueux] they may be to their deathbeds, their fate will be to stumble from the paradise of believers to artificial paradises. . . . Such doctrines are as *fertile* in the production of infirm dissenters as they are *sterile* in the production of citizens and, in sum, harmful for the discipline of minds" (102–3). Barrès's Baudelaire offers him no model for a collective embodiment of such impulses, for, while conducive to the formation of young rebels, such an aesthetics is one he deems detrimental to the reproduction of bodies necessary for any potential collective body. Readers will stumble, nationalist pupils will get lost, without a method or order.

However, Baudelaire is not his sole master in spirituality. Barrès also appeals to Jesuit masters. In *Un Homme libre*, the narrator's desire for a method, or a means, of channeling and directing intense energies (a way of interpreting them) is in fact satisfied. This occurs through diverting St. Ignatius of Loyola's *Spiritual Exercises*—his method of self-cultivation on the model of Christ via meditation, exercises, and actions—to a secular, purely egotistic cultivation of the self.[10] Loyola demands of the retreatant that he exert himself (i.e., become an exercitant) through a controlled *instrumentalizing of the five senses*, a humbling sensory experience central to his method of spiritual progress. Barrès reterritorializes Loyola's focus on sensory experiences, the instruction to the exercitant to "smell with the sense of smell the smoke, the brimstone, the filth, and the corruption," "to taste with the sense of taste bitter things, such as tears, sadness, and the worm of conscience" in order to sense hell. Despite Baudelaire and Loyola's common focus on exercising the senses, in every other way, they clearly make an ill-matched pair of masters for Barrès. However, his move toward Loyola provides Barrès with the tactic of imitation and models (absent from Baudelaire), the exercise of the senses within a limited semiotic system (one which excludes alternative readings); in sum, Loyola produces, as he and his method intend to produce, a mortifying straitjacketing, or hair-shirting, of Barrès's interest in Baudelairian synesthesia through redirecting it to Christomorphic imitation, an exercise of the senses, yet with interpretive closure, rather than interpretive expansion.

It is also clear that Barrès's subversion of Loyola's method undertakes several important innovations. After all, spirituality and literature rely on opposed understandings of signification: immediacy in one case, or mediation in the other. Rather than a manual, or syllabus, for the practice of spiritual exercises, *Un Homme libre* offers the narration of a personal exemplum, a fictional diary. Rather than the deliberately arid exposition of exercises intended for serious readers who seek to imitate Christ, *Un Homme libre* provides a seductive description of the narrator's progress as a model to readers and, in the move away from the Christian context, leaves unanswered the questions surrounding the model to be imitated. Is it the narrator? Is it each reader's own imagined model of self-realization? Michel Beaujour forcefully brings out the generic crossbreed with which we are dealing in Barrès's fictional method, or seductive pedagogy, when he observes that "the Barrèsian 'method' is not a workable machine or a working model: it is the fiction of a method, or a fiction about method. It modelizes the fantasies of an ego-trip" (342). By underscoring the character of the text as a "transgressive *rite de passage*" (331), Beaujour's analysis returns us to the scene Barrès constructs of his furtive, eroticized, dormitory reading list. In turn, Barrès's own fictions become "the antitextbook, an antidote to classroom ideology" (334), the self-narration of an exemplum, now rerouted *away* from Descartes's rationality, together with the machinery for activating the senses in spiritual self-realization, yet now rerouted *away* from Loyola's models and intercessors.

"The ideal condition is to be both clear-headed [clairvoyant] and impassioned [fiévreux]" (*Un Homme* 22): here, the by now familiar oxymoron presents the narrator's aspiration for a lucidity of mind enjoined to the exhilaration of emotional intensity. Earlier, we aligned Barrès's recourse to such dynamic oxymorons, or unresolvable oppositions, with a more general fin-de-siècle, *and* decadent, aesthetic of alterity. Michel Beaujour takes things a little bit further. First, he identifies the seductive, transgressive, and eroticized element in Barrès's rhetoric — its reliance on oxymorons to figure nondialectically resolved conflictual desires — with Georges Bataille's emphasis on heterology as a subversion of Hegelianism, an emphasis on excess, on what remains outside of thought, a resistance to the Hegelian impetus to reduce the unknown to the known.[11]

Barrès appeals to a heterological space of excess, which marshals rhetoric to gesture beyond its own limiting terms, yet which also seeks, in Loyolan fashion, to operate with a closed (nationalist) semiotic system. By understanding Barrès's seductive education in this way, it is easier to see the obstacles encountered by Barrès's conceptual framework and rhetorical strategies in the move to draft nationalist readers. For this transition from aestheticism to nationalism is marked first by an attempt to define, contain, and limit what is illimitable: the space of excess is henceforth relabeled as a culturally determinist national unconscious. It is then also marked by a move to prescribe, prohibit, and render productive the work of an unconscious that is characterized by its very tolerance of contradictions, and its very violation of prohibition. Barrès's fictionalized antimethod of *Un Homme libre*, which was already a fusing of seduction and education, a conscripting of nonproductive, or nonteleological, expenditure [la dépense] to resist assimilation to defining norms, runs into narrative and rhetorical problems at this point.

In the turn toward nationalism, in his best-known novel, *Les Déracinés* (1897), Barrès's narrative splits education from seduction and reserves the prerogative of education for nationalism — nationalism *as* an education — while figuring the forces that jeopardize it as a dangerous "Oriental" seduction. For Barrès, as for other right-wing nationalists at the turn of the century, the imagined "Oriental" threat and the recourse to the signifier "Oriental" serve to connote an array of internal elements: Jewishness, Protestantism, German Romanticism, and the 1789 Revolutionary legacy of democracy. While Barrès separates out two allegorical structuring poles — education and seduction — to produce a counter-model, a treacherous, seductive other as the constitutive outside to his desired education, the Barrèsian nationalist pedagogy nevertheless also retains, as its primary instrument, the earlier aesthete's fusion of education and seduction. In narrative terms, Barrès ends up with a moral battlefield of competing seductions, or rival readings. At this point, in response to the ideological demands to distinguish the *right* (nationalist) seduction from the *wrong* (unpatriotic) seduction, the text names decadence to designate errantly seductive readings, or misreadings, from a nationalist perspective.

Decadence, I am suggesting, in Barrès hands, names a waywardness or unproductiveness of eroticized energies aroused by reading. As the dormitory scenes suggest, the seduction of reading is presented through a potentially highly charged autoerotic scene, a schoolboy's sexual/textual arousal as the experience of being "all dressed up with no place to go." Indeed, in one of the rare passages where Barrès himself uses the term *decadence,* in *Amori et dolori sacrum* (1903), he reinforces connotations of a textually induced dormitory autoeroticism, and diagnoses what he refers to as the "elegant impotence" of decadence resulting when schoolboys' ambitions and desires are aroused but not given any collective channel through which to express themselves. Thus, Barrès uses decadence to define an imminent threat to young men when their supposedly masculine desires are aroused by reading literature — desires for passion, heroism, glory, power — yet when the initial arousal lacks a productive and/or collectively functional outlet: "Isn't this contradiction the essential secret to understanding the elegant impotence of our students, a phenomenon that has been noted, but not understood, and that has been called decadence?" (137). Taking too much pleasure in the overtures to sexual productivity, never getting beyond textual arousal, and then going nowhere (nationalistically) productive with it: these I would suggest are the connotations that Barrès gives to decadence and that I have been signaling in his references to readers getting lost, stumbling, and feeling disoriented.

To avert such decadent reading practices, the text also secures and fastens semantically — literally racinates — the newly nationalist splitting of education and seduction by restabilizing their respective associations with propriety or impropriety, order or transgression, nationalism or decadence. And finally, we, the external readers, are provided with the ministrations of an internal reader who patrols interpretive boundaries and who offers readers the "security" of knowing how to distinguish the right nationalist seduction from the wrong, decadent, "Oriental" one, and how to direct our textually aroused energies. The appearance of *propriety* and *impropriety* signals not only a heavy-handed moralizing tone but, more significantly, a substantial change in Barrès's implicit theorizing of language in order to juggle with these demands. In *Les Déracinés,* and a less well known later text, *Les Amitiés françaises,* subtitled *Notes sur l'acquisition par un petit Lorrain des sentiments qui donnent un prix à la vie* (1903), both of which deal most explicitly with the formation of nationalist subjects, individual and collective, past and present, we can see this change in his progressive rerooting, or regrounding, of language.

"Ce Bazar Intellectuel": Education Versus Seduction

In restoring propriety to nationalist education, Barrès attempts to demarcate its strategies and objectives from an unpatriotically sensual, literary seduction. Nationalist education is to entail the bringing out, eliciting, or developing of national consciousness from a condition of latent, rudimentary, or merely potential existence: the giving of form to an unconscious potential figured as "poetry." In this way, Barrès sets up what he intends as an instructive opposition between the drawing out of nationalist potential and the leading away, and astray, of the same. He sees seduction away from nationalist truths as the cause of a divided and fragmented community of readers, the leading of the community away from itself, leaving a community adrift, a community uprooted [les déracinés], or decadently misled on the wrong route away from its nationalist reading practices.

The Orientalizing metaphor, "ce bazar intellectuel," resonates as a densely overdetermined signifier for the negative elements threatening to seduce French youth away from Barrès's nationalist cultural economy. One of the narrator's central metaphors in his indictment of Republican national education in *Les Déracinés*, it turns Paris's Latin Quarter — not only hub of student life but also site of the Ecole Normale, which trains the nation's pedagogues — into a souk, an intellectual marketplace. It is just this (de)formative environment which greets the seven young student protagonists on their arrival from a provincial lycée education which has failed, from the narrator's perspective, to instil in them either a sense of their attachment to their provincial Lorraine roots or an accompanying interpretive groundedness. The initial cultural uprooting at the *lycée*, attributed to Kantian teachings, seems destined to continue through a further deracination or interpretive dis-orientation in the *Quartier latin*. *Le bazar* denotes not only an "Oriental" marketplace; it is an archaic slang term for *le lycée*, and it also connotes a brothel. Through these layers of connotations — qualified by the term *intellectuel*, which is always used pejoratively by Barrès — "ce bazar intellectuel" stigmatizes an adulteration of values he names as decadent in three discursive fields of the nationalist cultural economy: the monetary, the spiritual, and the sexual.[12] Where Barrès aspires to a collective investment in the ideals and values of the *poetry* of nationalism, he sees instead a decadently disorderly bartering over values and ideals in the democratic marketplace (a bankrupt nationalism). Since Barrès endows nationalism with a spirituality, the decadence of contemporary France is signaled, for him, by the dwindling of spirituality into mere intellectualism (words stifling feelings). Finally, where Barrès seeks to regulate the body and foster the literal and figurative reproduction of the nation, he sees, instead, the nation's youth threatened by the lure of a decadently wasteful, nonproductive expenditure of energies — precisely the seductive heterological impulses of *Un Homme libre* (sexual/textual stimulation, yet with no productive outlet).

The three discursive fields that merge in the Orientalizing metaphor "ce bazar intellectuel" also correspond in post-Enlightenment discourses to those operative in constructing the genealogy of fetishism. Fetishized concepts operate as negative cultural counter-models that reiterate and represent *internal* social variance as if it had *external* sources.[13] The naming of decadence, in Barrès's later writing, is just such a form of fetishizing. Domestic values *appear* to remain intact since the incongruous elements, and their menace of corrupt reading practices, are transferred elsewhere through the creation of a new discursive category — in Barrès's case, the ideological projection of a decadent Orient, one which overvalues material, as opposed to spiritual, objects. The Orientalized decadence connoted by "ce bazar intellectuel," functioning, as it does, as a fetishized concept, is figured repeatedly and ritualistically as a gesture of expulsion central to Barrès's definition of nationalism. If the "bazar intellectuel" (a Barrèsian figure for decadence) implies a sellout of nationalist values, an internal "Oriental" colonization of France, the betrayal of nationalist values to foreign investors, it also fetishizes, most significantly, specific uses of language that Barrès deems conducive to decadently errant readings, interpretations diverted by the materiality of language which are, therefore, antithetical to the closed semiotic system sought for his nationalist project.

As we have seen, Barrès accounts for the cultural predicament of deracination with an entangled knot of sociopolitical causes whose loose ends and stray threads are nevertheless bound together discursively by the figure of a supposed seduction away from nationalist truths. And in this figure, his arguments find consistency by ascribing such cultural deracination to an improper use of language, be it what he considers semantic deviation, rhetorical distortion, or narrative decoys. The presentation of nationalism as *nonrhetorical* is a strategy that one finds in many different aesthetic and political moves to "break with the past," from various avant-gardes to forms of fascism. Though it may be a political-aesthetic commonplace, an analysis of its specific formations in Barrès's texts is also crucial in understanding what he exactly designates as decadence. In Barrès's nationalist reluctance to acknowledge that rhetorical choices underlie *every use* of language, we see what Paolo Valesio defines as an obscuring ideology of "the rhetoric of anti-rhetoric": "The type of discourse that is explicitly contrary to rhetoric and tries to detach itself from its mechanism is completely under the sway of rhetoric[;] . . . it is actually more sophisticated and devious than the rhetoric from which it pretends to shy away" (59).

Sophisticated, devious, and duplicitous, Barrès's rhetoric certainly is; yet, true to his Loyolan departure point, he presents nationalist pedagogy as a supposedly nonrhetorical appeal to the direct impact of images, biographies, scenes: "Nationalism, regionalism remain theories too often. I will lead us to experience them [je les ferai sentir] not as doctrines, but as biographies, the shared biographies of all those of us who are French" (*Scènes* 9). In attempting to bypass the *mediation* of language, and to side-step the issue of the *inscription* of national biographies, Barrès appeals to the symbolic materiality of the cemeteries, the tombs, and the soil of the French provincial landscape, all of which claim to naturalize nationalism by their very visibility. Accompanying the making visible of nationness, he empha-sizes the affective bond of national consciousness as a life-giving source of nationalist rejuvenation. Already, we see the makings of a starkly Manichean metaphorical framework, and indeed Barrès's rhetorical strategies reserve the prerogative of generation, renewal, and rebirth for nationalism, while transferring a death-dealing pall to "Oriental" seduction: the impact of the Jews, Prussians, Protestants, and German philosophy on French culture. However, the starkly polarized metaphoric frame is constantly cracking open to reveal its dissimulations and contradictions.

By figuring the mutually transformative and generative recitation of the national myths as a giving birth to the nation and a reawakening of national-ist *poetry*, the text reasserts the pedagogic mission through a rhetoric of reproduction defined as generation. However, while masquerading rhetori-cally as life-giving generation, the idealist reproduction in question is in fact the duplication of the same (masculine ideal form). The originary scene of the mythic recitation constitutes the prototype of the pedagogic experi-ence, narrativized in terms of a classroom language drill, a securing of interpretive errancy through collective recitation. Nationalist *engagement*, the harnessing of poetry, which Barrès articulates in *Les Déracinés* and other texts written between the 1890s and 1900s, owes much to imagined scenes of mythic pedagogic recitation that fuses past and present generations. Fusion entails circularity in Barrès's nationalist politics of language, which in turn entails tautology, a process foregrounded here by the narrator in *Les Dé-racinés*: "Napoleon, our heaven, by means of a noble impulse, we create you, and you create us!" (67).

The circularity of Barrès's desired Nationalism binds together his na-tionalist pupils in a community that commemorates itself in the act of at once founding and affirming itself, a community where language provides what Jean-Luc Nancy calls "an exemplary site of monstrance and revela-tion" (113). Nancy's term "monstrance" foregrounds the instructive or pedagogic element in the founding myth: in showing, or giving symbols, the myth seeks to instruct. He calls the myth's circularity a "tautogorical" — as opposed to "allegorical" — feature, in that the myth doesn't seek to refer to another level of meaning, but instead constitutes itself in the saying, for example, the "Repeat after me" of the classroom drill (124). The myth in question here isn't mythological in any usual sense of the word. Rather, it is the means by which a nationalist pupil feels a sense of oneness with himself and with his past. Thus, for Nancy, the myth as foundational fiction harbors a nostalgia for the immediacy of presentation, for the bypassing of representation in order to find the "proper" meaning of words. The *impropriety* we associate with figurative language is, in fact, considered *proper* to such foundational myths, since such language claims to be appropriated from the truth and the founding fiction of the myth itself, a "self-fictioning of nature" (Nancy 134). It is in this sense that Barrès presents the symbols of the land and the cemeteries: as figures endowed with a foundational propriety in nationalist pedagogy, foundational in that they refer to themselves, produce the semblance of continuity through time, and are supposed to act apotropaically in semiotic terms, as do Loyola's images, as part of a code of images that wards off adulterated interpretations.

Nancy's analysis is particularly useful in understanding Barrès's claims that direct, unmediated expression *gives birth* to the nation, and *turns language into action*, both claims that are implicit in the rhetoric of reproduction as generation. In the chapter recounting a gathering around Napoleon's tomb (for Napoleon is designated one of the "master pedagogues"), the narrator reiterates these two aspects of the ritualized, collective commemorations of a single exemplary figure. "They [the students] love Bonaparte: unambiguously [nûment]" (*Les Déracinés* 167), comments the narrator, isolating the adverb *unambiguously*, which highlights the unmediated, spiritual relationship sought between teacher and nationalist pupil, nationalist fiction and reader, and signifier and signified. The transformation of words into acts emerges through the univocality of admiration marking the reciting of Napoleon's biography: "This gathering, near the tomb, it's more than a dialogue; an action" (175).

In both cases, Barrès's orchestration of the phrases is striking. We have a description from which he extracts and isolates the pertinent feature, and then gives it further emphasis by placing it at the end of the phrase: "unambiguously," and then "an action." His rhetorical method combines an opening clause, both in the sense that it precedes and that it invites interpretation, with subsequent interpretive closure — the immediate condensing and compacting into a single word. By curtailing interpretive exploration, the nationalist code reverses the earlier aestheticist fissuring and splintering of meaning. Yet the terms that are isolated in this way, although turned into foundational concepts in the nationalist code, are no less nebulous for that apparent concrete concision. The words possess a mnemonic power, are suggestive, yet leave pending the definition of an action — a poetics of suggestiveness, yet which produces duplicitous, interpretive smoke screens, rather than evocative Mallarméan smoke rings.

Within the code of nationalism, Barrès opposes two verbs: *dépenser* [to expend] and *consumer* [to use up, exhaust]. Of the lamentable majority who use up, or exhaust their potential of nationalist poetry, Barrès comments: "The immense herd exhausts its poetic potential in aspiring to become bureaucrats. Card-playing, quacking and inbibing alcohol, these half-men, or rather these effeminate creatures brought up by the administration just as it likes them, hang out in cafés, abjectly unproductive [vil désoeuvrement] waiting for nothing better than to be selected for a bureaucratic post" (*Les Déracinés* 65). Barrès feminizes those who deplete, dissipate, or otherwise squander their nationalist energy, for the potential community remains undefined, unformed, or unworked [désoeuvrée] and inoperative.[14] In sharp contrast to the squandering of national energy, profitable use of symbolic capital appears as expenditure — "une dépense" — the giving of oneself, albeit through death, to the defense of the idea of the nation. Through an idealist process of abstraction, material deaths are converted into life-giving symbolic capital (nationalist spirituality). At Napoleon's tomb, the narrator describes this, commenting that the students "get inebriated when they breathe in, through the triple coffin, the putrefaction of death [des miasmes de mort] which for them is like the arousing agent of immortality [des ferments d'immortalité] (165). As we saw from the dormitory reading scene, an eroticized seduction now channelled into patriotic fervor allows nationalist pupils to move beyond furtive semiotic autoeroticism to a nationalistically endorsed necrophilia.

Barrès's project of nationalist education offers a monumentalizing of death without an accompanying materializing. Most significantly, by highlighting the governing rhetorical duplicity, we trace the oxymoronic figurations of the unbounded, heterological self, give way to the anchoring of those opposing urges in a chiasmic rhetoric of predictably deceptive antitheses, where life (outside of nationalist "truths") means a figurative death, and literal (patriotic) death means immortal life (of the spirit of nationalism). Indeed, when we recall that Barrès was dubbed "prince de la jeunesse" [prince of French youth], while Baudelaire dubbed himself ironically "prince des cadavres" [prince of corpses], mocking his critics, after the unfavorable reception given "Une Charogne," one might quite legitimately suggest that our analysis discloses yet another reversal. Baudelaire's influence on young writers of the 1880s and 1890s turns, in Barrès's version, to a funereal aesthetics focusing on national corpses. Just as in Loyola's spiritual exercises — the excercitant is expected to be as receptive to the spirit as a corpse [perinde ac cadaver] — Barrès's nationalist pupil is required to do likewise, to empty the self in order to identify with successive moribund nationalist pedagogues, and Barrès himself, rather than Baudelaire, becomes perhaps the most significant "prince des cadavres." As we have seen, there is an absolutely rational logic at work, albeit in the guise of the spontaneity and immediacy of a national unconscious.

However, the self-fictioning of the community does not merely articulate the shaping of an ideal community around death. While the nationalist male type defines himself in the act of dying *in the name of the nation*, for every ideal and idealist figure in Barrès's texts, there is an accompanying untranscended negative countermodel: an enemy to be named and identified by category. Barrès figures the ideal national type as a source of tales of national self-definition, "a deposit [i.e., a savings account] of the past generations" [un dépôt des générations] (*Les Déracinés* 39), a figure for the increasingly rare reserves of symbolic cultural capital in the depleted nationalist bank of poetry. Nationalist language works by being hoarded, by gaining interest on itself, rather than by circulating in the marketplace in Barrès's idealist self-reproduction.

The banking metaphors we have used for Barrès's definition of nationalist language find an explicit commentary in *Les Amitiés françaises*, where the narrator addresses his pupil with the concern that he will grow up to find that there is no longer "an order in which to situate yourself, a community where words keep their meanings" (36–37). In this desired semiotic community of tautological self-fictioning, where words keep their meanings — or rather, where readers must decipher Barrès's nationalist twist on their meanings, alternative meanings — alternative fictional decoys constitute the Orientalized, decadent seduction that jeopardizes the idealist reproduction of the same. He literalizes the idea that a competing opinion can lure young people away from nationalist interests by presenting these ideas first as *ideological foreign commodities* on the market, and then as *ideological foreign bodies*: in other words, as Jewish and, in the fin-de-siècle context, Oriental imports: "Disorder is sown in our country by the import of exotic truths, when the only useful truths for us are those elicited from within us [tirées de notre fonds]" (*Les Déracinés* 34). Barrèsian protectionism demands exclusively homegrown ideologies on the market, yet, since the principles of 1789, Parliamentary democracy *are* precisely homegrown but antithetical to Barrès, he distances them by referring to them, along with Kant's philosophy, and Jewishness, as exotic imports. Through a combination of economic and physiological metaphors, and parallels between the individual and social body, his heavy-handed diagnosis pinpoints not only a bankrupt national reserve of poetry but also a sickly body: an ailing, degenerating, and ultimately, decadent national culture.

The metaphors of infection, degenerative disease, and interpretive unease, named and contained as decadence, function to distinguish the *corrosive* death carried by exotic, Oriental imports from the *glorious* death in defense of the nation. Where Barrès reserves for the latter the transcendent echoes that intensify and amplify the spirituality of the idealist community, in the former, principles alien to the ideal form of the spiritual community eat away at it. The ideal form consumes itself, wasting away to death as indeterminate, or unformed, untranscended matter, a decadently, feminized, ailing France that Barrès associates with the Jewish (Oriental) presence within national boundaries.

It comes then as no surprise that the most significant exotic import, a wealthy Turkish woman, Astiné Aravian — the novel's principal embodiment of "the foreign" and cosmopolitanism as threats — is described primarily in terms of materiality and contagion. More significantly, it comes as no surprise that the anxiety surrounding the "proper" use of language, the need to preserve categories through language, and the avoidance of errant readings, should crystallize around her and the Jewish presence in France. Astiné is remarkable for her material wealth, her jewelry, her "costly Turquoise gemstones" [TURQuoises de prix]. The text's repetitious enforcement of the "right" reading, through the choice of turquoise gem stones, draws attention to the source of these gems as the wealth of *une Turque*, a Jew. Astiné infects potential nationalist pupils through seduction with the "wrong" fictions, a contaminatedly dangerous use of language; the effect of her exotic narratives is described both as a virus and as "a goblet of poison" (*Les Déracinés* 94) seeping into the veins of the social body, staining the pages of the Nationalist book of myths, and her eventual assassination is deemed "natural" to the formation of the essential France: "it is natural that *an Astiné Aravian* should be assassinated" (304; emphasis added). Since, in Barrès's nationalist pedagogy, language functions through the creation of a nationalist code whose decrypting reveals a higher, spiritual truth, the implications of turning a word away from its nationalist meaning are equivalent to erasing the desired national boundaries, producing very defensive narrative reactions to potential leakages of capital, or boundary-betrayals.

In the following passage, the narrator describes the effect of Astiné's seduction-through-narrative on one of the young students, Sturel: "At first, he [Sturel] thought he could sense an intensification of his inner strength. His energy, no longer slumbering, was instead rushing through his veins. However, Astiné's words let their foreign elements flow through this organism in disarray. Sturel, who experienced the *enervating invasion of Asia*, believed at first that his *lucidity was heightened*. What a mistake!" (93; emphasis added). The narrator's obtrusive intervention signaling the boundary between education and seduction is absolutely essential at this point, since Barrès needs to establish starkly polarized values at two different levels: both within the diegesis, and between narrator and reader. The double objective, exhilaration [la fiévre] and lucidity [la clairvoyance] reappears from the early writings, almost unchanged in the words describing Astiné's impact on Sturel: "the enervating invasion of Asia" and the illusion of "a greater lucidity." However, lest readers should be misled, and lest the memories of the illicit reading practices of the school dorm should distract them from the novel's reformed nationalist pedagogic program, the manipulative narrator reinstates an authorized reading several times. A warning voice signals that the impression of exhilaration and lucidity from Astiné's Oriental tales is a delusion, that nationalist spiritual capital does not appreciate through the addition of foreign elements, or through alternative readings. Just as the nationalist pupils' adoration of Napoleon is "unambiguous," *Les Déracinés* attempts, in turn, to fulfill an unambiguously, and yet enticingly, nationalist pedagogic role in relation to the reader.

The "need" to repeatedly sacrifice *an* Astiné (one of a type or category, as the text puts it) constitutes a narrative motor that relates directly, and very significantly, to the naming of decadence as wayward reading. For in Barrès's would-be allegorical battlefield, Astiné represents the very alterity constitutive of language itself. And yet, to defend language against itself, to make of language's materiality an identifiable category to be named and denounced, will necessarily result in a repeatedly staged battle between education and seduction, and inevitably lead to a series of sacrifices to be recapitulated ritualistically. Oriental affairs relocate to the home-front, internal colonization drains the reserves of nationalist language and energy. Barrès's nationalist project is forced to channel its depleted energies into defusing *the* Oriental affair at home — the Dreyfus Affair — and the "intellectual" seduction of ideas antithetical to Barrèsian nationalism, those of the Dreyfusards, and not simply Astiné's seduction of nationalist pupils, its synecdochal fictional counterpart. Barrès describes the Dreyfus Affair as an example of internal colonization, and develops further the connotations of the "bazar intellectuel": "A babbling of idiocies together with the jargon of foreigners. We need to respond to these idiocies, and to these foreigners, with an education" (*Scènes* 96). Barrès's pedagogy seeks to eliminate from a desired unambiguous clarity of nationalist truths what he depicts as a babble of foreign tongues. For all the strenuous reader-addressed reminders that the allegorical battle pits nationalist spirit against (literal) foreign matter, and the proper education of natural instincts against an improper, decadent seduction of that potential, the strategy of *naming* decadence remains ineffective in preempting truant readings. Barrès's nationalist reading directives only reinforce the ways in which the so-called decadence of wayward reading is, one might suggest, simply *reading*, as opposed to following interpretive mandates.

To return to our opening questions about the "passerelles" between decadent literary strategies and political and cultural interventions, we need to emphasize the distinction we have analyzed between Baudelaire's *dynamic* textual strategies and the *static* models into which Barrès reduced them. There is nothing about Baudelaire's aesthetics that lends itself to Barrèsian nationalism; instead, Barrès consistently buttons down, literalizes, and freezes the dynamism of his decadent master's literary strategies. The synesthetic suggestiveness of poetic language, its ability to break with linguistic stereotypes and clichés, turns in Barrès's hands to quite the opposite: an appeal to the suggestiveness of poetry in order to consolidate national types, to produce a picture book of nationalism and its negative counterpart of categories of adversaries. Moreover, Barrès irons out the rhetorical oscillations of the decadent subject to give way to a luminously clear nationalist landscape constructed by externalizing and expelling the very antitheses that were constitutive of its decadent stage. Thus, in Barrès's literary project of naming and identifying by category, he uses the term *decadence* to accomplish a similarly didactic containment. And yet, since the supposed decadence in question is the practice of *reading* (as opposed to following interpretive directives), and therefore a generalized (rather than a localizable) phenomenon, it is one that cannot be quarantined by its naming. Naming decadence seems rather to render the phenomenon more contagious.

Notes

1. See Richard Gilman for an exploration of the confusion surrounding the term *decadence*. And on the connections between decadence and the suspension of epistemological certainties, see Charles Bernheimer's essay, "Unknowing Decadence," in this volume.

2. The texts referred to here are: Barrès's writings in the short-lived journal, *Taches d'encre*, which appeared in 1884, and from which his essay on Baudelaire, *La Folie de Charles Baudelaire*, was taken, and republished separately; *Sensations de Paris. Le Quartier latin. Ces messieurs. Ces dames* (1888); Barrès's three novels comprising the first trilogy, entitled *Le Culte du moi: Sous l'oeil des barbares* (1888), *Un Homme libre* (1889), and *Le Jardin de Bérénice* (1891); and *L'Ennemi des lois* (1893).

3. Here, the texts in question are various essays on travel in Spain and Italy in *Du sang, de la volupté et de la mort* (1894; reedited and supplemented in 1903) and *Amori et dolori sacrum* (1903), *Le Greco et le secret de Tolède* (1911), *Un Jardin sur l'Oronte* (1922), and *Enquête aux pays du Levant* (1923).

4. The texts of the second trilogy are *Les Déracinés* (1897), *L'Appel du Soldat* (1900), and *Leurs figures* (1902); also included here are *Scènes et doctrines du nationalisme* (1902) (a collection of articles and speeches) and *Les Amitiés françaises* (1903).

5. See also particularly Carroll's lucid analyses of precisely these questions in "The Use and Abuse of Culture: Maurice Barrès and the Ideology of the Collective Subject."

6. My use of the term *rhetoric* does not simply refer either to rhetorical figures or to the skills of persuading through speech. I follow Paolo Valesio's view of rhetoric as coextensive with discourse; therefore, "Rhetoric is all of language, in its realization as discourse" (7). As such, rhetoric implies, in Valesio's terms, "an integrated structure (embracing the topoi, the arguments, and the figures—without being confined to any of these three components alone)" (39). Again, following Valesio's view of rhetoric, ideology finds its meaning as a failure to recognize the workings of rhetoric.

7. See chapter 14 of *A rebours* [Against nature] for Des Esseintes's encounter with his literary "masters": Flaubert, Edmond de Goncourt, Zola, and Baudelaire.

8. "Isocolon (G. 'of equal member or clauses')—1. Repetition of phrases of equal length and usually corresponding structure" (Lanham 62).

9. A. E. Carter connects the dandyism associated with nineteenth-century aesthetes, their striving for aesthetic superiority, and the prophylactic dimension of self-definition, which lends itself to recontextualization in Barrèsian nationalism. See *The Idea of Decadence* (47).

10. In Barrès's novel, Sainte-Beuve, Benjamin Constant, and Baudelaire provide figures of secular, spiritual intercession, though the final one of the trio is subsequently dropped.

11. For Georges Bataille on Loyola's *Spiritual Exercises*, see *L'Expérience intérieure* (26). See Mark C. Taylor for a useful commentary on Bataille's heterology as oxymoron.

12. It is Barrès who *first* mobilizes the term *intellectuel* in a pejorative sense, and he does so at the time of the Dreyfus Affair.

13. See Anne McClintock.
14. See Nancy's *La Communauté désoeuvrée*, the title of which is translated as *The Inoperative Community*.

Works Cited

Barrès, Maurice. *Amori et Dolori Sacrum*. Paris: Félix Juven, 1903
———. *Les Amitiés françaises* 1903. Paris: Émile-Paul Frères, 1918.
———. "Examen des trois romans idéologiques." 1892. *Le jardin de Bérénice*. 1891. Paris: Flammarion, 1988.
———. *La Folie de Charles Baudelaire*. 1884. *Taches d'encre*. Paris: Les Écrivains réunis, 1926.
———. *Les Déracinés*. 1897. Paris: Union Générale. 1986.
———. *Un Homme libre*. 1889. Paris: Éditions Plon, 1957.
———. *Scènes et doctrines du nationalisme*. 1902. Paris: Librairie Plon, 1925.
Bataille, Georges. *L'Expérience intérieure*. Paris: Gallimard, 1954.
Beaujour, Michel. "Barrès, Loyola, and the Novel." In *The Reader in the Text: Essays on Audience and Interpretation*, ed. Susan R. Suleiman and Inge Crosman, 325–49. Princeton: Princeton University Press, 1980.
Buci-Glucksmann, Christine. *La raison baroque de Baudelaire à Benjamin*. Paris: Editions Galilée, 1984.
Carroll, David. "The Use and Abuse of Culture: Maurice Barrès and the Ideology of the Collective Subject." *Paragraph* 17 (March 1994): 153–73.
———. *French Literary Fascism: Nationalism, Anti-Semitism, and the Ideology of Culture*. Princeton: Princeton University Press, 1994.
Carter, A. E. *The Idea of Decadence in French Literature: 1830–1900*. Toronto: University of Toronto Press, 1959.
———. *Baudelaire et la critique française, 1868–1917*. Columbia: University of South Carolina Press, 1963.
Foyard, Jean. "Structures sémantiques du moi décadent chez Maurice Barrès." In *Fin-de-Siècle: Terme—Evolution—Révolution?*, ed. Gwenhaël Ponnau, 217–80. Toulouse: Presses Universitaires du Mirail, 1987.
Gilman, Richard. *Decadence: The Strange Life of an Epithet*. New York: Farrar, Straus and Giroux, 1979.
Huysmanss, Joris-Karl. *A rebours*. Ed. Marc Fumaroli. Paris: Gallimard, 1977.
Lanham, Richard A. *A Handlist of Rhetorical Terms: A Guide for Students of English Literature*. Berkeley: University of California Press, 1969.
Loyola, Ignatius. *Spiritual Exercises of St. Ignatius of Loyola*. Trans. W. H. Longridge. London: Mowbray, 1955.
McClintock, Anne. "Screwing the System: Sexwork, Race and the Law." *Boundary II* 19:2 (1992): 70–95.
Nancy, Jean-Luc. *La Communauté désoeuvrée*. Paris: Christian Bourgeois Editeur, 1986.
Taylor, Mark C. *Altarity*. Chicago: University of Chicago Press, 1987.
Valesio, Paolo. *Novantiqua: Rhetoric as a Contemporary Theory*. Bloomington: Indiana University Press, 1980.

Contributors

Emily Apter is professor of comparative literature and French at UCLA. She is the author of *André Gide and the Codes of Homotextuality* and *Feminizing the Fetish: Psychoanalysis and Narrative Obsession in Turn-of-the-Century France*, and *Continental Drift: From National Characters to Virtual Subjects*. She also co-edited *Fetishism as Cultural Discourse* with William Pietz.

Sharon Bassett is professor of English at California State University at Los Angeles, currently conducting research on the life and works of Walter Pater.

Charles Bernheimer was co-chair of the Comparative Literature and Literary Theory Program at the University of Pennsylvania. He is the author of *Flaubert and Kafka: Studies of Psychopoetic Structure*, *Figures of Ill Repute: Representing Prostitution in Nineteenth-Century France*, and numerous articles on nineteenth- and twentieth-century writers. He co-edited, with Clare Kahane, *In Dora's Case: Freud, Hysteria, Feminism*, and has edited a collection entitled *Comparative Literature in the Age of Multiculturalism*, which focuses on his influential report on the future of comparative literature.

Jennifer Birkett is professor of French at the University of Birmingham, England. She is the author of *The Sins of the Fathers: Decadence in France, 1870– 1914*, and editor and translator of *The Body and the Dream: French Erotic Fiction, 1464–1900*. She has co-edited, with Elizabeth Harvey, *Determined Women: Studies in the Construction of the Female Subject, 1900–1990*, and has also co-authored, with James Kearns, *The Macmillan Guide to French Literature: Early Modern to Postmodern*.

Hema Chari is assistant professor of English at California State University at Los Angeles. She teaches and publishes in colonial, postcolonial, gender, and film studies. Her book "Fabulous Artificers and the Forked Tongue of Postcolonial Realities" is forthcoming.

Liz Constable is assistant professor of French at the University of California, Davis. She has articles published on Flaubert, Catulle Mendès, and Rachilde in *MLN* and *L'Esprit Créateur*. She is currently working on a book-length project historicizing states of shame in nineteenth- and twentieth-century French literature and culture.

Dennis Denisoff is assistant professor of English at the University of Waterloo. He is the author of *Erin Mouré: Her Life and Works* and the editor of *Queeries*, the first anthology of Canadian gay male prose. He has recently completed a book-length study on sexual parody and aestheticism.

Melanie C. Hawthorne is associate professor of French and assistant department head at Texas A&M University. She translated Rachilde's *The Juggler*, and is coeditor (with Richard J. Golsan) of *Gender and Fascism in Modern France*. She is currently working on a biography of Rachilde.

Leonard R. Koos is associate professor of French at Mary Washington College. He is currently working on a book-length study of the decadent aesthetic entitled "Endgames: Decadence in the Fin de Siècle."

Sylvia Molloy is Schweitzer Professor of Humanities at New York University. She is the author of *At Face Value: Autobiographical Writing in Spanish America*, *Signs of Borges*, and an acclaimed novel, *Certificate of Absence* (*En breve carcel*). She is the co-editor of *Women's Writing in Latin America: An Anthology* and is currently writing a book on the construction of sexualities in fin-de-siècle Latin America.

Matthew Potolsky teaches in the Literature Program at Harvard University. He has articles published or forthcoming on Mallarmé, Pater, Yeats, and Sacher-Masoch, and is currently completing a book-length project on scenes of education in late nineteenth-century writing.

Michael Riffaterre is University Professor of French at Columbia University. His many publications include *The Semiotics of Poetry*, *Text Production*, and *Fictional Truth*, as well as numerous influential articles on poetry and literary theory.

Barbara Spackman is professor of Italian and comparative literature at the University of California, Berkeley. She is the author of *Decadent Genealogies: The Rhetoric of Sickness from Baudelaire to D'Annunzio* and *Fascist Virilities: Rhetoric, Ideology, and Social Fantasy in Italy*, as well as numerous essays and translations.

David Wayne Thomas is assistant professor of English at the University of Michigan, Ann Arbor. His writings on literary and theoretical topics have been published or are forthcoming in *Mosaic, PMLA*, and *Raritan*. He is completing a critical study of Oscar Wilde and is beginning work on a study of originality in Victorian Britain.

Marc A. Weiner is professor of Germanic studies, comparative literature, and film studies at Indiana University, Bloomington. He is the author of *Arthur Schnitzler and the Crisis of Musical Culture, Undertones of Insurrection: Music, Politics and the Social Sphere in the Modern German Narrative*, and *Richard Wagner and the Anti-Semitic Imagination*.

Index

Abbate, Carolyn, 132, 137
Adam, Paul, 201, 203, 211
Adelsward-Fersen, Baron, 165
Aldington, Richard, 278, 286
Alfred (the Great), 256–57
Allen, Maud, 159–61
Allison, David B., 30
Anderson, Benedict, 164, 167
Angenot, Marc, 163
Annales médico-psychologiques, 162
Antinoüs, 174
Apollinaire, Guillaume, 75, 143, 145
Apter, Emily, 271
Apuleius, 260, 261, 263, 264
Arbus, Diane, 153
Aristotle, 256, 263
Armani, Giorgio, 108
Arnold, Matthew, 256–58, 262, 266–67
Atget, Eugène, 145
L'Aube, 293
Aurangzebe, 220
Aurelius, Marcus, 24, 256–58

Badouin, Marcel, 198, 199
Bahr, Hermann, 29, 120
Bahti, Timothy, 117
Baird, David, 219, 227
Baju, Anatole, 12, 28, 211
Bal, Mieke, 63
Baldick, Robert, 44, 45, 286
Balzac, Honoré de, 142, 204
Banville, Théodore de, 71
Barbey d'Aurevilly, Jules, 28
Barker, Pat, 177
Barnes, Djuna, 25, 144, 148, 155, 235
Barney, Natalie Clifford, 144

Barrès, Maurice, 7, 23, 26, 201, 207, 289–308
Bartlett, Neil, 179
Bataille, Georges, 297, 307
Baudelaire, Charles, 5, 10, 13–14, 15, 16–18,
    20, 24–25, 29, 43, 70, 72, 74, 76, 77–78,
    145, 178, 185, 269–70, 272, 292, 293, 294,
    295, 296, 303, 306, 307
  Works: *Epaves*, 71; *Les Fleurs du mal*, 13, 17,
    65, 71, 75, 292, 293; "Notes nouvelles sur
    Edgar Allan Poe," 13, 251; *Le Peintre de la
    vie moderne*, 14; *Paris Spleen*, 77; *Petits Poèmes
    en prose*, 76–77
Baudrillard, Jean, 272
Baumont, Maurice, 165
Beardsley, Aubrey, 169, 173, 174, 175
Beaufils, Christophe, 274, 286
Beaujour, Michel, 296, 297
Beckson, Carl, 5–6, 7, 27
Bécquer, Gustavo Adolpho, 195
Beer-Hofmann, Richard, 120
Beethoven, Ludwig van, 120, 123–24, 126
Beizer, Janet, 63
Benjamin, Walter, 62, 63, 250–51, 272, 295
Benkert von Kertbeny, Karoly Maria, 162,
    177, 178, 179
Bergamín, José, 195
Bernhardt, Sarah, 171, 211
Bernheimer, Charles, 35, 38, 41, 46, 47–48,
    272, 285
Bhabha, Homi, 217
Billing, Noel Pemberton, 159–61
Binet, Alfred, 272, 286
Binet-Valmer, Lucien, 165
Bird, Alan, 160, 171, 172, 174, 178
Birkett, Jennifer, 271, 286
Bizet, Georges, 133

Blackwood's Monthly Magazine, 254
Bohringer, Richard, 103
Borchmeyer, Dieter, 137
Borie, Jean, 63
Borland, Maureen, 160, 169, 174, 178
Bouilhet, Louis, 53, 54
Boulanger, Georges Ernest, 200
Bourdieu, Pierre, 84, 109–10, 116, 117, 155
Bourget, Paul, 16, 29, 56
Bouzingos, 65
Brantlinger, Patrick, 228, 230
Brassaï, Georges, 22, 25, 143, 144, 145, 146, 149–55
Bréal, Michel, 199
Brecht, Bertolt, 148
Brett, Philip, 122, 137, 177
Broe, Mary Lynn, 155
Broomfield, Nick, 146
Bruant, Aristide, 142, 145
Buci-Glucksmann, Christine, 29, 63, 295
Burdett-Coutts, Angela, 230
Bürger, Peter, 28
Burne, Glen S., 278, 286
Butler, Judith, 29, 92, 99

Cahun, Claude, 146
Caithness, Lady, 274
Calinescu, Matei, 27, 28
Callas, Maria, 131, 138
Cameron, Julia Margaret, 99
Capes, W. W., 255
Cardon, Patrick, 177
Carroll, David, 290, 307
Carter, A.E., 4, 10, 293, 307
Casal, Julián del, 188
Casanova de Seingalt, Giovanni, 204
Castle, Terry, 145, 151, 193
Chabaneix, Paul, 278
Chaddock, Charles, 163
Chamberlain, Lord, 176
Chambers, Ross, 17
Charcot, Jean-Martin, 184, 191
Chatelain, Dr., 162
Cherbuliez, Victor, 204
Choissy, Abbé, 204
Clark, Larry, 153
Clayton, Douglas, 137
Clement, Catherine, 137
Cohen, Ed, 59, 94, 96, 162, 163, 168, 177
Collins, Wilkie, 23, 215–32
Constable, Liz, 63, 267
Constant, Benjamin, 307

The Cook, the Thief, His Wife & Her Lover. See Greenaway, Peter
Coppée, François, 200
Coquio, Catherine, 25
Corelli, Marie, 10
Courrière, Berthe, 279, 286
Coward, Noël, 145
Cowling, Mary, 99
Craft, Christopher, 48
Cresson, Edith, 167, 177
Curry, Tim, 179–80
Cycling World Illustrated, 87, 88, 90

Daily Telegraph, 93, 94, 169
D'Annunzio, Gabriele, 26, 30, 48, 119, 191, 194, 196, 207
Dante (Alighieri), 281
Darabont, Frank, 136
Darío, Rubén, 183, 185–86, 188, 189–90, 193, 195, 196
Darwin, Charles, 262
Dauphiné, Claude, 211
da Vinci, Leonardo, 165, 243
Davis, Lisa E., 195
Le Décadent, 12, 28, 200–201, 202, 211
Degas, Edgar, 145
de Joyeuse, Anne, 173
Deleuze, Gilles, 26, 270, 271, 272
Dellamora, Richard, 137, 251
de Maeztu, Ramiro, 187
de Man, Paul, 28
Demme, Jonathan, 23, 122, 123, 130–38
Denby, David, 138
de Quincey, Thomas, 218
Derrida, Jacques, 26, 30, 39, 251, 266
Dickens, Charles, 230, 291
Didi-Huberman, Georges, 184, 185
Dieulafoy, Madame, 211
Dijkstra, Bram, 137, 178, 269
Doane, Mary Ann, 138
Dollimore, Jonathan, 26
Donato, Eugenio, 63
Douglas, Alfred, 83, 84, 86, 87–94, 99, 159–60, 165, 169, 175, 180, 186, 193
Douglas, Francis, 91
Douglas, Norman, 165
Douglas, Percy, 91, 92
Dowlah, Suraga, 228
Dowling, Linda, 27, 178, 188, 237, 251, 262, 263
Doyle, Arthur Conan, 99
Doyle, Charles, 286

Dreyfus, Alfred, 306, 307
Dryden, John, 166
Dubarry, Armand, 168
Duchamp, Marcel, 69
Dumas, Alexandre, 142
Duncan, Ian, 230
du Plessys, Maurice, 28
Dupuy, M., 285

Eagleton, Terry, 61
The Egoist, 278
Eiser, Otto, 129, 138
Eliot, George, 254
Eliot, T. S., 229, 279, 286
Ellis, Havelock, 163, 177
Ellmann, Richard, 59, 83, 86, 89, 92, 169,
    170, 171, 175, 178, 179
Erber, Nancy, 178
Eulenburg, Philipp, 165
Evans, Lawrence, 254
Evening News, 92
Evening Standard, 94
Eyre, Edward, 228

Fellows, Jay, 251
Felski, Rita, 27, 29, 48
Féray, Jean-Claude, 162, 163, 177, 178, 179
Féré, Charles Samson, 286
Fewster, J.C., 29
Fischer-Dieskau, Dietrich, 138
Fischlin, Daniel, 137
Flaubert, Gustave, 53, 54, 55, 58, 61, 62, 63,
    307
    Works: *Bouvard et Pécuchet*, 55; *Madame Bov-
    ary*, 53; *Salammbô*, 52–55, 58, 63, 292; *L'Ed-
    ucation sentimentale*, 116; *Trois Contes*, 170
Flint, Kate, 169
Forrest, Denys, 229
Foucault, Michel, 90, 91, 117, 121–22, 134,
    161–63, 177, 217, 229, 269, 282
Foyard, Jean, 295
Freud, Sigmund, 36, 38, 48, 109, 184, 230,
    270–71, 272, 273, 276
    Works: *Civilization and Its Discontents*, 109;
    "The Disappearance of the Oedipus Com-
    plex," 40; "Infantile Genital Organiza-
    tion," 40; "Medusa's Head," 38; "Some
    Psychological Consequences of the Ana-
    tomical Distinction Between the Sexes,"
    40; *Three Essays on the Theory of Sexuality: I.
    The Sexual Aberrations*, 284–85
Frick, Patricia Miller, 229

Friedman, Barton R., 252
Froehner, M., 54
Fumaroli, Marc, 29–30

Gagnier, Regenia, 9
Gaillard, Françoise, 35, 36–38, 39, 41, 44, 46,
    47–48, 63
Gambon, Michael, 103
Gasché, Rodolphe, 30
Gaultier, Jean Paul, 108
Gautier, Théophile, 5, 10
    Works: *Comédie de la mort*, 65; *Emaux et
    camées*, 292; *Jeunes-France*, 65; *Mademoiselle
    de Maupin*, 14, 204; "Notice," 13
Gide, André, 178
Gilbert and Sullivan, 94, 166
Gilbert, Arthur, 177
Gilman, Richard, 12, 27, 51–52, 54, 63, 137,
    289, 307
Gilman, Sander L., 137, 138, 216, 217–18
Ginsburg, Michal, 63
Giordano, Umberto, 130, 132, 135
Gissing, George, 99
Gladstone, William, 91
Goldin, Nan, 22, 25, 143–44, 145, 146, 147–
    55
Gómez Carillo, Enrique, 187
Goncourt, Edmond de, 307
Gosse, Edmund, 266
Gossman, Lionel, 117
Gourmont, Remy de, 23, 25, 29, 268–73,
    278–84, 285
    Works: *Les Chevaux de Diomède*, 278; *La Cul-
    ture des idées*, 278, 286; *Histoires magiques*,
    286; "Le Joujou patriotisme," 285; *Le Latin
    mystique*, 279; *Litanies de la Rose*, 279; *Livres
    des masques*, 185; *Physique de l'amour. Essai
    sur l'instinct sexuel*, 286; *Portraits du prochain
    siècle*, 286; *La Problème du style*, 278; *Sixtine*,
    271, 273, 279–82, 283; "Stéphane Mal-
    larmé and the Idea of Decadence," 1, 12,
    235; "Stratagèmes," 282–84
Grace, Della, 146
Grand-Carteret, John, 177
Gras, Vernon, 117
Greenaway, Peter, 24, 25, 101–17
Greene, Thomas, 251
Gregor-Dellin, Martin, 138
Grein, J. T., 159, 160, 176
Griesser, Luitpold, 138
Grundmann, Roy, 138
Guaita, Stanislas De, 292

Guattari, Félix, 270, 272
Guszalewicz, Alice, 171
Gutman, Robert W., 138

Habšck, Franz, 137
Halévy, Jacques François Fromental Elie,
    126
Hall, Radclyffe, 145
Hals, Franz, 117
Hanks, Tom, 130, 131
Hannoosh, Michele, 27, 251
Hare, E. H., 138
Harris, Frank, 92
Harrison, John Smith, 244, 252
Hartley, Kelver, 179
Hawthorne, Melanie, 27, 210
Hegel, Georg Wilhelm Friedrich, 102, 106,
    111, 117, 297
Heine, Ferdinand, 125
Heine, Heinrich, 243, 244
Heller, Tamar, 226, 230
Hemingway, Ernest, 144
Henry III, 173, 174
Heriot, Angus, 137
Hernández, Felisberto, 185
Herzer, Manfred, 177, 178
Hibbert, Christopher, 230
Hill, Donald L., 254, 255, 266
Hoare, Philip, 177
Höch, Hannah, 144
Hofmannsthal, Hugo von, 29, 120
Holland, Merlin, 171, 176
Holland, Vyvyan, 162, 176, 178
Hollinrake, Roger, 138
Holroyd, Michael, 89
Homans, Margaret, 99
Homer, 13, 70, 79, 244
Horace, 8
Hough, Graham, 20
Household Words, 230
Howard, Alan, 103
Huas, Jeanine, 165
Hugo, Victor, 70, 73–74
Hutcheon, Linda, 137, 138
Hutcheon, Michael, 137, 138
Huysmans, Joris-Karl, 3, 5, 6, 7, 9, 10, 17, 18–
    19, 20, 21, 22, 25, 29, 30, 35–49, 55, 56, 60,
    61, 67–70, 76, 77–78, 79, 95, 119, 132, 145,
    166, 169, 170, 173–74, 201, 202, 203, 208,
    211, 281, 291–92, 307
Hyde, H. Montgomery, 93, 94, 159, 166, 175,
    186

Inden, Ronald, 230
Ingenieros, José, 191–96
Inman, Billie Andrew, 244, 252
Irigaray, Luce, 36, 48

Jacob, Max, 143
Jakobson, Roman, 48
James, William, 286
Jankélévitch, Vladimir, 6, 7, 8, 11
Johnson, Brian D. 138
Jouve, Séverine, 27, 29
Joyce, James, 144, 284
Juin, Hubert, 286
Jullian, Philippe, 212

Kant, Immanuel, 266, 292, 294, 304
Kaufman, Moisés, 87–89
Kaufmann, Stanley, 138
Kaufmann, Walter, 30
Keefe, Janice, 244
Keefe, Robert, 244
Kelly, Dorothy, 63, 209
Kertesz, André, 144
Kettle, Michael, 160, 177
Keyserling, Graf von, 120
Kimmelman, Michael, 147
Klawans, Stuart, 138
Knapp, Bettina L., 178
Koestenbaum, Wayne, 137, 138, 185
Kofman, Sarah, 26
Koos, Leonard R., 212
Koppen, Erwin, 138
Krafft-Ebing, Richard von, 145, 163
Krauss, Rosalind, 153
Kristeva, Julia, 26, 30, 272–73, 282, 284, 285
Kureishi, Hanif, 229

Labouchère, Henry, 179
Laforgue, Jules, 72–73, 74–76
Laird, W. W., 176
Lambroso, Cesare de, 191
Lamennais, Hugues-Félicité Robert de, 65
Lane, John, 169, 179
Lanham, Richard A., 307
Lanoff, Sue, 228, 229
Laplanche, Jean, 36, 40, 41
Larousse, 163
Latouche, Henri de, 204
Laugaa, Maurice, 211
Lautréamont, Comte de (Ducasse I.), 185,
    272, 284
La Vaudere, Jane de, 7, 27

Leavis, F. R., 189
Ledeen, Michael, 30
Lee, Vernon, 28
Le Galliene, Richard, 9
Lepelletier, Edmond, 196
L'Estoile, Pierre de, 173
Lever, Maurice, 164, 165, 173, 177
Leverson, Ada, 28
Levin, David J., 137
Lewis, James, 150
Linkman, Audrey, 85
Litvak, Joseph, 178
Lloyd George, David, 160
Locke, Ralph P., 137
London Quarterly Review, 254
Lorrain, Jean, 7, 203, 204–7, 210, 211, 212–13, 298
Louvet de Couvray, Jean Baptiste, 204
Louÿs, Pierre, 169, 170
Loy, Mina, 144
Lucan, 8
Lukács, Georg, 27, 53

McClary, Susan, 137
McClintock, Ann, 308
McConkey, Kenneth, 84–85, 97
McDougall, Joyce, 149, 155
McPherson, Heather, 85
Maeterlinck, Maurice, 68, 79, 171
Magraw, Roger, 269
Mahmoud of Ghizni, 220
Mallarmé, Stéphane, 1, 26, 29, 30, 170, 188, 201–2, 251, 272, 273, 281, 284, 302
Manet, Edouard, 145
Mann, Thomas, 119, 132
Mapplethorpe, Robert, 146
Marcus, Jane, 179
Marjoribanks, Edward, 93
Martí, José, 183, 187, 193
Marvick, Louis, 29
Marx, Karl, 112–13, 215, 229, 250, 272
Mass, Lawrence D., 137
Massenet, Jules, 172
Mathews, Elkin, 179
Mayne, Arthur 85
Medici, Catherine de, 165
Mehlman, Jeffrey, 285
Mehta, Jaya, 228, 230
Meltzer, Françoise, 178
Mendelssohn, Felix, 126
Mendès, Catulle, 25
Mercure de France, 285

Metcalf, Thomas, 230
Méténier, Oscar, 178
Meunier, Anna, 211
Meyer, Moe, 186
Meyerbeer, Jacques (or Giacomo), 126–27
Mill, John Stuart, 199
Miller, Henry, 143, 144, 151
Miller, J. Hillis, 241, 251
Millet, Kate, 179
Mirbeau, Octave, 143, 145
Mirren, Helen, 103
Mohr, Richard D., 137
Molinier, Pierre, 146
Molloy, Sylvia, 177, 187, 194, 196
Le Monde, 171
Mondragón, Miguel Guerra, 195
Monegal, Rodríguez, 195
Monsman, Gerald Cornelius, 243, 244
Montgomery, Sybil, 91
Montifaut, Marc de, 212
Moran, M. F., 241
Morand, Paul, 143, 151
Moréas, Jean, 201
Moreau, Gustave, 36, 47, 170
Morris, Mitchell, 131, 138
Morris, William, 9, 242, 244
Morrissette, Bruce, 211
Mosher, Frederic J., 211
Mosse, George, 27
Mozart, Amadeus, 136
Mussolini, Benito, 26
My Beautiful Laundrette. See Kureishi, Hanif
Myron, 243

Nadel, Ira, 99
Nancy, Jean-Luc, 301–2, 308
Nandy, Ashis, 230
Napoleon I, 302, 303, 305
National Observer, 1
Nattiez, Jean-Jacques, 137
Neefs, Jacques, 63
The New Freewoman, 278
Newall, Christopher, 99
Newman, John Henry, 259, 262, 266–67
New York Times, 147, 167, 177
Nietzsche, Friedrich, 14–16, 18, 20, 23, 25, 26, 29, 30, 54, 56, 62, 111, 112, 121, 122, 128–30, 133, 138, 191, 278, 279, 286
Works: *Case of Wagner*, 15, 16, 56; *Ecce Homo*, 15; *On the Genealogy of Morals*, 110, 111–12; "On the Uses and Disadvantages

Nietzsche, Friedrich (*cont.*)
   of History for Life," 54; *Preface to the Gay Science*, 39; *The Will to Power*, 56, 62
Nisard, Désiré, 8–9, 11, 13, 15, 24, 28, 235
Nodier, Charles, 199, 204
Nordau, Max, 2–6, 7, 9, 12, 15, 18, 24, 26, 27, 30, 52, 63, 83–84, 98, 142, 143, 145, 146–47, 148, 175, 191, 202, 235
Notker, Gotteschalk, 279, 281

Observer, 167
Oliphant, Mrs., 254
Opie, Catherine, 146
Origen, 281, 282
Outram, Dorinda, 252
Ovid, 241, 243, 245–49, 252
Owens, Craig, 151

Paglia, Camille, 62
Paige, D. D., 286
Palacio, Jean de, 7, 10
Parker, Harold T., 252
Pater, Walter, 10, 22, 24, 60, 170, 235–53, 254–67
   Works: "Apollo in Picardy," 236, 238–53; *Appreciations with an Essay on Style*, 266; *Greek Studies: A Series of Essays*, 243; *Imaginary Portraits*, 243, 244; *Marius the Epicurian*, 24, 237, 254–67; *Miscellaneous Studies*, 244; "Pico della Mirandola," 243; *Plato and Platonism*, 237, 243, 252; "Poems by William Morris," 242, 244; *The Renaissance: Studies in Art and Poetry*, 255; *Studies in the History of the Renaissance*, 10, 237, 243, 244, 245, 256, 257, 261, 266; "Two Early French Stories," 243
Paxton, Nancy L., 230
Péladan, Adrien, 274
Péladan, Adrien, Jr., 274
Péladan, Joséphin, 23, 211, 268–71, 273–77, 278, 279, 282, 285, 286
   Works: *A coeur perdu*, 275; *L'Androgyne*, 276; *Un coeur en peine*, 277; *Comment on devient fée: Erotique*, 275; *Comment on devient mage: Ethique*, 275; *Curieuse!* 275; *La Décadence latine*, 274; *L'Initiation sentimentale*, 275; *Mélusine*, 276; *La Science de l'amour*, 275; *Le Vice Suprême*, 275
Penrose, Roland, 151
Pérez de Ayala, Ramón, 187
Petersen, Antje, 137
Petronius, 47

Philadelphia. See Demme, Jonathan
Phoebus, 76
Picasso, Pablo, 143, 144
Pick, Daniel, 99
Pierrot, Jean, 3, 138, 236
Pigott, Edward F. Smyth, 172
Plato, 237, 243, 251, 252, 256
Poe, Edgar Allan, 13, 251
Ponce, Aníbal, 191
Porter, Roy, 269
Pouilliart, Raymond, 29
Pound, Ezra, 278, 279, 286
Powell, Kerry, 99, 172, 179
Praz, Mario, 3, 10–11, 28, 269
Price, Steven, 180
Proust, Marcel, 119, 132, 143, 178
Prudhomme, Sully, 200

Queensberry, ninth Marquess of (John Sholto Douglas), 1, 22, 83–100, 159, 169, 177, 186, 192
Quérard, Jean-Marie, 199

Rachilde, 7, 25, 28, 162, 174, 193, 200, 202–3, 207–10, 211, 212, 213
Ramos Mejía, José María, 192
Ray, Man, 144, 151
Raynaud, Ernest, 173, 200
Reed, John, 8, 229, 230
Renan, Ernest, 195
La Révolte, 273
La Revue scientifique, 198
Ribot, Théodule, 278, 281, 286
Richard, Noël, 174, 211
Ricketts, Charles, 161
Ricks, Christopher, 251–52
Riding, Alan, 167
Riffaterre, Michael, 79
Riley, Charles, 266
Rilke, Rainer Maria, 29
Rimbaud, Arthur, 145, 196, 211
Robbins, Tim, 136
Roberts, Brian, 91, 92, 93
Robespierre, Maximilien, 250
Robinson, Christopher, 178
Rocky Horror Picture Show. See Sharman, Jim
Rodó, José Enrique, 189–90, 193
Rolfe, Frederick, 9
Rollinat, Maurice, 201
Rosebery, Archibald Philip Primrose, Lord, 91
Ross, Robbie, 160, 169, 174

Rosselli, John, 137
Roudiez, Leon S., 285
Rousseau, Jean-Jacques, 10
Roy, Ashish, 219, 225, 230
Ruskin, John, 9
Russell, Ken, 179
Russell, Paul, 106
Ryals, Clyde de L., 8, 179

Saar, Ferdinand von, 120
Sacher-Masoch, Leopold von, 271
Sacks, Peter, 138
Sade, marquis de, 208
Sahib, Nana, 228
Said, Edward, 216, 229
Saint Ignatius of Loyola, 296, 297, 300, 303, 307
Saint Louis, 256–57
Sainte-Beuve, Charles, 52–53, 54, 55, 65, 307
Salessi, Jorge, 188, 196
Salomé's Last Dance. See Russell, Ken
Sand, Georges, 42
Sand, Michael, 151
Sante, Luc, 143, 147
Sarcey, Francisque, 200
Sartorius, Joachim, 147
Saturday Review, 257
Saul, John, 164
Schickling, Dieter, 138
Schiller, Friedrich von, 124
Schnitzler, Arthur, 29, 120
Schopenhauer, Arthur, 278
Schor, Naomi, 117
Schubert, Franz, 120, 124
Scott, Walter, 74
Sedgwick, Eve Kosofsky, 90, 121, 137, 165, 168, 169, 218, 225, 230
Séon, Alexandre, 277
Shāh, Nāder, 223
Shakespeare, William, 74
Sharman, Jim, 179–80
Sharpe, Jenny, 230
Shattuck, Roger, 286
Shaw, Bernard, 92
Shawshank Redemption. See Darabont, Frank
Shelley, Percy Bysshe, 189
Showalter, Elaine, 27, 171, 230
Shuter, William F., 251, 252
Sieburth, Richard, 286
Siegel, Sandra, 230
Silverman, Deborah, 269
Silverstolpe, Frederic, 177

Simon, John, 138
Simpson, Colin, 164
Sinai, Robert, 137
Sinfield, Alan, 166, 168, 177, 189, 195
Sinha, Mrinalini, 230
Smith, James M., 8, 235
Smith, Timothy d'Arch, 166
Söder, Hans-Peter, 27
Spackman, Barbara, 25, 27, 29, 251
Squiers, Carol, 147
Steakley, James, 165
Stein, Gertrude, 144
Stekel, Wilhelm, 138
Stoker, Bram, 99
Strachey, Lytton, 89–90
Strauss, Richard, 179
The Studio, 173
Subotnik, Rose Rosengard, 137
Suleri, Sara, 230
Sullivan, Andrew, 138
Sultan, Tipu, 219, 220, 223, 227, 228, 229
Swart, Koenraad, 27
Swinburne, Algernon, 10
Symons, Arthur, 4, 29, 188

Taches d'encre, 307
Tailhade, Laurent, 174
Taylor, Archer, 211
Taylor, Mark C., 307
Teich, Mikuláš, 269
Tel Quel, 285
Temple, Ruth, 27
Tennyson, G. B., 266
Tertullian, 43
Thornton, R. K. R., 27
Times, 257
Tisson, Simon-André, 138
Toulouse-Lautrec, Henri de, 143
Trajan, 257
Trumbach, Randolph, 137
Turner, Frank M., 256, 261
Tydeman, William, 160, 161, 180

Ulner, Arnold L., 188
Ureña, Henríquez, 183

Valesio, Paolo, 300, 307
Vallette, Alfred, 178
Van Ness, Peter H., 138
Van Roosbroeck, G. L., 235
Verlaine, Paul, 28, 71–72, 145, 193, 196, 211
Versace, Gianni, 146

Vicinus, Martha, 177, 178
Victoria, Queen, 99, 220
Vigilante, 159
Villiers de L'Isle-Adam, Auguste de, 185, 204, 281
Viollet, H. Roger, 171
Virgil, 8, 260
Viswanathan, Gauri, 230
Vogel, Martin, 138

Wagner, Cosima, 128, 129
Wagner, Richard, 23, 119, 121–30, 132, 133, 136, 137, 138, 277
Walkowitz, Judith R., 169
Wall, James M., 138
Wallen, Jeffrey, 236
Waller, Margaret, 285
Ward, Mrs. Humphrey, 254–55
Waugh, Alec, 176
Weedon, Ethel, 91
Weeks, Jeffrey, 195
Weill, Kurt, 148
Weiner, Marc A., 137, 138
Weininger, Otto, 126
Weir, David, 3, 27, 28
Wells, H. G., 99
Westernhagen, Curt von, 138
Westphal, Carl, 161, 162

Whissen, Thomas, 137
White, Hayden, 102, 116
Whitman, Walt, 193, 281
Wilde, Oscar, 1, 3, 5, 9, 10, 17, 18, 21, 22, 25, 26, 27, 29, 35, 44, 58, 59, 60, 62, 83–100, 159, 160, 162, 163, 164, 165, 168, 169, 177, 178, 179, 180, 183, 185–87, 188, 190, 191, 192, 193, 195, 272
  Works: "The Critic as Artist," 63; "Decay of Lying," 14; *De Profundis*, 92, 176; *The Importance of Being Earnest*, 90, 95, 168; *The Picture of Dorian Gray*, 17, 19–21, 30, 58–61, 87, 94–98, 99, 101, 132, 169, 173, 174, 236; "Portrait of Mr. W. H.," 96; *Salomé*, 23, 159, 160, 170–80, 195; *A Woman of No Importance*, 89
Wilhelm, Kaiser, 165
Williams, Carolyn, 251
Williams, Linda, 137, 138
Williams, Rosaline H., 28
Wojnarowicz, David, 143
Wordsworth, Jonathan, 254

Yellow Book, 29, 169, 170

Zagona, Helen Grace, 178
Zola, Emile, 10, 56–58, 61, 62, 63, 68, 281, 307